Personal Insurance

Personal Insurance

Eric A. Wiening, CPCU, ARM, AU
Assistant Vice President and Ethics Counsel
American Institute for CPCU/Insurance Institute of America

George E. Rejda, Ph.D., CLU
V. J. Skutt Distinguished Professor of Insurance
University of Nebraska—Lincoln

Constance M. Luthardt, CPCU, AAI, AIM
Director, Northeast Region
American Institute for CPCU/Insurance Institute of America

Cheryl L. Ferguson, Ed.D., CPCU, AU
Senior Director of Curriculum
American Institute for CPCU/Insurance Institute of America

First Edition

American Institute for Chartered Property Casualty Underwriters/
Insurance Institute of America
720 Providence Road, Malvern, Pennsylvania 19355

© 2002

American Institute for Chartered Property Casualty Underwriters/
Insurance Institute of America

First Edition • Third Printing • August 2003

Library of Congress Control Number: 2002110391
ISBN 0-89463-108-X

Printed in Canada

Foreword

The American Institute for Chartered Property Casualty Underwriters and the Insurance Institute of America are independent, nonprofit organizations serving the educational needs of the risk management, property-casualty, and financial services businesses. The Institutes develop a wide range of curricula, study materials, and examinations in response to the educational needs of various elements of these businesses. The American Institute confers the Chartered Property Casualty Underwriter (CPCU®) professional designation on people who meet its examination, ethics, and experience requirements. The Insurance Institute of America offers associate designations and certificate programs in the following areas:

- Accounting and Finance
- Agent Studies
- Business Writing
- Claims
- Global Risk Management and Insurance
- Information Technology
- Insurance Fundamentals
- Management
- Marine Insurance
- Performance Improvement
- Personal Insurance
- Premium Auditing
- Regulation and Compliance
- Reinsurance
- Risk Management
- Surety Bonds and Crime Insurance
- Surplus Lines
- Underwriting

The American Institute was founded in 1942 through a cooperative effort between property-casualty insurance company executives and insurance professors. Faculty members at The Wharton School of the University of Pennsylvania in Philadelphia led this effort. The CPCU designation arose from the same type of business and academic partnership at Wharton as the Chartered Life Underwriter (CLU) designation did in 1927.

The Insurance Institute of America was founded in 1909 by five educational organizations across the United States. It is the oldest continuously functioning national organization offering educational programs for the property-casualty insurance business. It merged with the American Institute in 1953.

The Insurance Research Council (IRC), founded in 1977, is a division of the Institutes. It is a not-for-profit research organization that examines public policy issues that affect property-casualty insurers and their customers. IRC research reports are distributed widely to insurance-related organizations, public policy authorities, and the media.

The broad knowledge base in property-casualty insurance and financial services created by the Institutes over the years is contained mainly in our textbooks. Although we use electronic technology to enhance our educational materials, communicate with our students, and deliver our examinations, our textbooks are at the heart of our educational activities. They contain the information that you as a student must read, understand, integrate into your existing knowledge, and apply to the tasks you perform as part of your job.

Despite the vast range of subjects and purposes of the more than eighty individual textbook volumes we publish, they all have much in common. First, each book is specifically designed to increase knowledge and develop skills that can improve job performance and help students achieve the educational objectives of the course for which it is assigned. Second, all of the manuscripts for our texts are reviewed widely before publication, by both insurance business practitioners and members of the risk management and insurance academic community. In addition, the revisions of our texts often incorporate improvements that students and course leaders have suggested. We welcome constructive comments that help us to improve the quality of our study materials. Please direct any comments you may have on this text to my personal attention.

We hope what you learn from your study of this text will expand your knowledge, increase your confidence in your skills, and support your career growth. If so, then you and the Institutes will truly be *succeeding together*.

Terrie E. Troxel, Ph.D., CPCU, CLU
President and CEO
American Institute for CPCU
Insurance Institute of America

Preface

This text begins with an overview of personal insurance, including property and liability loss exposures and personal risk management. Auto insurance is familiar to most people, and the study of personal insurance begins with this topic. Next, the text discusses homeowners insurance in detail, including alternative forms and endorsements. The text then introduces the student to other types of property and liability insurance. The final three chapters provide an introduction to financial planning, followed by a discussion of life, health, and disability insurance. Without these final topics, no study of personal insurance would be complete.

This edition of *Personal Insurance* is designated a first edition because it is assigned for the first time in the CPCU program as well as the INS program. Four previous editions of *Personal Insurance* were assigned solely in the INS program.

This new first edition of *Personal Insurance* incorporates a substantial rewrite of Chapters 5 through 7 to reflect the "Homeowners 2000" policy forms recently introduced by Insurance Services Office (ISO). Chapters 8 and 9 are also heavily revised, and several other changes or updates appear elsewhere in the text. In the fourth edition, published two years ago, Chapters 3 and 4 were rewritten to reflect the 1998 edition of the ISO Personal Auto Policy, and they are essentially unchanged for this edition. Most updates in the fourth and first editions were drafted by the undersigned, based on previous work by other authors.

We give special thanks to Insurance Services Office for its cooperation and help in the preparation and review of this manuscript. Stephen Anderson, CPCU, AIM, coordinated ISO's efforts for the current edition. We are also grateful to ISO for extending its permission to use ISO forms extensively as the basis for much of the material presented in this text.

Special thanks are due to Robert J. Prahl, CPCU, for his superb work in updating the material that refers to AAIS forms.

We are indebted to the following individuals, each of whom reviewed the initial draft of material changed in this edition. Numerous improvements resulted from their contribution to this project. Connie Luthardt is also a primary author of this text. David Ueeck and Andy Zagrzejewski are also current members of the Institute's INS Advisory Committee.

Daniel G. Bachman, CPCU

Ralph A. Maffei

R. Bryan Tilden, CPCU, CLU, ARM

David A. Ueeck, CPCU, ChFC, ARM

Andrew Zagrzejewski, CPCU, AIC

This edition, especially Chapters 3 and 4, also continues to benefit from the work of those who reviewed manuscripts for the fourth edition:

Jeff DeTurris, CPCU

Karen L. Hamilton, Ph.D., CPCU, CLU

George E. Rejda, Ph.D., CLU

Beth Gamble Riggins, CPCU, AIC, AAI

Although this preface names only those who participated in the fourth and new first editions, we remain grateful to the many individuals who reviewed manuscripts for the first three editions of *Personal Insurance* and were recognized in previous prefaces. The text continues to benefit from their dedication, diligence, and attention to detail.

We thank the members of the INS Advisory Committee, who continuously provide expertise and insight and give unselfishly of their time to promote insurance education and professionalism. Lastly, we wish to thank all the students and course leaders who have given us their constructive comments regarding the materials in previous editions of this text. We invite you to help shape the next edition by sending your comments to the Institutes. With your help, we can continue to improve this and other texts to give you the best educational tools for your study of the insurance business.

We sincerely hope that the hard work and expertise of the many people who worked on this text will provide you with a meaningful experience in your professional development.

Eric A. Wiening

Contributing Authors

The American Institute for CPCU, the Insurance Institute of America, and the authors of this text acknowledge, with deep appreciation, the work of the following contributing authors:

Donald R. Oakes, Ph.D., CPCU, ARM
Vice President
AICPCU/IIA

Anita W. Johnson, CPCU, CLU, ChFC
Director of Examinations
AICPCU/IIA

Mary Lou Speckheuer, CPCU, AMIM, CPIW
Vice President
Richard M. Marshall Insurance Agency, Inc.

Contents

Chapter 1

Direct Your Learning

Overview of Personal Insurance

After learning the subject matter of this chapter, you should be able to:

■ Describe and analyze the following aspects of property loss exposures that individuals and families might face:

- Property exposed to loss

- Causes of loss

- Financial consequences of property losses

■ Describe and analyze the following aspects of liability loss exposures that individuals and families might face:

- The possibility of a claim for money damages

- The financial consequences of liability losses

■ Describe and analyze the following aspects of risk management as they apply to individuals and families:

- Steps in the risk management process

- Insurance as a risk management technique

- Other techniques to treat loss exposures

Develop Your Perspective

What are the main topics covered in the chapter?

We all face personal loss exposures. This chapter identifies those personal loss exposures and describes how the exposures can be addressed by various risk management techniques, including insurance. An overview is provided of the personal insurance policies that are addressed in depth in the remaining chapters of the text.

Evaluate the role that personal insurance plays in protecting individuals and families.

- How would society change if personal insurance were not available?

Why is it important to know these topics?

Personal insurance policies address the loss exposures faced by individuals and families. However, insurance might not be the only method of effectively addressing such loss exposures. Risk management involves identifying and addressing loss exposures using a variety of techniques.

Assess the fire loss exposure for homeowners.

- Although insurance is an excellent risk management technique for addressing this exposure, what additional techniques might be applied to reduce homeowners insurance premiums or lower the chance of loss?

How can you use this information?

Examine your own loss exposures:

- What risk management techniques are you already applying to address exposures?

- What additional risk management techniques might you consider applying?

Chapter 1

Overview of Personal Insurance

Personal insurance is a subject that affects all of us—not only in our professional lives, but also in our personal lives. Without insurance, most of us could not buy our homes, finance our cars, pay our hospital and medical bills, or prepare for unexpected financial emergencies.

This chapter provides a brief overview of personal insurance. It begins by exploring the property and liability loss exposures faced by individuals and families. In addition, individuals and families face losses caused by death, illness, injury, disability, and unemployment; these exposures are commonly known as personal loss exposures (or human loss exposures). The term "personal loss exposures" can also be used in its broader sense to mean all loss exposures relating to an individual or a family unit, including the property and liability loss exposures discussed in this chapter. Chapter 10 discusses other personal (human) loss exposures (such as death, illness, and disability).

Chapter 1 also explains the basic concept of personal risk management and introduces various risk management techniques, including insurance. Finally, this chapter gives an overview of the various types of insurance policies used to treat personal loss exposures. Later chapters of the text discuss those policies in detail.

To understand the exposures that affect the typical family and the personal insurance coverages needed to cover them, consider the following scenario:

> Ted and Carrie Russell are a young married couple with one young child, Jason. The Russells currently rent an apartment, but they are house hunting in the hope of soon buying a home in the suburbs near Ted's office. They own two late-model cars, a Ford Explorer and a Nissan Sentra. Ted and Carrie do not own many items of unusually high value, but Carrie is very proud of her diamond engagement ring. Ted is equally proud of his extensive coin collection that he inherited from his grandfather. Ted's company provides health insurance for the family and a small amount of life insurance on Ted. Because Carrie works for a very small firm, she does not receive any such benefits.

What types of loss exposures do Ted and Carrie have? What personal risk management techniques should they use? What types of personal insurance are they likely to have? What other types of personal insurance might they need? This chapter explores the answers to these questions.

Personal insurance
Insurance that covers the financial consequences of losses to individuals and families caused by death, illness, injury, disability, and unemployment.

LOSS EXPOSURES OF INDIVIDUALS AND FAMILIES

Loss exposure
Any condition or situation that presents the possibility of a financial loss, whether or not loss occurs.

All individuals and families face **loss exposures.** How they handle those loss exposures varies according to individual preference, resources, knowledge, and often ignorance. This section examines the loss exposures that can cause property and liability losses.

What situations in Ted's and Carrie's lives present the possibility that a loss will happen? Certainly, they face the possibility that their belongings could be damaged or destroyed by fire or other disaster. If the Russells invite a guest to their apartment who slips on water that Ted spilled on the kitchen floor, they could be held financially responsible for the guest's injuries. Their automobiles could be stolen or damaged in an accident. Suppose either Ted or Carrie negligently causes an automobile accident and injures another driver. The Russells could be held liable for the other driver's injuries, the damage to the other driver's car, and even the driver's loss of income.

All of these situations, and many more, are loss exposures that the Russells and most other people face.

Property Loss Exposures

Cause of loss
Means by which property is damaged or destroyed (e.g., fire and theft); also called perils.

A property loss results when property is destroyed, damaged, stolen, lost, or otherwise suffers a decrease in value because of a particular **cause of loss** (or **peril**). **Property loss exposures** consist of three elements:

- The property exposed to loss
- The possible causes of loss
- The financial consequences of loss

Property Exposed to Loss

Property loss exposure
Any condition or situation that presents the possibility of a property loss.

Property is any item with value. Property can be divided into two basic categories: real property and personal property.

Real Property

Real property
Land, as well as buildings and other structures attached to the land or embedded in it.

A family might own several types of **real property** that give rise to property loss exposures. The Russells do not have a real property exposure because they do not own a home or other real estate. However, if they buy a house, they will own real property that will probably present their greatest property loss exposure. The land on which their home is built would also be considered real property. In addition, items embedded in the land, such as underground pipes or foundations, are real property. If the Russells were to acquire any separate structures on their land, such as a storage shed or detached garage, those buildings would also present real property exposures.

Other types of real property also create property loss exposures. For example, owners of condominium units have ownership rights to common areas of the condominium property, such as land, swimming pools, and recreational areas, in addition to the unit they own. Some people own vacation homes or rental properties that present real property loss exposures.

Personal Property

Listing all the kinds of **personal property** that individuals and families can own would be impossible. Think of the Russells—what types of personal property are they likely to own? Certainly, they have furniture in their apartment, as well as items such as televisions, radios, and small appliances, plus dishes, silverware, tools, and books. Their clothes could represent a substantial value. Carrie's ring and Ted's coin collection are special types of personal property. Their personal property also includes their two cars. In addition, personal property can include intangible property, such as a patent or a copyright.

Personal property
Tangible or intangible property that is not real property.

For the purpose of identifying and insuring personal property loss exposures, personal property can be divided into the following categories:

- *Dwelling contents*—the broadest category of personal property. A dwelling's contents might include furniture, appliances, kitchenware, groceries, clothing, sports equipment, tools, and many other items common to the use of a dwelling as a home. For insurance purposes, such items are generally insured as a group rather than individually.

- *High-value personal property*—items of personal property worth considerable sums of money. Examples include silverware, jewelry, furs, and firearms. These items may be partially covered under the category of dwelling contents. However, they usually require a more specific type of insurance, because many insurance policies limit the amount of coverage available for such items.

- *Property with unusual or intrinsic value*—items whose value comes from their unique characteristics. Examples of this type of property are antiques, works of art, and coin or stamp collections. Such items should be specifically listed for insurance purposes because most insurance policies limit the amount that an insurer will pay for this type of personal property. The value of these items must be established (usually by an appraisal) when insurance is purchased.

- *Business personal property*—personal property, such as office furniture and computer equipment, used for business purposes. Most personal insurance policies limit or exclude coverage for business personal property, so additional insurance coverage might be necessary for this exposure.

- *Motor vehicles, trailers, watercraft, and aircraft*—mobile property typically excluded (or covered only up to a certain limit) in policies covering dwellings and their contents. Because these items present unique loss exposures, they should be separately insured.

To keep the cost of personal insurance reasonable, personal insurance policies are designed to cover the loss exposures of the average person or family. If personal policies included unlimited coverage on all categories of personal property, insurance premiums needed to provide such coverage would be higher than most people could afford or would be willing to pay. Customers sometimes have trouble understanding why full coverage for expensive jewelry and other valuable items is not included in their policies. Insurance professionals can help by explaining that in order to keep insurance premiums reasonable for the average consumer, it is fair for those persons who own valuable or unusual items to pay an additional premium to insure them.

Causes of Loss Affecting Property

Many causes of loss could damage or destroy both real and personal property. In the Russells' case, their apartment could be badly damaged by fire, destroying their personal belongings. A severe windstorm could cause the roof of their apartment building to blow off, and rain could then damage the contents of their apartment. Their cars could be stolen or be damaged in an accident. Their luggage could disappear while they are on vacation, and their clothes with it. The diamond in Carrie's ring could fall out of its setting and be lost. Countless possible causes of loss could affect an individual's or a family's property.

Financial Consequences of Property Losses

When a loss happens to property, an individual or a family suffers one or more of the following consequences:

- *Reduction in value of property*—the difference between the value of the property before the loss (preloss value) and after the loss (postloss value). If Carrie severely damages the front end of the Nissan as a result of a collision with a tree, the car would be worth less than it was worth before the accident.

- *Increased expenses*—expenses in addition to normal living expenses that are necessary because of the loss. Increased expenses would include the cost of renting a vehicle if Carrie's Nissan is temporarily unusable following a collision.

- *Lost income*—loss of income that results if property is damaged. For example, if a hurricane damages a home rented to others, the owner might not be able to collect rent on the property until the house is repaired or replaced.

Liability Loss Exposures

Liability loss exposure
Any condition or situation that presents the possibility of a liability loss.

As disastrous as a severe property loss might be, the potential for loss created by a **liability loss exposure** is even greater. In a society such as the United States, where the legal climate encourages lawsuits, individuals and families face a severe drain on assets from the possibility of being sued or being held responsible for someone else's injury. To understand liability loss exposures, consider two elements of such exposures:

- The possibility of a claim for money damages
- The financial consequences that might occur from a **liability loss**

What are the Russells' liability exposures? What situations might give rise to a liability claim? First, their possession and use of their apartment create liability. If a guest in their home trips on a ball Jason left on the stairs and breaks his leg, the guest might expect the Russells to pay his medical bills and perhaps even his lost wages. The cars the Russells own could also create liability; if either Ted or Carrie is at fault in an auto accident, the Russells could become liable for damage to another car and injury to the other driver, as well as for injuries sustained by passengers in their vehicle or the other vehicle. Suppose Jason hits another child with his baseball bat and sends him to the hospital. Once again, the Russells could be liable for the financial consequences.

Liability loss
A claim for money damages because of injury to another party or damage to another party's property.

Possibility of a Claim for Money Damages

A liability loss exposure involves the possibility that one party, claiming injury or damage, will bring a claim for money damages against another party allegedly at fault for the injury or damage.

Claims for liability damages are governed by **civil law**. The settlement of disputes between individuals and the indemnification for wrongs committed against individuals are within the scope of civil law. By contrast, criminal law deals with conduct that endangers the public welfare, such as the crimes of murder, rape, and fraud. Because such criminal acts are generally not the subject of insurance, civil law provides the legal foundation of insurance. Several types of claims fall under civil law, but the most common involve tort liability, contractual liability, and statutory liability.

Civil law
Body of law that deals with the rights and duties of citizens regarding one another.

Tort Liability

When injury or damage results from a **tort**, the injured party has the right under civil law to seek payment from the wrongdoer.

An individual may face a claim for tort damages on the basis of any of the following:

- **Negligence**—the most common cause of liability losses. To prove that negligence has occurred, an injured party must prove that all four legal elements of negligence have occurred. Exhibit 1-1 illustrates these four elements.
- **Intentional torts**—regardless of whether the harm itself is intended, the intentional act can create liability. Exhibit 1-2 presents some examples of intentional torts.

Tort
A wrongful act, other than a crime or breach of contract, committed by one party against another.

Negligence
The failure to act in a manner that is reasonably prudent, causing damage to another.

Intentional tort
A deliberate act that causes harm to another person.

Absolute liability (strict liability)
Legal liability that arises from inherently dangerous activities or dangerously defective products that harm another, regardless of the degree of care used; does not require proof of negligence.

- **Absolute liability**—liability that does not involve proving negligence. For example, if a person keeps a pet alligator in a cage in his back yard and the alligator bites a neighbor, the owner of the alligator could be held liable whether or not negligence can be proved. Owners of dangerous animals are typically held liable for injuries the animals cause regardless of how carefully the owners confine them.

EXHIBIT 1-1

The Elements of Negligence

1. *A duty to act.* For example, the Russells have a duty to maintain their premises so as not to cause injury to a guest.

2. *A breach of that duty.* If the Russells allow Jason to leave an object, such as a ball, on the front entry steps, they may have breached their duty to keep the premises safe.

3. *An injury or damage occurs.* A guest trips on the ball left on the steps and breaks his leg.

4. *The breach of duty is the direct cause of the injury or damage* (in an unbroken chain of events). The direct cause of the guest's broken leg is the ball Jason left on the steps.

EXHIBIT 1-2

Some Examples of Intentional Torts

Libel—a written or printed *untrue* statement that damages a person's reputation. For example, Ted prints an article in a local community newsletter claiming that his neighbor, Paul, has been convicted of drunken driving, which is not true.

Slander—an oral *untrue* statement that damages a person's reputation. If, at a parent-teacher meeting, Susan publicly and wrongly accuses a local pharmacist of selling illegal drugs to teenagers, she may be guilty of slander.

Assault—the intentional and unlawful *threat* of bodily harm. If Mary threatens to hit Betty, and Betty believes that Mary is ready and willing to carry out her threat, Mary has committed an assault on Betty.

Battery—unlawful physical contact with another person. If Mary carries out her threat and hits Betty, she has committed a battery. Betty may sue Mary for damages because of assault and battery.

Trespass—the unauthorized possession or use of land. If Jacob parks his car in Chris's yard without Chris's permission, Jacob may be guilty of trespass.

Nuisance—the violation of a person's right to enjoy use of property without disruption from outside sources. For instance, if Juliette persistently gives noisy parties that last late into the night, her neighbors may seek an injunction against such activities under civil law.

Contractual Liability

The possibility of **contractual liability** arises when an individual enters into a contract or an agreement. Leases for homes and apartments, as well as rental agreements for autos, power tools, and other equipment, typically contain provisions that transfer the financial consequences of liability losses from the owner of the property to the renter. For example, the Russells' apartment lease may require the Russells to assume liability for any injury or damage that results to others, even if the owner of the property was the party at fault. Alternatively, their lease may require that they assume liability only when they are at fault.

Contractual liability
Liability assumed under any contract or agreement.

Statutory Liability

Statutory liability is liability that exists because of the passage of a statute or law. Most important to individuals and families are the laws dealing with liability arising out of automobile accidents. These laws vary by state, and a detailed explanation of individual state laws is beyond the scope of this text. However, motorists should know the laws that apply in the state or states in which they live and work. As the discussion of no-fault laws in Chapter 2 explains, such laws change the legal basis of liability in regard to negligence.

Statutory liability
Liability imposed by a specific statute or law.

Financial Consequences of Liability Losses

When a liability claim occurs, an individual or a family can suffer two major financial consequences:

- Costs of investigation and defense
- Money damages awarded if the defense is not successful (or if the claim is settled out of court)

Many liability claims are settled before they reach court. For cases settled out of court, parties to the claim negotiate the amount paid in damages, and the costs of investigation and defense are usually reduced. Because settling out of court is usually less expensive than going through a potentially long trial, insurance companies often try to reach out-of-court settlements.

Unlike most property loss exposures, liability loss exposures put all of an individual's financial resources at risk of loss. When a court orders an individual to pay liability damages, the amount of the damages is based on the loss the injured party suffers. The court is not concerned with the financial resources of the party at fault or with that party's ability to pay the damages. As a result, all of an individual's or a family's savings and property are exposed to loss because of the possibility that the individual or family might have to liquidate all available resources to pay large liability damages. In addition, courts have the power to garnishee a portion of an individual's wages, if necessary, to pay for liability damages. The fact that all of an individual's assets, plus his or her future income, may be required to pay for liability damages makes a liability loss a frightening possibility.

PERSONAL RISK MANAGEMENT

Risk management
The process of making and carrying out decisions that will decrease the adverse effects of potential losses.

Families and individuals who engage in **risk management** can minimize worry and ease the harmful effects of a loss. Risk management helps people identify loss exposures and decide how to protect against potential losses before they happen.

Basics of Personal Risk Management

Risk management involves the following steps:

- Identifying loss exposures
- Analyzing loss exposures
- Examining possible risk management techniques that can be used to treat loss exposures
- Choosing the appropriate techniques
- Implementing the chosen techniques in a risk management plan
- Monitoring and revising the plan, as needed

Personal risk management
The risk management process applied to the loss exposures of individuals or families.

The typical individual or family does not pay much attention to personal risk management. **Personal risk management** is often unplanned and unintentional. Individuals and families are likely to consider insurance as the only way to handle their loss exposures and to expect insurance to take care of all their exposures for them. They are not likely to identify all their loss exposures, study alternative risk management techniques, and select and implement other techniques. They are even less likely to monitor and revise their decisions. Large corporations are far more likely to have a formal risk management program than are families.

Errors and omissions
Negligent acts (errors) committed by a person while conducting insurance business that give rise to legal liability for damages; can also involve a failure to act (omission) that creates legal liability.

Some customers expect a personal insurance agent or company representative to serve as their risk manager. Although trained insurance personnel can help clients identify their loss exposures and suggest appropriate insurance coverages, customers should make their own coverage decisions. Customers—not insurance companies—should select the desired coverages. Insurance professionals who deal with the public should offer customers several optional coverages and limits and then let them choose the ones they want and can afford. Insurance personnel can become involved in **errors and omissions (E&O)** claims if they act as risk managers for their clients. Customers who think an insurance professional gave them misleading or incorrect advice might bring an E&O claim against the insurance agency or company they believe to be responsible.

Insurance as a Risk Management Technique

As stated above, the risk management process includes examining and selecting the appropriate risk management techniques for the exposures. One risk management technique is insurance. Unfortunately, many individuals think insurance is the only risk management technique available to handle loss exposures, and they do not explore other possibilities. They might also think that insurance should cover all losses, no matter what the cause or the circumstances. In reality, insurance covers only certain losses, and other risk management techniques are appropriate for treating many loss exposures. Like any other business, insurance companies intend and need to make a profit. In fact, if they covered all losses and charged premiums that everyone would consider reasonable, they would not have the financial strength to cover their losses and operate their organizations.

Insurance is an excellent risk management technique for individuals and families, as long as personal insurance clients understand that insurance will not cover all their loss exposures and that they must choose other techniques as well. Personal insurance can protect against many typical loss exposures the average person or family faces. This text explores the ways that personal insurance policies cover various property and liability loss exposures. It also examines how life and health insurance can cover personal loss exposures that property and liability insurance do not cover.

Other Techniques To Treat Loss Exposures

In addition to insurance, the following are typical risk management techniques that an individual or a family can consider:

- Loss control
- Avoidance
- Noninsurance transfer
- Retention

Loss Control

Loss control is one of the most important and most overlooked personal risk management techniques. Controlling loss exposures involves both loss prevention and loss reduction. Loss prevention measures seek to control the frequency of losses; loss reduction measures aim at controlling the severity of losses that do occur. For example, a simple loss prevention technique the Russells could use to prevent crime losses would be to have deadbolt locks installed in their apartment and to keep doors and windows locked at all times. Loss reduction cannot prevent losses, but it can help to reduce the dollar amount of losses that occur. For instance, by limiting the amount of cash they keep in their home, Ted and Carrie could reduce the amount of money they would lose in a burglary.

Loss control
Risk management technique to reduce the frequency or severity of losses.

Avoidance

Another way of handling loss exposures is **avoidance**. If Ted and Carrie buy a house located on a large lake, they will automatically take on the additional loss exposure of possible flooding. The Russells' homeowners policy will not cover flooding damage to either their home or its contents. The Russells

Avoidance
Risk management technique by which an individual or a family avoids a loss exposure by choosing not to own a particular item of property or not to engage in a particular activity.

could avoid exposure to flood losses by simply deciding not to buy a house on the lake; instead, they could purchase a house in an inland area at an elevation that is not subject to flooding.

Noninsurance Transfer

By use of a **noninsurance transfer**, individuals can transfer the potential consequences of a loss exposure to another party by contract. For example, suppose Ted and Carrie buy a small house and decide to rent it to others. This house would present both property and liability exposures. The Russells can transfer property (and even liability) exposures to the tenants by requiring in the lease that the tenants be responsible for any losses that happen to the property (or any liability losses that happen as a result of their use of the house). The lease would thus transfer exposures from the owners to the tenants, and the tenants might then purchase property and liability insurance on the house.

Retention

Retention is another risk management technique, but it is one that many individuals do not wish to use or one that they use unintentionally. Retention can be intentional or unintentional. By intentionally choosing higher deductibles on their homeowners and auto policies, the Russells could save substantial premium dollars. However, they must be prepared to pay the greater deductible amount for each loss that occurs. Unintentional retention occurs when insureds do not purchase coverage for a particular exposure (such as flood or earthquake) either because they do not know that their policies exclude these perils or because they do not know that specific insurance is available to cover them.

How a Personal Risk Management Program Works

A look at the Russells' situation will illustrate how a personal risk management program can work. First, Ted and Carrie need to identify and analyze the loss exposures their family faces. One of the best ways for a family to identify property loss exposures is to estimate the value of their motor vehicle(s) and make a complete home inventory, listing all items of furniture and other possessions, including when they were acquired and at what price. To make this process easier, the Russells can take pictures or home videos of every room in their home. Many insurance companies and agents offer inventory forms to help in this process and can recommend professional photographers. Once the inventory is complete, it should be kept off the residence premises so it is not destroyed if a loss to the premises occurs. The Russells can also analyze their driving patterns and other personal activities that could cause liability claims. Do they play any sports? Do they have frequent guests, especially small children? Do they have unusual hazards such as swimming pools or dogs? Do they engage in any activities, such as volunteer work, that could cause a liability claim? Once they have identified and analyzed all their known property and liability loss exposures, they can determine ways to treat them and select the best risk management techniques.

The Russells can purchase insurance, if appropriate, to cover property exposures such as fire or other damage to their home and contents and liability exposures arising from their home or autos. Then they need to determine what exposures are not covered. Have they specifically insured Carrie's diamond engagement ring? Is Ted's coin collection fully covered? Do they live in an area subject to flooding? Do they occasionally rent a car, and, if so, will their insurance cover this exposure? What would they do if a catastrophe, such as a hurricane or an earthquake, struck their apartment building?

In addition to purchasing insurance, the Russells should consider the following risk management techniques:

- Employ *loss prevention* measures—for example, periodically inspecting the brakes and tires on their cars

- Implement *loss reduction* measures, such as purchasing fire extinguishers to minimize fire damage

- *Avoid* the risk of a flood exposure by not buying a house on a lake

- Examine their lease to determine whether any *noninsurance transfers* apply to them

- *Retain* some of the risk of loss by raising the deductibles on their insurance policies

In exploring various techniques, the Russells should try not to retain any exposures out of ignorance but should become enlightened consumers using risk management to their advantage.

TYPES OF PERSONAL INSURANCE POLICIES

Personal insurance policies are often standardized and are usually written as a **package policy**, combining property and liability coverages at a reasonable price. Although many insurance consumers think that their policies will (or should) cover them for anything that might happen, such all-inclusive policies do not exist. Although standardized personal insurance policies meet the needs of most customers, no policy covers every potential loss exposure.

This text examines many of the typical policies used to insure loss exposures for individuals and families. It focuses initially on the two most commonly used personal policies: the personal auto policy (PAP) and the homeowners policy. Then it explores some of the policies that provide other types of protection, including the following:

- Dwelling policy
- Mobilehome insurance
- Farm insurance
- Flood insurance
- FAIR plans, beachfront and windstorm plans
- Inland marine insurance

Package policy
Policy that includes two or more lines of insurance. In personal insurance, such as property and liability, examples of package policies are the homeowners policy and the personal auto policy.

- Watercraft insurance
- Umbrella policies
- Life insurance
- Health insurance, including Medicare
- Disability income insurance

In studying these policies, consider the types of exposures that each is intended to cover. Note also the types of exposures that are not covered. Exhibit 1-3 lists some of the typical property and liability exposures and insurance policies for individuals and families, but it is by no means a comprehensive list.

EXHIBIT 1-3

Some Typical Property and Liability Exposures and Policies for Individuals and Families

Exposure	Policy	Some Major Exposures *Not* Covered
Automobiles	Personal Auto Policy	Regular use of a company car Driving outside North America Racing
Property: home and contents	Homeowners Policy	Flood, earthquake
Personal liability	Homeowners Policy	Business activities Professional liability
Personal liability: large lawsuits	Personal Umbrella Policy	Business activities Professional liability
Boat	Boatowners Policy	Racing events Liability for water-skiers
Vacation or rental home	Dwelling Policy with Liability Supplement	Theft coverage for personal property Business activities
Mobilehome and contents	Mobilehome Policy	Flood, earthquake Transportation of mobilehome
Mobilehome liability	Mobilehome Policy	Business activities Professional liability

Valuable items:
  jewelry, furs, coin collections,
  musical instruments,
  fine arts, etc.
	Scheduled Personal
	  Property Endorsement
	  (to Homeowners Policy)
	  or Personal Articles
	  Floater (PAF)
		Breakage of fragile fine arts
		Professional use of musical instruments

Damage to property from rising waters	National Flood Insurance Policy	Amounts over maximum limits set by law

Earthquake damage	Earthquake Policy
	  or Endorsement to
	  Homeowners Policy
		Flooding or tidal wave, even if
		  caused by earthquake

What types of insurance policies might the Russells need? With two automobiles in the family, they probably have a personal auto policy. As apartment dwellers, they should have a "tenant homeowners" policy (popularly known as a "renters policy"). (If they owned a home, they would probably have a homeowners policy.) However, because renters are not usually required to purchase insurance on their property, apartment dwellers often overlook this inexpensive yet valuable coverage. Ted has a group life insurance policy, but does he carry any individual life insurance? Is there any life insurance on Carrie and Jason? Given their circumstances, the Russells might overlook these coverages or consider them unaffordable. Ted's group health policy might be adequate, but does he have disability coverage in case he is unable to work because of an accident or illness? Additional coverages the Russells might consider include a personal umbrella policy, which would protect them against large liability claims, and a separate policy or endorsement on Carrie's ring and Ted's coin collection. This text will explain all of these coverages in more detail.

SUMMARY

Personal insurance consists of the insurance coverages designed to cover loss exposures of individuals and families. Personal loss exposures exist when personal resources are subject to causes of loss that might adversely affect an individual's or a family's financial condition. Personal loss exposures can include property and liability loss exposures as well as "human" loss exposures such as death, illness, and disability.

Property loss exposures consist of the following elements: the property exposed to loss, the possible causes of loss (perils), and the financial consequences of loss. Property losses can affect not only real property, such as houses and other structures, but also personal property, such as household contents. Other categories of personal property exposed to loss are high-value personal property, property with unusual or intrinsic value, business personal property, and mobile property such as autos and boats. All types of property are exposed to numerous causes of loss, many of which can be insured against. The financial consequences of property losses include reduction in the value of the property, as well as increased expenses and lost income that might result from such losses.

Liability loss exposures involve the possibility of a claim for money damages and the potentially large financial consequences of such a claim. A liability loss results when a claim for money damages is made against an individual for alleged injury to another or damage to another's property. Under civil law, which deals with the rights and duties of citizens with respect to each other, liability claims can be made on the basis of tort liability, contractual liability, and statutory liability. A person might face a claim for tort liability on the basis of negligence, or failing to exercise reasonable care; intentional torts, such as libel or slander; or absolute liability, which involves inherently dangerous activities. Financial consequences of liability claims can include costs of investigation and defense, as well as money damages if the defense is not successful or if the claim is settled out of court.

Personal risk management can minimize worry and ease the harmful effects of a loss. Risk management involves the following steps:

- Identifying loss exposures
- Analyzing loss exposures
- Examining possible risk management techniques
- Choosing the appropriate techniques
- Implementing the chosen techniques
- Monitoring and revising the plan

Insurance personnel can help a client identify loss exposures and can suggest appropriate insurance coverages, but they should not select coverages for the customer, or they might become involved in errors and omissions (E&O) claims. Although insurance is one effective risk management technique, others are loss control, avoidance, noninsurance transfer, and retention.

Personal insurance policies are designed to transfer the financial consequences of many personal loss exposures from individuals and families to insurance companies. The most common personal policies are standardized package policies, which combine property and liability coverages in one policy, such as the homeowners and personal auto policies. Although package policies meet the needs of most personal insurance customers, no policy covers every potential loss exposure. This text will examine many of the typical policies used to insure loss exposures for individuals and families.

Chapter 2

Direct Your Learning

Automobile Insurance and Society

After learning the subject matter of this chapter, you should be able to:

■ Describe various problems associated with automobile insurance.

■ Describe and evaluate each of the following approaches to compensating automobile accident victims:
  - Tort liability system
  - Financial responsibility laws
  - Compulsory insurance laws
  - Unsatisfied judgment funds
  - Uninsured motorists coverage
  - Underinsured motorists coverage
  - Low-cost auto insurance

■ Describe each of the following:
  - Characteristics of no-fault automobile insurance laws, including benefits provided
  - Types of no-fault automobile insurance laws
  - Arguments favoring and opposing no-fault automobile insurance

■ Describe the methods used to provide automobile insurance to high-risk drivers.

■ Explain why and how states regulate personal automobile insurance.

■ Describe the factors used to rate personal automobile insurance, and explain how competition affects rates.

Develop Your Perspective

What are the main topics covered in the chapter?

This chapter examines automobile insurance issues as they relate to society. Problems involving the high frequency and cost of automobile accidents have led to systems designed to ensure that auto accident victims are compensated for their losses and injuries.

Analyze the problems associated with automobile insurance.

Could these problems be remedied by no-fault insurance as it is described in the chapter?

Why is it important to know these topics?

Compensating innocent automobile accident victims requires systems that hold negligent drivers accountable for their actions. However, insurance companies are unwilling to insure drivers with poor driving records. Thus, residual markets are created to make insurance available for high-risk drivers. Also, automobile insurance is highly regulated to ensure that the public is treated fairly by insurance companies.

Consider how your state makes certain that automobile accident victims are compensated for their injuries and financial losses.

How can you use this information?

Determine the minimum limits of automobile coverage required in your state.

- If another automobile insured for minimum limits struck your vehicle and injured you, would the limits be sufficient to compensate you for the value of your vehicle and your possible injuries?

- If not, what action might you take to ensure that you and your vehicle are adequately covered?

Chapter 2

Automobile Insurance and Society

This chapter begins with the subject of automobile insurance, one of the best known and most used types of personal insurance. Millions of individuals are injured or disabled each year in auto accidents, and thousands are killed. The high cost of medical services, the unexpected death of a family member, and the loss of or damage to an auto can all have profound financial effects on an individual or a family. This chapter examines these and several other important problems concerning autos and auto insurance.

After examining some of the problems associated with auto insurance, this chapter discusses various systems that have been designed to compensate auto accident victims. Following the discussion of other compensation systems, the chapter explores no-fault insurance laws and residual (nonstandard) markets for insuring high-risk drivers. Finally, this chapter describes the regulation and rating of personal auto insurance.

PROBLEMS ASSOCIATED WITH AUTOMOBILE INSURANCE

Most of the millions of Americans who own autos have purchased insurance policies to protect against the financial consequences of auto accidents. Auto insurers, however, have experienced many problems in their efforts to insure the driving population. In addition, some drivers have difficulty obtaining insurance they can afford. Following are some of the problems associated with auto insurance that this chapter addresses:

- High frequency of auto accidents
- High costs of auto accidents
- Underwriting losses
- Irresponsible drivers
- Availability and affordability of auto insurance

High Frequency of Automobile Accidents

According to the National Safety Council, an estimated 25 million drivers per year—more than one of every eight licensed drivers—are involved in auto accidents in the United States. A motor vehicle death occurs, on average, every thirteen minutes and an injury, every sixteen seconds. The good news is that the number of fatalities per 100,000 registered vehicles has been steadily declining during the past decade.[1]

Drivers under the influence of alcohol or drugs cause many fatalities. Other poor driving habits such as speeding, following too closely (tailgating), falling asleep at the wheel, using cellular phones, and failing to yield right of way also account for a large number of accidents. A distressing modern trend, particularly in urban traffic areas, is that of accidents and deaths caused by driver aggression—too many people under too much stress with too little respect for other human beings.

High Costs of Automobile Accidents

The economic costs of motor vehicle accidents are well over $50 billion per year. Insured losses include the costs of property damage, medical expenses, lost income, emergency services, and legal fees. Additional costs include lost productivity, public assistance programs, and insurance administrative expenses. Increases in medical costs, automobile repair costs, and legal costs have contributed to the steadily rising cost of automobile accidents.

Underwriting Losses

Underwriting loss
An insurer's loss incurred when losses and expenses for a given period are greater than its premium income for the same period.

Standard market
Insurers who voluntarily offer insurance coverages at rates designed for customers with average or better-than-average loss exposures.

Insurers' auto insurance underwriting results vary by state and over time. Some automobile insurers have experienced consistent **underwriting losses** in some states.

Because of underwriting losses, many auto insurers periodically increase premiums and tighten their eligibility requirements for accepting auto insurance customers. As a result, some motorists have considerable difficulty obtaining necessary coverages from insurers in the **standard market**.

Irresponsible Drivers

Irresponsible drivers are another part of the automobile insurance problem. These drivers fall into three main groups, and some drivers might belong to more than one of these groups:

- Drivers with no automobile insurance
- Drivers under the influence of alcohol or drugs
- Other high-risk drivers

Drivers With No Automobile Insurance

According to one study, 14 percent of drivers in the United States were uninsured.[2] Uninsured drivers are a major problem, because when uninsured drivers cause accidents that injure other persons or damage property of others, they usually cannot pay for the injuries or damage they have caused. When innocent accident victims have no compensation available to them, society must address the problem.

Drivers Under the Influence of Alcohol or Drugs

Alcohol and drug abuse is widespread in the United States as well as in many other countries. Drivers under the influence of alcohol or illegal drugs are also responsible for a large number of nonfatal automobile accidents. In addition to the use of illegal drugs, the use of legal drugs, such as sedatives and even decongestants, can also impair driving ability and has caused many automobile accidents.

Many states have tightened their drunk-driving laws, increased the penalties for first-time offenders, and passed laws holding servers of alcohol legally liable for accidents caused by drunk customers and guests. Groups such as Mothers Against Drunk Drivers (MADD), Students Against Drunk Drivers (SADD), and the Insurance Institute for Highway Safety (IIHS, which is supported in part by casualty insurance companies and trade associations) are effective in aggressively pushing for measures to remove drunk drivers from the roads.

Other High-Risk Drivers

Other high-risk drivers include those who habitually violate traffic laws, those who are involved in an excessive number of traffic accidents, and those who are convicted of certain serious offenses, such as reckless driving and driving with a suspended license. Insuring these individuals is extremely difficult for private insurers because of the high probability of a high-risk driver killing or seriously injuring other persons.

Availability and Affordability of Automobile Insurance

A final problem is that some individuals are unable to buy auto insurance at affordable premiums in the standard market. Because of large underwriting losses and the potential of large liability judgments, auto insurers restrict the sale of auto insurance to certain groups, or they make the coverages available to certain drivers at premiums that are substantially higher than standard premiums.

Those who cannot purchase auto insurance at standard rates include drivers convicted of serious or multiple traffic violations and other high-risk drivers. Insurers commonly consider young and inexperienced drivers, especially young unmarried male drivers, as undesirable insureds because statistics show that such inexperienced drivers have a greater-than-average probability of having automobile accidents.

COMPENSATION OF AUTO ACCIDENT VICTIMS[3]

Under the legal system in the United States, persons who are injured or who incur property damage losses because of the negligence of the owner or operator of an automobile are entitled to compensation and damages. Both automobile insurers and state governments have designed various approaches to compensating auto accident victims, including the following:

- The tort liability system
- Financial responsibility laws
- Compulsory insurance laws
- Unsatisfied judgment funds
- Uninsured motorists coverage
- Underinsured motorists coverage
- Low-cost auto insurance

In addition to using these methods, many states have enacted no-fault laws.

Contributory negligence law
Law that prevents a person from recovering damages if that person contributes in any way to his or her own injury. Thus, if Driver A is judged to be 20 percent responsible for an accident, and Driver B is judged to be 80 percent responsible, Driver A cannot collect any damages.

Comparative negligence law
Law that requires both parties to a loss to share the financial burden of the injury according to their respective degrees of fault. For example, under one type of comparative negligence law, if Driver A is judged to be 20 percent responsible for an accident and Driver B is judged to be 80 percent responsible, Driver A can collect for his or her injury, but the damages to which Driver A would otherwise be entitled are reduced by 20 percent. In a number of states, if Driver A is 50 percent or more responsible for the accident, he or she can collect nothing from Driver B.

> ### Reminder
>
> A *tort* is a wrongful act, other than a crime or breach of contract, committed by one party against another.
>
> *Negligence* is acting differently from the way a reasonably prudent person would act under similar circumstances. An individual is negligent when he or she fails to exercise the appropriate degree of care under given circumstances.

The Tort Liability System

The tort liability system, based on fault, is the traditional and most commonly used method in the United States of seeking compensation for injured auto accident victims. As discussed in Chapter 1, the most common cause of *tort* liability is *negligence*. If someone operates an auto in a negligent manner that results in damage to another's property or in bodily injury to another person, the operator can be held legally liable for the damages incurred by the injured person. To avoid legal liability, auto owners and operators must exercise a high degree of care to protect others from harm.

Under the tort liability system, injured auto accident victims must prove that another party was negligent before they can collect damages. A few states, however, have **contributory negligence laws** that make it difficult for an accident victim to collect damages.

Because of the harshness of contributory negligence laws, most states have enacted some type of **comparative negligence law** that allows injured persons to recover damages even though they might have contributed to the accident. Although comparative negligence laws vary by state, they all share the common element that negligence on the part of the injured party does not necessarily prevent recovery for damages.

Critics have attacked the tort liability system, arguing that it is unfair and has many defects. One type of **tort reform** that several states have proposed and enacted is no-fault insurance, which this chapter discusses later.

Financial Responsibility Laws

Financial responsibility laws require motorists to provide proof of financial responsibility (such as liability insurance) under the following circumstances:

- After the occurrence of an auto accident involving bodily injury or property damage exceeding a certain dollar amount
- After a conviction for certain serious offenses, such as drunk driving, reckless driving, or losing a driver's license because of repeated violations
- Upon failure to pay a judgment that results from an auto accident

If motorists do not provide the required proof of financial responsibility, they face suspension of both their driver's license and vehicle registration.

Although financial responsibility laws provide some protection against irresponsible drivers, critics point out the following defects:

- *Most financial responsibility requirements become effective only after an accident, a conviction, or a judgment.* Thus, the law does not guarantee that a negligent driver will be able to pay a judgment to an accident victim.
- *Financial responsibility laws do not guarantee payment to all accident victims.* Accident victims might not be compensated if uninsured drivers, hit-and-run drivers, or drivers of stolen cars injure them.
- *The legal system might cause considerable delay in compensating accident victims.* Delays caused by clogged courts can result in considerable financial hardship for some automobile accident victims.
- *Injured persons might not be fully indemnified for their injuries.* Most financial responsibility laws require only minimum amounts of financial responsibility, which might not fully compensate the injured person.

Compulsory Insurance Laws

Many states have enacted **compulsory auto insurance laws** that require auto liability insurance for all motorists to drive legally in the state. Alternatively, a motorist can post a bond or deposit cash or securities to guarantee financial responsibility in the event of an accident.

Many people consider compulsory insurance laws superior to financial responsibility laws because motorists must provide proof of financial responsibility *before* an accident occurs. Critics of compulsory insurance laws, however, argue

Tort reform
Proposed or actual legislation intended to reduce legal costs or settlement awards resulting from negligence lawsuits.

Financial responsibility law
Law that requires motorists, under certain circumstances, to provide proof that they have the ability to pay, up to certain minimum amounts, for damage or injury that they might cause as a result of operating a vehicle.

Compulsory auto insurance law
Law that requires the owners or operators of automobiles to carry automobile liability insurance at least equal to certain minimum limits before the vehicle can be licensed or registered.

that compulsory insurance laws have serious defects, including some defects that financial responsibility laws share. The following are frequently cited as problems related to compulsory insurance:

- *Compulsory insurance laws do not guarantee compensation to all accident victims.* For example, persons might be injured by hit-and-run drivers, drivers whose insurance has lapsed, out-of-state drivers with no insurance, drivers of stolen cars, or drivers of fraudulently registered vehicles.

- *Compulsory insurance laws provide incomplete protection.* The required minimum amount of insurance might not meet the full needs of accident victims. Exhibit 2-1 shows the minimum limits required by compulsory insurance or financial responsibility laws.

- *There can be considerable delay in the legal system before accident victims are compensated.* Because compulsory insurance is based on the tort system, delays caused by an overburdened court system can result in considerable financial hardship for some automobile accident victims.

- *Compulsory insurance laws might not reduce the number of uninsured motorists.* Some drivers do not insure their vehicles because insurance is too costly. Others let coverage lapse after demonstrating proof of insurance to satisfy vehicle registration requirements.

- *Insurers argue that compulsory laws restrict their freedom to select profitable insureds.* In addition, insurers fear that state regulators might deny needed rate increases, resulting in underwriting losses.

- *Consumer advocates argue that if insurers are allowed to increase rates to accept all applicants for insurance, rates might become unfairly high for good drivers.* In other words, good drivers could be subsidizing rates for the high-risk drivers that insurers are required by law to insure.

- *Compulsory insurance laws do nothing to prevent or reduce the number of automobile accidents.* This argument expresses one of the most serious problems associated with automobile insurance.

Unsatisfied Judgment Funds

A few states (all of which have compulsory insurance laws) have established **unsatisfied judgment funds**. These funds have the following common characteristics:

- The injured person must obtain a judgment against the negligent driver and show that the judgment cannot be collected.

- The maximum amount paid is generally limited to the state's minimum compulsory insurance requirement. In addition, most funds reduce the amount paid by any amount collected from other collateral sources of recovery, such as payments from a workers compensation law or from insurance.

- The negligent driver is not relieved of legal liability when the unsatisfied judgment fund makes a payment to the insured person. The negligent

Unsatisfied judgment funds
Funds established by some states to compensate auto accident victims who have obtained a court judgment that is uncollectible because the negligent party cannot pay.

EXHIBIT 2-1

Automobile Financial Responsibility/Compulsory Limits by State

State	Liability limits[1]	State	Liability limits[1]
Alabama	20/40/10	Montana	25/50/10
Alaska	50/100/25	Nebraska	25/50/25
Arizona	15/30/10	Nevada	15/30/10
Arkansas	25/50/25	New Hampshire[5]	25/50/25
California[2]	15/30/5	New Jersey[6]	15/30/5
Colorado	25/50/15	New Mexico	25/50/10
Connecticut	20/40/10	New York[7]	25/50/10
Delaware	15/30/5	North Carolina	30/60/25
D.C.	25/50/10	North Dakota	25/50/25
Florida[4]	10/20/10	Ohio	12.5/25/7.5
Georgia	25/50/25	Oklahoma	10/20/10
Hawaii	20/40/10	Oregon	25/50/10
Idaho	25/50/15	Pennsylvania	15/30/5
Illinois	20/40/15	Rhode Island	25/50/25
Indiana	25/50/10	South Carolina	15/30/10
Iowa	20/40/15	South Dakota	25/50/25
Kansas	25/50/10	Tennessee[3]	25/50/10
Kentucky	25/50/10	Texas	20/40/15
Louisiana	10/20/10	Utah	25/50/15
Maine	50/100/25	Vermont	25/50/10
Maryland	20/40/15	Virginia	25/50/20
Massachusetts	20/40/5	Washington	25/50/10
Michigan	20/40/10	West Virginia	20/40/10
Minnesota	30/60/10	Wisconsin[5]	25/50/10
Mississippi	10/20/5	Wyoming	25/50/20
Missouri	25/50/10		

[1]The first two figures refer to bodily injury liability and the third figure, to property damage liability. For example, 20/40/10 means coverage up to $40,000 for all persons injured in an accident, subject to a limit of $20,000, for one individual, and $10,000 coverage for property damage. [2]Low-cost policy limits for Los Angeles and San Francisco low-income drivers in the California Automobile Assigned Risk Plan are 10/20/3. This is a pilot program effective from July 1, 2000, until January 1, 2004. [3]Although legally defined as financial responsibility, Tennessee's law is similar to a compulsory law because drivers can be fined if stopped by police or after crashes if they cannot show proof of financial responsibility. [4]Only property damage liability is compulsory. [5]Liability insurance not compulsory; limits are for financial responsibility. [6]Drivers may choose a Standard or Basic Policy. Basic Policy limits are 10/10/5. [7]50/100 if injury results in death.

Source: *Insurance Information Institute Fact Book 2002*, based on information obtained from Alliance of American Insurers, American Insurance Association, National Association of Independent Insurers, and Insurance Information Institute.

driver must repay the fund or lose his or her driver's license until the fund is reimbursed for the payments made.

Several methods are used to finance the benefits paid under unsatisfied judgment funds. States obtain funds by assessing insurers based on the amount of auto liability insurance premiums written in the state, by charging each motorist a fee, by assessing the uninsured drivers in the state, and by surcharging motorists convicted of moving violations.

Unsatisfied judgment funds offer the advantage of ensuring that injured accident victims have some protection against irresponsible motorists. In addition, states with such funds attempt to keep uninsured drivers off the road by suspending their driving licenses until they reimburse the unsatisfied judgment fund.

Those who oppose unsatisfied judgment funds point out the following major disadvantages:

- Financing is inequitable because insured motorists within the state are charged a fee.
- Administration of the funds is often cumbersome and slow.
- Amounts that uninsured motorists repay into the fund are relatively small.
- Some funds have experienced financial problems because of inadequate funding.

Uninsured Motorists Coverage

Uninsured motorists (UM) coverage
Coverage that reimburses an insured auto accident victim who sustains bodily injury (and, in some states, property damage) caused by an uninsured motorist, a hit-and-run driver, or a driver whose insurer is insolvent.

Uninsured motorists (UM) coverage is an approach for compensating automobile accident victims that appears to work reasonably well as a technique for providing some financial protection against an uninsured driver. UM insurance is mandatory in many states and optional in the rest. Most states require that all automobile liability policies contain UM coverage unless the insured voluntarily waives the coverage in writing. Details of UM insurance are included in the discussion of the personal auto policy in Chapter 3.

However, uninsured motorists coverage has several defects as a technique for compensating injured auto accident victims:

- *As with other compensation methods previously mentioned, an injured person might not be fully compensated for his or her economic loss.* Unless the insured has purchased higher UM limits, the maximum paid for a bodily injury claim is limited to the state's financial responsibility or compulsory insurance law requirement.
- *Before the injured person can collect under the UM coverage, legal responsibility of the uninsured motorist for the accident must be established.* This responsibility might be difficult to establish in some cases and could be expensive if the injured person hires an attorney.
- *Property damage is excluded in most states.* In such states, if a negligent uninsured motorist fails to stop for a red light and damages another car,

the owner of the damaged car would collect nothing for this property loss under the UM coverage. In some states, UM property damage coverage can be added at the insured's option.

- *The victim is paying for insurance to protect against the failure of others to act responsibly.* In effect, UM insurance provides coverage similar to the liability insurance that the negligent party failed to buy.

Underinsured Motorists Coverage

Underinsured motorists coverage provides additional limits of protection to the victim of an auto accident when the negligent driver's insurance limits are insufficient to pay for the damages. It can be added by endorsement to an automobile insurance policy and in some states is included automatically. Chapter 4 includes a discussion of the underinsured motorists endorsement and other endorsements to the personal auto policy.

For example, Tony has underinsured motorists coverage in the amount of $100,000 and is injured by a negligent driver who has a bodily injury liability limit of $50,000. If Tony is entitled to damages of $75,000 for his injury, he would recover a maximum of $50,000 from the negligent driver's insurer because that is the applicable limit of liability. He would collect the remaining $25,000 from the underinsured motorists coverage his own insurer provides.

Although *underinsured motorists* insurance is sometimes combined with *uninsured motorists* insurance, the two coverages should not be confused. They do not overlap or duplicate each other. An insured can collect under one coverage or the other, depending on the situation, but not both. As stated earlier, the UM coverage applies when the bodily injury is caused by an uninsured motorist, by a hit-and-run driver, or by a driver whose insurer is insolvent. In contrast, underinsured motorists coverage applies only when the other driver has liability insurance, but the liability limits carried by the negligent driver are lower than the limits provided by the injured person's underinsured motorists coverage.

In most states, the underinsured motorists coverage can be written only if certain conditions are satisfied, such as the following:

- Uninsured motorists coverage must be included in the policy.
- The insured must purchase increased limits for the uninsured motorists coverage that are higher than the state's minimum financial responsibility limits.
- The limits for the uninsured and underinsured motorists coverages must be the same.
- The underinsured motorists coverage must apply to all automobiles covered under the policy.

Underinsured motorists coverage
Coverage that applies when a negligent driver has liability insurance at the time of the accident but has limits lower than those of the injured person's coverage.

Low-Cost Auto Insurance

Low-cost auto insurance is intended to decrease the number of uninsured drivers by making minimal liability coverage available at a reduced cost. In New Jersey, for example, a basic policy offers $15,000 in personal injury protection, up to $250,000 in medical benefits for catastrophic injuries, and $5,000 property damage liability. Uninsured and underinsured motorists coverage is not available. In Colorado, a no-fault state, a low-cost plan provides first-party medical expense or personal injury protection coverage with a maximum benefit of $25,000. A pilot program in California offers bodily injury liability coverage up to $10,000 per person and $20,000 per accident, and property damage liability coverage with a $3,000 limit.

To date, low-cost auto policies have not been highly successful in attracting low-income drivers who have few assets to protect and little money to pay auto insurance premiums.

NO-FAULT AUTOMOBILE INSURANCE[4]

No-fault automobile insurance
Insurance that covers automobile accident victims on a first-party basis, allowing them to collect damages from their own insurers regardless of who was at fault.

No-fault automobile insurance is another approach for compensating auto accident victims. Today, many states have some type of no-fault auto insurance law with restrictions on filing lawsuits. Other states allow some type of *first-party* automobile insurance but do not restrict lawsuits. Exhibit 2-2 shows the jurisdictions that have various forms of first-party automobile insurance.

Under a no-fault system, an injured person does not need to establish fault and prove negligence in order to collect payment for damages. In addition, a true no-fault law places some restrictions on the right to sue the negligent driver who causes the accident. If a claim is below a certain **monetary threshold** (a relatively low limit, such as $2,500), an injured motorist would collect for the injury from his or her own insurer. If the loss exceeds the threshold amount, the injured person has the right to seek compensation from the negligent driver, which could include suing for damages resulting from the accident. A few states with no-fault laws use a **verbal threshold** (rather than a monetary threshold), which specifies what types of injuries qualify for compensation from a negligent party. In these states, persons with injuries other than those specified are not entitled to recover damages from a negligent driver but must collect from their own insurers.

Monetary threshold
The level of monetary damages in a no-fault system at which one injured party can seek compensation from the at-fault party.

Verbal threshold
The level of severity of injury in a no-fault system, including death and certain specified injuries, such as disfigurement or dismemberment, at which the injured party can seek compensation from the at-fault party.

Characteristics of No-Fault Laws

Although no-fault laws vary widely among states, certain characteristics are common to these laws. They all seek to limit the need to prove negligence so that benefits can be paid quickly. They also define the conditions under which a victim might be entitled to additional compensation from the party at fault.

EXHIBIT 2-2

State Auto Insurance Laws Governing Liability Coverage

"True" No-Fault	First-party benefits Compulsory	First-party benefits Optional	Restrictions on lawsuits Yes	Restrictions on lawsuits No	Thresholds for lawsuits Monetary	Thresholds for lawsuits Verbal
Colorado	X		X		X	
Florida	X		X			X
Hawaii	X		X		X	
Kansas	X		X		X	
Kentucky	X		X	X[1]	X[1]	
Massachusetts	X		X		X	
Michigan	X		X			X
Minnesota	X		X		X	
New Jersey	X		X	X[1]		X[1,2]
New York	X		X			X
North Dakota	X		X		X	
Pennsylvania	X		X	X[1]		X[1]
Utah	X		X		X	
Puerto Rico	X		X		X	

Add-on						
Arkansas		X		X		
Delaware	X			X		
D.C.		X	X[3]	X[3]		
Maryland	X			X		
New Hampshire		X		X		
Oregon	X			X		
South Dakota		X		X		
Texas		X		X		
Virginia		X		X		
Washington		X		X		
Wisconsin		X		X		

In the following twenty-seven states, auto liability is based on the traditional tort liability system. In these states, there are no restrictions on lawsuits:

Alabama
Alaska
Arizona
California
Connecticut
Georgia
Idaho
Illinois
Indiana
Iowa
Louisiana
Maine
Mississippi
Missouri
Montana
Nebraska
Nevada
Nevada
New Mexico
North Carolina
Ohio
Oklahoma
Rhode Island
South Carolina
Tennessee
Vermont
West Virginia
Wyoming

[1]"Choice" no-fault state. Policyholder can choose a policy based on the no-fault system or traditional tort liability. [2]Verbal threshold for the Basic Liability Policy and the Standard Policy where the policyholder chooses no-fault. The Basic Policy contains lower amounts of coverage. [3]The District of Columbia is neither a true no-fault nor add-on state. Drivers are offered the option of no-fault or fault-based coverage, but in the event of an accident, a driver who originally chose no-fault benefits has sixty days to decide whether to receive those benefits or file a claim against the other party.

Source: *Insurance Information Institute Fact Book 2002,* based on information obtained from American Insurance Association.

Typical No-Fault Benefits

Personal injury protection (PIP) endorsement

Endorsement to an auto insurance policy describing the no-fault benefits that are provided.

Insurers provide no-fault benefits by adding an endorsement to an auto insurance policy. The endorsement is typically called a **personal injury protection (PIP) endorsement.** (In some states, the endorsement is called "basic reparations.") Benefits the endorsement provides are limited to the injured person's actual *economic* loss, including payment of medical expenses, a percentage of lost wages, and certain other expenses. The injured person can seek compensation from the responsible party for *noneconomic* losses that are not measurable in dollars (such as pain and suffering, inconvenience, and mental anguish) only if the monetary threshold is exceeded or the verbal threshold is met.

The following are typical no-fault benefits:

- Medical expenses—usually paid up to some maximum limit
- Rehabilitation expenses—usually paid in addition to medical expenses
- Loss of earnings—a proportion of the insured person's lost earnings (usually subject to a maximum amount and time limit)
- Expenses for essential services—benefits paid for expenses incurred or certain necessary services the injured person normally performs, such as housework and house repairs
- Funeral expenses—usually paid up to a certain limit (In some states, this benefit is part of the medical expense limit.)
- Survivors' loss benefits—periodic income payments that partially compensate certain survivors for the death of a covered auto accident victim

Some states require that higher optional no-fault benefits be available to persons who want benefits above the prescribed minimums. In addition, some states require insurance companies to provide optional deductibles that can be used to reduce or eliminate certain no-fault benefits.

Right To Seek Compensation From the Party at Fault

The right to seek compensation from the party at fault depends on the type of no-fault law. States with add-on plans do not restrict the right to sue. In the majority of states that have enacted modified no-fault laws, the injured person may sue if the injury exceeds the threshold. The insured person usually has the option of continuing to receive the no-fault benefits instead of seeking compensation from the negligent party. No-fault laws typically allow the no-fault insurer to collect payment from the party at fault or from the negligent driver's insurer to the extent that no-fault benefits are paid. Like other no-fault provisions discussed here, the insurer's right to collect from the party at fault varies by state.

Exclusion of Property Damage

No-fault laws generally apply only to injuries and not to damage to property. (One exception to this rule is Michigan, which requires that property damage be included in no-fault coverage.) Thus, if a negligent motorist damages a person's property, that person has a right to seek compensation from the party at fault. No-fault laws generally exclude property damage for several reasons:

- Property damage is relatively small and is usually confined to vehicles.
- The amount of damage to property can usually be determined without great difficulty.
- Auto insurers can usually settle claims for damage to their insureds' property quickly.

Types of No-Fault Laws

When no-fault insurance was first proposed as a means of eliminating or at least reducing the high costs of auto liability suits, the proponents of no-fault anticipated a pure no-fault system. A **pure no-fault system** would have abolished the tort liability system for bodily injuries resulting from auto accidents. However, many people thought a pure no-fault system would be unfair, and no state has yet enacted a pure no-fault law. Instead, certain states have enacted one of two types of no-fault laws: add-on plans and modified no-fault laws.

Add-On Plans

An **add-on plan** is appropriately named, because it adds benefits to auto insurance policies but takes nothing away. Such a plan is not a true no-fault law because the injured person retains the right to seek compensation from the negligent person who caused the accident. For example, Virginia's add-on plan allows an optional first-party coverage for limited medical expenses and loss of income. Under this law, all insurers that sell auto insurance in the state must offer every auto policyholder this coverage, but policyholders are not obligated to purchase it. Whether they purchase the add-on coverage or not, policyholders can seek compensation from the negligent party.

Modified No-Fault Laws

Modified no-fault laws limit an injured person's right to recover damages from negligent parties but do not completely eliminate it. This type of law is the one most commonly used in states—such as Michigan and Florida—that have adopted some form of no-fault insurance.

Choice No-Fault Plans

Under a **choice no-fault plan**, an insured has the option, at the time the auto insurance policy is purchased or renewed, of choosing whether to be covered on a no-fault basis. If no-fault coverage is selected, premium reductions are offered in return for limitations on the right of tort recovery for certain types of auto injuries. If no-fault coverage is not selected, the insured retains full rights to seek compensation from a party at fault, but the insured pays a higher premium.

Pure no-fault system
System that would prevent an injured person from seeking compensation for damages from the at-fault party, regardless of the injury's severity; the injured person would collect no-fault benefits directly from his or her own insurer.

Add-on plan
Endorsement that provides certain benefits to injured automobile victims regardless of fault; the injured person retains the right to seek compensation from the negligent party who caused the accident.

Modified no-fault laws
Laws that prevent an injured person from seeking compensation for damages from a negligent driver unless damages exceed the monetary or verbal threshold; if the claim is below the threshold, the injured person collects benefits from his or her own insurer.

Choice no-fault plan
Plan that gives an insured the option, at the time an auto insurance policy is purchased or renewed, of choosing whether to be covered on a no-fault basis.

Evaluation of No-Fault Laws

No-fault automobile insurance has been controversial since its conception. This section presents arguments both in favor of and against no-fault laws.

Arguments in Favor of No-Fault Laws

Those who favor no-fault laws argue that such laws are necessary because of serious defects in the present tort liability system based on fault. Proponents believe that no-fault laws correct some of these defects by doing the following:

- *Eliminating the need to determine fault.* Auto accidents occur suddenly and unexpectedly, and determining who is at fault is often difficult, especially when more than one driver contributes to the accident.

- *Eliminating inequities in claim payments.* Those who favor no-fault argue that the present tort liability system is marred by inequities in claim payments. Under the present system, small claims might be overpaid, and serious claims might be underpaid.

- *Correcting the limited scope of the present system.* Many seriously injured persons or the beneficiaries of those killed in auto accidents do not collect, or collect less than their full economic loss, under the current tort liability system.

- *Decreasing the proportion of premium dollar used for claim investigation and legal costs.* Under the tort liability system, a large proportion of the liability coverage premium dollar is used to pay for attorneys, claim investigation expenses, and other costs of determining who was at fault.

- *Avoiding delays in payments.* Many claims take months or even years to settle under the tort liability system, which often involves lengthy court trials and delays in the legal system.

Arguments Against No-Fault Laws

Supporters of the present tort liability system, however, present various arguments against no-fault laws, including the following:

- *Defects of the present tort liability system are exaggerated.* Some people argue that the present system works reasonably well because most auto claims are settled out of court.

- *Claims of premium savings and greater efficiency are overstated and unreliable.* Premiums for auto insurance have not decreased significantly and, in some cases, have increased in states that have implemented no-fault plans. Opponents of no-fault laws fear that premium savings are unlikely to occur with any new no-fault legislation.

- *No-fault might penalize safe drivers.* The rating system used for no-fault insurance might unfairly allocate accident costs to the drivers who are not responsible for the accidents, thus increasing the premiums for good drivers.

- *No-fault benefits do not include payment for pain and suffering.* Attorneys representing injured auto accident victims argue that the dollar amount of medical expenses and lost wages does not always represent the true loss to the victim, because this amount does not include damages for pain and suffering.

- *The present tort system needs only to be reformed, not replaced.* Reform could take the form of limiting attorneys' fees, increasing the number of courts and judges, and using arbitration panels rather than the courts to settle claims.

AUTOMOBILE INSURANCE FOR HIGH-RISK DRIVERS

As stated earlier, high-risk drivers frequently cannot obtain auto insurance in the standard market. However, these drivers can usually purchase insurance in the **residual market** (also called the **shared market**).[5]

Several plans are available for high-risk drivers:

- Automobile insurance plans
- Joint underwriting associations (JUAs)
- Reinsurance facilities
- Specialty insurers

Automobile Insurance Plans

Most states have an **automobile insurance plan** for high-risk drivers who cannot obtain auto insurance in the standard market. These automobile insurance plans were formerly called "assigned risk plans," but insurers no longer officially use or recommend that term because it might have a negative connotation for the drivers assigned to the plan.

Although state automobile insurance plans vary, they usually have the following common characteristics:

- Applicants must show that they have been unable to obtain auto liability insurance within a certain number of days (usually sixty) of the application.

- The minimum limits of insurance offered are at least equal to the state's financial responsibility or compulsory insurance requirement. (Most plans offer optional higher limits, as well as medical payments and physical damage coverages.)

- Certain persons may be ineligible for coverage. For example, persons convicted of a felony within the preceding thirty-six months, persons engaged in illegal activities, and persons who are habitual violators of state and local laws may be ineligible for coverage.

- Premiums are generally higher than premiums in the standard market. High-risk drivers are rated on the basis of their driving records and are charged accordingly.

Residual market (shared market)
Term referring collectively to insurers and other organizations that make insurance available to those who cannot obtain coverage in the standard market.

Automobile insurance plan
Plan for insuring high-risk drivers in which all auto insurers doing business in the state are assigned their proportionate share of such drivers based on the total volume of auto insurance written in the state. For example, if one insurer writes 10 percent of all the auto insurance in the state, it would be assigned 10 percent of the state's high-risk drivers.

Joint Underwriting Associations (JUAs)

Joint underwriting association (JUA)
Organization created in a few states that designates servicing insurers to handle high-risk auto insurance business; all auto insurers in the state are assessed a proportionate share of the losses and expenses based on their percentage of the voluntary auto insurance premiums written in the state.

A few states have established **joint underwriting associations (JUAs)** that make auto insurance available to high-risk drivers. Under this arrangement, the JUA sets the insurance rates and approves the policy forms to be used for high-risk drivers. Although JUAs vary by state, a limited number of insurance companies are generally designated as servicing insurers to handle high-risk business. Agents and brokers submit applications for high-risk drivers to the JUA or to a designated servicing insurer. The servicing insurer usually receives applications, issues policies, collects premiums, settles claims, and provides other necessary services. All auto insurers in the state pay their proportionate share of underwriting losses and expenses based on each company's share of voluntary auto insurance written in the state.

Reinsurance Facilities

Reinsurance facility
A state-wide reinsurance pool to which insurers can assign premiums and losses for high-risk drivers; original insurers service the policies, but all insurers in the pool share the losses and expenses of the facility in proportion to the total auto insurance they write in that state.

A few states, such as Massachusetts, have enacted laws to establish a special **reinsurance facility** for high-risk drivers. Under this arrangement, insurers accept all auto insurance applicants who have a valid driver's license; the insurers issue policies, collect premiums, and settle claims. However, if an applicant for auto insurance is considered a high-risk driver, the insurer has the option of assigning the premiums and losses for the driver to the reinsurance facility. All auto insurers doing business in the state share any underwriting losses. Although the high-risk driver is assigned to the reinsurance facility, the original insurer pays any claims and continues to service the policy.

Specialty Insurers

High-risk drivers may also be able to obtain auto insurance from certain private insurers that specialize in insuring motorists with poor driving records. These specialty insurers typically insure inexperienced drivers, drivers who have been canceled or refused insurance, drivers convicted of driving under the influence of alcohol or drugs, and other high-risk drivers.

Because high-risk drivers have a greater probability of having an accident, automobile insurance policies from specialty insurers for high-risk drivers generally have several common characteristics:

- Premiums are substantially higher than premiums charged in the standard market.
- The amount of insurance is at least equal to the state's financial responsibility or compulsory insurance law, and many specialty insurers offer optional higher limits.
- Medical payments coverage may be limited.
- Collision insurance may be available only with a high deductible.

Many specialty insurers have safe driver rating plans to encourage high-risk drivers to drive responsibly. Under these plans, premium credits are given to insureds who have no auto accidents or traffic convictions within a certain time period; however, insureds who incur traffic convictions or have at-fault accidents must pay higher premiums.

REGULATION AND RATING OF PERSONAL AUTO INSURANCE

Automobile insurers are in business to make a profit. Accomplishing this objective requires effective underwriting and appropriate rating. Insurance company underwriters accept or reject applicants based on the company's underwriting standards. The basic objective of *underwriting* is to select a group of insureds whose losses will not exceed those anticipated in the rates and will thus be profitable for the insurer. However, the goal of profitability can conflict with the public's perceived right to buy insurance.

Underwriting is the process by which insurers decide which potential customers to insure and the coverage that insureds will be offered. Underwriting activities include selecting insureds, pricing coverage, determining policy terms and conditions, and monitoring underwriting decisions.

Most drivers view auto insurance as a necessity for two reasons. First, motorists need auto insurance for protection against financial hardships from liability suits. Second, the state government may require auto insurance in order to operate a vehicle legally in that state. For most drivers, the purchase of auto liability insurance is the only practical way to meet state financial responsibility or compulsory insurance laws. Thus, motorists generally believe that purchasing auto insurance is a right, not a privilege.

However, because of the underwriting goal of profitability, auto insurers do not make unlimited amounts of auto insurance available to the public. Auto insurance in the standard market is not available to all drivers. Based on their underwriting guidelines, insurers reject some drivers with a high potential for loss. Other high-risk drivers might be able to obtain insurance only by paying substantially higher premiums than average drivers pay.

The conflict between the public's belief that it has a right to buy auto insurance and the insurers' goal of profitability is often resolved by government regulation. In addition to the types of state regulation already mentioned (such as financial responsibility laws, compulsory insurance laws, and regulation of various residual market plans), states regulate auto insurance in other ways, such as cancellation restrictions, nonrenewal restrictions, and rate regulation.

Restrictions on Cancellation and Nonrenewal

All states have laws that restrict an insurer's right to cancel or nonrenew an automobile insurance policy. These laws reflect a desire to protect the public from actions that are thought to be unfair to policyholders, such as the following:[6]

- An insurer's decision to stop offering coverage in a certain geographic area
- An insurer's decision to stop writing auto insurance for certain groups, such as young drivers

- An insurer's decision to eliminate the authority of a particular agent to sell auto policies
- The cancellation of a policy by an insurer after a single loss

Restrictions on Cancellation

Cancellation refers to a decision by the insurer or the insured to terminate coverage during the policy period (before the expiration date of the policy).

Restrictions on *cancellation* by insurers generally do not apply to new policies that have been in force for less than a certain period (such as sixty days). During that period, which gives them time to complete their initial underwriting and investigation of the applicant's qualifications, insurers can usually cancel new policies. However, after the new policy has been in force for the stated period, cancellation is permitted only for reasons specified in the state's insurance laws and regulations. These reasons vary by state, but cancellation is usually permitted for the following reasons:[7]

- Nonpayment of premium
- Suspension or revocation of a driver's license
- Submission of a false or fraudulent claim
- *Material misrepresentation* of relevant underwriting information
- Conviction for certain offenses, such as driving under the influence of alcohol or drugs
- Violation of policy terms or conditions

A *material misrepresentation* is a false statement by an insured of an important (material) fact on which the insurer relies to make an underwriting decision.

Most states require that an insurer provide written notice of cancellation to the insured a certain number of days before the cancellation becomes effective. Often, the reason for cancellation must be stated in the notice or provided at the insured's request. In addition, most states require the insurer to indicate on the cancellation notice that coverage might be available from an automobile insurance plan or from some other residual market facility.

Restrictions on Nonrenewal

Nonrenewal refers to an insurer's decision to terminate coverage on the expiration date of the policy; in other words, the insurer refuses to renew the policy when it expires.

Regulations restricting an insurer's right to *nonrenew* an auto policy vary by state. Some states specify reasons for which insurers can nonrenew policies that are similar to the reasons for which policies can be canceled. Insurers usually have the right to refuse renewal of an auto insurance policy, subject to restrictions such as the following:

- The insurer must give the insured written notice that the policy will not be renewed.
- A certain number of days of advance notice is required.
- Many states require the insurer to give the reason for the nonrenewal or to provide the reason on request.

Most states prohibit insurers from refusing to renew a policy solely because of an insured's age, sex, race, color, creed, national origin, occupation, or place of residence.

Rate Regulation

Automobile insurers do not have unlimited freedom to charge any price they desire for the coverages they provide. Rating laws in each state require that automobile insurance rates meet certain statutory standards. State rating laws vary, but in general they require that rates be adequate and reasonable (not excessive) for the exposure presented. States also require that rates not be *unfairly discriminatory*.

Rating Automobile Insurance

Rating systems vary by state and also by insurer. This section of the chapter examines typical factors used in rating personal auto insurance. Although the rating of personal auto insurance today is often computerized, an understanding of the factors that contribute to auto rating is essential for anyone who works with auto insurance.

Primary Rating Factors

The major factors (called "primary factors") that most states and companies use for determining the cost of personal auto insurance are listed below. Although each of these factors has been used for many years in rating auto insurance, several states no longer permit the use of some of them, such as age and gender, on the grounds that they are unfairly discriminatory.

Unfair discrimination involves applying different standards or methods of treatment to insureds that have the same basic characteristics and loss potential. Examples of unfair discrimination in auto insurance rating would include charging higher-than-normal rates for an applicant based solely on the applicant's race, religion, or ethnic background.

- *Age*—As previously mentioned, young drivers have less driving experience and tend to be involved in accidents more frequently than older drivers. Therefore, rates for younger drivers are often higher than those for more experienced drivers.

- *Sex*—Women have tended in the past to have fewer accidents than men in the same age categories, particularly among youthful drivers, so rates are often lower for women than for men. However, this tendency is changing as more women are driving and having accidents.

- *Marital status*—Usually a factor only among younger drivers. Young married males tend to have fewer accidents than young unmarried males, and rates often reflect this tendency.

- *Territory*—Determined by where the vehicle is normally used and garaged (parked overnight); territory is usually defined by the location of the insured's residence. Rural territories often have lower rates than urban territories because losses and claim expenses tend to be higher in cities.

- *Use of the auto*—Autos are usually classified for farm, pleasure, driving to work, or business use. Rates are generally lowest for farm and highest for business use, reflecting typical accident statistics for various uses of automobiles.

- *Good student discount*—A premium credit based on statistics showing that good students typically have fewer accidents than poor or average students.

- *Driver education credit*—A premium discount (usually 10 percent) given for young drivers who complete an approved driver education course. Such training can help reduce the number and severity of automobile losses.

Other Rating Factors

In addition to the preceding primary rating factors, insurers use several other factors to rate personal automobile insurance:

- Driving record—Probably the most important factor of all. Almost all insurers use an individual's driving record to determine whether an applicant is acceptable and at what rate. Many insurers have safe driver plans in which premiums are based on the insured's driving record.
- Type of vehicle—The performance, age, and damageability of a vehicle can affect the rates for physical damage coverage on the vehicle. For instance, a new sports car would cost more to insure for collision coverage than an older station wagon, because the sports car would be more expensive to repair and might be damaged more easily.
- Number of vehicles—Most companies give a multi-car discount when more than one vehicle is insured under the same policy. This discount is based on the assumption that two or more vehicles owned by the same insured will not be driven as often as a single vehicle.
- Deductibles—Insureds who choose higher deductibles for collision and other physical damage coverage on their vehicles can expect a credit, sometimes a significant one.
- Liability limits—Rates are generally based on the minimum liability limits required in the state, and premiums increase if the insured chooses higher limits. (However, doubling liability limits does not mean doubling the premium, and higher limits are often a bargain compared to minimum limits.)

Other Discounts and Credits

Some insurers also give credits, such as the following:

- Anti-theft devices
- Passive restraints (airbags)
- Defensive driving courses
- Senior citizens
- Farmers
- Nonsmokers
- Number of years of continuous coverage with the insurer (called a renewal or anniversary discount)
- Having more than one type of policy with the same insurer (called a multi-policy or account discount)

- Reduced vehicle use by students because of their attendance at schools over a specified distance from home (provided they do not have an insured vehicle with them at school)

Matching Price to Exposure

Insurers often divide auto insurance applicants into several rating categories, such as "preferred," "standard," and "nonstandard," to reflect different levels of exposure to loss. For example, applicants considered to be better-than-average drivers who will probably have fewer losses than average are categorized as preferred and are charged a lower rate than other applicants. In this way, insurers hope to attract and retain good customers.

Conversely, drivers with higher-than-average loss exposure are considered nonstandard and are charged higher rates. Usually the same insurer will also have a standard rating class for drivers with average loss exposure. Insurers commonly have two or more rating categories with different rates for differing levels of loss exposure. The intent is to match the price of insurance with the loss exposure. Regulators usually approve these rating categories on the grounds that policyholders receive equitable treatment: preferred drivers pay less for their protection, and nonstandard drivers pay more.

Competition Among Insurers

Competition for profitable automobile business is often intense among insurers. When underwriting losses are low and profits are favorable, insurers compete with each other by lowering rates. However, insurers cannot decrease rates to the point at which they can no longer cover the costs of losses and expenses. In times of high underwriting losses and low profits, insurers must raise rates, restrict the number and type of new applicants they will accept, or take other steps to become more profitable.

Despite this tendency of insurers to consider competitive cycles in pricing personal automobile insurance, rates are still subject to regulatory approval or disapproval. Insurers' rates must always meet the state requirements for rates that are adequate, reasonable, and not unfairly discriminatory.

SUMMARY

Automobile insurance presents a problem for insurers and for society for several reasons, including:

- The high frequency of automobile accidents
- The high costs of automobile accidents
- Large underwriting losses
- Irresponsible drivers, including drivers with no insurance, drivers under the influence of alcohol or drugs, and other high-risk drivers
- The lack of availability and affordability of automobile insurance

Traditionally, persons injured in auto accidents through the negligence of others have relied on the tort liability system, based on fault, to collect damages. In an effort to ensure that negligent drivers carry insurance to pay for such damages, states have enacted financial responsibility and compulsory insurance laws. Some states have established unsatisfied judgment funds to provide compensation for auto accident victims. Uninsured and underinsured motorists coverages are also possible sources of recovery for some accident costs of the injured individual. Low-cost auto insurance is another approach to increasing the number of motorists purchasing insurance.

In contrast to these traditional approaches to compensating auto accident victims, some states have enacted no-fault auto insurance laws. Under no-fault insurance, each party injured in an automobile accident collects from his or her own insurance company, regardless of who was at fault. No-fault add-on plans do not restrict the right to collect damages from the negligent party. Under a modified no-fault plan, an injured victim can sue only if the monetary threshold is exceeded or the verbal threshold is met. The personal injury protection (PIP) endorsement adds no-fault coverage to the personal auto policy. Insurers pay benefits, as specified in the state law, for economic losses, such as medical expenses and loss of earnings resulting from bodily injury to the insured. Noneconomic losses, such as pain and suffering, inconvenience, and mental anguish, are not paid under the PIP endorsement. However, no-fault laws allow for recovery of noneconomic losses from the negligent party after a monetary or verbal threshold is exceeded.

Several types of residual (or shared) market insurance plans are available. The most common form of residual market plan is the automobile insurance plan. In addition, some states have established a joint underwriting association (JUA) for high-risk drivers. A few states have an arrangement that allows the insurer of a high-risk driver to reinsure the business in a reinsurance facility supported by all auto insurers in the state. In addition, specialty insurers specialize in insuring drivers who cannot purchase insurance in the standard market.

State governments regulate the personal automobile insurance industry in several ways. In addition to having financial responsibility and compulsory insurance laws, all states have laws that restrict the right of insurers to cancel or nonrenew automobile insurance policies. States also regulate the rates charged for auto insurance and require that rates be adequate, reasonable (not excessive), and not unfairly discriminatory.

Numerous factors determine the cost of automobile insurance, such as age, gender, marital status, territory, use of the auto, and good student and driver education credits. In addition, insurers use other factors such as driving record, type and number of vehicles, deductibles, and liability limits to determine rates. Some insurance companies also offer discounts and credits for certain characteristics of the autos, such as anti-theft devices and airbags. Insurers often divide auto insurance applicants into several rating categories in an attempt to match the price of insurance with the exposure. Thus, rates may be reduced for better-than-average drivers and increased for below-average drivers. Companies also compete for profitable automobile insurance business by lowering rates when underwriting losses are low and profits are favorable. Conversely, insurers may increase rates during periods of high underwriting losses and low profits. Despite these competitive cycles, however, rates are still subject to regulatory approval or disapproval.

CHAPTER NOTES

1. Insurance Information Institute, *The I.I.I. Insurance Fact Book 2002* (New York: Insurance Information Institute, 2002), pp. 97, 100.

2. Insurance Research Council, *Public Attitude Monitor 2001*, Issue 2 (Malvern, Pa.: Insurance Research Council, 2001), p. 17.

3. This section is based largely on material drawn from George E. Rejda, *Principles of Risk Management and Insurance*, 5th ed. (New York: HarperCollins College Publishers, 1995), Chapter 11; *Fire, Casualty & Surety Bulletins*, Personal Lines Volume, Personal Auto section (Cincinnati, Ohio: The National Underwriter Company, February 1996); and David L. Bickelhaupt, *General Insurance*, 11th ed. (Homewood, Ill.: Richard D. Irwin, Inc., 1983), Chapter 19.

4. The section on no-fault insurance laws is based largely on the sources cited in Note 3.

5. The material on residual (shared) market plans for high-risk drivers is based largely on the sources cited in Note 3.

6. Frederick G. Crane, *Insurance Principles and Practices*, 2d ed. (New York: John Wiley and Sons, 1984), p. 121.

7. Crane, pp. 121-122.

Chapter 3

Direct Your Learning

Personal Auto Policy, Part I

After learning the subject matter of this chapter, for a given auto liability case involving the ISO personal auto policy (1998 version), you should be able to:

- Explain whether the loss is covered.
- Determine the amount the insurer would pay for covered losses.
- Identify the types of information typically contained on the declarations page.
- Define the words and phrases included in the definitions section of the policy.
- Explain what is covered and what is limited or excluded under:
  - Part A—Liability Coverage
  - Part B—Medical Payments Coverage
  - Part C—Uninsured Motorists Coverage

Develop Your Perspective

What are the main topics covered in the chapter?

This chapter introduces the personal auto policy (PAP) and provides a review of the declarations; the definitions; and the liability, medical payments, and uninsured motorists coverages. The remainder of the personal auto policy is addressed in the next chapter.

Scrutinize the liability, medical payments, and uninsured motorists coverages.

- Who is covered?

- What coverages are provided, and under what circumstances are coverages excluded?

Why is it important to know these topics?

The PAP is a standard contract purchased, in some form, by most auto owners, and the policy is designed to meet the needs of most auto owners. Coverage is excluded for those exposures that are not commercially insurable and for coverage that most individuals and families do not need.

Consider the coverage needs of average people.

- Do the coverages included in the policy meet their needs?

- Is coverage excluded for activities in which they engage?

How can you use this information?

Compare your own auto insurance needs to the coverages provided by the PAP:

- Does the PAP cover all of the users of your auto?

- Are any coverages provided of which you were unaware?

- Do you have any auto-related loss exposures that are excluded from the PAP?

Chapter 3

Personal Auto Policy, Part I

This chapter begins the study of the personal auto policy (PAP), which covers personal loss exposures arising out of the ownership or operation of an auto. The discussion is limited to the PAP drafted by Insurance Services Office (ISO), a policy used widely throughout the United States. Although it is used by many different insurers, the standard PAP studied here is not universal. The PAP is not used by all insurance companies, the PAP is not used in all states, and state variations exist.

OVERVIEW OF THE PERSONAL AUTO POLICY (PAP)

The personal auto policy was introduced in several states in 1977. It was designed to be easier to read and understand than earlier personal auto policy forms. The PAP has been revised several times since it was introduced. The following discussion is based on the edition introduced in 1998 and bearing a 1997 copyright date. This edition of the policy form is numbered PP 00 01 06 98.[1]

The PAP is designed to insure private passenger autos—vehicles such as cars, vans, station wagons, and sport utility vehicles designed primarily for use on public roads—as well as pickup trucks and full-size vans, subject to restrictions that might vary from one insurer to the next.

The PAP can also be used, if allowed by the state and the insurer, to cover motorcycles, golf carts, snowmobiles, motor homes, and other vehicles by adding an appropriate endorsement to the policy. Chapters 3 and 4 introduce endorsements in shaded boxes when describing the policy sections to which they apply. Chapter 4 discusses these and other endorsements in greater detail.

Summary of Coverages

The PAP consists of a declarations page, an agreement and definitions page, and six separate parts. The six parts are as follows:

- *Part A—Liability Coverage*: provides coverage that protects the insured against a claim or suit for bodily injury or property damage arising out of the operation of an auto.
- *Part B—Medical Payments Coverage*: provides coverage for reasonable and necessary medical expenses incurred by an insured because of bodily injury caused by an auto accident.

- *Part C—Uninsured Motorists Coverage*: provides protection if an insured is injured by an uninsured motorist, a hit-and-run driver, or a driver whose insurer is insolvent.
- *Part D—Coverage for Damage to Your Auto*: provides coverage for physical damage to a covered auto and to certain nonowned autos. Coverage for damage to your auto is also referred to as **physical damage coverage**.
- *Part E—Duties After an Accident or Loss*: outlines the duties required of an insured after an accident or a loss.
- *Part F—General Provisions*: contains certain general provisions, such as cancellation and termination of the policy and the policy period and territory.

Only Parts A, B, and C are examined in this chapter. Chapter 4 discusses the remaining parts.

In addition to the coverages outlined above, options, such as towing and labor costs coverage, can be added. Chapter 4 discusses the optional coverages.

Declarations

The **declarations page** personalizes each policy by identifying the parties and vehicles involved and the coverages provided. Although each insurance company designs its own declarations page, the information discussed in this section is typically included.

Insurance Company

The declarations page shows the name of the insurance company providing the coverage. The name of the insurance agent or broker who sold the policy may also be included, along with an address and a telephone number.

Named Insured

The declarations page shows the name of the policyholder or **named insured** and the named insured's mailing address. The named insured can be an individual, a husband and wife, or other parties. When a married couple purchases insurance, the husband's name, the wife's name, or both names might appear in the declarations.

Policy Period

The policy period is the time during which the policy provides coverage. The policy period starts at 12:01 A.M. standard time at the address of the policyholder on the date the policy becomes effective and ends at 12:01 A.M. standard time on the date the policy expires. The policy period is usually six months or one year.

Physical damage coverage
Coverage for damage to your auto.

Declarations page
A required component of an insurance policy; in an auto policy, it provides information about the insured, a description of the insured autos, a schedule of coverages, and other important details.

Named insured (as used in the PAP)
Policyholder whose name (or names) appears on the declarations page.

Description of Insured Autos

The declarations page identifies each of the vehicles and trailers that is to be specifically insured under the policy. This description usually includes the year, make, model, and vehicle identification number. It might also include body type, annual mileage, use of the vehicle, date of purchase, and other information about each vehicle.

Schedule of Coverages

The schedule of coverages indicates the coverages and limits that apply to each listed vehicle, along with the premium for each coverage. If physical damage coverage applies, the deductibles are also shown.

Applicable Endorsements

The declarations page also lists any endorsements that are attached to the policy. For example, if the policyholder owns a snowmobile that is covered under the policy, the snowmobile endorsement would be listed along with the premium for the coverage.

Lienholder

Whether it is owned or leased, the vehicle might be financed through a bank, savings and loan association, credit union, or other organization that holds the title to the vehicle until the loan is paid off. In such a case, the name of the lender, or lienholder, is usually shown on the declarations page.

Garaged Location

The location where the described auto is primarily "garaged" may be shown if that location is different from the insured's mailing address stated on the declarations page. The garaging location is used for rating purposes. "Garaging" often does not involve a garage; a vehicle may be "garaged" on the street in front of the insured's home.

Rating Information

The rating class for the vehicle and any applicable credits and discounts may be shown. Premiums can be reduced by discounts for multiple cars, driver training, a good scholastic record, a defensive driving course, passive restraints, anti-theft devices, and other factors as mentioned in Chapter 2.

Signature

The signature of an authorized legal representative of the insurer is usually shown at the bottom of the declarations page.

Agreement and Definitions

Page 1 of the personal auto policy contains a general agreement and the definitions of several terms used throughout the policy.

Agreement

A brief general agreement serves as an introduction to the policy and states that the insurer's obligations are subject to all the terms of the policy and depend on the payment of the premium by the insured.

Definitions

Specific definitions apply to the entire policy. The definitions are written in simple language designed to be easily understood. This section of the policy defines the following words and phrases:

A. *You and your*. The words "you" and "your" refer to the named insured shown on the declarations page. "You" and "your" also include an unnamed spouse of the named insured—provided that he or she is a resident of the same household.

   If a married couple divorces, an unnamed partner is no longer a spouse, and it is obvious the term "you" no longer applies to that person. However, an unnamed spouse who moves out of the household for any reason but remains married to the named insured is considered "you" for another ninety days or until the policy expires—whichever comes first. Coverage ceases if he or she is named on another policy.

B. *We, us, and our*. The words "we," "us," and "our" refer to the insurance company that is providing insurance under the contract, generally the company named in the declarations.

C. *Owned includes leased*. The third definition clarifies what the policy includes when it refers to an owned auto. A leased private passenger auto, pickup, or van is deemed to be an owned auto if it is leased under a written agreement for a continuous period of at least six months. Thus, a car that the insured leases for two years would be considered an owned auto under the PAP. However, a car rented during a two-week vacation would not be an owned auto.

D. *Bodily injury*. **Bodily injury** is bodily harm, sickness, or disease, including death.

E. *Business*. Business includes a trade, a profession, or an occupation.

F. *Family member*. A family member is a person who is related to the named insured or spouse by blood, marriage, or adoption and resides in the named insured's household. This definition also includes a ward or a foster child.

G. *Occupying*. Occupying is defined as in, upon, getting in, on, out, or off. This definition is used in connection with Part B—Medical Payments Coverage and Part C—Uninsured Motorists Coverage.

Bodily injury (BI) (as used in the PAP)
Bodily harm, sickness, or disease, including death that results.

H. *Property damage.* **Property damage** is physical injury to or destruction of tangible property.

I. *Trailer.* A **trailer** is a vehicle designed to be pulled by a private passenger auto, a pickup, or a van.

J. *Your covered auto.* An extremely important definition applies to the vehicles that are covered under the PAP. **Your covered auto** includes four classes of vehicles that can be covered:

1. Any vehicle shown in the declarations
2. A trailer owned by the insured
3. A temporary substitute auto or trailer
4. A newly acquired auto (as separately defined)

Your covered auto includes *any vehicle listed in the declarations.* Covered vehicles can include a private passenger auto—such as a car, minivan, station wagon, sport utility vehicle, pickup truck, or full-size van owned by the named insured.

A *trailer owned by the named insured* is a covered auto. As mentioned, a trailer is a vehicle designed to be pulled by a private passenger auto, pickup, or van.

As the label suggests, a **temporary substitute vehicle** is one that is used as a short-term substitute for another covered auto that is out of service. A temporary substitute auto is covered under the PAP. For physical damage coverage, discussed in Chapter 4, a temporary substitute vehicle is treated the same as other nonowned autos. For all other coverages, a temporary substitute vehicle is considered a covered auto.

K. *Newly acquired auto.* A **newly acquired auto** is an eligible private passenger auto, pickup, or van that becomes an owned vehicle during the policy period. Remember, a leased vehicle is the same as an owned vehicle. The coverage that applies to newly acquired autos is also discussed in the definition.

For *liability, medical payments, uninsured motorists,* or any other coverage except the coverage for damage to your auto, a newly acquired auto automatically receives coverage equal to the broadest coverage indicated for any vehicle shown in the Declarations. Often, people sell one car when they purchase another to replace it, but sometimes they just purchase one more car. A replacement auto must be distinguished from an additional auto, because they are treated differently.

- An *additional auto* is automatically covered for fourteen days after the named insured becomes the owner. The insured must request coverage beyond fourteen days.

- A *replacement auto* is covered for the remainder of the policy period, even if the insured does not ask for coverage.

The situation is different with *coverage for damage to your auto.* Many people drop physical damage coverage on older cars with a reduced value, but they might need the coverage when purchasing a newer car.

Property damage (PD) (as used in the PAP)

Physical injury to or destruction of tangible property. It also includes loss of use of tangible property.

Trailer (as used in the PAP)

A vehicle designed to be pulled by a private passenger auto, a pickup, or a van; farm wagon or farm implement when towed by one of these vehicles.

Your covered auto (as used in the PAP)

Any vehicle shown in the declarations; a trailer owned by the insured; a temporary substitute auto or trailer; a newly acquired auto (subject to certain restrictions).

Temporary substitute vehicle (as used in the PAP)

A nonowned auto or trailer that the insured is using because of the breakdown, repair, servicing, loss, or destruction of a covered vehicle.

Newly acquired auto (as used in the PAP)

An eligible private passenger auto, pickup, or van of which the named insured becomes the owner or that the named insured leases during the policy period; it can be a replacement auto or an additional auto.

Damages
Monetary award that one party is required to pay to another who has suffered loss or injury for which the first party is legally responsible.

Compensatory damages
Damages, including both special damages and general damages, that are intended to compensate a victim for harm actually suffered.

Special damages
Compensatory damages allowed for specific out-of-pocket expenses, such as doctor and hospital bills.

General damages
Compensatory damages awarded for losses, such as pain and suffering, that do not have a specific economic loss.

Punitive damages
Damages awarded by a court to punish wrongdoers who, through malicious or outrageous actions, cause injury or damage to others; some states do not permit insurers to award payment for punitive damages because such payment would not punish the insured.

Split limits (as used in the PAP)
The maximum amounts a PAP insurer will pay for the insured's liability for bodily injury per person, bodily injury per accident, and property damage per accident.

Single limit
Maximum amount an insurer will pay for the insured's liability for both bodily injury and property damage per accident.

- An insured who *does not* carry collision or other-than-collision coverage on at least one auto receives automatic physical damage coverage on a newly acquired auto for *four* days, subject to a $500 deductible.

- An insured who *does* carry collision or other-than-collision coverage on at least one auto receives automatic coverage on a newly acquired auto for *fourteen* days. The coverage that automatically applies is equal to the broadest coverage (that is, the smallest deductible) on any vehicle currently shown in the policy declarations.

PART A—LIABILITY COVERAGE

The liability coverage of the PAP provides protection against an insured's legal liability arising out of the ownership or operation of an auto. Because the financial consequences of a liability loss are potentially far greater than any damage that could occur to the insured's auto, Part A offers particularly valuable protection for the insured. Part A—Liability Coverage is summarized in Exhibit 3-1.

Insuring Agreement

In the liability coverage insuring agreement, the insurer agrees to pay **damages** for bodily injury or property damage for which an insured is legally responsible because of an auto accident. Damages may include both **compensatory damages** (**special damages** and **general damages**) and **punitive damages.** The policy limits applicable to this coverage can be expressed either as split limits or as a single limit.

Most policies are written with **split limits**, in which the amounts of insurance apply separately to bodily injury and property damage. For example, split limits of $100/$300/$50 mean that the insured has bodily injury liability limits of $100,000 per person and $300,000 for each accident, and a limit of $50,000 for property damage liability per accident.

Some policies are written with a **single limit** that applies per accident to the total of both bodily injury and property damage liability. For example, a policy might have a single limit of $300,000 that applies to bodily injury and property damage liability. A single liability limit endorsement modifies the policy to provide coverage on a single-limit basis.

> The *single liability limit endorsement* (PP 03 09) modifies the liability coverage of the PAP to provide coverage on a single-limit basis.

EXHIBIT 3-1

Summary of Part A—Liability Coverage

Insuring Agreement	Persons Insured	Exclusions
Pays damages for bodily injury and property damage for which the insured is legally liable because of an auto accident Legal defense costs paid Supplemental payments: Up to $250 for the cost of a bail bond; interest accruing after a judgment; up to $200 daily for the loss of earnings due to attendance at a hearing or trial; and other reasonable expenses incurred at the company's request	Named insured and resident family members[a] Any person using a covered auto with permission Any person or organization legally responsible for acts or omissions of an insured while using a covered auto on behalf of that person or organization Any person or organization legally responsible for acts or omissions of an insured while using any auto or trailer on behalf of that person or organization (other than a covered auto or auto owned or hired by that person or organization)	Intentional bodily injury or property damage Damage to property owned or transported by an insured Property rented to, used by, or in the insured's care (except a residence or private garage) Injury to an employee during the course of employment Using a vehicle as a public or livery conveyance (exclusion does not apply to a share-the-expense car pool) Vehicles used in the automobile business (exclusion does not apply to the operation, ownership, or use of covered autos) Other business vehicles used in any business other than farming or ranching (exclusion does not apply to an owned or nonowned private passenger auto, pickup or van, or trailer used with the preceding vehicles) Nuclear energy exclusion Vehicle with fewer than four wheels, or one designed for use off public roads[b] Any vehicle, other than a covered auto, owned by, furnished, or made available for the named insured's regular use Any vehicle, other than a covered auto, owned by, furnished, or made available for a family member's regular use (exclusion does not apply to the named insured's use of a vehicle owned by a family member, or a vehicle made available for a family member's regular use) Vehicle located inside a racing facility to compete, practice, or prepare for a prearranged racing contest

a. The 1998 PAP extends coverage for ninety days to a spouse who is no longer a resident of the named insured's household.
b. Exclusion does not apply to use of the vehicle in a medical emergency, to a trailer, or to a nonowned golf cart.

Exhibit by George E. Rejda, Ph.D., CLU, used with permission.

Prejudgment interest
Interest on damages that accrues between the time the accident or suit occurs and when a judgment is rendered indicating that the insured is responsible for damages; subject to the policy limit of liability.

Structured settlement
Periodic and guaranteed payments made for damages over a specified time period; an alternative to lump-sum payment.

The damages covered also include any **prejudgment interest** awarded against the insured. The laws of many states allow plaintiffs (injured persons) to receive interest on a judgment from the time an accident occurs, or a lawsuit is filed, to the time the judgment is handed down. Prejudgment interest adjusts the amount recovered to put the claimant into the same position as if he or she had received payment for damages at the time of the accident or suit.

Prejudgment interest is considered to be part of the award for damages and is subject to the policy limit of liability. For example, assume an insured who is legally liable for bodily injury in an auto accident has a PAP with liability limits of $100/$300/$50. If the insured is legally liable for a $50,000 judgment involving bodily injury to one person, plus $5,000 in prejudgment interest, the insured's PAP insurer will pay the full $55,000. However, if the insured is legally liable for a $95,000 judgment plus $10,000 in prejudgment interest, the insured's PAP will pay only $100,000—the per-person liability limit.

Damages are usually paid in a lump sum. However, a **structured settlement** may be used when a large bodily injury claim is involved.

Structured Settlements

Awards for damages resulting from bodily injury liability claims are increasingly being paid as structured settlements. Unlike a one-time cash payment for damages, a structured settlement consists of periodic and guaranteed payments over a specified time. The auto insurer generally purchases an annuity from a life insurer that pays periodic and guaranteed payments to the injured accident victim. For example, in one case, an injured twenty-five-year-old plaintiff received a lifetime income of $400 monthly with twenty years of guaranteed payments and a $250,000 retirement benefit at age sixty. The annuity provided total guaranteed payments of $346,000 to the injured person. However, the cost of the annuity to the auto insurer was less than $60,000.

Structured settlements have advantages to both injured victims and auto insurers. The injured person receives the periodic annuity payments income-tax free; he or she is protected against squandering a large lump-sum payment; and the payments are guaranteed, which provides protection for the injured person against an unprofitable investment.

Auto insurers also benefit because claim costs can be reduced. Also, by offering a flexible and attractive benefit, insurers can often reach a settlement agreement with an injured person more quickly, thereby avoiding costly court expenses and delays.

Besides agreeing to pay damages for which an insured is legally liable, subject to policy limits, the insurer also agrees to defend the insured and pay all legal defense costs—even if the combined figure exceeds the policy limits. In other words, the insurer is obligated to pay defense costs *in addition to* the policy limits. When a large claim is involved, the insurer cannot simply offer or "tender" its policy limits and be relieved of any further duty to defend the insured. However, the insurer's duty to settle or defend the claim ends when the limit of liability has been exhausted by the payment of judgments or settlements. Once the policy limits (including prejudgment interest) have been *paid*, the insurer has no further obligation to settle or defend the claim.

The insurer also has no obligation to defend any claim that is not covered under the policy. For example, the PAP specifically excludes intentionally caused bodily injury or property damage. If an insured intentionally causes bodily injury or property damage and is sued, the insurer has no obligation to defend the insured.

Insured Persons

Four categories of persons and organizations are insured for liability coverage under the PAP:

- The named insured and any family member (as defined)
- Any person using a covered auto
- Any person or organization, but only for legal liability arising out of an insured person's use of a covered auto on behalf of that person or organization
- Any person or organization legally responsible for the named insured's or a family member's use of any auto or trailer (other than a covered auto or an auto owned by that person or organization)

The *named insured and family members* are covered under Part A—Liability Coverage. As noted when the definition of "you" was examined, the named insured also includes the spouse of the named insured if he or she is a resident of the same household or has recently moved out. Family members, as defined, are persons related to the named insured by blood, marriage, or adoption, as well as a ward or a foster child, any of whom live in the insured's household. Children who are temporarily away from home, as when attending college, are still covered under their parents' policy.

Any person using the named insured's covered auto is also covered. Generally, liability coverage applies if that person has a reasonable belief that he or she has the insured's permission to use the covered auto. For example, assume that Mary has allowed her roommate to drive her car several times during the past month. If Mary is not around and the roommate drives Mary's car believing that Mary would have granted permission, the roommate would be an insured under Mary's policy.

Any person or organization legally responsible for the acts of a covered person while using a covered auto is covered. For example, assume that Mary, Bob's employer, asks Bob to drive his car to the post office to pick up a package. While driving his own covered auto on company business, Bob negligently injures another person. Bob's liability would be covered by his personal auto policy. Moreover, Mary, as Bob's employer, is also covered under Bob's PAP, and if the employer is sued, Bob's insurer is obligated to defend Mary and pay any damages assessed against her because of Bob's accident.

Finally, *any person or organization legally responsible for the named insured's or family member's use of any auto or trailer* (other than a covered auto or an auto owned or hired by that person or organization) is also covered. For example, Cheryl, the named insured, injures a pedestrian while driving a car she borrowed from Bill to do errands for a nursing home. Cheryl would have liability coverage under her PAP for her use of a nonowned auto. Because neither Cheryl nor the nursing home owns or hired the car, Cheryl's PAP will also defend the nursing home against any allegation of its liability for the injury to the pedestrian and pay any damages for which the nursing home might be held responsible.

Although Cheryl's PAP provides coverage for both her and the nursing home, Cheryl's coverage would be excess over any coverage Bill has on his car. Cheryl's insurer would not pay a liability loss unless it exceeded the liability limit on Bill's PAP, because Bill's policy is primary. This point is clarified in the "other insurance" provision of the PAP, discussed later.

Supplementary Payments

Supplementary payments (as used in the PAP)
Amounts paid in addition to the liability limits for items such as premiums on bail bonds and appeal bonds, postjudgment interest, loss of earnings for attendance at trials, and other reasonable expenses incurred at the insurer's request.

The following **supplementary payments** may be paid *in addition to* the liability limits and other legal defense costs:

- Cost of bail bonds
- Premiums on appeal bonds and bonds to release attachments
- Interest accruing after a judgment
- Loss of earnings because of attendance at trials
- Other reasonable expenses incurred at the insurer's request

An insured who is arrested might have to stay in jail unless he or she can furnish a bail bond. The *cost of a bail bond* for an insured can be paid up to $250 because of an accident that results in bodily injury or property damage. Bail bond premiums are not paid for speeding tickets or other moving violations unless bodily injury or property damage results.

Premiums on appeal bonds and bonds to release an attachment of property in a lawsuit defended by the insurer are covered as a supplementary payment. If a court awards a judgment against an insured, the insured might appeal that decision to a higher court. An appeal bond guarantees that, if the insured loses the appeal, the insured will pay the original judgment and the cost of the appeal. During legal proceedings, an attachment or lien may be placed by the plaintiff on the insured's property, such as a house. A release of attachment bond guarantees that the insured will pay any judgment, permitting a release of the attachment on the insured's property.

Postjudgment interest
Interest in damages that accrues after a judgment has been rendered and before the damages are paid; can be in addition to the liability limits and other legal defense costs.

If interest accrues after a judgment (known as **postjudgment interest**), the accrued interest is also paid as an additional payment. For example, if the insured appeals the judgment, he or she is responsible for the payment of any interest that accrues while the appeal is pending; this postjudgment interest is covered as a supplementary payment. (As previously mentioned, prejudgment interest is part of the limit of liability under the PAP.)

The insurer also pays up to $200 per day for *an insured's loss of earnings* (but not other income) because of attendance at a hearing or trial at the insurer's request.

Other reasonable expenses incurred at the insurer's request are also paid. For example, an insured might incur travel and transportation expenses to testify at a trial at the insurer's request. These expenses are paid as a supplementary payment.

Prejudgment and Postjudgment Interest

Both prejudgment interest and postjudgment interest compensate a liability insurance claimant for the interest that might have been earned on money if the claimant had received it earlier.

Prejudgment interest: Long delays sometimes occur between an accident and a court trial. When a court award is finally made, the court may award both damages and an additional sum of money representing the interest that could have been earned if the claimant had received compensation at the time of injury or damage rather than at the time of the judgment. This additional sum is prejudgment interest, and in the PAP it is subject to the policy limit.

Postjudgment interest: Sometimes an insurer appeals a judgment to a higher court, rather than paying it when it is awarded. If the appeal is successful, the insurer ultimately pays no damages. But when the higher court upholds the initial judgment, the claimant may be entitled not only to the amount of the initial judgment, but also to compensation for the interest that could have been earned on the money if the insurer had paid it at the time of the first judgment. Because this interest would have been earned after the judgment, it is called postjudgment interest. In the PAP, postjudgment interest is paid as a supplementary payment, and it is not subject to policy limits.

Liability Coverage Exclusions

As with most insurance policies, the insuring agreement of Part A describes broad coverage that is narrowed by exclusions. The major exclusions that apply to the liability coverage under the PAP are summarized here.

Intentional Injury

Bodily injury or property damage that is intentionally caused is specifically excluded. For example, if Cleve, who is enraged because he is caught in a traffic jam, deliberately rams the vehicle in front of him, Cleve's responsibility for any intentional property damage to the other motorist's car would not be covered under Cleve's PAP.

Property Owned or Transported

Liability coverage does not apply to damage to property owned or being transported by an insured. For example, if Alice's suitcase and clothes are damaged in an auto accident while she is driving on vacation, the loss to these items is not covered under Alice's PAP. (A homeowners policy will cover them.)

Property Rented to, Used by, or in the Care of the Insured

Liability for property rented to, used by, or in the care of the insured is not covered under the PAP. For example, if Don plans a party and rents glassware and china that are later damaged when his car is involved in an accident, his liability for damage to the rented glassware and china is not covered by his PAP.

This exclusion does not apply to damage to a residence or private garage. Thus, if Don rented a vacation house and accidentally backed his car into the side of the house, his liability for the damage to the rented house would be covered by his PAP.

Bodily Injury to an Employee of an Insured

The liability coverage also excludes bodily injury to an employee of an insured if that employee is injured during the course of employment. Compensation for the employee's injury should be provided for under a workers compensation law. However, injury to a domestic employee injured in the course of employment is covered if workers compensation benefits are not required or available.

Public or Livery Conveyance

A public or livery conveyance is one that is indiscriminately offered to the public (usually to carry people or property for a fee), such as a taxi or a bus. Liability insurance does not apply to an insured's ownership or operation of a vehicle while it is being used as a public or livery conveyance. For example, if local taxicab drivers are on strike and Harry decides to capitalize on the situation by transporting persons in his car for a fee, Harry's PAP liability coverage does not apply to this activity. The exclusion does not apply to share-the-expense car pools. Ordinary business use of a car, such as newspaper or pizza delivery or use by a traveling sales representative, is not public or livery conveyance and is not excluded by this exclusion.

Liability Coverage and Car Pools

PAP premium rates are not designed to include the increased exposure to the insurer if an insured owns or operates an auto used as a public taxi or livery conveyance for hire by the general public. For this reason, the PAP excludes legal liability arising out of ownership or operation of a vehicle while it is being used for these purposes. However, share-the-expense car pools are an exception. If Barbara picks up several persons and transports them to work in an organized car pool with each person sharing the auto expenses, the liability coverage of Barbara's PAP still applies. Likewise, if Barbara and several friends go on a vacation in her car and the friends reimburse her for car expenses, her liability coverage is not affected.

Garage Business

Liability insurance does not apply to any insured while employed or engaged in the business of selling, repairing, servicing, storing, or parking vehicles designed for use mainly on public highways. This exclusion also applies to road testing and delivery of vehicles. For example, if an auto mechanic has an accident while road testing a customer's car, the mechanic's PAP liability coverage does not apply. Likewise, if a parking lot attendant accidentally injures someone while parking a customer's car, the loss is not covered under the attendant's PAP. The intent is to exclude a loss exposure that should be covered by a commercial policy, such as a garage policy, purchased by the owner of the business.

The garage business exclusion does not apply to the insured's covered auto when it is being driven by the named insured, a family member, or any partner, agent, or employee of the named insured or family member. For example, if an auto mechanic drives his covered auto (rather than a customer's auto) to a parts shop to pick up a part for his employer and he injures someone on the way, the mechanic's PAP liability insurance would cover the loss.

Other Business Use

Liability coverage does not apply to any vehicle other than a private passenger auto, a pickup, a van, or a trailer (while it is being used with a covered vehicle) that is maintained or used in any business other than farming or ranching. The intent is to exclude liability coverage for commercial vehicles and trucks used in a business. For example, if an insured drives a city bus or operates a large commercial truck, the insured's PAP liability coverage does not apply. Coverage for such vehicles is available through business auto policies.

Using a Vehicle Without Reasonable Belief of Being Entitled To Do So

If an insured uses a vehicle without reasonable belief that he or she is entitled to do so, the liability coverage does not apply. For example, if Jake's teenage son sees that the keys have been left in a stranger's car at a mall, takes the car for a joy ride, and causes an accident, Jake's PAP does not provide liability coverage.

This exclusion does not apply when another family member (as defined) uses the owned auto of a named insured. For insurance purposes, it is assumed that one family member has permission to use another family member's car.

Nuclear Energy Liability Losses

The PAP excludes liability for bodily injury or property damage for which an insured is covered under a special nuclear energy liability contract.

Vehicles That Have Fewer Than Four Wheels or Are Designed Primarily for Off-Road Use

Liability arising out of the ownership, maintenance, or use of any vehicle that has fewer than four wheels is excluded. Also excluded is liability coverage for any vehicle, other than a nonowned golf cart, that is designed primarily for use off public roads. The coverage for nonowned golf carts recognizes that vacationers at a resort sometimes are provided with a golf cart to get around the resort, and the cart might be used on a public road.

Although this provision excludes coverage for motorcycles, mopeds, and motorscooters, those vehicles can be covered, if an insurer agrees to provide coverage for them, by adding an endorsement to the PAP.

> The *miscellaneous type vehicle endorsement* (PP 03 23) provides coverage for miscellaneous vehicles, such as motor homes, motorcycles, dune buggies, or golf carts.
>
> The *snowmobile endorsement* (PP 03 20) covers the named insured, family members, and other persons for liability arising out of the use of any snowmobile.
>
> These endorsements are discussed in Chapter 4.

Other Vehicles Owned by the Named Insured or Available for the Named Insured's Regular Use

It is probably obvious that a person should not have liability coverage on a car without paying for the insurance, but it is necessary to state this point in the policy. Liability coverage is excluded for any vehicle owned by the named insured that is not a covered auto. A person who owns two vehicles but lists only one in the policy declarations would have coverage only for the vehicle listed, unless the other vehicle is a newly acquired auto or a trailer.

Any vehicle, other than a covered auto, that is furnished to or made available for the named insured's regular use is also excluded. The named insured can occasionally drive another person's auto and have coverage under his or her own policy. However, if the nonowned auto is furnished for the insured's regular use, the insured's liability coverage does not apply. This exclusion is intended to encourage policyholders to disclose accurately the number of vehicles they own or regularly operate. Without this provision, a person could insure and pay premiums for only one vehicle but have liability coverage for several cars he or she regularly drives. Without this exclusion, the insurance company's exposure could be substantially increased.

Many employees are furnished with "company cars," owned by their employers but available for the employees' regular use. Although the unendorsed PAP excludes coverage for these vehicles, the coverage can be added by using the extended non-owned coverage for named individual endorsement.

The *extended non-owned coverage for named individual endorsement* (PP 03 06), discussed in Chapter 4, provides coverage (on an excess basis) for certain vehicles otherwise excluded, such as a vehicle furnished for the named insured's regular use.

Vehicles Owned by or Available for Regular Use of Any Family Member

A similar exclusion applies to a vehicle (other than a covered auto) that is owned by any family member or that is furnished or made available for the regular use of any family member. However, the exclusion does not apply to the named insured and spouse while maintaining or occupying such a vehicle. Therefore, if Bill borrows a car owned and insured by his daughter who lives with him, the liability insurance under Bill's PAP would cover him while using his daughter's car. As explained later, Bill's coverage would apply as excess over the liability limit in his daughter's policy.

Racing

The PAP liability coverage does not apply to any vehicle that is located inside a racing facility for the purpose of preparing for, practicing for, or competing in any organized racing or speed contest.

Limit of Liability

As previously explained, coverage is most commonly provided on a split-limits basis. Three dollar limits are stated:

- The first limit applies to bodily injury to each person.
- A second limit applies to bodily injury to all persons in each accident.
- A third limit applies to all property damage in each accident.

Although split limits are most commonly used, a single limit is often substituted by adding a single liability limit endorsement to the PAP.

The PAP states that the limits of liability for the policy will not be increased regardless of the number of insured persons, claims made, vehicles or premiums shown, or vehicles involved in an auto accident. The most any claimant can recover for one accident is the applicable limit(s) stated in the declarations. For example, if Betty were doing an errand for the Red Cross in her personal auto and caused an accident, the claimant might sue both Betty and the Red Cross, because Betty was acting on its behalf. Betty's insurer would handle the claim and respond to a lawsuit on behalf of both Betty and the Red Cross. However, Betty's insurer would not pay more than the limits of liability on her PAP even though it is responding on behalf of two parties. (The Red Cross might also have its own coverage.)

Examples of Split Limits and Single Limit

Split Limits

Jessica has a personal auto policy with the following split limits:

Bodily Injury

$100,000 each person

$300,000 each occurrence

Property Damage

$50,000 each occurrence

Jessica is liable for a covered auto accident resulting in injuries to Richard, the driver of the other car, and Marcy, his passenger. When the case went to trial, the court awarded $200,000 in bodily injury damages to Richard and $150,000 to Marcy. In addition, the damage to Richard's car amounted to $10,000, which Jessica was also ordered to pay. Jessica's insurer would pay $110,000 to Richard ($100,000 each person limit for bodily injury plus $10,000 for property damage) and $100,000 to Marcy (the each person limit). Thus, the insurer would pay a total of $210,000 for this accident (plus Jessica's defense costs, which are paid in addition to the policy limits in a personal auto policy). Jessica would have to pay the remaining bodily injury damages of $150,000 from her own pocket.

Single Limit

If Jessica's personal auto policy had a single limit of $300,000 in lieu of the split limits shown above, her insurer would pay a total of $300,000 to Richard and Marcy for both bodily injury and property damage (plus defense costs) in the above accident. (A determination of exactly how much each party receives would depend on the circumstances of this particular claim.)

In this situation, Jessica's insurer would pay more under the single limit policy than the split limits policy, but such is not always the case. For example, if three people had had bodily injury of $150,000 each plus the $10,000 property damage, the insurer would have paid a total of $310,000 under the split limits policy ($100,000 bodily injury for each person plus $10,000 property damage); under the single limits policy, the insurer would pay only $300,000, the maximum payable for any one occurrence.

The limit of liability provision specifically states that no one is entitled to receive duplicate payments for the same elements of loss under Part A—Liability Coverage, Part B—Medical Payments Coverage, Part C—Uninsured Motorists Coverage, or any underinsured motorists coverage provided by the policy. This provision keeps an insured from collecting twice for one loss under the same policy.

Out-of-State Coverage

Out-of-state coverage (as used in Part A of the PAP)
Provision that automatically provides any higher limits and types of coverage required by the state in which an auto accident occurs if such an accident occurs in a state other than the one in which the covered auto is principally garaged.

The PAP contains an **out-of-state coverage** provision that applies when an auto accident occurs in a state other than the one in which the covered auto is principally garaged. If the accident occurs in a state that has a financial responsibility law or a similar law that requires higher liability limits than the limits shown in the declarations, the PAP automatically provides the higher required limits for that accident. In addition, if a state has a compulsory insurance or a similar law that requires a nonresident to maintain coverage whenever a nonresident uses a vehicle in that state, the PAP provides the required minimum amounts and types of coverage.

This provision assures customers that their policy complies with an out-of-state law and will provide the required benefits. For example, a driver who is not required to have "no-fault" personal injury protection (PIP) coverage in his or her home state would have PIP coverage when driving in a state that requires it.

Compliance With Financial Responsibility Laws

As mentioned in Chapter 2, many states have financial responsibility laws that require certain motorists, such as those who have been involved in accidents, to provide some form of proof of financial responsibility for the future. Most people use liability insurance as their proof. When the PAP is used to demonstrate financial responsibility, the policy will comply with the law to the extent required. Thus, if the financial responsibility law is changed to require higher minimum limits, the PAP will automatically comply with the new law.

Other Insurance

Part A of the PAP has a provision that addresses situations in which more than one auto policy covers a liability claim. In an unusual situation in which the insured has other applicable liability insurance on an *owned vehicle*, the insurer pays only its pro rata share of the loss. The insurer's share is the proportion that its limit of liability bears to the total of all applicable limits.

If other liability insurance is available on a *nonowned vehicle*, the PAP coverage is excess over any other collectible insurance. For example, Ken borrows Patti's car with her permission. Ken has a PAP with $100,000/$300,000/$50,000 liability limits, and Patti has a PAP with $50,000/$100,000/$25,000 liability limits. Ken negligently injures another motorist and must pay a judgment of $60,000. Patti's insurance is primary and Ken's is excess. Each insurer pays as follows:

Patti's insurer (primary)—$50,000 (Patti's per person limit)

Ken's insurer (excess)—$10,000 (the excess over Patti's limit)

PART B—MEDICAL PAYMENTS COVERAGE

Medical payments coverage is an option that can be added to the PAP. Under this coverage, the insurer pays medical expenses up to a specified limit for certain people who are injured in an auto accident. The limit is typically between $1,000 and $10,000 per person. The limit applies separately to each insured person who is injured in any one auto accident.

Part B—Medical Payments Coverage is summarized in Exhibit 3-2.

EXHIBIT 3-2

Summary of Part B—Medical Payments Coverage

Insuring Agreement	Persons Insured	Exclusions
Pays reasonable medical and funeral expenses incurred by an insured for services rendered within three years of the accident	Named insured and resident family members while occupying a motor vehicle or if injured as a pedestrian by a motor vehicle designed for use mainly on public roads Other persons while occupying a covered auto	Occupying a motorized vehicle with fewer than four wheels Using a covered auto as a public or livery conveyance (exclusion does not apply to a share-the-expense car pool) Using the vehicle as a residence or premises Injury occurring during the course of employment if workers compensation benefits are required or available Vehicle furnished or made available for the named insured's regular use Vehicle furnished or made available for the regular use of any family member Occupying a vehicle without a reasonable belief of being entitled to do so Vehicle used in the business of an insured (exclusion does not apply to a private passenger auto, an owned pickup or van, or trailer used with any of the preceding vehicles) Nuclear weapons, war, nuclear reaction or radiation Occupying a vehicle located inside a racing facility for the purpose of competing in or preparing for a prearranged racing contest

Exhibit by George E. Rejda, Ph.D., CLU, used with permission.

Insuring Agreement

The insurer will pay reasonable and necessary medical and funeral expenses incurred by an insured because of bodily injury caused by an accident. The insurer will pay only those expenses incurred for services rendered within three years from the date of the accident. The types of expenses payable include those incurred for medical, surgical, X-ray, dental, and funeral services.

Medical payments coverage applies without regard to fault. Thus, whether or not the accident is caused by the insured, medical payments benefits may be paid for both the insured and other injured occupants of the insured's covered auto.

Insured Persons

Two groups of persons are considered insured persons for medical payments coverage. They are (1) the named insured and family members and (2) any other person while occupying a covered auto.

The *named insured and family members* are covered for their medical expenses if they are injured while **occupying** a motor vehicle or are injured as pedestrians when struck by a motor vehicle designed for use mainly on public roads. Examples of covered losses include payment of medical expenses when the named insured is injured in an auto accident, when a child's hand is injured when the insured's car door shuts on it, and when a guest of the insured breaks a leg while getting out of the insured's vehicle. If the named insured or any family member is a pedestrian when struck by a motor vehicle or trailer, his or her medical expenses are also paid. However, if an insured is struck by a farm tractor, for example, medical payments coverage does not apply because the tractor is not designed for use mainly on public roads.

Occupying (as used in the PAP)
In, upon, getting in, on, out, or off.

Any other person while occupying a covered auto is also insured. Therefore, medical expenses of passengers in a covered auto are covered. For example, if Mary owns her car and is the named insured, all passengers in her car are covered for their medical expenses under her policy. However, if Mary is operating a *nonowned vehicle*, passengers in the car (other than family members) are not covered under Mary's medical payments coverage. Passengers in the nonowned vehicle should seek protection under their own policies or under the medical payments coverage that applies to the nonowned vehicle.

Medical Payments Exclusions

Numerous exclusions apply to Part B—Medical Payments Coverage. Many of these exclusions are similar to those under Part A—Liability Coverage.

Motorized Vehicles With Fewer Than Four Wheels

Medical expenses for bodily injury that any insured sustains while occupying a motorized vehicle with fewer than four wheels are excluded. For example, if an insured is injured while operating a motorcycle, medical payments coverage does not apply.

Public or Livery Conveyance

Medical payments coverage does not apply while a covered auto is being used as a public or livery conveyance. The exclusion does not apply to share-the-expense car pools.

Vehicles Used as a Residence or Premises

If the injury occurs while the vehicle is located for use as a residence or premises, the medical payments coverage of the PAP does not apply. For example, Steve's apartment building burns down, and he decides to live in a van covered by his PAP while he looks for a new apartment. If Steve burns himself while cooking on a small stove in the van, the medical payments coverage of the PAP does not apply to this injury arising out of Steve's use of the covered vehicle as a residence.

Injury During the Course of Employment

If the injury occurs during the course of employment and workers compensation benefits are required or available, medical payments coverage does not apply. For example, if an insured is injured while driving his or her car on company business and workers compensation benefits are available, the medical payments coverage of the PAP does not apply.

Other Vehicles Owned by the Named Insured or Available for the Named Insured's Regular Use

Medical payments coverage does not apply to an injury sustained by an insured while occupying, or when struck by, any vehicle (other than a covered auto) that is owned by the insured or is furnished or available for his or her regular use. The intent is to exclude medical payments coverage on an owned or regularly used vehicle that is not described in the policy and for which no premium is paid.

Vehicles Owned by or Available for Regular Use of Any Family Member

A similar exclusion applies to any vehicle (other than a covered auto) that is owned by or is furnished or available for the regular use of any family member. However, there is an important exception. The exclusion does not apply to the named insured and spouse. For example, assume that a son living at home owns a car that is separately insured. If the parents are injured while occupying the son's car, their medical expenses are covered under their own PAP (as excess over any medical payments coverage in the son's policy).

Occupying a Vehicle Without Reasonable Belief of Being Entitled To Do So

If an insured sustains an injury while using a vehicle without a reasonable belief that he or she is entitled to do so, medical payments coverage does not apply.

For example, Harry works at a hotel and takes a guest's car from the garage for use on a brief errand. Neither Harry's PAP nor the guest's PAP will provide coverage if Harry is injured while using the guest's car without permission.

As with the liability coverage, this medical payments exclusion does not apply when another family member (as defined) uses the owned auto of a named insured. For insurance purposes, it is assumed that one family member has permission to use another family member's car.

Vehicles Used in the Business of an Insured

Medical payments coverage does not apply to bodily injury sustained by an insured while occupying a vehicle used in the insured's business. However, this exclusion does not apply to a private passenger auto, an owned pickup or van, or a trailer used with these vehicles. The intent is to exclude medical payments coverage for commercial vehicles used in the business of an insured. (Coverage for such injuries should be provided by a commercial policy or by a workers compensation policy.)

Bodily Injury From Nuclear Weapons or War

Injury from the discharge of a nuclear weapon (even if accidental) or from war, insurrection, rebellion, or revolution is excluded from medical payments coverage.

Nuclear Radiation Exclusion

Bodily injury caused by nuclear reaction, radiation, or radioactive contamination is also excluded. For example, if an insured drives a covered auto near a public utility plant when an accidental release of radiation occurs, injuries resulting from the radiation exposure would not be covered.

Racing

Also excluded from medical payments coverage is bodily injury that occurs while an insured is occupying any vehicle that is located inside a racing facility for the purpose of preparing for, practicing for, or competing in any organized racing or speed contest.

Limit of Liability

The limit of insurance for medical payments coverage is stated in the declarations. This limit, typically between $1,000 and $10,000, is the maximum amount that will be paid to *each injured person* in a single accident regardless of the number of insured persons, claims made, vehicles or premiums shown, or vehicles involved in the auto accident. The intent is to prevent an insured person from collecting more than the stated medical payments limit for any one accident.

In addition, the limit of liability provision specifically states that no one is entitled to receive duplicate payments for the same elements of loss under

Part B—Medical Payments Coverage, Part A—Liability Coverage, Part C—Uninsured Motorists Coverage, or any underinsured motorists coverage provided by the policy. This provision avoids a double payment for the same medical expenses. For example, assume Janice has a limit of $5,000 for medical payments coverage, and she is injured by an uninsured motorist. Janice's medical bills are $5,000. Without this provision, Janice could collect $10,000—that is, $5,000 under the medical payments coverage and another $5,000 under the uninsured motorists coverage (discussed in the next section) for the same bills.

Other Insurance

If other auto medical payments insurance should apply, the insurer would pay its pro rata share based on the proportion that its limit of liability bears to the total of applicable limits.

With respect to a *nonowned vehicle*, however, medical payments coverage under a PAP is *excess* over any other collectible auto insurance that provides payment for medical or funeral expenses. For example, assume that Mary is driving her own car and Pam is her passenger. From Pam's perspective, Mary's car is a nonowned vehicle. Mary hits a patch of ice and skids into a tree. Mary has a $5,000 limit of medical payments coverage under her PAP, and Pam (under her own personal auto policy) has a medical payments limit of $10,000. If Pam's medical expenses are $6,000, Mary's insurer pays $5,000 as primary insurance and Pam's insurer pays the remaining $1,000 as excess insurance.

PART C—UNINSURED MOTORISTS COVERAGE

Uninsured motorists (UM) coverage, summarized in Exhibit 3-3, is designed to compensate an insured for bodily injury caused by an uninsured motorist, a hit-and-run driver, or a driver whose insurer is insolvent.

Insuring Agreement

The insurer agrees to pay compensatory damages that the insured person is legally entitled to recover from the owner or operator of an uninsured motor vehicle because of bodily injury caused by an accident. Such compensatory damages could include medical expenses, rehabilitation expenses, lost wages, and other losses resulting from the insured's bodily injury. Only compensatory damages are covered. To emphasize this point, punitive damages are specifically excluded, as noted later.

UM coverage applies only if the uninsured motorist is legally responsible for the accident. Although a covered person is not required to sue the uninsured driver, that driver's legal liability must be established.

Although the standard PAP provides uninsured motorists coverage only for bodily injury claims, in some states uninsured motorists coverage for property damage claims is also included. In such states, the UM property damage coverage is subject to a deductible, such as $200 or $300.

EXHIBIT 3-3

Summary of Part C—Uninsured Motorists Coverage

Insuring Agreement	Persons Insured	Exclusions
Pays compensatory damages that an insured is legally entitled to recover from the owner or operator of an uninsured motor vehicle because of bodily injury sustained by an insured caused by an accident	Named insured and resident family members Any other person while occupying a covered auto Any person legally entitled to recover damages because of bodily injury to a person described above	No uninsured motorists coverage on a motor vehicle owned by an insured No coverage for a family member who occupies, or is struck by, a motor vehicle owned by the named insured that is insured for uninsured motorists coverage on a primary basis by another policy Settling a claim without the insurer's consent Using a covered auto as a public or livery conveyance (exclusion does not apply to a share-the-expense car pool) Using a vehicle without a reasonable belief that the insured is entitled to do so No benefit to workers compensation insurer No punitive damages paid

Exhibit by George E. Rejda, Ph.D., CLU, used with permission.

Insured Persons

Three groups of persons are considered insureds under the uninsured motorists coverage:

1. The named insured and family members
2. Any other person occupying a covered auto
3. Any person legally entitled to recover damages because of bodily injury to a person described in 1. or 2.

The *named insured* and *family members* are covered if injured by an uninsured motor vehicle while occupying a covered auto or nonowned auto. They are also covered as pedestrians.

Any other person who is injured while occupying a covered auto is also covered. Thus, passengers in the insured's car have coverage for bodily injury caused by an uninsured motorist.

Finally, an insured includes *any person legally entitled to recover damages* as a result of bodily injury caused by an uninsured motorist to any insured person as described above. For example, if an insured person is killed by an uninsured motorist, a surviving spouse could collect damages under the uninsured motorists coverage.

Uninsured Motor Vehicles

Uninsured motor vehicle
Any type of land motor vehicle or trailer that is not insured for bodily injury liability, is insured for less than the financial responsibility limits, is a hit-and-run vehicle, or whose insurer denies coverage or becomes insolvent.

The uninsured motorists coverage clearly specifies the types of vehicles that are considered **uninsured motor vehicles**. An uninsured vehicle is a land motor vehicle or trailer of any type that meets any of the following criteria:

1. No bodily injury liability insurance or bond applies to the vehicle at the time of the accident.

2. A bodily injury liability policy or bond is in force, but the limit for bodily injury liability is less than the minimum amount required by the financial responsibility law in the state where the named insured's covered auto is principally garaged.

3. The vehicle is a hit-and-run vehicle, whose operator or owner cannot be identified, that hits (a) the named insured or any family member, (b) a vehicle that the named insured or family member is occupying, or (c) the named insured's covered auto.

4. A bodily injury liability policy or bond applies at the time of the accident, but the insurance or bonding company (a) denies coverage or (b) is or becomes insolvent. For example, if Tom has a valid claim against a negligent motorist whose liability insurer becomes insolvent before the claim is paid, Tom can collect for his bodily injury damages under the uninsured motorists coverage of his PAP.

Certain vehicles, however, are not considered to be uninsured motor vehicles. If an insured were injured by one of these vehicles, uninsured motorists coverage would not apply. The definition of uninsured motor vehicle does not include:

1. Vehicles owned or furnished or available for the regular use of the named insured or any family member

2. Vehicles owned or operated by a self-insurer under any applicable motor vehicle law, except a self-insurer that is or becomes insolvent

3. Vehicles owned by a governmental unit or agency

4. Vehicles operated on rails or crawler treads

5. Vehicles designed mainly for use off public roads (while not on public roads)

6. Vehicles located for use as a residence or premises

Uninsured Motorists Exclusions

The uninsured motorists coverage has several general exclusions. The following is a summary of these exclusions:

1. *No uninsured motorists coverage on vehicle.* There is no UM coverage for bodily injury sustained by an insured who occupies or is struck by a motor vehicle or trailer owned by that insured if that vehicle does not have uninsured motorists coverage under the policy.

2. *Primary coverage under another policy.* There is no UM coverage for a family member who occupies or is struck by a vehicle the named insured owns that is insured for uninsured motorists coverage on a primary basis under another policy.

3. *Claim settled without insurer's consent.* The uninsured motorists coverage does not apply to a claim that is settled without the insurer's consent. The purpose of this exclusion is to protect the insurer's right to settle the claim.

4. *Covered auto used as public or livery conveyance.* If a person is injured while occupying a covered auto when it is being used as a public or livery conveyance, the uninsured motorists coverage does not apply. The exclusion does not apply to a share-the-expense car pool.

5. *Vehicle used without reasonable belief of being entitled to do so.* The uninsured motorists coverage does not apply to any person who uses a vehicle without a reasonable belief that the person is entitled to do so. Family members need not obtain explicit permission to use a covered auto.

6. *Cannot benefit workers compensation insurer.* The uninsured motorists coverage cannot directly or indirectly benefit any insurer or self-insurer under a workers compensation law or disability benefits law.

   In some states, if an employee is injured and workers compensation benefits are paid, the workers compensation insurer has a legal right to recover from a negligent third party the amounts paid by the insurer. The process of recovering from the negligent third party is known as *subrogation.* Thus, the workers compensation insurer could sue the uninsured driver or attempt to make a claim under the injured employee's uninsured motorists coverage. This exclusion prevents the workers compensation insurer from obtaining reimbursement under the injured worker's uninsured motorists coverage.

7. *Punitive damages not paid.* The PAP excludes payment for punitive damages under the uninsured motorists coverage. Therefore, only compensatory damages are paid under this coverage.

Limit of Liability

The minimum amount of uninsured motorists coverage available under the PAP is the amount required by the financial responsibility or compulsory insurance law of the state in which the named insured's covered auto is principally garaged. Higher limits can be purchased for an additional premium.

The limit of liability for uninsured motorists coverage is shown in the declarations. Uninsured motorists coverage is normally written on a split-limits basis, but single-limit coverage is available by endorsement.

The limits shown are the most that will be paid regardless of the number of insured persons, claims made, vehicles or premiums shown in the declarations, or vehicles involved in the accident. This provision prevents the "stacking" of uninsured motorists payments under a policy that covers more than one car owned by the named insured. Stacking refers to situations in which the insured maintains that, because the policy covers two (or more) vehicles, he or she should collect up to twice the stated limit since a separate premium has been paid for each vehicle. For example, assume the insured owns three cars that are covered by a PAP with an uninsured motorists limit of $25,000 per person. If the insured is injured by an uninsured motorist, the most the insured can recover is $25,000, not $75,000.

The uninsured motorists section specifically states that no person will receive duplicate payments for any loss under Part A—Liability Coverage, Part B—Medical Payments Coverage, or Part C—Uninsured Motorists Coverage, or under any underinsured motorists coverage provided by the policy. For example, if Christine is injured by a hit-and-run driver and incurs $5,000 in medical expenses, she cannot collect $5,000 under her medical payments coverage and then collect an additional $5,000 for the same expenses under her UM coverage. (She can, however, attempt to collect any *additional* damages under her UM coverage as long as they do not duplicate the expenses for which the insurer has already paid under her medical payments coverage.) Likewise, the insurer will not make duplicate payment under the uninsured motorists coverage if payment has been made by the person or organization legally responsible for the accident or if the injured person is entitled to receive payment under a workers compensation or disability benefits law.

Other Insurance

If other applicable uninsured motorists insurance is available under one or more policies, the following provisions apply to the payment for damages:

- The total amount paid will be no more than the highest limit of any of the policies that provide coverage.

- Coverage for an accident involving a vehicle the named insured does not own is provided on an excess basis over any collectible insurance providing coverage on a primary basis. For example, assume that Louis has uninsured motorists coverage with limits of $50,000/$100,000 under his PAP. (These limits indicate $50,000 per person and $100,000 per accident for bodily injury. No property damage limit is given because uninsured motorists coverage does not usually include property damage.) He is injured by an uninsured motorist while riding in Gayle's car. Gayle has $25,000/$50,000 of uninsured motorists coverage. If Louis is entitled to $35,000 for his bodily injuries, Gayle's insurer pays the first $25,000 as primary insurer of her owned vehicle, and Louis's insurer pays the remaining $10,000 as excess insurance (because Louis does not own the vehicle).

- When the named insured's policy and the other policy (or policies) provide coverage on a primary basis, each policy will contribute proportionally to the insured's recovery. Each insurer's share is equal to the proportion its UM limit bears to the total amount available under all applicable coverages provided on a primary basis.

- When the named insured's policy and the other policy (or policies) provide coverage on an excess basis, each policy will contribute proportionally to the insured's recovery, based on the excess limits each policy provides.

Arbitration

If the insurer and insured cannot agree on whether the insured is entitled to recover damages under uninsured motorists coverage or on the amount of damages, the dispute can be settled by **arbitration**. However, both the insurer and the insured must agree to arbitration.

Each party selects an arbitrator, and the two arbitrators select a third arbitrator. If the two arbitrators cannot agree on a third arbitrator within thirty days, either party can request that the selection be made by a judge of a court having jurisdiction. Each party pays the expenses it incurs, and both parties share the expenses of the third arbitrator.

A decision agreed to by two of the three arbitrators is binding as to (1) whether the insured is legally entitled to recover damages and (2) the amount of damages. However, this decision is binding only if the amount of damages does not exceed the minimum limit for bodily injury specified by the state's financial responsibility law. If the amount of damages exceeds that limit, either party can demand the right to a trial within sixty days of the arbitrators' decision. Otherwise, the arbitrators' decision is binding.

Arbitration (as used in the PAP)
Process for settling disputes between the insured and the insurer concerning whether or for what amount uninsured motorists coverage applies.

SUMMARY

The personal auto policy (PAP) consists of a declarations page, an insuring agreement, definitions, and six separate parts. Endorsements can be added to the policy. To be eligible for coverage under the personal auto policy, the vehicle to be insured must be owned, or leased for at least six months, by an individual or individuals. The PAP is designed to insure private passenger autos, as well as pickup trucks and vans, subject to certain restrictions.

The PAP declarations page identifies the named insured, his or her address, and the location where the vehicle is garaged. It also describes the covered vehicles and lists the premiums, limits of liability, applicable endorsements, and other information. The definitions clarify certain terms used in the policy.

Part A—Liability Coverage of the PAP pays damages for bodily injury or property damage for which the insured is legally responsible because of an auto accident. When the policy has split limits of liability, the limits are available per person for bodily injury, per accident for bodily injury, and per accident for property damage to pay damages for which the insured is legally liable. The insurer also agrees to defend the insured and pay all legal defense costs, in addition to the policy limits, until the limits have been exhausted by settlement or payment of a judgment.

Four groups of persons are insured under the PAP liability coverage:

- The named insured and family members;
- Persons using the named insured's covered auto;
- Persons or organizations held responsible for liability arising out of an insured's use of a covered auto on behalf of persons or organizations; and
- Persons or organizations legally responsible for the named insured's or a family member's use of any auto or trailer other than a covered auto or one owned by those persons or organizations.

Excluded from liability coverage are:

- Intentional injury
- Damage to the insured's own property
- Nonowned property in the care of the insured
- Bodily injury to an employee of the insured
- Bodily injury or property damage when the vehicle is being used as a public or livery conveyance
- Claims arising out of the use of the auto by someone in the garage business
- Claims relating to the preparation or use of a vehicle where speed contests are held

Other business uses of the auto are also excluded, with certain exceptions. Additional exclusions relate to nuclear energy liability losses, motorized vehicles with fewer than four wheels, vehicles made available for the insured's regular use, and vehicles owned by or furnished or available for the regular use of any family member.

Part B—Medical Payments Coverage pays medical expenses, up to a specified limit, of insured persons who are injured in an accident involving an auto. The medical expenses must be incurred for services rendered within three years of the date of the accident. The insureds under this part of the policy are the named insured and family members, as well as any other person while occupying a covered auto. A number of exclusions mentioned above also apply to the medical payments coverage.

Part C—Uninsured Motorists Coverage pays for bodily injury to an insured who is injured by an uninsured motorist, a hit-and-run driver, or a driver whose insurer becomes insolvent. Some states also include property damage as part of the uninsured motorists (UM) coverage. The minimum amount of uninsured motorists coverage is the amount of the state's financial responsibility or compulsory insurance law. The named insured, family members, and any other person occupying a covered auto are insured under the uninsured motorists coverage. Vehicles that qualify as uninsured motor vehicles and those that do not qualify are described in the policy. UM coverage has a special set of exclusions, such as punitive damages.

CHAPTER NOTE

1. The first four digits of an ISO form are the form number, and the last four digits represent the month and year of the edition of the form. The 1998 edition of the PAP (00 01 06 98) was drafted during 1997 and bears a 1997 copyright date.

Chapter 4

![Direct]
Direct Your Learning

Personal Auto Policy, Part II

After learning the subject matter of this chapter, for a given auto physical damage case involving the ISO personal auto policy (1998), you should be able to:

■ Determine whether the loss is covered and the amount the insurer would pay for covered losses.

■ Explain the insured's duties after an accident or a loss.

■ Explain the general provisions in Part F of the PAP.

■ Explain how the endorsements described in this assignment can change coverage.

Develop Your Perspective

What are the main topics covered in the chapter?

This chapter completes the review of the personal auto policy (PAP) by describing coverage for damage to your auto, conditions of the policy, and common endorsements to the PAP.

Review sections of the PAP policy described.

- What coverage is provided to protect an insured's automobile?

- What duties must an insured perform for coverage to apply?

Why is it important to know these topics?

The PAP is a package of coverages that includes protection for the auto damage loss exposures that most individuals and families face. However, there are significant limitations in the coverage. Also, the PAP conditions define specific actions required of the policyholder.

Consider the auto damage coverage needs of average auto owners.

- For what value does the PAP provide coverage for a vehicle?

- What exclusions limit the coverage provided?

- What must an insurer do following an accident?

How can you use this information?

Compare your own auto insurance needs to the coverages provided by the PAP:

- Does the PAP provide adequate coverage for the value of your vehicle?

- Do you have any auto damage loss exposures that are excluded by the PAP?

- Would you consider adding any endorsements to your PAP?

Chapter 4

Personal Auto Policy, Part II

This chapter continues the discussion of the personal auto policy (PAP) by examining the remaining coverages and provisions, including Part D—Damage to a Covered Auto, Part E—Duties After an Accident or Loss, and Part F—General Provisions. The chapter also examines some common endorsements that can be added to the PAP to modify various coverages and to better meet the needs of some insureds.

The discussion of the PAP and endorsements in this chapter is based on the edition introduced in 1998 and bearing a 1997 copyright date. The policy form and edition is numbered PP 00 01 06 98.

PART D—COVERAGE FOR DAMAGE TO YOUR AUTO

Part D of the personal auto policy provides **physical damage coverage** for damage to or theft of a covered auto. Coverage under Part D also applies to nonowned autos used by an insured, including temporary substitute vehicles. Part D—Coverage for Damage to Your Auto is summarized in Exhibit 4-1.

Physical damage coverage ("coverage for damage to your auto")
Insures against loss resulting from damage to or theft of an auto owned or operated by the insured; a type of property insurance that includes both collision coverage and "other-than-collision" coverage.

Insuring Agreement

In the insuring agreement of Part D, the insurer promises to pay for any direct and accidental loss to a covered auto or a nonowned auto, including its equipment, minus the deductible shown on the declarations page. Three coverage alternatives are usually available:

- No physical damage coverage
- Other-than-collision coverage
- Both collision and other-than-collision coverage

It would be unusual for an insurer to write collision coverage without other-than-collision.

Coverage for other-than-collision losses is effective only if the declarations page indicates that other-than-collision coverage is provided for that auto. Likewise, collision losses are covered for a specified auto only if the declarations page indicates that collision coverage is in effect for that auto. If the insured purchases both coverages, the premium for each coverage is shown

EXHIBIT 4-1

Summary of Part D—Coverage for Damage to Your Auto

Insuring Agreement	Persons Insured	Exclusions

Pays for direct and accidental loss to a covered auto or to a nonowned auto, including its equipment, minus any deductible, caused by a collision or other-than-collision. Declarations must indicate such coverage is provided for each vehicle.
 	
Loss caused by the following is considered other-than-collision:
 	
  Missiles or falling objects
  Fire
  Theft or larceny
  Explosion or earthquake
  Windstorm
  Hail, water, or flood
  Malicious mischief or
    vandalism
  Riot or civil commotion
  Contact with a bird or animal
  Breakage of glass
 	
Transportation Expenses:
  Pays up to $20 daily, to a maximum of $600, for transportation expenses because of loss to a covered auto caused by collision or other-than-collision.
 	
  Declarations must indicate such coverage is provided for each vehicle.
 	
Also pays expenses for which the insured is legally liable because of loss to a nonowned auto.
	Part D does not specifically mention the persons insured. However, coverage applies to the named insured and spouse, resident family members, and any person using a covered auto with permission.	Loss to a covered auto or nonowned auto while being used as a public or livery conveyance (exclusion does not apply to a share-the-expense car pool)
		
		Damage from wear and tear, freezing, and mechanical or electrical breakdown
		
		Radioactive contamination or war
		
		Electronic equipment and accessories designed for the reproduction of sound—including radios, stereos, tape decks, or compact disc players—unless permanently installed in the auto. Certain other exceptions apply.
		
		Other electronic equipment, including citizens band radios; telephones; two-way mobile radios; scanning monitor receivers; television monitor receivers; videocassette recorders; or personal computers*
		
		Tapes, records, and discs used with the preceding equipment
		
		Government destruction or confiscation
		
		Loss to a trailer, camper body, or motor home now shown in the declarations (except if newly acquired and reported within fourteen days)
		
		Loss to nonowned auto used without a reasonable belief of permission
		
		Radar or laser detection equipment
		
		Custom furnishings or equipment in a pickup or van
		
		Nonowned auto maintained or used in the automobile business
		
		Vehicle located inside a racing facility for the purpose of competing in or preparing for a prearranged racing contest
		
		Loss to a rental car if a state law or rental agreement precludes the rental company from recovering from the insured

* Exclusion does not apply to electronic equipment for the normal operation of the auto, or to a permanently installed car telephone.

Exhibit by George E. Rejda, Ph.D., CLU, used with permission.

separately on the declarations page. Additional physical damages coverages can be added by endorsement.

> A popular coverage option can be added to the PAP endorsement. The *towing and labor costs coverage endorsement* (PP 03 03) provides coverage for towing and labor costs, up to a specified limit, for a covered auto that is disabled.

The distinction between collision and other-than-collision coverage is relevant: many motorists purchase only other-than-collision coverage, because collision insurance is more expensive. Also, the other-than-collision coverage often has a lower deductible than does collision coverage.

Collision Loss

Collision coverage is examined first, because other-than-collision coverage by definition applies to losses that are not collisions. The following are examples of **collision** losses covered under Part D of the PAP:

Collision (as used in the PAP)
The upset of a covered auto or a nonowned auto or its impact with another vehicle or object.

- An auto collides with another vehicle.
- An auto smashes into a telephone pole.
- A driver loses control of an auto, causing it to overturn.
- An owner parks an auto and goes shopping; when the owner returns, the rear fender of the auto is dented.
- A person opens a car door in a parking lot, and the door is damaged when it hits a vehicle parked next to it.

Collision losses are paid regardless of fault. For example:

- If Frank is responsible for an accident that damages his car, his collision coverage will pay for any physical damage to his own car, minus any deductible that applies.

- If the driver of another car causes the accident resulting in damage to Frank's car, Frank can collect either from the other driver (or the driver's insurer) or from his own insurer. If Frank collects from his own insurer, his insurer then has the right to recover payment from the other driver who caused the accident (or the driver's insurer). This recovery involves the *subrogation* process, discussed later in this chapter.

If two or more autos, for which the same policy provides collision coverage, are damaged in the same collision, only one deductible applies. If the collision coverage deductible on one of the vehicles is higher than the others, the larger deductible applies. For example, Bob owns three cars, all of which are covered under the same PAP. While pulling into his driveway during a winter storm, Bob's car skids on the snow and collides with both of his other cars. Bob's PAP includes a $250 collision deductible on two of the cars and a $500 collision deductible on the third car. In settling this loss, Bob's PAP insurer will apply a single $500 deductible to the total damage to all three cars.

Other-Than-Collision Loss

Other-than-collision (OTC) coverage covers auto physical damage losses that are not caused by collision and are not specifically excluded in the policy. This coverage was previously called **"comprehensive,"** and insurance practitioners still use that label frequently. However, the name was changed because "comprehensive" implies coverage for everything. Like virtually all other coverages, other-than-collision coverage is subject to exclusions.

While collision is specifically defined in the PAP, other-than-collision is not. The policy does, however, list certain causes of loss that are considered other-than-collision:

- Missiles or falling objects
- Fire
- Theft or larceny
- Explosion or earthquake
- Windstorm
- Hail, water, or flood
- Malicious mischief or vandalism
- Riot or civil commotion
- Contact with a bird or another animal
- Breakage of glass

Two points are especially important. First, *colliding with a bird or animal is not a collision loss*. Thus, if Anna hits a bird, deer, or cow with her car, any physical damage to her car is considered to be an other-than-collision loss. Second, *if glass breakage is caused by a collision, the insured can elect to have the glass breakage considered as part of the collision loss*. By electing to treat the glass breakage as part of the collision loss, only one deductible has to be satisfied. Otherwise, the insured would have to absorb two deductibles.

The preceding list provides examples of other-than-collision loss that are covered by the PAP; it does not list all possible perils. Any "direct and accidental loss" that is not due to collision and is not specifically excluded would be covered as an other-than-collision loss. For example, if a car is used to take a bleeding person to the hospital and blood stains the car's upholstery, other-than-collision coverage would apply. Other-than-collision coverage would also apply to exterior damage to a covered auto when it is splattered with paint while it is parked next to a house being painted.

Physical Damage Coverage for Nonowned Autos

The Part D coverages also apply to a **nonowned auto**. Therefore, if Lois borrows a car that belongs to her friend Dick, any physical damage coverage

Other-than-collision (OTC) coverage
Coverage for auto physical damage losses that are not caused by collision and that are not specifically excluded by the policy.

Nonowned auto (as used in the physical damage coverage section of the PAP)
Any private passenger auto, pickup, van, or trailer that is not owned by or made available for the regular use of the named insured or any family member. Physical damage coverage applies to such a vehicle while it is in the custody of or is being operated by the named insured or any family member. With respect to physical damage coverage, a temporary substitute vehicle is also considered a nonowned auto.

that applies to Lois's covered auto also applies to the borrowed vehicle. (However, Lois's coverage would be excess over any physical damage coverage Dick has on his car. This concept is explained later in this chapter.)

An insured can occasionally drive a rented or borrowed auto, and the insured's physical damage insurance will cover the vehicle. However, if the vehicle is driven regularly or is made available for an insured's regular use, the insured's coverage does not apply. For example, if an employer furnishes an insured with a company car, or if a car is made available for the insured's regular use in a carpool, the Part D coverages of the insured's PAP do not apply. The deciding factor is not how frequently the insured drives a nonowned auto, but whether the nonowned auto is made available for the insured's regular use.

The definition of nonowned auto also includes any auto or trailer that is being used as a temporary substitute for a covered auto or trailer that is out of normal use because of its breakdown, repair, servicing, loss, or destruction. For example, if Jim's car is in the shop for repairs and he is furnished with a loaner car, his physical damage insurance applies to the loaner car.

If there is a loss to a nonowned auto, the PAP provides the broadest coverage applicable to any covered auto shown in the declarations. For example, assume that Oscar owns two cars that are insured by his PAP. One car is covered for both collision and other-than-collision losses, while the second car is covered only for other-than-collision losses. If Oscar borrows his neighbor's car, the borrowed car is covered by Oscar's PAP for both collision and other-than-collision losses.

Deductibles

A flat deductible of $100, $250, $500, or some higher amount specified in the policy declarations typically applies to each covered collision loss. A separate deductible applies to other-than-collision losses. The deductible for other-than-collision losses is often a lower amount than the collision deductible. For example, an insured might have a PAP with a $500 collision deductible and a $250 other-than-collision deductible.

Deductibles require the insured to share covered losses with the insurer. Deductibles are used for Part D to (1) reduce small claims, (2) hold down premiums, and (3) encourage the insured to be careful in protecting his or her car against damage or theft.

Transportation Expenses

Part D also provides an additional coverage known as **transportation expenses**. The transportation expenses coverage provides reimbursement of up to a maximum of $600 for each covered loss. For a loss to a *covered auto*, the insurer will reimburse the insured for temporary transportation expenses, such as auto rental fees or taxi fares, up to $20 per day. When the

Transportation expenses (as used in the PAP)
Additional coverage reimburses up to $20 per day, to a maximum of $600, for temporary travel expenses for each covered physical damage loss.

loss involves a *nonowned auto* and an insured is legally responsible to the owner of that auto for the owner's transportation expenses, the insured's PAP will pay, subject to a daily limit of $20. Likewise, if the owner of a nonowned rental car claims a loss of income because the car cannot be rented while it is being fixed and the named insured is legally responsible for the renter's loss of income, coverage applies—subject to the $20 daily limit.

If the insured has purchased only other-than-collision coverage, the PAP provides transportation expenses coverage in the event of any other-than-collision loss. If the insured has also purchased collision coverage, transportation expenses coverage also applies to collision losses.

The PAP states that transportation expenses coverage is provided "without application of a deductible." No dollar-amount deductible applies. However, transportation expenses coverage is subject to a waiting period, which is essentially a deductible stated in time rather than in dollars. While a forty-eight-hour waiting period applies to theft losses, a twenty-four-hour waiting period applies to loss by other perils.

Theft

If transportation expenses are incurred because of the total theft of a covered auto or a nonowned auto, the insurer will pay for these transportation expenses beginning forty-eight hours after the theft. Coverage ends when the stolen auto is returned to use or the insurer pays for the auto. Because stolen cars often require repairs after they are recovered, transportation expenses coverage extends until the time the stolen auto is actually returned to use (or the insurer pays for the auto). For example, Sally's covered auto is stolen and is not recovered until seventeen days later. Her car has been damaged, and repair parts must be ordered. Sally's car is in the shop a total of twenty days for repairs. Her PAP, which includes other-than-collision coverage, will pay Sally's transportation expenses for thirty-five days (17 + 20 – 2 = 35; 17 days before the car is recovered, plus 20 days in the shop, minus 2 days' deductible), up to $20 per day, but subject to a maximum of $600.

Other Than Theft

If transportation expense is incurred because of a covered loss other than theft, the insurer will pay transportation expenses beginning twenty-four hours after the auto is withdrawn from use. The intent is to pay for transportation expenses or loss of use only during the period necessary to repair the car, subject to a twenty-four-hour waiting period. For example, suppose Tom borrows Pete's car and causes an accident, and Pete has no physical damage insurance. Beginning twenty-four hours after Pete's auto was withdrawn from use and while it was being repaired, Tom's insurer would pay Pete up to $20 per day for his transportation expenses, subject to a maximum of $600.

Exclusions

Most insurance policies provide very broad statements of coverage that is then narrowed through exclusions. The exclusions that narrow the broad coverage in the PAP Part D insuring agreement are summarized below.

Public or Livery Conveyance

Physical damage insurance does not apply while the vehicle is used as a public or livery conveyance. For example, if Ken uses his covered auto as a taxi on the weekends, any physical damage loss to the auto while it is being used as a taxi is not covered under Part D of Ken's PAP. As with comparable exclusions under other coverages, this exclusion does not apply to a share-the-expense car pool.

Wear and Tear, Freezing, Mechanical or Electrical Breakdown, and Tire Damage

Damage caused by and confined to wear and tear, freezing, mechanical or electrical breakdown or failure, and road damage to tires is excluded. The intent is to exclude regular maintenance expenses. This exclusion does not apply if the damage results from the total theft of a covered auto or non-owned auto. If the tires on Bill's covered auto are damaged beyond repair because he strikes a pothole, the cost of replacing the tires because of this road damage would not be covered. However, if a thief damages the tires by driving the wrong way across the spikes in a parking lot, the tire loss would be covered because it results from the car's theft.

Radioactive Contamination or War

Loss due to radioactive contamination, discharge of a nuclear weapon, war (declared or undeclared), civil war, insurrection, rebellion, or revolution is excluded. For example, if a covered auto is damaged from radioactive con-tamination because of a nuclear accident at a public utility plant, the damage is excluded.

Electronic Equipment Designed for the Reproduction of Sound

Generally speaking, the PAP covers the sound reproduction equipment normally provided by an auto manufacturer, as well as replacements or upgrades, but excludes or limits coverage on certain custom equipment. For example, sound reproduction equipment permanently installed in a covered auto or nonowned auto is covered. However, sound reproduction equipment installed in locations not used by the auto manufacturer is subject to a $1,000 limit.

Also covered is electronic equipment that is "removable from a housing unit which is permanently installed in the auto" and that operates only from the power of the auto's electrical system, provided the equipment is in or on the covered auto or nonowned auto at the time of the loss. This equipment would include pull-out compact disc players. While in the auto, they are covered by the PAP. When they have been removed from the auto for protection against theft, they might be covered under a homeowners policy or other policy providing coverage on personal property.

Except as noted above, the PAP excludes many types of sound reproduction equipment such as radios and stereos, tape decks, and compact disc players, as well as any related accessories. For example, unless they are permanently installed, speakers riding in the back of a station wagon or hatchback would not be covered, even if they are connected to the car's audio system.

Equipment Designed for the Reception and Transmission of Audio, Visual, or Data Signals

Generally, telephones, two-way radios, police-radio scanners, televisions, computers, videocassette recorders, and audiocassette recorders are excluded from coverage under the PAP. Such equipment is not contemplated in the premium charge because it is not part of a typical car.

However, the exclusion does not apply to electronic equipment, such as a factory-installed electronic ignition system, that is necessary for the normal operation of the auto. Also not excluded—and therefore covered—is a permanently installed telephone operated by the auto's electrical system.

Media and Accessories

Tapes, records, discs, or other media used with sound, video, or data equipment are not part of the auto, and they are not covered under the PAP. For example, the theft of videotapes or computer software from an insured's car is not covered even if the car is locked.

> The *coverage for excess sound reproducing equipment, audio, visual and data electronic equipment, and tapes, records, discs and other media endorsement* (PP 03 13) can be added to the PAP to provide coverage for some otherwise excluded electronic equipment and accessories. This endorsement is examined later in this chapter.

Government Destruction or Confiscation

The PAP excludes coverage for a total loss to a covered auto or nonowned auto due to destruction or confiscation by governmental or civil authorities. However, this exclusion does not apply to the interests of any loss payees (such as banks or other lending institutions) in the covered auto.

For example, a kidnapper's van is destroyed by a gasoline fire that ignites during a gun battle with police. The PAP would provide no coverage for the owner of the van. However, coverage would be provided to the bank through which the van was financed, to the extent of the remaining balance on the loan.

The insured does not have to be engaged in illegal activities for this exclusion to apply. Any destruction or confiscation by governmental or civil authorities is excluded.

Camper Body or Trailer Not Shown in the Declarations

If the policy contains appropriate endorsements (discussed later), a motor home, camper, or trailer might be shown in the declarations as a covered auto. Physical damage loss to a motor home, camper, or trailer that is not shown in the declarations is excluded. However, the exclusion does not apply to a nonowned trailer. Also not excluded, and therefore covered, is a camper body or trailer acquired during the policy period if the insurer is asked to cover it within fourteen days after the insured becomes the owner.

> Several endorsements, discussed later in this chapter, can be used to provide coverage for motor homes, campers, trailers, and other recreational vehicles: *miscellaneous type vehicle endorsement* (PP 03 23), *trailer/camper body coverage (maximum limit of liability) endorsement* (PP 03 07), *customizing equipment coverage endorsement* (PP 03 18), and *snowmobile endorsement* (PP 03 20).

Nonowned Auto Used Without a Reasonable Belief of Permission

As with other coverages, the PAP provides no physical damage coverage for loss to a nonowned auto when it is used by the insured or a family member who does not reasonably believe that he or she is entitled to use it.

Radar and Laser Detection Equipment

Loss to equipment designed for the detection of radar or laser beams is excluded. Therefore, theft of or damage to a radar or laser detection device in the insured's auto is not covered. The exclusion is based on the theory that these devices promote unsafe driving.

Customizing Equipment

Many pickup trucks and vans are customized with special equipment. However, Part D excludes loss to any custom furnishings or equipment in or on any pickup or van. Custom furnishings and equipment include but are not limited to:

- Special carpeting or insulation
- Furniture or bars
- Height-extending roofs
- Custom murals, paintings, or other decals or graphics

If a covered auto is a pickup, the customized equipment exclusion does not apply to a cap, cover, or bedliner.

> The *customizing equipment coverage endorsement* (PP 03 18) can be purchased to provide coverage for custom furnishings and equipment.

Nonowned Auto Used in the Auto Business

Also excluded under Part D is loss to a nonowned auto maintained or used in the business of selling, repairing, servicing, storing, or parking vehicles designed for use on public highways, including road testing and delivery. For example, if Ross is employed as an auto mechanic and damages a customer's car while road testing it, the physical damage loss to the car is not covered under Ross's PAP. This commercial loss exposure should be insured by the repair shop.

Racing

Loss to a covered auto or a nonowned auto is excluded if the auto is damaged while located in a facility designed for racing if the auto is being used to prepare for, practice for, or compete in any prearranged racing or speed contest. For example, if Andrew drives his car a few laps around a race track to test the track conditions in preparation for a later race, he would have no coverage under his PAP if he damages his car by colliding with the guardrail at the track.

Rental Vehicles

If an insured's PAP provides physical damage coverage for an owned auto, the policy also provides physical damage coverage for nonowned vehicles—including rental vehicles. However, if the rental agreement includes a collision damage waiver or if applicable state law precludes the rental company from recovering from the insured for the loss, then this exclusion makes it clear that the PAP will not pay for loss to, or loss of use of, a rental auto.

Auto rental companies usually offer their customers a collision damage waiver (CDW) at substantial extra cost. If purchased, this waiver eliminates or substantially reduces the individual's financial obligation to the rental company for damage to the car in an auto accident. Physical damage protection for rental autos is also provided as a benefit by some credit card companies, provided their card is used to charge the rental.

Arranging appropriate liability and physical damage insurance on rented vehicles is a complex topic, and the best advice for any situation might depend on state laws, rental contracts, and other variables beyond the scope of this text. Discussion here is limited to the coverage provided under the PAP.

Limit of Liability

The insurer's limit of liability for a physical damage loss to a covered auto is the lower of (1) the **actual cash value** of the damaged or stolen property or (2) the amount necessary to repair or replace the property with other property of like kind and quality. In determining actual cash value, an adjustment is made for depreciation and physical condition of the damaged property.

Actual cash value (ACV) Replacement cost of property minus an allowance for depreciation and obsolescence.

When a vehicle has only a partial loss (such as a damaged fender), the cost of repairing the vehicle is usually the amount the insurer will pay, less any applicable deductible. However, if the physical damage to the vehicle is extensive and the cost of repairs exceeds the vehicle's actual cash value, the car may be declared a total loss. In such cases, the amount the insurer will pay is limited to the actual cash value of the damaged vehicle, less any applicable deductible.

> The *coverage for damage to your auto (maximum limit of liability)* endorsement (PP 03 08) can be used to establish the car's insurable value when the policy is written. This endorsement is usually used for antique cars, restored show cars, and other cars with unusually high values. The endorsement limits the maximum amount an insurer will pay for a covered vehicle to the amount stated in the endorsement.

The insurer's maximum obligation for sound reproduction equipment installed in locations not used by the original manufacturer is limited to $1,000. Also, as noted earlier, the maximum amount paid for a physical damage loss to a *nonowned trailer* is $500. For example, if an insured rents a trailer to move his or her personal property to another house and the trailer is damaged in an accident, no more than $500 will be paid under the insured's PAP for damage to the trailer.

Betterment

If a repair or replacement results in better than like kind or quality, the insurer will not pay for the betterment.

Diminution in Value

A vehicle that is damaged and repaired is sometimes considered to have a lower market value than one that has never been in an accident. Although the policy does not specifically provide diminution coverage, during recent years many claimants have requested payment for **diminution in value**. ISO has filed a clarifying endorsement in many states noting that coverage for diminution in value is specifically excluded.

Diminution in value Actual or perceived loss in market or resale value resulting from a direct and accidental loss.

> The *personal auto coverage for damage to your auto exclusion endorsement* (PP 13 01) clarifies that coverage is not provided for any loss in market or resale value (sometimes referred to as "diminution in value") that results from a direct and accidental physical damage loss to an auto covered under the policy. Many insurers add this clarifying endorsement to all PAPs in states where the endorsement has been approved.

Payment of Loss

The insurer has the option of paying for the loss in money or repairing or replacing the damaged or stolen property. If the insurer returns a stolen auto, the insurer pays the cost of returning the stolen car or its equipment to the insured and also pays for any damage resulting from the theft. However, the insurer has the right to keep all or part of the stolen property and pay the insured an agreed or appraised value. If the insurer pays for the loss, that payment will include the applicable sales tax for the damaged or stolen property.

Payment of Loss, Betterment, and Diminution in Value

The right rear door on April's Ford was damaged in an intersection accident caused by another driver. Although the other driver's insurer paid for the damage, April did not have the door repaired but kept the money and continued to drive the car with a damaged door. Subsequently, April's car skidded off the road into a guardrail, damaging the entire right side of the car. April submitted a collision claim to the insurer under her PAP policy.

The insurer will not pay the costs of repairing the previously-damaged right rear door, to the extent these repairs result in *betterment*. Assuming the remaining cost of repairs does not exceed the value of the car, April's insurer will pay those costs, less the deductible, of repairing April's car for damage sustained *in this accident*.

April is not entitled to any additional compensation for *diminution in value*, even if the market value of her car is reduced because it has been damaged and repaired.

No Benefit to Bailee

Bailee
Person or business that has in its care, custody, or control, property belonging to another.

The no benefit to bailee provision states that the policy will not benefit, either directly or indirectly, any **bailee** (a person who assumes custody of the property of others for business purposes). If one of Midtown Parking Garage's employees negligently damages Donna's car while it is in Midtown's custody, Donna's PAP insurer will pay for the damage to her car. The no-benefit-to-bailee clause preserves the right of Donna's insurer to recover from Midtown if the garage was negligent. Although Donna receives prompt recovery, Midtown does not benefit from Donna's insurance.

Other Sources of Recovery

If other sources of recovery also cover a loss, the PAP insurer will pay only its share of the loss. Its share is the proportion that its limit of liability bears to the total applicable limits. For example, a trailer with an actual cash value of $3,000, owned by an insured, is destroyed by a fire in the insured's garage. The insured's other-than-collision coverage applies to the loss. The PAP insurer's limit of liability for the loss would be $3,000, the actual cash value of the trailer. The insured's homeowners insurance also covers the fire loss to the trailer, subject in this case to a $1,000 sublimit. The total applicable limits are $3,000 + $1,000, which equals $4,000. The PAP insurer's proportional share of the loss is $3,000/$4,000 or 75 percent. Thus, the PAP insurer's share is 75 percent of $3,000, which equals $2,250. The loss payment would be reduced by the amount of the insured's other-than-collision deductible.

Any physical damage insurance provided by the PAP for a nonowned auto is excess over any other collectible source of recovery. Other sources of recovery include coverage provided by the owner of the nonowned auto, any other applicable physical damage insurance, and any other source of recovery that applies to the loss. For example, if Andy borrows Barry's car and damages it, Barry's physical damage insurance applies first, and Andy's insurance is excess, subject to his deductible. If Barry's collision deductible is $200 and Andy's collision deductible is $100, and the damage is $1,000, Barry's policy pays $800 ($1,000 – $200), and Andy's policy pays $100 ($200 – $100). The remaining $100 would have to be paid either by Andy or by Barry. In effect, if Barry's collision deductible is larger than Andy's deductible, Andy's insurer will pay the difference between the two deductibles.

Appraisal

In some cases, the named insured and the insurer cannot agree on the amount of the loss. This is especially true if the insured claims that the car is above average and in "mint condition" and has a value that exceeds the value listed in the various publications of car prices. In the event of a disagreement on the amount of loss, either party may demand an **appraisal** of the loss. According to the appraisal provision in the PAP, each party selects a competent appraiser. The two appraisers then select an "umpire." If the appraisers cannot agree on the actual cash value and the amount of loss, any differences are submitted to the umpire. A decision by any two of the three is binding on all. Each party pays its chosen appraiser and shares equally the expenses of the appraisal and the umpire. If the insurer agrees to an appraisal, it does not waive any of its rights under the policy.

PARTS E AND F—PERSONAL AUTO POLICY CONDITIONS

The conditions of the PAP are found in two sections at the end of the policy. Part E concerns duties of the policyholder after a loss, and Part F concerns general provisions applicable to the policy.

Appraisal (as used in Part D of the PAP)
A provision that describes how the insured and insurer will settle disputes about the amount of loss. Each party selects a competent appraiser, and the two appraisers select an umpire. A decision by any two of the three is binding. Procedurally, the appraisal process resembles the arbitration process described under uninsured motorists coverage.

Part E—Duties After an Accident or Loss

Part E of the PAP outlines a number of duties the insured must perform after an accident or a loss. The insurer has no obligation to provide coverage unless the insured fully complies with these duties. Additional duties are imposed if the insured is seeking protection under Part C—Uninsured Motorists Coverage or Part D—Coverage for Damage to Your Auto.

General Duties

A person seeking coverage must comply with the following general duties after an accident or a loss in order to receive payment under all the coverages of the policy:

- *Prompt notice.* The insurer must be notified promptly of how, when, and where the accident or loss occurred. The notice should also include the names and addresses of any injured persons and witnesses.

- *Cooperation with the insurer.* The person seeking coverage must cooperate with the insurer in the investigation, settlement, or defense of any claim or suit.

- *Submission of legal papers to the insurer.* The person seeking coverage must promptly submit to the insurer copies of any notices or legal papers received in connection with the accident or loss.

- *Physical examination.* The person seeking coverage must agree to submit to a physical examination at the insurer's expense.

- *Examination under oath.* The person seeking coverage must agree to an examination under oath if required by the insurer.

- *Authorization of medical records.* The person seeking coverage must authorize the insurer to obtain medical reports and other pertinent records.

- *Proof of loss.* The person seeking coverage must submit a proof of loss when required by the insurer. A "proof of loss" is a written statement giving the pertinent facts of the claim.

Additional Duties for Uninsured Motorists Coverage

A person seeking benefits under Part C—Uninsured Motorists Coverage must perform two additional duties:

1. *Notify police.* That person must notify the police if a hit-and-run driver is involved. This requirement is designed to reduce fraudulent claims. When an accident is subject to police investigation, the possibility of a fraudulent claim is reduced.

2. *Submit legal papers.* If the person seeking coverage sues the uninsured motorist, a copy of the legal papers must be sent to the insurance company.

Additional Duties for Physical Damage Coverage

Three additional duties are required under Part D—Coverage for Damage to Your Auto:

1. *Prevent further loss.* The person seeking coverage must take reasonable steps after a loss to protect a covered auto or nonowned auto and its equipment from further loss. The insurer will pay the reasonable expenses incurred to protect the vehicle from further damage. For example, the insurer will pay the cost of having a tow truck transport the damaged car to another location for safekeeping.

2. *Notify police.* If a covered auto or nonowned auto is stolen, the person seeking coverage must promptly notify the police of the theft. Prompt notification significantly increases the possibility of recovering the stolen vehicle.

3. *Permit inspection and appraisal.* The person seeking coverage must permit the insurer to inspect and appraise the damaged property before its repair or disposal. Some insurers have drive-in claim centers where damaged but driveable vehicles may be appraised. For more severely damaged cars, appraisers usually see the car at home or at the garage or body shop where the car has been taken. For small losses, the insurer sometimes waives its right to inspect and appraise the damaged auto and allows the person seeking coverage to submit two or three repair estimates that provide as the basis for the loss settlement.

Part F—General Provisions

Part F—General Provisions is the final part of the PAP. It contains general provisions and conditions that apply to the entire policy.

Bankruptcy of Insured

The insurer is not relieved of any obligations under the policy if the insured declares bankruptcy or becomes insolvent. For example, if the insured is sued for an amount exceeding the policy limits and declares bankruptcy to escape payment of the rest of the judgment, the insurer is still required to pay the part of the judgment covered by insurance.

Changes in the Policy

The policy contains all the agreements between the named insured and the insurer. The terms of the policy cannot be changed except by an endorsement issued by the insurer. If the change requires a premium adjustment, the adjustment is made in accordance with the manual rules of the insurer. Changes during the policy term that can result in a premium increase or decrease include changes in:

1. The number, type, or use of insured vehicles
2. The operators of insured vehicles

3. The place of principal garaging of insured vehicles
4. The coverage, deductibles, or limits of liability

Another portion of the changes provision, sometimes referred to as a *liberalization clause*, automatically provides broadened coverage under some conditions. According to this provision, if the insurer makes a change to the PAP that broadens PAP coverage without an additional premium, the change automatically applies to the insured's existing policy on the date the revision is effective in the insured's state. However, this provision does not apply to changes that include both broadenings and restrictions of coverage and are implemented in a general program revision either by a new edition of the policy or by an amendatory endorsement.

Fraud

The PAP contains a specific provision dealing with fraud. No coverage exists for any insured who makes fraudulent statements or engages in fraudulent conduct in connection with any accident or loss for which a claim is made. For example, if a car owner deliberately abandons a covered auto and reports the car as stolen, the insurer does not provide coverage for the car owner for that claim.

Legal Action Against the Insurer

In the event of a dispute, an insured might wish to sue the insurer. However, the PAP states that no legal action can be brought against the insurer until the insured has fully complied with all of the policy terms. In addition, under Part A—Liability Coverage, no legal action can be brought against the insurer unless the insurer agrees in writing that the insured has an obligation to pay damages or the amount of the insurer's obligation has been finally determined by a judgment after a trial. No person or organization has any right under the policy to involve the insurer in any action to determine the liability of an insured.

Insurer's Right to Recover Payment

The policy provision regarding an insurer's right to recover payment provision is often called a *subrogation clause*. If the insurer makes a loss payment to a person who has a right to recover damages from a negligent third party, the insurer has a legal right of **subrogation** against that third party. The covered person must do whatever is necessary to enable the insurer to exercise its subrogation rights. In addition, the person to whom the loss payment is made is not allowed to do anything after the loss that would prejudice the insurer's right of subrogation.

Subrogation
Insurer's right to recover payment from a negligent third party. When an insurer pays an insured for a loss, the insurer takes over the insured's right to collect damages from the other party responsible for the loss. The insurer has the right to subrogate against the party directly responsible for the loss.

The subrogation provision does not apply to physical damage coverages in regard to any person who is using a covered auto with a reasonable belief that he or she is entitled to do so. For example, if Kent borrows Patti's car with her permission and damages the car in a collision, Patti's collision coverage will pay for the damage to the car. According to the terms of this provision, Patti's insurer cannot subrogate against Kent or his insurer.

Finally, if a person receives a loss payment from an insurer and also recovers damages from another party, that person is required to hold the proceeds of the second recovery in trust for the insurer and to reimburse the insurer to the extent of the insurer's loss payment.

Policy Period and Territory

The PAP applies only to accidents and losses that occur during the policy period and within the policy territory. The policy period is stated in the declarations and is usually a six-month or one-year period.

The policy territory includes the United States, U.S. territories and possessions, Puerto Rico, and Canada. The policy also applies to a covered auto while being transported among ports of the United States, Puerto Rico, or Canada. Coverage does not apply anywhere outside the policy territory. For example, if Alfred drives his car into Mexico, he will not have coverage under his PAP. Alfred should purchase valid liability insurance from a Mexican insurer. Under Mexican law, a motorist from the United States who has not purchased valid insurance from a Mexican insurer and is involved in an accident can be detained in jail, have his or her car impounded, and be subject to other penalties.

> The insured can purchase the *limited Mexico coverage endorsement* (PP 03 21), discussed later, to extend PAP coverage to an insured who is involved in an accident in Mexico within twenty-five miles of the U.S. border on a trip of ten days or fewer. This endorsement does not eliminate the need to purchase primary liability coverage from a Mexican insurer.

Termination

The PAP contains a provision that applies to termination of the policy by either the insured or insurer. The termination provision consists of four parts:

- Cancellation
- Nonrenewal
- Automatic termination
- Other termination provisions

As explained in Chapter 2, all states have laws that restrict the insurer's right to cancel or nonrenew an auto policy. In many states, these laws differ from the termination provision in the PAP. Changes mandated by state laws are usually incorporated into the policy by means of a state endorsement that must be attached to all auto policies in the state. Whenever state laws and the policy conflict, state law supersedes the policy provisions.

Cancellation

The *named insured* normally can cancel anytime during the policy period by returning the policy to the insurer or by giving advance written notice of the date the cancellation is to become effective.

The *insurer* has more limited cancellation rights. If the policy has been in force for fewer than sixty days and is not a renewal or continuation policy, the insurer can cancel by mailing a cancellation notice to the named insured. Thus, the insurer has sixty days to investigate and determine whether a new applicant meets the insurer's underwriting standards. If the cancellation is for nonpayment of premium, the insurer must give the named insured at least ten days' notice; in all other cases, at least twenty days' notice must be given.

After the policy has been in force for sixty days, or if it is a renewal or continuation policy, the *insurer* can cancel the policy only for one of three reasons:

1. The premium has not been paid.

2. The driver's license of an insured has been suspended or revoked during the policy period (or since the last annual anniversary of the original effective date if the policy is for other than one year).

3. The policy has been obtained by a material misrepresentation. For example, if an insured knowingly provides false information to the insurer, the insurer has the right to cancel that person's coverage after the correct information is discovered.

Nonrenewal

Rather than cancel, the insurer may decide to let the policy remain in force during the policy period but not renew the policy for another term. If the insurer decides not to renew, the named insured must be given at least twenty days' notice before the end of the policy period. The times when the insurer can nonrenew vary with the length of the policy period.

- If the policy period is less than six months, the insurer has the right to nonrenew every six months, beginning six months after the policy's original effective date.

- If the policy period is six months or longer, but less than a year, the insurer has the right to nonrenew at the end of the policy period.

- If the policy period is one year or longer, the insurer has the right to nonrenew at each anniversary of the policy's original effective date.

Automatic Termination

Under the automatic termination provision, if the insurer offers to renew the policy but the named insured does not accept the insurer's offer to renew, the policy automatically terminates at the end of the current policy period. Failure to pay the renewal premium means that the named insured has not accepted the insurer's offer to renew the policy. Thus, once the named insured is billed for another period, the premium must be paid, or else the policy automatically terminates on its expiration date. Although in practice some insurers allow a short period of time for an insured to pay an overdue premium, the policy itself provides no grace period.

If the named insured obtains other insurance on a covered auto, the PAP coverage on that auto automatically terminates on the effective date of the other insurance. Suppose, for example, that Dennis has a PAP covering his sedan. He later buys a sports car and purchases a new auto policy covering both the sports car and the sedan. Dennis's original PAP automatically terminates on the effective date of his new policy, even if he does not notify his PAP insurer. If Dennis becomes involved in a serious accident while driving his sedan, he cannot claim coverage under both policies.

Other Termination Provisions

Several additional termination provisions are stated in the policy:

1. The insurer may choose to deliver the cancellation notice rather than mail it. However, proof of mailing (to the named insured at the address shown on the declarations page) of any cancellation notice is considered sufficient proof of notice.

2. If the policy is canceled, the named insured may be entitled to a premium refund. Any premium refund is computed according to the insurer's manual rules. Making or offering to make the refund is not a condition of cancellation.

3. The effective date of cancellation stated in the cancellation notice becomes the end of the policy period.

Transfer of Insured's Interest in the Policy

The "transfer of your interest in this policy" provision limits **assignment** of the policy by an insured. The named insured's rights and duties under the policy cannot be assigned to another party without the insurer's written consent. However, if the named insured dies, the coverage is automatically continued to the end of the policy period for both the surviving spouse, if a resident of the same household at the time of the named insured's death, and the legal representative of the deceased person (but only with respect to the representative's legal responsibility to maintain or use a covered auto).

Assignment
The transfer of a policy from the named insured to another party; insurer's written consent is required.

Two or More Auto Policies

If two or more auto policies issued to the named insured by the same insurer apply to the same accident, the insurer's maximum limit of liability is the highest applicable limit of liability under any one policy. For example, suppose Denise has two auto insurance policies issued by the same insurer, each providing coverage on a different auto. If Denise has an accident while driving a nonowned auto, the most the insurer will pay is the highest limit of liability under either of the policies. The intent of this provision is to prevent the "stacking" (adding) of policy limits when two or more auto policies are issued by the same insurer.

ENDORSEMENTS TO THE PERSONAL AUTO POLICY

Because of various eligibility restrictions, exclusions, and limitations, the unmodified PAP does not completely meet the auto insurance needs of some people. Several coverage additions or modifications are available by adding an endorsement to the PAP.[1] The PAP endorsements drafted by Insurance Services Office (ISO) are identified by two letters and eight digits. The letters are PP for the Personal Auto Policy. The first four digits are the endorsement number. The last four digits indicate the month and year that version of the endorsement was introduced. Because new versions of endorsements are frequently introduced, only the first four digits are used here. Various insurers have also drafted endorsements that they add to a PAP, and some endorsements are used only in a particular state. These endorsements often differ from the ISO endorsements described in this text.

The endorsements discussed in this section of the chapter are arbitrarily divided into four groups:

- Endorsements covering motorcycles, recreational vehicles, and customizing equipment
- Other endorsements affecting multiple coverages
- Underinsured motorists coverage endorsement
- Endorsements affecting physical damage coverage

Endorsements Covering Motorcycles, Recreational Vehicles, and Customizing Equipment

Many people own motorcycles, motor homes, and other vehicles that are ineligible for coverage under an unendorsed PAP. Also, motor homes, vans, and pickup trucks may include custom equipment that is not covered under an unendorsed PAP. This section of the chapter examines several coverages that might be used alone or in combination, depending on the circumstances:

- Miscellaneous type vehicle endorsement (PP 03 23)
- Trailer/camper body coverage (maximum limit of liability) endorsement (PP 03 07)
- Customizing equipment coverage endorsement (PP 03 18)
- Snowmobile endorsement (PP 03 20)

Miscellaneous Type Vehicle Endorsement

The *miscellaneous type vehicle endorsement* to the PAP provides coverage for a motor home, a motorcycle or similar type of vehicle, an all-terrain vehicle, a dune buggy, or a golf cart. Coverage for snowmobiles requires a different endorsement, examined later. The miscellaneous type vehicle endorsement can be used with one of the vehicles aforementioned to provide the coverages found in the PAP, including liability, medical payments, uninsured motorists, collision, and other-than-collision coverages. Each covered vehicle is listed in a schedule that states the applicable coverages, premiums, and limits of liability.

An optional passenger hazard exclusion, which excludes liability for bodily injury to anyone occupying the covered vehicle, can be activated as part of the miscellaneous type vehicle endorsement. For example, a motorcycle owner who never carries passengers can elect this exclusion in exchange for a lower premium.

Under the miscellaneous type vehicle endorsement, the amount paid for physical damage losses is limited to the lowest of:

1. the stated amount shown in the schedule or declarations,

2. the actual cash value of the stolen or damaged property, or

3. the amount necessary to repair or replace the property (less any deductible).

In determining the actual cash value, an adjustment is made for the depreciation and physical condition of the damaged vehicle.

When the PAP is used to insure a motor home, an amending endorsement is added to the miscellaneous type vehicle endorsement. The *miscellaneous type vehicle amendment (motor homes)* (PP 03 28) specifically addresses the issue of coverage while the motor home is rented to another party. Motor home owners who rent or lease their vehicles to others can obtain coverage through this amendment for an additional premium shown on the schedule in the amendment. If no premiums are shown, there is no coverage while the vehicle is rented or leased to another party.

Trailer/Camper Body Coverage Endorsement

A different endorsement is designed to provide physical damage coverage for trailers and/or camper bodies. Under the *trailer/camper body coverage (maximum limit of liability) endorsement*, the insurer agrees to pay for direct and accidental loss to a trailer or camper body described in the declarations of the policy or the schedule of the endorsement. Also covered are related facilities or equipment, including but not limited to cooking, dining, plumbing, or refrigeration facilities, as well as awnings or cabanas. Loss to clothing or luggage, business or office equipment, and sales samples or articles used in exhibitions are excluded. The PAP exclusions for electronic equipment and media, radar detectors, and custom furnishings or equipment still apply. If necessary, such items can be covered under other endorsements, discussed separately in this chapter.

The provisions of this endorsement regarding the amount paid for physical damage losses are essentially the same as those of the miscellaneous type vehicle endorsement described earlier.

Customizing Equipment Coverage Endorsement

Part D of the PAP specifically excludes coverage for custom furnishings and equipment in or upon a pickup or van. This exclusion can be deleted by adding the *customizing equipment coverage endorsement* to the PAP. Under this endorsement, the insurer agrees to pay for direct and accidental loss to customized furnishings or equipment including, but not limited to:

- Special carpeting or insulation
- Furniture or bars
- Height-extending roofs
- Custom murals, paintings, or other decals or graphics

For example, if the insured has other-than-collision coverage, the loss caused by a fire that damages built-in cabinets in a van would be covered by this endorsement.

Snowmobile Endorsement

Snowmobile coverage can be obtained by adding the *snowmobile endorsement* to a PAP. A snowmobile is defined as a land motor vehicle propelled solely by wheels, crawler-type treads, belts, or similar mechanical devices and designed for use mainly off public roads on snow or ice. A vehicle propelled by airplane-type propellers or fans is not considered to be a snowmobile.

Available coverages include liability, medical payments, uninsured motorists, collision, and other-than-collision coverages. Each covered snowmobile is listed in a schedule that states the applicable coverages, premiums, and limits of liability.

The named insured and family members are covered for liability arising out of their use of any snowmobile. However, other persons are covered only while using the insured's owned or temporary substitute snowmobile. They are not covered while using a snowmobile rented or leased by the named insured. For example, if Gaston is operating Jacques' owned snowmobile and someone is injured through Gaston's carelessness, the liability portion of Jacques' PAP with the snowmobile endorsement would provide coverage. If Jacques rents a snowmobile and lends it to Gaston and someone is injured through Gaston's negligence, Jacques' PAP would not provide coverage to Gaston.

The liability coverage for snowmobiles has several exclusions and modifications:

- Coverage does not apply if the snowmobile is used in any business.
- Coverage is excluded for any person or organization, other than the named insured, while renting or leasing a snowmobile.
- Coverage does not apply when the snowmobile is used in a race or speed contest or in practice or preparation for the race, regardless of whether the race is prearranged or organized.
- A passenger hazard exclusion can be activated, which excludes liability for bodily injury to any person while occupying or being towed by the snowmobile.

The provisions of this endorsement regarding the amount paid for physical damage losses are essentially the same as those of the miscellaneous type vehicle endorsement described above.

Other Endorsements Affecting Multiple Coverages

Even though they might not apply to specialized vehicles, certain available endorsements affect more than one coverage under the PAP:

- Named non-owner coverage endorsement (PP 03 22)
- Extended non-owned coverage for named individual endorsement (PP 03 06)
- Limited Mexico coverage endorsement (PP 03 21)

Named Non-Owner Coverage Endorsement

The *named non-owner coverage endorsement* is used in conjunction with the PAP to provide liability, medical payments, and uninsured motorists coverage—but not physical damage coverage—for a driver who does not own an auto. Some people who do not own a car regularly or occasionally drive another person's car or a rental car. These people can secure their own insurance coverage for their loss exposures arising out of the use of a nonowned auto by purchasing a PAP with the named nonowner coverage endorsement.

As suggested by the name of the endorsement, it provides liability, medical payments, and uninsured motorists coverage only for a person who is actually *named* in the endorsement. The spouse and other resident family members are not automatically covered. If they need coverage, a spouse, family members, or other individuals should also be named in the endorsement.

The liability insurance under the PAP with the named nonowner endorsement is excess over any other applicable liability insurance on the nonowned auto. The endorsement provides important protection to the named insured who drives a nonowned auto with inadequate liability limits, or perhaps no insurance at all.

If the named nonowner turns into an owner by buying a car, he or she has liability, medical payments, and uninsured motorists coverage on the car for up to fourteen days. Coverage automatically terminates when the named insured purchases insurance on the newly acquired car.

Extended Non-Owned Coverage for Named Individual Endorsement

The unendorsed PAP excludes liability and medical payments coverage for vehicles furnished or made available for the regular use of the named insured and family members. The PAP also excludes the use of a nonowned vehicle (other than a nonowned private passenger auto) for business purposes. These exclusions can be eliminated by adding the *extended non-owned coverage for named individual endorsement* to the PAP. The coverage applies only to the individual(s) named in the endorsement. The liability coverage provided by the endorsement is excess over any other applicable insurance on the nonowned vehicle. The endorsement also contains a provision for broadening medical payments coverage.

Several loss exposures otherwise excluded under the PAP are covered when the endorsement is added:

1. Use of a nonowned car furnished or made available for the regular use of the named individual is covered. For example, an individual may be furnished with a company car, have regular access to a car in a carpool, or regularly drive a state car on government business. These loss exposures are covered under the endorsement.

2. A nonowned vehicle used in business is covered, except vehicles used in the auto business. Although the unendorsed PAP provides such coverage for nonowned private passenger autos and trailers, other types of vehicles, such as certain vans and trucks, are provided coverage by this endorsement. For example, if Terry drives a truck for her employer, she would have coverage under her PAP while driving the nonowned truck if she adds the endorsement. Her PAP coverage would apply as excess over the employer's policy on the truck.

3. Use of a nonowned vehicle as a public or livery conveyance is covered. For example, a taxicab driver has coverage under this endorsement while driving a company taxicab. The liability coverage is excess over any other applicable insurance on the taxi.

4. The individual named in this endorsement also has protection against a fellow-employee suit arising out of a work-related accident. For example, Rudy might be driving a company truck, and a fellow employee in the truck is injured when Rudy is involved in an accident with another motorist. If the injured employee sues Rudy, Rudy has coverage for his legal liability.

Limited Mexico Coverage Endorsement

The unendorsed PAP does not provide any coverage in Mexico. However, the *limited Mexico coverage endorsement* can be added to the PAP to extend PAP coverages to an insured who is involved in an accident or loss in Mexico within twenty-five miles of the United States border on a trip of ten days or less. (Some insurers automatically include similar Mexico coverage without the need to purchase a special endorsement.)

The coverage provided by this endorsement does not meet Mexico's auto liability insurance requirements. The endorsement is effective only if primary liability coverage is also purchased from a licensed Mexican insurer. Mexican insurance can be purchased from a licensed agent at the border.

The liability insurance provided by the endorsement is excess over the Mexican insurance and over any other valid and collectible insurance. The major advantage of the endorsement is that it provides additional liability insurance beyond that provided by the Mexican policy, as well as providing the other standard PAP coverages, such as physical damage coverage.

Underinsured Motorists Coverage Endorsement

The *underinsured motorists coverage endorsement* (PP 03 11) can be added to the PAP to supplement uninsured motorists coverage. Underinsured motorists coverage must be distinguished from uninsured motorists coverage. Unlike *un*insured motorists coverage, *under*insured motorists coverage becomes important in situations when a negligent driver is insured but has liability limits that are insufficient to pay the insured's damages. The underinsured motorists coverage endorsement applies when *the negligent driver carries liability insurance limits that are lower than the limits provided by the underinsured motorists coverage of the injured person.*

For example, assume that Patricia has underinsured motorists coverage in the amounts of $100,000 per person and $300,000 per occurrence and is injured by a negligent driver who has bodily injury liability limits of $25,000 per person and $50,000 per occurrence, which satisfy the state's minimum financial responsibility requirement. If Patricia's actual damages are $75,000, she would recover a maximum of $25,000 from the negligent driver's insurer, because that is the applicable limit of liability per person. Patricia would receive the additional $50,000 from her own insurer under her underinsured motorists coverage.

Provisions for underinsured motorists coverage vary by state. In some states, the underinsured motorists coverage endorsement can be added to the PAP to provide coverage as a supplement to the uninsured motorists coverage already in the PAP. In several states, however, a single endorsement providing both uninsured and underinsured motorists coverages replaces the uninsured motorists coverage of the standard PAP. Some states mandate that the underinsured motorists coverage be provided on all auto liability policies, but the coverage remains optional in many other states. The limits available (or required) for underinsured motorists coverage also vary by state. Insurance practitioners need to remain familiar with the laws in their state regarding both uninsured and underinsured motorists coverages.

Endorsements Affecting Physical Damage Coverage

Part D—Coverage for Damage to Your Auto can also be modified by adding certain endorsements to the PAP. The following are some of the more widely used physical damage endorsements:

- Towing and labor costs coverage endorsement (PP 03 03)
- Coverage for excess sound reproducing equipment, audio visual and data electronic equipment, and tapes, records, disks and other media endorsement (PP 03 13)
- Coverage for damage to your auto (maximum limit of liability) endorsement (PP 03 08)

Towing and Labor Costs

Under the *towing and labor costs coverage endorsement*, the insurer pays for towing and labor costs when a covered auto or nonowned auto is disabled, up to some stated amount such as $25, $50, or $75. For example, if an insured's car will not start because of a dead battery and a repair truck is called, the roadside assistance costs are covered up to the stated limit. The cost of labor is covered only when it is performed at the place of disablement. Labor costs for work done at a service station or garage are not covered, even if the disabled vehicle is first towed there.

If a nonowned auto being used by an insured becomes disabled, the insurer provides the broadest towing and labor costs coverage that applies to any covered auto shown in the schedule or declarations. For example, Abby has two cars insured under her PAP and has elected collision and towing and labor coverages for the older car only. If Abby borrows Grace's uninsured car and it breaks down, Abby's PAP insurer will pay necessary charges for towing Grace's car—up to the stated limit.

The towing and labor endorsement can be added to the PAP for a specified auto only if the insured has purchased other physical damage coverages on that auto. Usually collision coverage is required. Some insurers automatically include towing and labor coverage on any vehicle to which collision coverage applies.

Electronic Equipment and Tapes

The unendorsed PAP excludes or limits coverage on a wide variety of electronic equipment, as well as tapes, records, and other media. Coverage for such equipment can be obtained by adding the *coverage for excess sound reproducing equipment, audio, visual and data electronic equipment, and tapes, records, discs and other media endorsement* to the PAP.

This endorsement can be used to add any or all of three coverages. A premium is shown in the schedule of the endorsement for each of the following coverages that applies.

Excess Sound Reproducing Equipment

Recall that the unendorsed PAP includes a $1,000 limit on sound reproduction equipment and accessories that are installed in locations not used for that purpose by the auto manufacturer. The endorsement can increase the limit on such equipment from $1,000 to a limit shown in the schedule.

Audio, Visual, and Data Electronic Equipment

Under this coverage, the insurer will pay, without any deductible, for direct and accidental loss to electronic equipment that receives or transmits audio, visual, or data signals and is not designed solely for the reproduction of sound. This endorsement can be used to cover a citizens band radio, car telephone, videocassette recorder (VCR), television receiver, personal computer, and similar electronic equipment if installed as required. For the coverage to apply, the electronic equipment must either be:

- permanently installed in the covered auto, or
- removable from a housing unit permanently installed in the covered auto and designed to operate solely from the auto's electrical system. Equipment in this category must also be in or upon a covered auto—or any nonowned auto—at the time of loss.

Radios and stereos, tape decks, and compact disc (CD) players that are not permanently installed or that are not in a permanently installed housing are excluded under the unendorsed PAP and are also excluded under this endorsement. Such nonautomotive equipment would usually be covered property under a homeowners policy.

The maximum amount payable under this coverage for the total of all losses to electronic equipment and accessories under this coverage is the least of:

- the stated amount shown in the schedule or declarations,
- the actual cash value of the stolen or damaged property—with allowance for depreciation, or
- the amount necessary to repair or replace the property. The insurer does not pay for any betterment that results from repairing or replacing lost or damaged property.

Tapes, Records, Discs, and Other Media

If the items are in a covered auto at the time of loss, the insurer will pay, without any deductible, for direct and accidental loss to tapes, records, discs, or other media owned by the named insured or family member. The insurer will pay the lesser of the actual cash value or the replacement cost of stolen or damaged property, subject to a maximum limit of $200 for all such media.

Stated Amount

Some people own high-value antique cars or restored show cars. To establish the car's insurable value when the policy is written, a stated amount of insurance can be inserted in the policy. This is done by adding a *coverage for damage to your auto (maximum limit of liability) endorsement* to the PAP. Under this endorsement (often called a "stated amount" endorsement), each vehicle is described, and a stated amount of insurance is shown that applies to collision loss and other-than-collision loss.

Even though a stated amount of insurance is indicated, the endorsement does not create a policy in which the insurer pays that amount in the event of a total loss to the vehicle. Rather, the insurer's maximum limit of liability for a covered loss is limited to the lowest of:

- the stated amount shown in the schedule or in the declarations,
- the actual cash value of the stolen or damaged property, or

- the amount necessary to repair or replace the property with property of like kind and quality.

If, for example, the stated amount is less than the actual cash value or the amount necessary to repair or replace the property, the stated amount is used as the basis of the loss settlement. However, if the stated amount is greater than the actual cash value or the amount necessary to repair or replace the property, the lower amount is the basis for payment. In any case, the amount paid is reduced by any applicable deductible shown in the schedule or declarations.

SUMMARY

Under Part D—Coverage for Damage to Your Auto of the personal auto policy (PAP), the insurer agrees to pay for direct and accidental loss to a covered auto or nonowned auto, less the applicable deductible. Any auto described in the policy declarations can be covered for other-than-collision loss, for both collision and other-than-collision loss, or for neither physical damage coverage. When physical damage coverage is purchased, limited coverage is also provided for transportation expenses in the event that a covered auto is damaged or stolen.

If a nonowned auto is being operated by an insured, the insured's coverage is available to pay losses in excess of any physical damage coverage carried by the owner of that auto. If a nonowned auto replaces a covered auto that is out of use because of breakdown, loss, or destruction, the replacement vehicle is considered a temporary substitute vehicle, and Part D coverage also applies to it.

A long list of exclusions narrows the coverage of the Part D insuring agreement. Physical damage coverage is excluded when the vehicle is being used as a public or livery conveyance or is damaged from wear and tear, freezing, mechanical and electrical breakdown, radioactive contamination, or war. Additional exclusions or limitations apply to:

- Electronic equipment designed for the reproduction of sound unless the equipment is installed in the space used by the auto manufacturer. Coverage on equipment installed in other places is limited to $1,000.
- Certain electronic equipment, including citizens band radios, telephones not permanently installed, television receivers, videocassette recorders, and similar equipment
- Tapes, records, discs, or other media used with excluded electronic equipment
- Loss to the vehicle due to destruction or confiscation by a governmental authority
- Loss to a camper body or trailer not shown in the declarations
- Damage to nonowned vehicles used without permission
- Loss to awnings and cabanas

- Loss to radar and laser detection equipment
- Loss to customized furnishings or equipment in a van or pickup
- Nonowned autos used in the auto business
- Nonowned autos (other than private passenger autos or trailers) used in any business
- Losses arising out of racing activities

The insurer's liability for physical damage losses is the lesser of the actual cash value of the property or the amount necessary to repair or replace it with property of like kind and quality. If the cost of repairs exceeds the auto's value, the auto may be declared a total loss. Provisions dealing with loss payment, other sources of recovery, and appraisal are also included in Part D.

Part E—Duties After an Accident or Loss lists six general duties of a person seeking coverage under the personal auto policy:

- Give prompt notice to the insurer.
- Cooperate with the insurer.
- Submit legal papers to the insurer.
- Submit to a physical examination or an examination under oath.
- Authorize the release of medical records.
- Submit a proof of loss.

If payment is sought under the uninsured motorists coverage, the person seeking coverage must also notify the police of the accident and submit to the insurer any legal papers involved in a suit against the uninsured motorist. A person seeking coverage under the auto physical damage coverage is required to prevent further damage to the vehicle, notify the police if the auto has been stolen, and permit the insurer to inspect and appraise the damaged auto before its repair.

The final part of the personal auto policy, Part F—General Provisions, contains provisions and conditions that apply to the entire policy. They include bankruptcy of the insured, changes in the policy, fraud, legal action against the insurer, the insurer's right to recover payment, and policy period and territory. The termination provision has four sections: cancellation, nonrenewal, automatic termination, and other termination provisions. Additional general provisions concern transfer of the insured's interest in the policy and the liability of the insurer if two or more auto policies issued by the same insurer apply to any one accident.

The coverage of the personal auto policy can be changed by endorsement. Several endorsements may be used to cover motorcycles, recreational vehicles, and customizing equipment:

- Miscellaneous type vehicle endorsement (PP 03 23)
- Trailer/camper body coverage (maximum limit of liability) endorsement (PP 03 07)

- Customizing equipment coverage endorsement (PP 03 18)
- Snowmobile endorsement (PP 03 20)

Other endorsements affect multiple coverages:

- Named non-owner coverage endorsement (PP 03 22)
- Extended non-owned coverage for named individual endorsement (PP 03 06)
- Limited Mexico coverage endorsement (PP 03 21)

The underinsured motorists coverage endorsement supplements the uninsured motorists coverage in the policy. This endorsement provides coverage when a negligent driver injuring the named insured or family members has liability insurance limits that are insufficient and lower than the named insured's underinsured motorists limits.

Several endorsements affect only the physical damage coverage. They include:

- Towing and labor costs coverage endorsement (PP 03 03)
- Coverage for excess sound reproducing equipment, audio visual and data electronic equipment, and tapes, records, discs and other media endorsement (PP 03 13)
- Coverage for damage to your auto (maximum limit of liability) endorsement (PP 03 08)

CHAPTER NOTE

1. This section is based on PAP endorsements copyrighted by Insurance Services Office.

Direct Your Learning

Homeowners Insurance: Section I

After learning the subject matter of this chapter, for the ISO homeowners HO-3 policy (HO 2000), you should be able to:

- Explain what is covered and what is limited or excluded under Section I—Property Coverages.

- Given a case involving a property loss:

  - Explain whether the loss is covered.

  - Determine the amount the insurer would pay for covered losses.

- Explain the structure of the HO-3 policy.

Develop Your Perspective

What are the main topics covered in the chapter?

Section I of the HO-3 homeowners policy is described in this chapter. Included in this description are illustrations of property coverages, additional coverages, perils insured against, and Section I conditions.

Analyze the property coverage provided by the HO-3 policy.

- What property is covered, and what is excluded or limited?

- Can endorsements be used to provide coverage that is excluded or limited by the policy?

Why is it important to know these topics?

Homeowners policies, and specifically the HO-3, are insurance policies used commonly to provide coverage to homeowners for a wide range of loss exposures. To apply the policy and ensure that an individual or a family's loss exposures are appropriately addressed, you must first understand what coverage is provided.

Compare the loss exposures of most individuals and families to the coverage provided by the HO-3 policy.

- Are most property and perils covered?

- What is excluded?

- Why might these property and perils be excluded?

How can you use this information?

Apply the Section I HO-3 coverages to your own property exposures or to those of a family member or a friend.

- Are all property exposures covered by the HO-3? If not, why?

- Are all perils covered by the HO-3? If not, why?

- Can any of the excluded property or perils be covered by an endorsement attached to the HO-3?

Chapter 5

Homeowners Insurance: Section I

The homeowners policy provides a highly versatile tool for insuring real property and personal property owned by individuals or families, as well as their personal liability exposures. The homeowners policy includes coverages for a house, its contents, and the occupants' liability. A homeowners policy is designed to be broad enough to cover the property and liability insurance needs that most families face. The coverages of the standard policy form can be modified by endorsement to meet a given policyholder's specific needs.

Three chapters in this text review a standard homeowners contract. Chapter 5 addresses the property section (Section I) of the policy, Chapter 6 reviews the liability section (Section II) and conditions common to both Sections I and II, and Chapter 7 addresses homeowners variations and endorsements and provides some basic information regarding rating. Chapters 5 and 6 focus on a homeowners policy form developed by Insurance Services Office (ISO), an advisory organization serving insurers throughout the United States. Some insurers use homeowners policy forms developed by the American Association of Insurance Services (AAIS), an advisory organization similar to ISO. Other insurers develop their own policy forms.

One of the most widely used homeowners policy forms is ISO's Homeowners 3 Special Form (HO 00 03), commonly known as the "HO-3," which is the basis for the discussion in this chapter and in Chapter 6. In Chapter 7, other policy forms and endorsements are discussed and compared to the HO-3.

Students reading Chapters 5 and 6, which discuss the HO-3 policy form, will find it helpful to refer to a copy of the complete form as they read.

HOW THE HOMEOWNERS POLICY EVOLVED

Before the 1950s, owners of private residences had to purchase separate policies if they wished to cover their various needs. For example, a typical homeowner might have purchased a fire policy (often separate fire policies covered the dwelling, other structures, and personal property), a theft policy, and a personal liability policy. He or she might also have considered separate policies to cover such items as window glass, jewelry, and furs. During the 1950s, standard homeowners policies were developed to cover most types of private residences and personal property, as well as to provide liability insurance for owners of such property. Soon many insurers provided standard homeowners policies.

Before the 1970s, insurance policies used a writing style similar to that of other legal contracts. Insurers used wording that had already been interpreted through many court decisions. In the 1970s, the need grew for insurance contracts containing simplified language so that policyholders could better understand the policies they were purchasing.

In 1976, ISO introduced a simplified homeowners policy series called the *Homeowners 76 Series*. The 1976 policy series was not adopted throughout the United States. The 1984 edition of the ISO homeowners policy, using simplified policy language, was filed and approved in all states except Texas. A 1991 edition with simplified language was issued subsequently. Extensive policy revisions usually require that a policy be reprinted entirely, as with the 1984 and 1991 editions. In other cases, changes are introduced by policy endorsements rather than by a complete rewriting of the policy. In 1994, ISO introduced multistate revisions in the form of endorsements to be attached to the 1991 homeowners policies. Each state reviewed the multistate revisions, and more than forty states adopted the endorsements or a version of them also containing other language specific to a state.

The "Homeowners 2000" policy program incorporates these multistate revisions, broadens many coverages of the 1991 form, and restricts other coverages. The policy forms in the Homeowners 2000 program bear a 1999 copyright date. Chapters 5 and 6 examine the Homeowners 2000 version of the ISO HO-3 policy.

THE HOMEOWNERS 3 SPECIAL FORM (HO-3)

The HO-3 policy is designed for the owner-occupants of a one- to four-family dwelling used as the residence of the named insured. The policy is not intended for owners who do not occupy the dwelling. Persons who purchase a dwelling under a long-term installment contract, without legal title to the property, are eligible in the same manner as owners with title to the property. A dwelling under construction may also be insured under the HO-3 if the named insured is the intended owner-occupant.

Occupants with a life estate arrangement, which allows them to live in the house for the rest of their lives, are also eligible for a homeowners policy. New to the HO-2000 program is the option to issue a homeowners policy in the name of a trust when it is the sole owner of the dwelling and the trustee, grantor, and/or beneficiary reside on the premises, using an endorsement that is examined in Chapter 7.

Structure of the HO-3 Policy

Exhibit 5-1 diagrams the structure of the HO-3 policy. The policy is divided into two major sections:

*   Section I—Property Coverages, which is discussed in this chapter, specifies the property covered, the perils for which property is covered, and the exclusions and conditions that affect property coverages and losses.

EXHIBIT 5-1

Homeowners Policy Structure

| Agreement | establishes this document as a contract exchanging insurance for premium and compliance with provisions |
| Definitions | defines terms that are used within the policy that have a specific meaning within the policy |

Section I—Property

Section I—Property Coverages	explains the categories of property covered, property subject to special limits, property not covered, and additional coverages
Section I—Perils Insured Against	describes the perils covered (and some excluded perils) for direct loss to covered property
Section I—Exclusions	lists the perils that are uniformly excluded for all covered property
Section I—Conditions	establishes the insurer's and policyholder's responsibilities and defines how losses will be settled

Section II—Liability

Section II—Liability Coverages	explains in broad terms the personal liability and medical payments to others coverages
Section II—Exclusions	lists the exposures excluded for personal liability and medical payments to others coverages
Section II—Additional Coverages	lists additional liability coverages that are available
Section II—Conditions	establishes the insurer's and policyholder's responsibilities and defines how limits apply

| Sections I and II—Conditions | provides overall conditions that apply to Sections I and II, including policy period, cancellation, and nonrenewal |

- Section II—Liability Coverages, which is discussed in Chapter 6, provides information regarding liability coverages, exclusions, and conditions.

The policy begins with segments that establish the policy insuring agreement and the definitions of words used in the policy. The policy ends with conditions that apply to both property and liability coverage sections.

Modifying Endorsements

The homeowners policy is a self-contained insurance policy; it is a single document that forms a complete contract. The HO-3 meets most, but not all, needs of many individuals and families. Endorsements can be used to alter the policy language to add, delete, or modify the coverage.

In Chapters 5 and 6, various endorsements that can be used to modify the policy are mentioned in shaded boxes with the name of the endorsement in italics and the form number in parentheses. These endorsements are identified in Chapters 5 and 6 to indicate which coverages can be modified by endorsement. The endorsements are more specifically described in Chapter 7.

Declarations Page

The HO-3 policy form is attached to the declarations page, which provides essential information about the insured, the property covered, and the limits of coverage provided. The declarations page answers the following questions:

- Who is the policyholder?
- Where is the policyholder's residence?
- What are the coverage limits?
- What is the premium?
- What is the Section I deductible?
- What is the effective date of the policy?
- What forms and endorsements apply to the policy?
- Who is the mortgage holder?

Agreement

The "agreement" (also known as the insuring agreement), the first sentence in the policy form, reads as follows:

> We will provide the insurance described in this policy in return for the premium and compliance with all applicable provisions of this policy.

This agreement establishes the basis for the contract and specifies what the insurer and the policyholder will do for each other. The insurer agrees to provide coverage, and the policyholder agrees to pay the premium and comply with the policy conditions.

Definitions

Certain words or phrases appear in the policy within quotation marks. Words in quotation marks are defined in the definitions section of the policy. Defined words have special meanings when they are used within the policy, and it is important to pay attention to these definitions. A defined word or phrase might have a meaning that is different, narrower, or broader than the dictionary definition. Different insurance policies, or different coverages within a single policy, might define the same word or phrase in different ways.

If a word is used within a policy and no definition is provided, the word is given its common meaning. The definition in a dictionary is the meaning of such a word as it appears within the policy.

Any ambiguities in an insurance policy are construed against the party that wrote the contract. Because the homeowners policy is drafted by or on behalf of the insurer, any ambiguity is interpreted in favor of the insured.

The terms "you" and "your" are defined in the HO-3 as referring to the "named insured" shown in the declarations and the spouse if a resident of the same household. The terms "we," "us," and "our" refer to the insurer providing the coverage.

A few definitions are discussed under the following headings, because they are important in interpreting Section I of the policy. This chapter and the next examine other specific definitions of words and phrases as they are encountered in the homeowners policy.

"Named Insureds" and Other "Insureds"

The authors of the homeowners policy were careful to distinguish between insureds and named insureds. Students and insurance practitioners should also pay careful attention to the distinction, because the named insured has somewhat more protection than other insureds.

As mentioned above, the terms "you" and "your" refer to the "named insured" shown in the policy declarations and his or her resident spouse, even if the spouse is not named. The definition of "insured" encompasses not only a named insured ("you"), but also other insureds, including:

- Relatives who are residents of the named insured's household.
- Other persons under the age of twenty-one in the care of a named insured or a resident relative.
- A full-time student who lives away from home but resided in the household before leaving to attend school, provided the student is either a relative under the age of twenty-four or someone in the care of the named insured or a resident relative and under the age of twenty-one.

When the policy refers to "an insured," it means "one or more insureds."

This textbook sometimes uses the term "policyholder" to refer to "you" or the named insured. This is a matter of convenience, and it makes for smoother reading. The term "policyholder" has no special meaning in the homeowners policy.

"Residence Premises" and "Insured Location"

The distinction between "residence premises" and "insured location" is worth noting. "Residence premises" does not include as many places as "insured location," and both terms are used in the homeowners policy.

Residence premises includes only the location shown as "residence premises" in the declarations and means:

- The one- to four-family dwelling where the named insured resides in at least one of the units.
- That part of any other building (such as an apartment building) where the named insured resides.
- Other structures and grounds at that location.

"Insured location" includes the "residence premises" and also includes:

- An unlisted residence acquired by the named insured during the policy period.
- A nonowned premises where any insured is temporarily residing (such as a hotel room).
- Vacant land, other than farm land, owned by or rented to any insured.
- An insured's land on which a one- to four-family residence is being constructed.
- Individual or family cemetery plots.
- Any part of a premises occasionally rented to an insured for nonbusiness use (such as a hall rented for a wedding reception).

Deductible

Following the definitions, the policy begins with a statement that the insurer will pay only property losses that exceed the deductible amount shown in the declarations. The deductible that appears on the declarations page is a specific amount to be deducted from payment for a loss covered under Section I, with two exceptions described later in this chapter. The standard deductible is $250, but the insured can choose a higher deductible in exchange for a lower premium.

The most used deductible amounts are $250 and $500. They apply to all perils insured against under Section I of the policy. Many insurers in catastrophe-prone areas also use special higher deductible amounts that apply to specified perils.

Residence premises
(as defined in ISO HO policies)
The one-family dwelling where the named insured resides; the two-, three-, or four-family dwelling where the named insured resides in at least one of the units; that part of any other building where the named insured resides; and other structures and grounds; all at the location shown in the declarations.

The deductible is subtracted once from the total of all loss payable under Section I—Property Coverages caused by a single loss event. Of course, the insurer will not pay more than the applicable policy limits.

Section I—Property Coverages

Section I is divided into the following property coverages:

- Coverage A—Dwelling
- Coverage B—Other Structures
- Coverage C—Personal Property
- Coverage D—Loss of Use
- Additional Coverages

Collectively, these coverages describe property and expenses the HO-3 would cover. An insured, an agent, or a claim representative who might need to determine whether a tool shed, a shotgun, a coin collection, or any other item is covered property would look in this section.

Coverage A—Dwelling

Coverage A applies to the dwelling on the "residence premises" listed on the declarations page. As noted, residence premises includes not only a one-family dwelling, but also a two-, three-, or four-family dwelling, shown in the declarations, where the named insured resides in at least one of the units. Thus, the HO-3 could cover the entire building for a policyholder who owns a four-family home, lives in one unit, and rents the other units to tenants.

Coverage A also applies to structures attached to the dwelling—such as a garage or a deck—as well as to materials and supplies that are located on or next to the covered dwelling that are used to construct or repair the dwelling.

The land at the residence premises is specifically excluded from property coverage. Land is not susceptible to most of the perils that cause damage to the building and other property, and the value of the land should not be included when determining the amount of insurance to purchase. Even if the building itself would be covered by insurance, there would be no insurance coverage for land destroyed by, say, lava flowing from a volcano.

When buying insurance, a homeowner should determine the Coverage A limit based on the cost to replace the dwelling; the cost of the land should *not* be included. The key question should be, what would it cost to rebuild this dwelling at this location if the dwelling were destroyed?

Coverage B—Other Structures

While Coverage A includes structures that *are* attached to the dwelling, Coverage B applies to **other structures** on the residence premises that *are not* attached to the dwelling and are separated from the dwelling "by clear space." A fence, utility line, or similar connection linking another structure with the

Other structures
Structures on the residence premises, other than the dwelling building, that are not attached to the dwelling.

dwelling building does not make it an attached building. Examples of other structures include storage sheds, detached garages, and swimming pools.

Coverage for other structures is automatically provided under the HO-3 with a limit that is 10 percent of the limit for Coverage A. This 10 percent limit applies collectively to all "other structures" at the residence premises. The limit applies in addition to the Coverage A limit. So, if the dwelling building is covered for $200,000 under Coverage A, all other structures combined are covered for another $20,000.

> The *other structures—increased limits endorsement* (HO 04 48) provides higher limits for specified other structures.

Coverage B has three important exclusions. No coverage is provided for other structures:

- *Rented to anyone who is not a resident of the dwelling (unless it is rented as a garage)*. Therefore, an insured who has converted a detached garage into an apartment that is rented to a college student would have no coverage for that structure under an unendorsed HO-3.

> The *structures rented to others endorsement* (HO 04 40) provides coverage for other structures rented to others for use as a private residence.

- *From which any "business" is conducted*. "Business" is defined as a full-time, part-time, or occasional trade, profession, or occupation or any other activity engaged in for money or compensation, except for volunteer activities or home daycare services involving no compensation beyond payment of expenses, the mutual exchange of daycare services, or home daycare services for a relative. Also excepted are business activities in which any insured received more than $2,000 in total compensation for the twelve months before the inception date of the policy. Thus, an insured who operates a print shop or an auto repair business in his detached garage would have no coverage for the garage under the HO-3, unless the business earned less than $2,000 during the year preceding the policy year.

> The *permitted incidental occupancies endorsement* (HO 04 42) or the *home business insurance coverage endorsement* (HO 07 01) can provide coverage for other structures used for business.

- *Used to store "business" property*. A structure containing business property is covered if the business property is solely owned by an insured or a tenant of the dwelling, provided that business property does not include gaseous or liquid fuel—except for fuel in the tank of a vehicle or craft parked or stored in the structure. ("Craft" refers to watercraft, aircraft, and hovercraft.) Coverage would therefore apply to the detached garage of a music teacher who stores sheet music and music stands in the garage.

In effect, the exceptions to this last exclusion provide limited coverage for structures with some business exposure—coverage that was not provided in other recent editions of the homeowners policy. An increasing number of people now keep some business property in detached garages or barns, and this has become a coverage they need.

Coverage C—Personal Property

Coverage C applies to the policyholder's personal property anywhere in the world. Personal property includes items that the policyholder owns or uses. For example, Coverage C provides coverage for property that is borrowed and used by the insured, just as it would for owned property. An insured traveling in Switzerland would have coverage for his or her luggage if it is stolen; borrowed skis that are stolen would also be covered.

Coverage C provides coverage, if the named insured requests it after a loss, for personal property owned by others while it is on the residence premises. For instance, an insured who is storing a friend's furniture in the attic could elect to cover a loss to that furniture under the insured's HO-3.

An insured can also provide coverage for personal property owned by a guest or residence employee while the property is in *any residence* occupied by the insured. If the insured's visiting aunt has her luggage stolen from a beach house he has rented and occupied for a family vacation, the named insured could choose to cover the aunt's luggage under his HO-3 policy.

Whether to cover someone else's property is a decision that the insured would make after a loss has occurred. An insured who has a total fire loss might need all of the Coverage C limit available to replace the insured's own damaged contents; providing coverage for a friend or a guest might not be practical.

The standard limit for Coverage C is 50 percent of the Coverage A limit and applies in addition to the Coverage A limit. The Coverage C limit can be increased simply by changing the amount appearing on the declarations page. No endorsement is required to increase the Coverage C limit, but an additional premium is charged.

Only 10 percent of the limit for Coverage C, or $1,000 (whichever is greater), is provided for property usually located at a residence other than the residence listed on the declarations page. For example, an insured who has a $100,000 Coverage C limit would have $10,000 available for property normally located at a secondary residence or dorm room. Notice that this limitation applies only to property usually located at another *residence*. An insured who has property in a self-storage warehouse would have the full amount of Coverage C available, because a warehouse is not a residence.

> The *increased limit on personal property in other residences endorsement* (HO 04 50) increases the limit for personal property at another residence.

The 10 percent or $1,000 limitation does not apply to personal property that is moved from the residence premises because the house is being repaired, renovated, or rebuilt and is not fit to live in or store property in. So, if the insured's home is damaged by a tornado and salvageable contents are moved to a friend's basement during repairs, they are covered in the friend's house for the full Coverage C limit.

 An insured who is moving from one principal residence to another will have the full limit of Coverage C (*without* the 10 percent limit) available at both locations for thirty days. This generally allows enough time for the insured to purchase homeowners coverage at the new location.

Special Sublimits

Some categories of personal property are subject to smaller sublimits, called "special limits of liability," within the Coverage C limit of liability. Items within these categories might have potentially high values or be targets for theft. (Some items have limitations for only the theft exposure.) The special smaller limits for each category are intended to provide an adequate dollar amount of coverage for the exposures of a typical family.

> The *Coverage C increased special limits of liability endorsement* (HO 04 65) increases the limits of coverage for certain special limit items.

The following are the special limits of liability within Coverage C:

1. *$200 on money and precious metals:* This limitation applies not only to cash but also to related items, such as bank notes, bullion, coins, medals, scrip, stored value cards, and smart cards, as well as silver, gold, and platinum (other than silverware, goldware, and platinumware). A few terms here might be new to many readers:

    - *Scrip,* often used as a fund raiser by various organizations, is sold to members or donors for a percentage of the redeemable value, with the difference being donated by a retailer.

    - *Stored value cards,* unlike credit or debit cards, have a magnetic strip or computer chip that is loaded with a value that can be spent. An example is a prepaid phone card.

    - A *smart card* looks like a credit card but has an embedded computer chip capable of storing personal medical or financial information that can be updated as the card is used.

    These items are subject to the "money" limitation, rather than the securities limitation, because they are increasingly used as a substitute for money.

2. *$1,500 on securities, documents, records, and stamps:* The policy lists many items in this category, including evidences of debt, letters of credit, manuscripts, personal records, passports, tickets, and stamps. Coverage is provided regardless of the medium, so paper airline tickets would be

subject to the $1,500 limit, as well as personal records stored on computer software. This limit also includes the cost to research and replace the information that has been lost.

3. *$1,500 on watercraft:* This limitation applies to watercraft of all types, including their trailers, equipment, and motors.

4. *$1,500 on trailers:* This limitation applies to trailers or semi-trailers other than those used with watercraft.

Note: The next three limitations apply only to the peril of theft.

5. *$1,500 for **theft** of jewelry and furs:* Jewelry, watches, furs, and gems are prime targets for theft. The $1,500 limit does not apply to other covered perils. For example, an insured who loses $10,000 in jewelry and furs in a fire would have the full Coverage C limit available for the loss.

6. *$2,500 for **theft** of firearms and related items:* Guns are another popular theft item; therefore, a limitation applies for theft of firearms and accessories such as telescopic sights, cases, and ammunition.

7. *$2,500 for **theft** of silverware, goldware, platinumware, and pewterware:* Flatware, tea sets, trophies, and the like made from or plated with precious and semiprecious metals are also targeted theft items.

> The *scheduled personal property endorsement* (HO 04 61) increases the limits and perils provided for specifically scheduled items. This endorsement can be used for certain special limit items, as well as other valuable or collectible items.

8. *$2,500 for property on the residence premises used primarily for any business purpose:* This limitation applies to any business property, whether the property is used in a business owned by the insured or whether the property is owned by another business. For example, a policyholder who works from an office in his home would have this limitation on the computer and equipment provided by his employer.

> The *increased limits on business property endorsement* (HO 04 12) increases the limits of coverage for business property at and away from the residence for a business that is *not* conducted on the premises.
>
> The *home business insurance coverage endorsement* (HO 07 01) removes the $2,500 special limit for personal property on the residence premises used in a business (which must be specifically named in the endorsement) conducted on the premises.

9. *$500 for property away from the residence premises used for business purposes:* This limitation applies to business property that is owned or used by the policyholder but that is not at the residence premises. For example, a portable computer that is used by a contractor to calculate building estimates would have a $500 coverage limit while it is away from the residence. (This limit does not apply to items described in 10 and 11.)

10. *$1,500 for electronic apparatus and accessories equipped to be operated by power from a motor vehicle, while in or upon a motor vehicle,* and

11. *$1,500 for electronic apparatus equipped to be operated by power from a motor vehicle, used primarily for business while away from the residence premises but not in or upon a motor vehicle:* The limitations under both 10 and 11 reduce the coverage available for electronic equipment that can be operated by the power of a motor vehicle and can also be operated independently (as from a battery). Coverage on this equipment is limited while it is in the vehicle. It is also limited when it is removed from the vehicle if it is not at the residence and is used primarily for business purposes (such as a portable two-way radio, carried to job sites, that can be plugged into a vehicle's cigarette lighter). Included in limitations 10 and 11 are the accessories, antennas, tapes, records, and discs for use with this electronic equipment.

Property Not Covered

The policy specifically excludes all coverage for some categories of personal property. In most cases, these items are best insured through policies other than the homeowners policy.

1. *Articles insured elsewhere:* Items that are specifically insured "in this or other insurance" are excluded under Coverage C, regardless of the limit available under other insurance. For example, a policyholder might schedule a piece of jewelry under the *scheduled personal property endorsement* (HO 04 61). A ring that is listed and covered under that endorsement for $500 is no longer covered under Coverage C, even if it is worth $2,500 when it is destroyed in a fire. This exclusion eliminates the possibility of duplicate coverage from a single policy or from multiple policies.

2. *Animals, birds, or fish:* The homeowners policy does not provide property coverage on living creatures.

3. *Motor vehicles:* Motor vehicles—including equipment and parts, as well as electronic equipment that operates *solely* from the vehicle's electrical system (including the accessories, antennas, tapes, records, and discs used with that electronic equipment), are excluded under Coverage C while they are in or on the motor vehicle. A pickup truck's loose spare tire, riding in the bed of the pickup truck, is not personal property covered under the homeowners policy.

   An exception is made—in other words, coverage is provided—for vehicles that are not required to be registered for use on public roads or motor vehicles that are used solely to service an insured's residence (such as a riding lawn mower) or are designed to assist the handicapped (such as a motorized wheelchair).

4. *Aircraft:* All aircraft and their parts are excluded from the policy, with the exception of model and hobby aircraft.

5. *Hovercraft:* Self-propelled motorized ground effect vehicles and their parts are specifically excluded.

Coverage for Electronic Apparatus

Notice the combined effect of the homeowners motor vehicles exclusion, the homeowners $1,500 limitation on electronic apparatus, and the Personal Auto Policy (PAP). To simplify points covered in detail elsewhere:

- Equipment that operates solely from the vehicle's electrical system is covered under the PAP and excluded under the homeowners policy. Example: factory-installed car radio.

- Equipment capable of operating from vehicle power or other power sources is covered by the homeowners policy when such equipment:

  - Is *not* used primarily for business and, at the time of loss, is in or upon a motor vehicle. In this case, it is subject to a $1,500 limit; when away from a motor vehicle, that it is subject to Coverage C limits.

  - Is used primarily for business. In this case, it is subject to a $1,500 limit, provided that at the time of loss, it is:

    - In or upon a motor vehicle; or

    - Not in or upon a motor vehicle but away from the residence premises.

6. *Property of roomers or boarders unrelated to an insured:* A policyholder who rents an apartment or a room to a tenant will not find coverage under the HO-3 for the tenant's property. However, a policyholder who rents a room or an apartment to a relative will have coverage for that relative's property. An example is an insured who has converted a garage into an apartment for an adult son who pays rent. The son's property would be covered by the insured's HO-3.

7. *Property in an apartment rented to others:* A policyholder who rents a furnished apartment to a tenant will not have protection under Coverage C of the HO-3 for the furnishings. (Up to $2,500 coverage is provided for the landlord's furnishings under the Additional Coverages section, discussed later.)

8. *Property rented or held for rental to others off the residence premises:* Any property rented to others away from the premises is excluded from coverage. For example, a policyholder who purchases a garden tiller might try to recoup the expense of the tiller by renting it to neighbors and friends. While the tiller is away from the residence premises (either rented or offered for rent), it is excluded from property coverage.

9. *Business data:* There is no coverage for business data—including drawings, stored either on paper or electronically. However, coverage is provided for the cost of blank recording and storage media and the cost of pre-recorded computer software programs available on the retail market.

10. *Credit card or electronic fund transfer card:* Coverage C does not apply to losses arising from unauthorized use of a credit or fund transfer card or for access devices used solely for deposit, withdrawal, or transfer of funds.

The reference to unspecified access devices recognizes that computers, cell phones, and other electronic devices are now frequently used to transfer funds from one account to another. (Although protection under Coverage C is precluded, some limited coverage is provided under the Additional Coverages section of the homeowners policy, discussed later.)

11. *Water or steam:* Water and steam are not covered property. The homeowners policy provides no property coverage for the cost of replacing water in a damaged swimming pool that must be drained and replaced, and it does not provide coverage for the cost of water, billed by a utility company, that escapes from a burst pipe.

Coverage D—Loss of Use

Coverage D applies to the policyholder's exposure to financial loss, apart from the property damage itself, if the residence premises where the insured resides are damaged so badly that they are "not fit to live in." A dwelling should be safe, sanitary, and secure; a dwelling that fails to meet those criteria is not fit to live in. For example, a dwelling with a roof that is collapsing as a result of a windstorm is no longer safe. A dwelling that is filled with soot as a result of a fire is probably no longer sanitary. A dwelling with a wall missing after a vehicle struck the house is no longer secure. In any of these situations, a family would probably need to live elsewhere until repairs to the dwelling could be completed.

Coverage D applies only if the damage is the result of a loss that is covered under Section I of the policy. Those losses cited in the examples in the preceding paragraph are covered losses under Section I of the HO-3. A family with a flood-damaged dwelling might also have damage that would require them to move elsewhere, but flood is *not* a covered cause of loss under the HO-3; therefore, Coverage D would *not* apply.

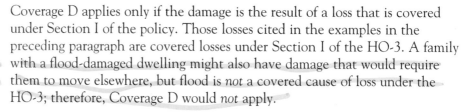

Coverage D is automatically provided at a limit that is 30 percent of the Coverage A limit and applies in addition to the Coverage A limit. The Coverage D limit can be increased simply by changing the amount appearing on the declarations page. No endorsement is required to increase the Coverage D limit, but an additional premium is charged.

Three coverages are grouped under Coverage D:

- *Additional living expense:* If the family must live elsewhere until the dwelling has been repaired, Coverage D pays for any necessary *increase* in living expenses required to maintain the household's normal standard of living. A claim representative might help the individual or family relocate to a temporary residence that is similar to the insured residence. The rent for the temporary residence would be an increase in expenses that would be covered by Coverage D. If the family relocates temporarily to a hotel (which might be reasonable if the repairs could be completed in a few weeks), eating at restaurants would cost more than their normal groceries. This difference between a reasonable cost of eating out and the family's normal food costs would also be covered by Coverage D. Note that Coverage D does not cover *all* living expenses while the insured is unable to live in the insured dwelling. Instead, it covers only the *necessary and increased* expenses caused by the temporary relocation; in other words, only the difference between the insured's normal living expenses and the higher expenses because of the relocation is covered.

Payment is made for the shortest time required to repair the dwelling or to permanently relocate the household.

• *Fair rental value:* If part of the residence is rented to others and a covered loss makes that part of the residence "not fit to live in," the insurer will reimburse the policyholder the lost rental value (minus expenses that do not continue) until repairs are made.

For example, an HO-3 might be used to insure a duplex where the policyholder lives in one half and rents the other half. A fire that damages the rented portion of the duplex could make it unfit to live in until repairs are made. While the repairs are taking place, Coverage D will provide coverage for the lost rent minus expenses that do not continue.

Assume that the fair value of the lost rent is $500 per month and that the policyholder had been paying an average of $100 per month for heating and water expenses that would not continue during the repair period. If the reasonable time to repair the duplex is three months, the policyholder would be compensated under Coverage D as follows:

$500 per month lost rent × 3 months =	$1,500
100 noncontinuing monthly expenses × 3 months =	−300
Total payment =	$1,200

Note that fair rental value coverage applies even to units not currently rented to a tenant as long as the unit is "held for rental."

• *Loss of use due to civil authority:* Occasionally, civil authorities prohibit property owners from using their residence premises because neighboring property is damaged, even though a policyholder's own property might be undamaged. For example, a forest fire threatening an area could cause civil authorities to evacuate a neighborhood that has not yet been damaged. Coverage D will reimburse the policyholder both additional living expenses and fair rental value (as previously described) for no more than two weeks for the loss of use due to civil authority.

For this coverage to apply, the threat to the property must come from a peril insured against by the HO-3. Flooding that causes the authorities to order an evacuation would not create a loss covered by Coverage D, because flood is not a covered peril. (Covered perils are discussed later.)

Additional Coverages

The following additional coverages are included in the HO-3 to provide protection, subject to certain limitations, in the event of specific perils and types of losses:

1. *Debris removal:* When property is damaged or destroyed, it is often necessary to remove debris before the repair or restoration can begin.

For example, if property is damaged by a covered peril or by ash from a volcanic eruption, the policyholder incurs expenses to remove the debris or ash. Likewise, an insured whose house was partially damaged by fire must remove the burned portion of the structure before repairs can be made. These are both examples of debris removal.

The cost of debris removal is included within the Coverage A, B, or C limit for the damaged property. If the debris removal cost plus the damage to the property exceeds the applicable limit, the additional coverage for debris removal comes into play. Under these circumstances, an additional 5 percent of the limit is available under the additional coverage. For example, an insured has a Coverage B limit of $10,000 when a detached garage is destroyed. If the cost of replacing the garage with another of like kind and quality exceeds the $10,000 limit, the insured would also have an additional $500 available to pay for removing debris of the original garage.

This coverage also pays for reasonable expenses up to a total of $1,000 for removal from the residence premises of (a) the insured's trees felled by windstorm, hail, or the weight of ice, snow, or sleet, or (b) a neighbor's trees felled by a Coverage C peril (discussed later in this chapter). For the loss to be covered, the tree must either damage a structure described in Coverage A or B, block a driveway, or block a handicap access ramp or similar structure. No more than $500 will be paid for the removal of any one tree.

2. *Reasonable repairs:* If the policyholder's property is damaged by a covered peril, this coverage will reimburse the policyholder for the reasonable cost of measures taken to protect the property from further damage. According to the Section I—Conditions, the policyholder is *required* to make reasonable and necessary repairs to protect the property from further damage following a loss. For example, an insured whose home has been damaged by a windstorm should promptly cover the broken windows and the hole in the roof to prevent further damage. This additional coverage will pay for the costs of hiring a repair person and purchasing the material needed to complete the temporary repairs.

3. *Trees, shrubs, and other plants:* Trees, shrubs, and other plants on the residence premises are covered for the perils of fire, lightning, explosion, riot, civil commotion, aircraft, vehicles (not owned or operated by a resident), vandalism, malicious mischief, or theft. Weather-related losses are *not* covered, such as those resulting from windstorm, hail, freezing, and the weight of ice, sleet, and snow. (The additional coverage for debris removal applies to wind, hail, and ice damage to trees but only for the cost to remove a tree and only when the tree damages a covered structure or handicapped access fixture.) Coverage is limited to 5 percent of the Coverage A limit and not more than $500 for any one tree, plant, or shrub.

4. *Fire department service charge:* Some homeowners must enter into an agreement or contract for fire department services. If the fire department is called to protect the property and the homeowner is billed for that response, this additional coverage pays up to $500 for that charge. If the property is located within the city or district furnishing the fire department response, this additional coverage does not apply.

5. *Property removed:* If an insured's home is endangered by a covered peril (such as a brush fire), the insured might attempt to save some contents by removing them from the home. To support that activity, which is intended to eliminate loss otherwise payable by the insurer, the insurer will cover the removed contents under this additional coverage for thirty days for *any peril,* even a peril not normally covered (such as marring, mildew, or flood).

6. *Credit card, electronic fund transfer card or access device, forgery, and counterfeit money:* An insured is covered up to $500 for the following types of losses:

    • Legal obligations because of the theft or unauthorized use of the insured's credit card

    • Loss resulting from the theft or unauthorized use of a fund transfer card or access device

    • Loss caused by forgery or alteration of a check

    • Loss through acceptance of counterfeit U.S. or Canadian money

No coverage is provided for losses arising out of business use or the dishonesty of an "insured." The definition of "insured" includes resident relatives and people under twenty-one in the insured's care, so unauthorized credit card use by a child of the named insured would not be covered.

> The *credit card, electronic fund transfer card or access device, forgery and counterfeit money coverage endorsement* (HO 04 53) increases the limit for this additional coverage.

7. *Loss assessment:* Loss assessments are proportional charges made against a property owner for losses to property owned by members of a group. For example, homeowners in a subdivision might belong to a homeowners association through which all homeowners collectively own common property, such as the fences and signs at the entrance. If an unknown vehicle hits and damages the entrance sign, the association could assess each property owner for his or her portion of the cost for repairs. Under this additional coverage, the insurer will pay the insured's share—up to $1,000—of a loss assessment made by a corporation or association of property owners if the loss is a result of a peril insured against under Coverage A and the damaged property is of a type insured under this policy (the fence would qualify).

> The *loss assessment coverage endorsement* (HO 04 35) increases the limit for this additional coverage.

8. *Collapse*: Collapse and glass breakage are not really *causes* of loss, but the result of some peril. Therefore, they are treated as additional coverages. The collapse additional coverage insures against damage to buildings and personal property caused by the collapse of part or all of an insured building. This is an additional coverage, because collapse is not an insured peril under Section I—Perils Insured Against of the HO-3. Collapse is explicitly defined to mean an abrupt falling down or caving in of a building or any part of a building so that it cannot be occupied for its intended purposes. The costs of repairing a building that is still standing or one that is in danger of collapsing do not qualify for payment under this additional coverage.

Collapse is covered only when it was caused by certain specific perils:

- The named perils insured against in Coverage C—personal property
- Hidden decay of which an insured was not aware
- Hidden insect or vermin damage of which an insured was not aware
- Weight of contents, equipment, animals, or people
- Weight of rain on a roof
- Use of defective building material or construction methods if collapse occurs during construction.

Coverage is subject to policy limits applicable to the covered property.

9. *Glass or safety glazing material*: Coverage is provided for the breakage of glass or safety glazing material (safety glass, etc.) and for the damage caused by that breakage. Coverage is excluded if the dwelling has been vacant for more than sixty days before the loss.

10. *Landlord's furnishings*: As noted earlier, a landlord's furnishings (including carpeting and appliances) in tenants' apartments are excluded from coverage under Coverage C. However, under this additional coverage, they are covered up to $2,500 per apartment for loss by the same perils applicable to other property under Coverage C, except that theft coverage is not included.

> The *landlord's furnishings endorsement* (HO 05 46) can be used to increase the limit on coverage for landlord's furnishings.

11. *Ordinance or law*: An individual who owns a home in an older, a historical, or a recently rezoned neighborhood could discover after a loss that repairs must be made in compliance with current ordinances or laws. For example, an insured with a home containing aluminum wiring could find that the home must be rewired with copper wire. The problem is not limited to older homes. More laws are being enacted affecting property in earthquake, hurricane, or flood zones.

> The *ordinance or law—increased amount of coverage endorsement* (HO 04 77) increases the total percentage of Coverage A that applies to this additional coverage.

Other provisions in the HO-3 provide coverage for the replacement cost of the building that was in place before the loss; they do not address the additional expense of upgrading a building to meet current building ordinances or laws. Where such an ordinance or law applies, this additional coverage provides an additional 10 percent of the Coverage A limit to pay for:

- The added cost of construction, demolition, remodeling, renovation, or repair due to damage as a result of a covered peril.

- The demolition, reconstruction, remodeling, removal, or replacement of the undamaged part of a covered building or other structure when the entire building must be rebuilt, following damage to another part of the building.

- The remodeling, removal, or replacement of the undamaged part of a covered building or other structure when it's necessary to complete the work being done to the damaged area.

- Related debris removal expenses.

Specifically excluded are losses in value to the building and costs associated with pollutants.

Ordinance or Law Example

Andy and Donna Baker own a thirty-year-old home with a replacement cost value of $250,000 and an actual cash value of $200,000. It is insured under an unendorsed HO-3 policy with a Coverage A limit of $250,000. The building code in their community requires that an automatic fire-extinguishing sprinkler system be installed in both new homes and older homes that are substantially remodeled.

A windstorm seriously damages the north side of the Bakers' home. It would cost $150,000 to restore the home to its preloss condition. However, the Bakers are not permitted to just restore the house. They must also install an automatic sprinkler system throughout the entire house. Their homeowners policy will pay the $150,000 repair cost plus up to $25,000 (10 percent of the Coverage A limit) for the added cost of installing an automatic sprinkler system in both the new and the undamaged portion of the house.

---

12. *Grave markers:* Grave markers do not clearly qualify as either personal property or real property that would be covered elsewhere in the HO-3 policy, so they are treated as an additional coverage. For loss caused by the Coverage C perils—including vandalism—$5,000 in coverage applies to grave markers and mausoleums on or away from the residence premises. Although the policy does not specify whose grave markers are covered, they would presumably be those in which the policyholder has an insurable interest.

General Comments on Additional Coverages

Most of these additional coverages are given special treatment because they do *not* fit neatly into Coverage A, B, C, or D groups. Others address items that have been excluded from the full coverage otherwise available under Coverage C (such as credit cards and landlord's furnishings) but instead receive "additional coverage" subject to reduced limits and limited perils. Furthermore:

- Some additional coverages create additional coverage limits, but others do not.
- Some additional coverages are subject to the deductible, but others are not.
- Some additional coverages are available only after a covered loss has occurred, but others are independent of any other covered loss.

Exhibit 5-2 makes it easier to understand the application of these coverages.

Section I—Perils Insured Against

Section I—Perils Insured Against has the following divisions:

- Coverage A—Dwelling and Coverage B—Other Structures
- Coverage C—Personal Property

Each division describes the covered perils that might damage or destroy the covered property. To determine whether windstorm, fire, or water damage is an insured peril, one would look in this segment of the policy.

No covered perils are listed in this section for Coverage D—Loss of Use or for the additional coverages, because Coverage D and three of the additional coverages apply only when other covered losses occur. The remaining additional coverages individually describe when coverage applies.

Perils Insured Against for Coverages A and B: Direct Physical Loss

This section begins with the following broad statement:

> We insure against direct physical loss to property described in Coverages A and B.

Insured Perils for Coverage A—Dwelling and Coverage B—Other Structures are grouped together because the items insured under these two coverages include real property items with similar exposures to loss. The approach to describing the perils insured against for Coverages A and B is known as **special-form coverage**.

Special-form coverage
Coverage for any direct physical loss to property unless the loss is caused by a peril specifically excluded by the policy; also called "all-risks" or open perils coverage.

Next, a list of excluded perils is provided. If a peril is not listed within these exclusions, it is covered. This method provides a broad range of perils that the policy could cover. For example, if an insured accidentally spilled bleach on the floor and ruined the wall-to-wall carpet, the damage would be covered because no exclusion appears for that type of loss. Wall-to-wall carpet is covered under Coverage A because it is attached to the structure.

EXHIBIT 5-2

Application of Additional Coverages

Additional Coverages	Does this coverage create an additional limit?	Does the deductible apply?	Is this coverage dependent on another covered loss?
1. Debris Removal	Yes, an additional 5 percent of the limit of liability is available.	Yes*	Yes, damage from a covered peril or volcanic ash must occur for this coverage to apply.
2. Reasonable Repairs	No, the coverage for expenses incurred does not increase the limit of coverage that applies to the covered property.	Yes*	Yes, a loss from a covered peril must occur for this coverage to apply.
3. Trees, Shrubs, and Other Plants	Yes, up to $500 is provided for each item up to a total of 5 percent of the Coverage A limit.	Yes*	No
4. Fire Department Service Charge	Yes, payment up to $500 is an additional limit.	No	No, there must be a threat of a covered peril, but there is no requirement that the peril actually occur.
5. Property Removed	No	Yes*	No, there must be a threat of a covered peril, but there is no requirement that the peril actually occur.
6. Credit Card, Electronic Fund Transfer Card or Access Device, Forgery, and Counterfeit Money	Yes, an additional total of $500 is available for any series of acts committed by any one person. Defense coverage is also provided for the insured if needed.	No	No
7. Loss Assessment	Yes, for an additional $1,000.	No	No, not to property of the insured. But there must first be a loss from a covered peril to association property.
8. Collapse	No	Yes *	No, other property need not be damaged, but the collapse must result from a covered peril.
9. Glass or Safety Glazing Material	No	Yes*	No, other property need not be damaged, but the glass breakage must result from a covered peril.
10. Landlord's Furnishings	No	Yes*	No
11. Ordinance or Law	Yes, an additional limit of 10 percent of Coverage A is available.	Yes*	Yes, this coverage is dependent on a covered loss occurring.
12. Grave Markers	No	Yes*	No

*Not a separate deductible. Only one deductible is subtracted from the total loss of a covered event.

Perils Excluded

The excluded perils for Coverages A and B are described under the following headings.

Perils Listed in the Section I Exclusions.
Another section of the policy, discussed later in this chapter, contains exclusions applicable to Coverages A, B, C, and D.

Collapse.
Although collapse is excluded as a *cause* of loss, coverage for collapse that *results* from another cause is provided under a Section I additional coverage, as explained earlier.

Freezing of a Plumbing, Heating, Air Conditioning or Sprinkler System, or a Household Appliance.
Freezing can cause pipes and hoses to burst or leak, causing extensive damage. If the insured fails to take reasonable precautions against freezing, such as keeping the heat on or shutting the water off and draining the system, coverage is excluded for any resulting damage.

Draining an automatic fire-protection sprinkler system would make it useless. Therefore, for homes protected by automatic sprinkler systems, the insured is required to use reasonable care to continue the water supply and maintain heat in the building, in order for "freezing" coverage to apply.

Freezing, Thawing, Pressure or Weight of Water or Ice.
Damage to external property (such as fences, pavement, patios, decks, swimming pools, foundations, piers, and docks) caused by freezing, thawing, and the pressure of water or ice is excluded.

Theft of Construction Materials.
Building materials and supplies for a home under construction are valuable and are attractive to thieves. Theft of these items is excluded until the dwelling is finished and occupied.

Vandalism and Malicious Mischief to Vacant Dwellings.
Vacant dwellings are targets for vandalism. Coverage for vandalism, including ensuing losses such as a fire, is excluded for dwellings that have been **vacant** for more than sixty consecutive days.

Vacancy Versus Unoccupancy

A **vacant** dwelling is unfurnished and has no occupants. An **unoccupied** dwelling is furnished but has no occupants. If an insured who lives in Vermont spends the winter in Florida, the Vermont dwelling is unoccupied, but not vacant, while the insured is in Florida. The insured would have to take precautions to prevent freezing in the Vermont dwelling, but it would be covered for **vandalism** damage during the winter.

Some people remember the difference between **vacancy** and **unoccupancy** by observing that the "vacancy" sign outside some motels is wrong. Unless the motel rents unfurnished rooms, the sign should read, "no unoccupancy."

Mold, Fungus, or Wet Rot.   Although mold is nothing new, it has recently become the focus of an increasing number of property insurance claims. Coverage for loss by these causes is excluded unless the mold, fungus, or rotting is hidden and results from an accidental leak of water or steam from a plumbing, heating, or air conditioning system or household appliance or from a storm drain or water, steam, or sewer pipes off the residence premises. Sump pumps, roof drains, and the like do not qualify as plumbing systems or household appliances in this context.

Natural Deterioration.   Dwellings naturally age and deteriorate over time. They require maintenance to keep them in good shape and prevent serious damage. Losses caused by age and natural deterioration are called "maintenance losses" and are not covered. The policy specifically excludes the following: wear and tear, marring, deterioration, mechanical breakdown, latent defect, or **inherent vice**—or any quality in property that causes it to damage or destroy itself. Also excluded are smog, rust, other corrosion, and dry rot.

Inherent vice
Type of deterioration that is characteristic of a material; e.g., the tendency of metal to rust.

Smoke From Agricultural Smudging or Industrial Operations.   Damage that results from smoke caused by agricultural smudging or industrial operations is excluded from coverage. Agricultural smudging intentionally creates a dense smoke to prevent plants from frost.

Pollutants.   The policy excludes property coverage for damage caused by pollutants, whether they are solid, liquid, gaseous, or thermal. An exception is made if the pollutants are released or escape as the result of any of the perils insured under Coverage C, discussed later in this chapter. The following are examples of excluded and covered pollution losses:

- Because a worker opened the wrong valve, a chemical plant accidentally released chemicals into the air that damaged the siding of the insured's home. This pollution loss is excluded by the HO-3 because a worker's error is not a peril insured under Coverage C.
- Because of an explosion (a peril insured under Coverage C), a chemical plant accidentally released chemicals into the air. The HO-3 would cover resulting damage to the insured's siding.

Settling of the Dwelling.   Losses that result from the settling, shrinking, bulging, or expansion of foundations, footings, patios, pavements, bulkheads, and the building structure are excluded from coverage.

Animals.   As mentioned earlier, the HO-3 does not cover damage *to* animals, because they are not covered property. The HO-3 also excludes damage caused *by* animals that an insured owns or keeps, or by birds, vermin, rodents, or insects. For example, the damage caused by a pet iguana that defecates on the carpet would not be covered. Likewise, damage caused by a squirrel (a rodent) that enters the dwelling and builds a nest in the wall would not be covered. Also, the damage caused by the insured's cat that sharpens its claws on the door is not covered. However, the policy does cover a loss caused by a deer (not owned by the insured and not on the list of excluded animals) that breaks through the glass door of the dwelling and causes damage to the wall-to-wall carpet.

Exception to Excluded Perils—Water Damage Coverage

Unless the loss is otherwise excluded, the HO-3 covers water damage to buildings or other structures that results from an accidental discharge or overflow of water or steam. The water or steam must come from a plumbing, heating, air conditioning, or sprinkler system; from a household appliance on the residence premises; or from a storm drain or water, steam, or sewer pipe off the residence premises. Coverage is provided for damage caused by the water and also for the cost of tearing out and replacing any part of the building or other structure necessary to make repairs. However, the loss to the damaged system or appliance is not covered.

The following examples demonstrate how this exception applies:

- If a water line inside a wall ruptures and causes flooding in the basement, coverage is provided for the resulting water damage and the cost to tear out the wall and repair the damage. The insurer will not pay for replacing or repairing the pipe itself.

- If a dishwasher suddenly leaks water and damages the kitchen floor, coverage is provided to tear out the damaged floor and repair the damage. The insurer will not pay for repairs to the dishwasher.

- If a water line under a paved driveway breaks and the escaping water damages a building on the premises, coverage is provided for the cost to (a) repair the damage to the building, (b) break through the driveway to access the plumbing break, and (c) repair the damaged area of the driveway. The insurer will not pay for replacing or repairing the pipe.

Ensuing Losses Covered

Ensuing losses not specifically excluded by the HO-3 are covered. For example, settling of foundations is excluded, but if a settling foundation causes a water pipe to break, the ensuing water damage would be covered.

Ensuing loss
Loss caused by a peril that occurs after or as a result of an initial peril; e.g., fire damage following an earthquake.

Perils Insured Against for Coverage C

Coverage C applies to the contents of a home and other personal property. The perils covered for Coverage C—Personal Property differ significantly from the special-form (open perils) coverage previously described for Coverages A and B. Remember, special-form coverage provides coverage for any direct loss to property unless the loss is caused by a peril specifically excluded by the policy. Under Coverage C, only named perils are covered.

Named Perils

Named perils
Perils listed and described in the policy as being covered; also called specified perils or specified causes of loss.

Named perils, to which Coverage C applies, are listed and described in the policy. Only losses caused by those listed perils are covered. Therefore, coverage for personal property under the HO-3 is not as broad as coverage for dwellings and other structures. To illustrate, an insured who accidentally spilled bleach on wall-to-wall carpeting (part of the building, covered under Coverage A) would be compensated for the loss because that peril is not excluded under Coverage A. However, if the spilled bleach also ruined the sofa and coffee table (Coverage C—personal property items), no coverage would apply for these items because spilled bleach is *not* one of the named perils for Coverage C.

> The *Homeowners 5—Comprehensive Form* (HO-5) closely resembles the HO-3 but changes the coverage for Coverage C from named perils to "special-form coverage" (risk of direct physical loss unless excluded). The HO-5 is examined in Chapter 7.

Named Perils Covered

The named perils for which coverage is provided for personal property items under Coverage C are listed below. Examples are provided for perils for which coverage is qualified in some way.

1. *Fire or lightning*
2. *Windstorm or hail:* Damage to personal property caused by rain, snow, sleet, sand, or dust is covered only if wind (including hurricane and tornado) or hail first damages the building and causes an opening in a roof or wall through which the rain, snow, sleet, sand, or dust enters. For example, there is no coverage if water damages a sofa, television, and stereo because rain came through a window that was left open. However, if windstorm or hail first damaged the building by breaking a window, by tearing shingles off the roof, or by causing a tree to fall and break through the roof, the resulting water damage to the sofa and other personal property would be covered.

    Coverage for windstorm or hail damage to watercraft, their trailers, furnishings, and equipment is provided only while these items are inside a fully enclosed building. Windstorm or hail damage would not be covered unless the building is first damaged.

3. *Explosion:* Explosion means a rapid chemical reaction with the production of noise and heat and the violent expansion of gases. An explosion sometimes occurs as a result of natural gas accumulation in a dwelling. Coverage may also be provided for damage to property as a result of a gunshot or rifle shot, because these can be interpreted to be within the definition of "explosion."[1]

4. *Riot or civil commotion*
5. *Aircraft*
6. *Vehicles:* Damage to personal property in the back seat of a car involved in an auto accident would be covered, as would damage to a bicycle backed over by a garbage truck or by the insured's own vehicle.

7. *Smoke:* Sudden and accidental smoke damage to personal property is covered. Soot, fumes, or vapors from a boiler or furnace are included as smoke for purposes of this peril. Loss caused by smoke from agricultural smudging or industrial operations is excluded.

8. *Vandalism or malicious mischief*

9. *Theft:* Theft includes losses of personal property as a result of burglary or robbery. It also includes "mysterious disappearance," loss of property that has disappeared from its last known location if it is likely that the property has been stolen. Coverage applies if the circumstantial evidence is strong enough to establish that theft is the cause of the loss.[2]

   The following types of theft are excluded for personal property:

   • Theft coverage is excluded if the theft is committed by an "insured." As mentioned previously, the definition of "insured" includes resident relatives and people under the age of twenty-one in the insured's care. So, a theft of covered property by a teenager who lives in the household would not be covered.

   • Theft from a building under construction and theft of construction materials are not covered under Coverage C. (Building materials can also be covered property under Coverage A, but a specific theft exclusion, mentioned earlier, also precludes theft coverage there.)

   • Theft from that part of the insured premises rented to someone other than another insured is not covered. For example, if the named insured rents a room to an unrelated college student, the student's belongings will not be covered if they are stolen.

   • Theft of personal property from another residence the insured owns, rents, or occupies is not covered unless the insured is temporarily living there. For example, theft of property at an insured's vacation home at the beach is not covered when the insured is not occupying it. However, the insured's property stolen from a hotel room while the insured is staying there on vacation would be covered.

   • Theft of property belonging to an insured who is a student at a residence away from home (such as a dormitory room at a college) is not covered if the student has not been there for more than sixty days. For example, if the insured's twenty-one-year-old daughter left her own furniture and stereo in her unoccupied dorm room over the summer, she would not have coverage for theft of her belongings occurring seventy-five days after she left the dorm.

   • Theft is excluded for watercraft, including its furnishings and equipment, away from the residence premises (such as a boat at a dock or boat landing).

   • Theft of trailers, semi-trailers, and campers is excluded. Coverage for these items can be provided under a personal auto policy.

10. *Falling objects:* Coverage is provided for losses to personal property if a falling object breaks through the dwelling's roof or wall and damages the

contents. Coverage would be provided for damage to a dining room table crushed beneath a tree that has first broken through the roof. Coverage would *not* be provided for damage to a table if a chandelier dropped onto the table, because no falling object penetrated the building.

11. *Weight of ice, snow, or sleet:* Coverage applies only to damage to property contained in a building.

12. *Accidental discharge or overflow of water or steam:* Personal property is covered if it is damaged by water or steam that is accidentally released by a plumbing, heating, air conditioning or fire-protective sprinkler system, or by a household appliance. For example, furniture damaged as a result of overflow from a dishwasher or clothes washer would be covered. However, damage caused by mold, fungus, or wet rot is not covered unless it is hidden by walls, ceilings, or floors. Damage by water from a sump pump or roof drain is not covered.

13. *Sudden and accidental tearing apart, cracking, burning, or bulging:* Personal property is covered if damaged by water or steam released from a hot water heating system, an air conditioning system, or an automatic fire protective sprinkler system. For example, personal property damaged by a ruptured water heater would be covered.

14. *Freezing:* Damage to personal property that results from the freezing of a plumbing, heating, air conditioning, or fire protective sprinkler system or of a household appliance is covered as long as the insured has taken reasonable precautions to maintain the heat or has shut off and drained the system or appliances.

15. *Sudden and accidental damage from artificially generated electrical current:* This peril does not include loss to tubes, transistors, or electronic components or circuitry of appliances, computers, or home entertainment equipment. It would, for example, cover loss to a window air conditioner's compressor resulting from a power surge or a brownout.

> The *special computer coverage endorsement* (HO 04 14) changes the named perils coverage to "special coverage" (risk of direct loss unless excluded) for electronic hardware and equipment, software, and media. Direct damage caused by a power surge is covered, in addition to other perils.

16. *Volcanic eruption:* This peril does not include loss caused by earthquake or tremors. Damage caused by airborne shock waves and ash, for example, would be covered.

Section I—Exclusions

Some perils are excluded for both buildings and personal property covered under Section I. The list of these exclusions begins with the following statement:

> We do not insure for loss caused directly or indirectly by any of the following. Such loss is excluded regardless of any other cause or event

contributing concurrently or in any sequence to the loss. These exclusions apply whether or not the loss event results in widespread damage or affects a substantial area.

This statement, combined with the exclusions that follow, is intended to address a thorny issue in special-form insurance coverage. As mentioned earlier, any loss under a policy with special-form (open perils) coverage is not precluded unless the cause of loss is specifically excluded. This can raise questions when two or more perils, simultaneously or in sequence, combine to cause a loss, and one peril is covered while the other is excluded. For example, vandals blow up a dam, releasing surface water that causes damage to downstream property. Vandalism and explosion are covered perils, but flood is an excluded peril, as explained later. Without this provision, the damage might be considered a covered vandalism or explosion loss. However, the policy language makes it clear that any flood loss is excluded, even if another peril is associated with it. Although one normally thinks of floods that cover many square miles, this provision would also clearly apply to water escaping from a pond on the insured's own property.

Concurrent causation
A loss involving two or more perils, occurring either simultaneously or sequentially.

Concurrent causation is the term used for a loss involving two or more perils, occurring either at the same time or in sequence. Except as otherwise noted, special-form property insurance policies tend to make it clear that loss involving flood, earthquake, war, and nuclear reaction are excluded even if another, prior cause can also be identified. However, some ensuing losses, resulting from and following an excluded peril, are specifically covered. These introductory comments should become clearer as each of the Section I exclusions is examined.

Perils Excluded Under Section I

The following are excluded perils under Section I.

Ordinance or Law

Other than the coverage that is provided in the additional coverages section of the policy, loss that results from the enforcement of an ordinance or a law is excluded.

Earth Movement

Earthquake and other types of earth movement, such as landslides, mudslides, mudflows, mine subsidence, and sinkholes, are excluded perils. However, damage caused by an ensuing fire or explosion is covered, and theft is not excluded. For example, an earthquake ruptures a gas line in a house. The gas then ignites and the house is burned. The damage caused by the earthquake is excluded, but the fire damage is covered.

> The *earthquake endorsement* (HO 04 54) can be added to cover the earthquake peril.

Water Damage

The water damage exclusion eliminates coverage for losses caused by flood, surface water, waves, and water or water-borne material such as sewage that backs up through sewers and drains. However, ensuing losses from fire, explosion, or theft resulting from water damage are covered. Assume, for example, that a homeowner must evacuate a flooded home. Thieves subsequently enter the home and steal several items of property. The theft would be covered.

> The *water back up and sump discharge or overflow endorsement* (HO 04 95) provides a $5,000 limit of coverage for loss caused by water that backs up through sewers or drains or by water that overflows from a sump.

Power Failure

An insured who loses electrical power or utility service because of a problem away from the residence premises will not be covered for the resulting damage. However, a loss is covered if power is interrupted by an insured peril that occurs on the premises. These examples help to illustrate this exclusion:

- A storm causes power lines to break ten miles from the insured's home. The loss of electrical power causes the food in the insured's freezer to thaw and spoil. Coverage for this loss is excluded because the power failure occurred off the residence premises.
- A windstorm causes a tree on the insured's property to fall, breaking the electrical lines that enter the house. The loss of electrical power causes the food in the freezer to thaw and spoil. This loss is covered because it was caused by a covered peril (windstorm) on the residence premises.

Neglect

An insured is expected to use all reasonable means to protect property at the time of a loss and after a loss occurs. There is no coverage for losses that result from the insured's failure to provide this protection. As mentioned earlier, the insurer agrees to pay the cost of reasonable repairs under an additional coverage.

War

Property losses that result from war, including the discharge of nuclear weapons, are excluded.

Nuclear Hazard

Property losses that occur because of a nuclear hazard are excluded. A nuclear hazard is defined in the Section I—Conditions portion of the policy as any nuclear reaction, radiation, or contamination.

Intentional Loss

No coverage, for any insured, applies to a loss that any insured commits or conspires to commit with the intent to cause a loss. For example, if the named insured intentionally sets fire to his home (perhaps with the intent of collecting an insurance payment), his homeowners policy would not cover the loss. Even if only one insured (for example, the husband) was involved in the arson, no other insured (such as his wife) is entitled to coverage. Likewise, coverage is excluded if a teenager becomes angry at her parents and sets the house on fire, because the teenager is an insured.

Governmental Action

Property described in Coverages A, B, and C is not covered against the destruction, confiscation, or seizure by order of any governmental or public authority. For example, if law enforcement officials seize a policyholder's personal computer to search for files that might be related to a crime, the policyholder may not successfully submit a theft claim on the computer.

This exclusion does not preclude coverage for governmental action taken to prevent the spread of fire. If the insured's home is burned by a fire set by government authorities in order to limit a raging wildfire, a fire claim would be payable under the HO-3 policy.

The next three exclusions apply only to Coverage A—Dwelling and Coverage B—Other Structures. The policy excludes losses from these perils, but any ensuing loss is covered as long as the policy does not preclude coverage for that ensuing loss. Examples of covered ensuing losses are provided.

Weather Conditions

Weather is an excluded peril if it contributes to any of the previously excluded perils. Therefore, torrential rain that causes a mudslide would not be a covered peril, because earth movement (mudslide) is an excluded peril. However, if the weight of rain water collected after a heavy downpour on a roof causes the roof to collapse, coverage is provided because collapse caused by the weight of rain on a roof is covered as an additional coverage.

Acts or Decisions

Acts or decisions of other people, organizations, or governmental bodies that cause property damage are not covered. For example, if a city government grants building permits for buildings to be constructed over an unstable landfill, no coverage is provided when shifting soil causes a house to collapse. However, if an agency or organization responsible for the public water supply fails to provide water pressure to fire hydrants, and a home is destroyed because firefighters could not get water to extinguish a fire, the fire damage would be covered.

Faulty Workmanship

Damage that results from faulty construction, planning, or materials is excluded. The exclusions specifically listed are faulty planning, zoning, surveying, design specifications, workmanship, construction, renovation, materials, and maintenance. Thus, if an insured's house floods because rainwater is diverted into the house because faulty surveying led to a drainage problem, no coverage is provided. However, if faulty construction of a chimney in the insured's house results in an ensuing fire, the damage caused by the fire would be covered.

Section I—Conditions

The Section I—Conditions of the policy describe the conditions applying to Section I that both the policyholder and the insurer must meet. The conditions are important for several reasons. This section explains how property will be valued in the event of a loss. A claim representative would review this section to determine how losses to contents or buildings should be settled. After a property loss, an insurance agent might also review this section with an insured to explain the steps that will be taken in settling a loss.

Insurable Interest and Limit of Liability

The definition of "insured" encompasses many people. This Section I condition limits the maximum payment for any single loss to the applicable limits shown on the declarations page, regardless of the number of insureds who might have an **insurable interest** in the property. This condition further limits loss payment to any insured to the extent of that insured's insurable interest in the property at the time of the loss.

Insurable interest
Interest in property that exists if a person could suffer a financial loss if the property is damaged or destroyed or cannot be used.

Your Duties After Loss

This portion of the Section I—Conditions establishes the insured's duties after a property loss. The first sentences read:

> In case of a loss to covered property, we have no duty to provide coverage under this policy if the failure to comply with the following duties is prejudicial to us. These duties must be performed either by you, or your representative, or by an "insured" seeking coverage, if not you.

The cooperation of an insured is essential to the investigation, settlement, or defense of any claim. This wording makes it clear that the insurer can deny coverage when an insured fails to fulfill his or her contractual duties and this failure is harmful to the insurer.

In any given claim settlement, the insurer's claim representative might not require that all of the listed items be completed, but this clause entitles the representative to require these activities if he or she feels they are helpful in the loss settlement process. The listed duties follow:

a. *Give prompt notice:* After a loss has occurred, the insured must notify the insurance company or its agent promptly. No specific time frame is given.

b. *Notify the police:* If a loss is by theft, the insured must report the loss to the police.

c. *Notify the credit card, electronic fund transfer card company, or access device company:* If the loss involves a credit card or fund transfer card or access device, the insured must notify the company that issued the card or provides the service.

d. *Protect the property from further damage:* The insured must protect damaged property from further loss. If necessary, the insured must make reasonable repairs to protect the property. During this process, the insured must keep an accurate record of the expenses incurred for the repairs. These expenses are considered part of the loss. One of the additional coverages (reasonable repairs) applies to these expenses.

e. *Cooperate with the insurer:* The insured must cooperate with all reasonable requests of the insurer.

f. *Prepare an inventory:* The insured must prepare an inventory of the damaged personal property. That inventory should include (for each item) the quantity, description, value, and amount of the loss. Bills, receipts, and related documents that justify the amounts shown in the inventory must be attached.

Preparing an Inventory

It is difficult for most policyholders to complete an inventory after a substantial loss. Imagine a policyholder, after a large fire, for example, attempting to make a list of every item he or she owned, when the property was received, and how much it cost. Some insurers and producers encourage policyholders to make a videotaped inventory of their home every year and store the tape at a location other than the home. In the event of a loss, this video can help a policyholder prepare an inventory, verify the ownership of the items listed, and justify the values of the items.

---

g. *Verify the loss:* An insured is expected to cooperate with the insurer in the settlement of a loss. As often as the insurer requires, the insured must show the adjuster the damaged property, allow the insurer to make copies of records and documents, and submit to an examination under oath.

Proof of loss
Document that describes the details of the loss, property values, and interest(s) in the property.

h. *Sign a sworn proof of loss:* Within sixty days of the insurer's request, the insured is expected to sign a sworn **proof of loss**. This is a form provided by the insurer that establishes the time and cause of the loss, the insured's insurable interest in the property, other insurance that might cover the loss, the inventory of the damaged personal property, information supporting additional living expenses, and information regarding a credit card, fund transfer card, or access device loss.

Loss Settlement

This portion of the Section I—Conditions establishes how the amount that will be paid for property after a loss will be determined. There are two settlement methods: one method is established for Coverage C—personal property items and other miscellaneous items, and the other method is established for Coverage A or B—buildings and other structures.

> *Reminder*: The deductible amount shown on the declarations page is subtracted once from the total of all loss payable under Section I caused by a single loss event. (No deductible applies to two additional coverages—fire department service charge and credit cards, etc., as noted earlier in this chapter.)

Coverage C and Miscellaneous Items

Losses to personal property listed under Coverage C, as well as awnings, carpeting, appliances, antennas, outdoor equipment, structures that are not buildings, and grave markers or mausoleums, are settled at the *lesser* of the following:

- Actual cash value (ACV) at the time of the loss
- The amount required to repair or replace the items

> The *personal property replacement cost endorsement* (HO 04 90) changes the loss settlement basis for Coverage C and miscellaneous items to replacement cost instead of ACV.

For example, a claim representative working with an insured who has a damaged range as the result of a kitchen fire might first determine the ACV of the range. This valuation can be determined by checking to see what the stove would cost new and then subtracting a percentage of that value based on depreciation. Depreciation of a range is largely determined by age and also by the circumstances of its use. For example, if a new kitchen range costs $800 but the damaged one was five years old, the adjuster might calculate that the old range depreciated 50 percent (appliances are sometimes estimated to have a useful life of ten years). The ACV of the stove would then be $800 × 0.50, or $400. If the claim representative then determined that it would cost $500 to repair the range, he or she would settle the loss for the lesser amount of $400.

Coverages A and B

The amount payable for a building loss might be one of three amounts: (1) the replacement cost, (2) the actual cash value, or (3) an amount that falls between these two numbers. It all depends on how the limit of insurance compares to the replacement cost value of the damaged building at the time of the loss.

The methods for determining the loss settlement for a building are as follows:

- *If the limit of insurance is 80 percent or more of the replacement cost:* The insurer will pay for the replacement cost of the damage up to the limit of coverage.

- *If the limit of insurance is less than 80 percent of the replacement cost:* The insurer will pay the *greater* of (1) the ACV of the damage or (2) the proportion of the cost to repair or replace the damage that the limit of insurance bears to 80 percent of the replacement cost. This second method is sometimes easier to understand as a formula:

$$\frac{\text{Limit of insurance}}{80\% \times \text{Replacement cost}} \times \text{Replacement cost of the loss} = \text{Loss payment}$$

Loss Settlement Example

The following are examples of how the loss settlement for a dwelling would be determined. (These simple examples ignore any deductible that might apply.)

Example 1. Dwelling limit equals or exceeds 80 percent of the replacement cost: An insured has a home with a $200,000 replacement cost and an HO-3 with a Coverage A limit of $180,000. Lightning strikes the central air conditioning unit and destroys it beyond repair. The unit has a replacement cost of $5,000 and is five years old. The dwelling is insured for more than 80 percent of replacement cost ($180,000 is 90 percent of $200,000).

The insured would receive $5,000 to replace the unit.

Example 2. Dwelling limit is less than 80 percent of the replacement cost: If this same insured has an HO-3 with a Coverage A limit of $100,000 (50 percent of the replacement cost), the insured's coverage would be below the 80 percent replacement cost requirement, and the second loss settlement method would be used. The insured would then receive the *greater* of the following:

- The ACV of the air conditioner. The ACV would be the $5,000 replacement cost minus depreciation. If a central air conditioner has a useful life of ten years and is now five years old, this air conditioner would depreciate by 50 percent. The ACV would equal $2,500.

- The limit developed by the formula is:

$$\frac{\$100,000}{80\% \times \$200,000} \times \$5,000 = \$3,125$$

The insured would receive the greater amount of $3,125.

Except for small losses (generally under $2,500), the insurer will not pay more than the actual cash value until repairs are completed. An insured who has not decided whether to rebuild can initially seek loss settlement on an actual cash value basis and has up to 180 days after the loss to tell the insurer he or she intends to complete the repairs and make settlement on a replacement cost basis.

The insured is not required to rebuild a damaged or destroyed building on the same location. However, if the building is rebuilt on different premises, the insurer will pay no more than it would if the building were repaired or replaced at the original premises.

Regardless of the method used to determine the loss settlement amount, the limit of coverage shown on the declarations page is the maximum amount that will be paid for any loss.

> The *additional limits of liability for Coverages A, B, C, and D endorsement* (HO 04 11) increases the Coverage A limit to equal the current replacement cost of the dwelling if that amount exceeds the limit appearing on the declarations page. The limits of liability for Coverages B, C, and D will be increased by the same percentage applied to Coverage A.

Loss to a Pair or Set

Often, items that are in pairs or sets are more valuable together than the items are individually. Because of the increased value of pairs or sets, a policy provision establishes the amount an insurer will pay if an item that is part of a pair or set is damaged or lost.

For example, Cindy has a custom-made brass lantern on each side of her driveway. The matching lanterns were recently fabricated at a cost of $2,000. As a pair, the lanterns have an ACV of $2,000. One lantern, by itself—not part of a pair, would have an ACV of $300 or could be exactly reproduced for $1,500. If one of Cindy's lanterns is stolen, the insurer can elect to do either of the following:

- Replace the missing lantern for $1,500 and restore the pair to its original value.
- Pay Cindy the difference between the ACV of the lanterns as a pair and the ACV of the remaining single lantern ($1,700).

Replacing the missing lantern for $1,500 is the logical choice for the insurer in this case. However, if the missing lantern could not be replaced—perhaps the craftsman who made it has died—the insurer might have no choice other than to pay $1,700 to compensate Cindy for the value lost. The deductible would be subtracted in each example.

Appraisal

If the insured and the insurer cannot agree on the amount of a loss, this segment of the Section I—Conditions outlines a method for resolving the disagreement. This method is commonly called the **appraisal** process and is performed as follows:

- The insurer and the policyholder each choose an appraiser to prepare an estimate of the value of the loss. Each party pays for its own appraiser.

Appraisal
A procedure, prescribed by a provision in a property insurance policy, for the insured and the insurer to settle disputes regarding the value of a covered loss.

- If the estimates differ, the two appraisers submit their differences to an umpire. The umpire is an impartial individual (often another appraiser or a judge) who resolves the differences. An agreement by any two of the three will set the amount of loss. The insurer and the policyholder share the cost of the umpire.

Other Insurance and Service Agreement

If two or more insurance policies cover the same loss, this condition explains that the loss will be shared proportionally by all policies. The following example demonstrates how this situation might occur.

Other Insurance

John Green has an HO-3 with an $80,000 Coverage A limit. Maryanne Green, John's wife, did not realize that John had purchased a homeowners policy. She also purchased a homeowners policy with a $120,000 Coverage A limit.

A fire destroys the home, which has a $100,000 replacement cost at the time of the loss. After the fire, the Greens discover that two policies exist to cover their home. A total of $200,000 in coverage is available ($80,000 from John's policy plus $120,000 from Maryanne's policy).

The two policies will share the loss proportionally as follows:

- The insurer that issued John's policy will pay 40% of the loss ($80,000/$200,000 = 0.40) or $40,000.

- The insurer that issued Maryanne's policy will pay 60% of the loss ($120,000/$200,000 = 0.60) or $60,000.

An insured home or item of personal property might also be covered by some type of service plan, property restoration plan, home warranty, or service warranty agreement. The homeowners policy makes it clear that homeowners insurance coverage applies as excess over any amounts payable under any such agreement. For example, Marcy's new big-screen TV is covered by a one-year service warranty that does not exclude lightning damage. If lightning strikes the power lines near Marcy's house and damages the TV, her homeowners insurer will pay nothing, even though lightning is a covered peril. The service agreement is expected to cover Marcy's loss.

Suit Against Us

An insured may not bring legal action against the insurance company unless all policy provisions have been complied with. Any legal action must be started within two years of the loss.

Our Option

Usually, insurers settle claims with money, and the insured is responsible for repairing or replacing the property. However, the insurer reserves the right to repair or replace damaged property with similar property. Sometimes insurance companies exercise this right because they can purchase repairs or obtain replacement items at a deep discount. Repairing or replacing property is the *insurer's* option. The insured cannot require the insurer to repair or replace damaged property.

Loss Payment

The insurer will adjust all losses with the policyholder or spouse (unless another person is named in the policy or is legally entitled to receive payment). A loss is payable sixty days after the insurer receives a proof of loss and either (1) the insurer and the policyholder have reached an agreement or (2) a court judgment or an appraisal award has been entered. (Some states require a different time period.)

Abandonment of Property

If the insured abandons the property after it is damaged or destroyed, the insurer need not take over responsibility for it. An insured might prefer to take the insurance proceeds, walk away from a burned-out home in a neighborhood where property values have declined, and turn the property over to the insurance company, rather than remain liable for the damaged building, but the insurance company is not obligated to accept the property.

Mortgage Clause

This condition establishes the following rights of the mortgagee listed on the declarations page:

* If a loss occurs to property covered by Coverages A or B, the loss will be payable jointly to the mortgagee and the policyholder. Typically, the mortgagee relies on this right to ensure that the policyholder uses the money to repair the property. The mortgagee is satisfied as long as the property is repaired and the policyholder continues to make mortgage payments.

* A mortgagee has rights that are independent of the policyholder's rights. If the insurer denies the policyholder's loss (if, for example, arson by the policyholder is discovered), the mortgagee retains the right to collect from the insurer its insurable interest in the property.

* If the insurer cancels or nonrenews the policy, the insurer must mail notice to the mortgagee (in addition to notice sent to the insured) at least ten days before the cancellation or nonrenewal.

No Benefit to Bailee

A bailee who holds the property of an insured is responsible for the care of that property. For example, a dry cleaner who negligently damages an insured's clothing cannot avoid responsibility for the damage because the insured has coverage under the homeowners policy.

Nuclear Hazard Clause

This condition defines the nuclear hazard, for which coverage is excluded in the Section I—Exclusions. Excluded nuclear hazards encompass any resulting radiation, contamination, explosion, or smoke. A direct loss by fire resulting from the nuclear hazard is covered.

Recovered Property

If the insurer pays a claim for the loss of property, and the insurer or the policyholder later recovers the property, the policyholder has the option of taking the property and returning the claim payment or keeping the claim payment and allowing the insurer to take over the property.

Volcanic Eruption Period

All volcanic eruptions that occur within a seventy-two hour period are considered to be one volcanic eruption. If multiple eruptions should occur within that period, only one coverage limit and one deductible would apply.

Policy Period

Coverage applies only to losses that occur during the policy period.

Concealment or Fraud

No insured is covered under this policy if *any* insured conceals or misrepresents any material information, engages in fraudulent conduct, or makes false statements relating to the insurance. This condition applies whether the conduct occurred before or after a loss.

Loss Payable Clause

A homeowner who uses leased or rented furniture, for example, might be requested to have the furniture leasing company named as an additional insured for this property. This information would appear in the policy declarations. In this policy provision, the insurer agrees to include the named loss payee when a claim is paid involving that property. Normally, this means that a claim draft would be payable to both the named insured and the loss payee. The loss payee is also entitled to notification if the policy is canceled or nonrenewed.

SUMMARY

The homeowners policy is a versatile insurance contract that provides a broad set of coverages designed to meet the property and liability needs of many individuals and families.

This chapter explores Section I—Property Coverages of the ISO homeowners special form (HO-3) in detail. Endorsements that can be used to modify the coverages discussed are introduced in shaded boxes; these endorsements are described in greater detail in Chapter 7.

The HO-3 policy is divided into two major sections. Section I specifies the property covered, the perils for which property is covered, and the exclusions and conditions that apply to property coverages. Section II—Liability Coverages is the topic of Chapter 6.

The HO-3 policy form is attached to the declarations page, which provides essential information about the insured, the property covered, and the limits of coverage provided. The HO-3 begins with the policy agreement, which states that the insurer will provide coverage if the policyholder pays the premium and complies with the policy provisions. Following the agreement are specific definitions of important words that appear in the policy in quotation marks.

Section I includes the following property coverages:

- Coverage A—Dwelling
- Coverage B—Other Structures
- Coverage C—Personal Property
- Coverage D—Loss of Use

Following a description of the items covered under Coverages A, B, C, and D, the policy lists eleven additional coverages, which include such coverages as debris removal; reasonable repairs; and trees, shrubs, and other plants. The chapter included a chart showing the additional coverages and how they apply.

The next segment of the policy shows the perils insured against in Section I. For Coverages A and B, the covered perils are known as "special-form coverage," which means that any direct physical loss to described property is covered as long as it is not specifically excluded in the policy. Because this coverage is so broad, the policy lists a number of excluded perils. The perils insured against for Coverage C are "named perils," which means that only losses caused by perils specifically listed in the policy are covered.

Some perils are excluded for both buildings, other structures, and personal property, and these are specifically listed in the next segment of the policy. Following these exclusions are the Section I conditions, which describe the conditions applying to the property coverages that both the policyholder and the insurer must meet. The conditions section also includes a loss settlement condition, which explains how property will be valued in the event of a loss.

CHAPTER NOTES

1. *FC&S Bulletins*, Personal Lines Volume (Cincinnati, Ohio: The National Underwriter Company, 2000), p. A. 4-3.
2. *FC&S Bulletins*, Personal Lines Volume, p. A. 4-6.

Chapter 6

Direct Your Learning

Homeowners Insurance: Section II and Sections I and II Conditions

After learning the subject matter of this chapter, for all ISO homeowners forms (Homeowners 2000 series, ©1999), you should be able to:

■ Explain who is covered under Section II coverages.

■ Explain what is covered and what is limited or excluded under Section II—Liability Coverages.

■ Given a case involving a loss,

  • Explain whether the loss is covered by Section II.

  • Determine the amount the insurer would pay for covered losses.

■ Explain the effect of conditions that apply to both Section I and Section II.

Develop Your Perspective

What are the main topics covered in the chapter?

This chapter continues the examination of the homeowners policy. Section II of the policy includes personal liability and medical payments to others coverages. Section I and II—Conditions are also examined.

Compare first-party Section I and third-party Section II homeowners coverages.

- How does the coverage provided by each of these sections protect an insured from loss?
- How do the "insureds" covered by each of these sections differ?

Why is it important to know these topics?

The homeowners policy provides a broad package of coverages that most individuals and families who own homes require. Section II coverages are an essential part of that package. These coverages protect homeowners from potentially devastating losses. To apply Section II coverages effectively, you must thoroughly understand the exclusions that clarify the coverages.

Contrast the personal liability and medical payments to others coverages.

- What events trigger coverage?
- Who might receive payments?
- What losses are excluded?

How can you use this information?

Analyze your own homeowners policy or the policy of a family member:

- Do the exclusions in Section II eliminate coverage for loss exposures present in the household or the activities of family members?
- Can an endorsement be attached to the homeowners policy to provide coverage for excluded loss exposures?

Chapter 6

Homeowners Insurance: Section II and Sections I and II Conditions

Chapter 5 introduced the homeowners policy and explored in depth Section I—Property Coverages of ISO's HO-3 policy. This chapter examines the remainder of the ISO homeowners policy. Section II of the policy, which is identical in all ISO homeowners policy forms, addresses coverages for personal liability and medical payments to others. Like Section I, Section II has additional coverages and conditions. Also like Section I, the Section II coverages can be modified by endorsement. These endorsements and their basic content are introduced in shaded boxes in this chapter the same way endorsements were presented in Chapter 5. A more detailed discussion of the endorsements appears in Chapter 7.

This chapter ends by examining the final segment of the homeowners policy, Section I and II—Conditions, which apply to the entire policy.

Students reading this chapter will find it helpful to refer to a copy of the complete HO-3 policy as they read.

SECTION II COVERAGES

Section II—Liability Coverages consist of two principal coverages, plus a few additional coverages:

- Coverage E—Personal Liability
- Coverage F—Medical Payments to Others
- Section II—Additional Coverages, also included in this section, provide four miscellaneous liability-related coverages.

The Section II coverages differ from the Section I coverages in three significant ways:

1. Section I includes **first party** insurance that provides coverage for loss to property owned or used by an insured. Section II provides **third party** coverages; the insurance company pays a claimant who is injured or whose property is damaged by an insured. Damages for claims covered under Section II coverages are not payable *to* an insured; rather, they are paid *on behalf of* an insured.

First party
The insured.

Third party
Someone not party to the insurance contract who might assert a claim against a first party.

2. A deductible applies to most of the coverages provided under Section I, but no deductible applies to Section II.

3. Section I contains detailed descriptions of covered property and perils. Section II contains much less detail, broadly describing personal liability and medical payments to others coverages and then clarifying coverage through exclusions.

Coverage E—Personal Liability

All homeowners policies automatically include Coverage E—Personal Liability for a basic limit generally set at $100,000 per occurrence. This limit can be increased for an additional premium by showing the higher limit on the declarations page; no endorsement is required.

Who Is an Insured for Liability Coverage?

Bodily injury (BI)
(as used in HO policies)
Bodily harm, sickness, or disease, including required care, loss of services, and death that result.

Property damage (PD)
(as used in HO policies)
Physical injury to, destruction of, or loss of use of tangible property.

Personal liability coverage is provided if a claim is made or a suit is brought against an insured because of **bodily injury** or **property damage** allegedly caused by the insured. "Insured" has a specific meaning, which is given in the definitions section of the homeowners policy.

> The *personal injury endorsement* (HO 24 82) adds a definition for "personal injury" and modifies the liability coverage of the homeowners policy to include not only bodily injury and property damage but also "personal injuries" such as libel, slander, malicious prosecution, wrongful eviction, and violating a person's right of privacy.

The definition of "insured" is broader for Section II—liability than it is for Section I—property. The following are included as insureds for Section II coverages:

- The policyholder (the named insured) shown on the declarations page and the named insured's spouse if a resident of the same household. The policyholder and resident spouse are identified as "you" in the policy.

- Residents of the household who are relatives of the named insured or spouse.

- Residents of the household who are under the age of twenty-one and in the care of the named insured or resident relatives.

- A full-time student who resided in the household before moving out to attend school. This person must be either under the age of twenty-one and in the care of the named insured or resident relatives, or a relative of the named insured under the age of twenty-four. The policyholder's twenty-two-year-old daughter who is a full-time college student would therefore qualify as an "insured."

- Any person or organization legally responsible for animals or watercraft that are covered by the policy and owned by a person defined in the first three bulleted items above. For example, a neighbor who walks the named insured's dog while the insured is on vacation is protected as an insured for liability coverage under the named insured's homeowners policy if the dog causes an injury while in the neighbor's care.

- Anyone employed by a person defined in the first three bulleted items, with respect to any motor vehicle covered by the policy. For example, a gardener who accidentally hits a neighbor's car, while using the named insured's riding lawn mower and mowing the named insured's lawn, is an insured for liability coverage under the named insured's homeowners policy.

- Other persons using any vehicle covered by the policy on an insured location, with the consent of the named insured or spouse, are insureds for liability coverage. For example, if a neighbor takes the named insured's all-terrain vehicle for a test drive in the named insured's yard and accidentally strikes and injures a child, the neighbor becomes an insured for liability coverage under the named insured's homeowners policy.

Events That Trigger Liability Coverage

The homeowners policy provides personal liability coverage, up to the policy limit, for damages for which an insured is legally liable. This coverage, which applies anywhere in the world, covers bodily injury and property damage arising from the insured's activities or premises. In most instances, such liability arises from the insured's negligence.

Liability might be obvious from the circumstances surrounding a loss. For example, if a policyholder's poodle bites and seriously injures a neighbor's one-year-old child who is playing in the child's own yard, the insured will almost certainly be held liable for the resulting injuries and damages. In this example, a claim notice to the insurance company will probably be sufficient for the insurer to investigate and settle the loss. However, if the dog bites a teenager who enters the insured's fenced yard and mistreats the animal, the insured's liability might be questionable. In the second example, the insurer might deny the claim on the grounds that the insured does not appear to be liable for the injury. If the injured teenager brings a suit against the insured, the insurer would be obligated to provide a defense and pay damages if the insured is, indeed, found to be liable.

Defense Costs Coverage

In addition to paying up to the limit of liability, the insurer pays defense costs if an insured is presented with a lawsuit that involves a claim that is covered under the policy. This defense cost coverage is provided even if the suit is groundless, false, or fraudulent. Consider the preceding example regarding the teenager allegedly bitten by the insured's dog; the dog might have been incapable of causing such an injury (perhaps the dog was so old that it no longer had teeth). The insured would still have to respond to the suit, which usually requires retaining an attorney. The defense of a suit can cost thousands of dollars. The insurance company will provide this defense for an occurrence to which the coverage would apply.

The insurer retains the right to investigate and settle any claim in a way that the insurer decides is appropriate. Continuing the example of the teenager and the dog, the insurance company could attempt to show, by defending the case in court, that the insured is not liable for damages. Alternatively, the insurance company could attempt to settle the claim with the teenager, perhaps by offering to pay $500 for the teenager's injury. The insured might not agree with a decision to pay the teenager for injuries that seem to result from the teenager's own acts, but the policy makes it clear that the insurer has the right to determine what is appropriate in settling a liability claim or suit.

Suppose, rather, that the dog's bite led to facial disfigurement and a large claim for damages. The insurer cannot simply offer to pay the policy limit and abandon the insured. Rather, the insurer is required to defend the insured against damages resulting from this occurrence until a settlement or judgment is reached. However, once the insurer has *paid* a judgment or settlement that exhausts the total limit of Coverage E—Personal Liability, the insurer is not required to provide a further defense. Suppose the teenager claims $250,000 in damages, and the homeowners policy has a $100,000 limit. The insurer cannot simply pay $100,000 and avoid further litigation. Rather, the insurer must defend the insured until a settlement is reached. If, say, the teenager ultimately agrees to settle the claim for $150,000, the insurer's obligations end when it pays defense costs and *pays* the teenager $100,000 in damages (the policy limit).

Coverage F—Medical Payments to Others

Medical payments to others
A homeowners coverage for necessary medical expenses incurred by others (not an insured) within three years of an injury.

Medical payments to others covers the necessary medical expenses incurred by others (not an insured) within three years of an injury. These medical expenses include reasonable charges for medical, surgical, X-ray, dental, ambulance, hospital, professional nursing, and funeral services and for prosthetic devices.

Medical Payments Coverage—Avoiding Confusion

Medical payments to others is often referred to as simply "medical payments" within the insurance industry. This abbreviation can cause confusion, because the personal auto policy and the homeowners policy differ greatly in regard to medical payments coverage.

- The personal auto policy *medical payments coverage* protects the insured, family members, and other passengers of the insured automobile.

- The homeowners *medical payments to others coverage* is a third-party coverage that applies to others, but provides *no* protection for injuries to the named insured and residents of the named insured's household.

Referring to the homeowners coverage by its full name, *medical payments to others,* creates less confusion.

In a way, medical payments to others coverage overlaps with bodily injury liability coverage. However, liability coverage applies only when an insured is legally responsible for damages. Claims for medical payments are often paid when the insured feels a moral obligation to another person, although the insured is not negligent and has no legal responsibility. In other cases, a bodily injury claim involves a relatively small amount of money, and paying it as a medical payments to others claim keeps matters simple by eliminating any need to determine whether an insured was responsible for the injuries.

Coverage F—Medical Payments to Others is automatically included in all homeowners policies for a limit generally set at $1,000 per person for a single accident. This limit can be increased for an additional premium. The limit for Coverage F is shown on the declarations page.

Who Might Receive Medical Payments to Others?

Medical payments to others covers the necessary medical expenses incurred by others (not an insured) within three years of an injury. It does not apply to the named insured or other regular residents of the household except "residence employees" (a discussion follows to explain this term).

Events That Trigger Medical Payments to Others Coverage

Medical payments to others coverage differs from personal liability coverage because there is no requirement that the insured be legally liable in order for medical payments to others coverage to apply. Legal liability *is* required for personal liability coverage to apply.

Coverage F applies to people who are injured in the following situations:

- A person is on an "insured location" (a discussion follows to explain this term) with the permission of an insured. Permission to be on the property might be implied permission. For example, a neighbor might walk into the insured's yard without a specific invitation but with implied permission because the neighbors often visit each other.

- A person off the insured location is injured because of conditions on the insured location; for example, an insured is burning leaves and allows the smoke and flames to spread to a neighbor's yard, causing injury to the neighbor.

- A person off the insured location is injured by an insured's activities; for example, an insured hits a golf ball while on a golf course and causes injury to another golfer.

- A person off the insured location is injured by a residence employee of the insured during the course of employment; for example, the insured's gardener cuts a tree limb that drops and injures a neighbor's child in the adjacent yard.

- A person off the insured location is injured by an animal owned by or in the care of an insured. For example, an insured who is riding her horse through the neighborhood allows children to pet her horse. The horse kicks and injures a child.

Residence Employees Versus Other Employees

Coverage F—Medical Payments to Others applies to insured "residence employees," but not to other "employees." Both terms are defined. **Residence employees** include domestic workers whose duties relate to maintaining or using the household premises or performing domestic or household services. This definition clarifies that a residence employee is a person whose duties relate to the insured's residence. There is no requirement that the employee reside at the premises. A part-time gardener, babysitter, plumber, or maid might be considered a residence employee. A temporary employee substituting for a residence employee is not included in this definition.

Four exclusions discussed later—locations that are not insured, motor vehicles, watercraft, and aircraft—do not apply to bodily injury sustained by a "residence employee" in the course of employment by an insured. Therefore, Coverages E and F will cover a residence employee's injuries in some situations.

An **employee**, as defined, is an employee of an insured who is not a residence employee. If a freelance writer hires a secretary to work in his home and transcribe some manuscripts, the secretary is an "employee," but not a "residence employee," so far as the writer's homeowners policy is concerned.

Insured Locations

An "insured location" is a defined term in the HO-3 policy definitions section. Eight locations are included in this definition. Exhibit 6-1 provides a list of these locations as well as examples.

Exclusions

Section II—Liability Coverages begins with a complex set of exclusions for losses arising out of motor vehicles, watercraft, aircraft, and hovercraft, as well as exceptions to the exclusions. With respect to all these vehicles or craft, there is no coverage for bodily injury, property damage, or medical claims arising out of:

- The ownership, maintenance, occupancy, operation, use, loading, and unloading of a motor vehicle or craft by any person unless it appears in a specific exception to the exclusion. Some observers have noted that this exclusion would preclude coverage for "host liability" claims against a policyholder that might result from an incident in which a guest of the insured becomes inebriated at a party at the insured's house and is later involved in an auto accident on the way home.
- Negligent entrustment, by an insured, of an excluded motor vehicle or craft.
- An insured's failure to supervise, or negligently supervising, a person.
- An insured's "vicarious liability" for the actions of a child or minor.

Residence employees
Domestic workers whose duties include maintaining or using the household premises or performing domestic or household services.

Employee (as used in HO policies)
An employee of an insured who is not a residence employee.

EXHIBIT 6-1

Definition of "Insured Location" in the HO-3

Insured Locations	Examples
a. The residence premises	"Residence premises" is defined as the insured's home, which might be a one-family dwelling (or a two- to four-family dwelling where the insured resides in at least one of the units). The insured's home that is shown in the declarations, and also the other structures and grounds, are included.
b. The part of other premises, other structures, and grounds used by the policyholder as a residence that is either shown in the declarations or acquired during the policy period	Such other premises might be the insured's vacation home listed in the declarations or a beach house acquired during the policy period.
c. Any premises used by the policyholder in connection with the residence premises or in connection with insured location b. described above	Premises used in connection with the residence might be a garage or a self-storage unit rented by the insured.
d. The part of a premises not owned by an insured and where an insured is temporarily residing	A temporary residence might be a hotel room used for a weekend or a cottage rented for a vacation.
e. Vacant land other than farmland that an insured owns or rents	Vacant land would include undeveloped land owned by an insured. In this context, the term "vacant" generally means free from any man-made structure or activity.[1]
f. Land owned by or rented to an insured on which a one-, two-, three-, or four-family dwelling is being constructed as the insured's residence	While an insured is constructing a new residence, the land owned for that purpose is an insured location.
g. Individual or family cemetery plots or burial vaults of an insured	The cemetery plots or vaults owned by an insured are considered insured locations.
h. Any part of a premises occasionally rented to an insured for nonbusiness use	A hall rented by the insureds for their daughter's wedding reception is an insured location.

[1] *FC&S Bulletins*, Personal Lines Volume, Dwellings (Cincinnati, Ohio: The National Underwriter Company, 2000), p. A.2–5.

Motor Vehicles

As defined, a motor vehicle is a self-propelled vehicle, including an attached trailer. Most excluded motor vehicle exposures can be insured under a personal auto policy (PAP). Coverage does not apply to motor vehicles that:

- Must, by law, be registered for use on public roads or property.
- Are involved in an organized race.
- Are rented to others.
- Are used to carry persons or cargo for a charge.
- Are used for any business purpose, except for motorized golf carts used on a golf course.

Unless the vehicle is excluded under one of the preceding categories, it might be covered under one of the exceptions to the motor vehicle exclusion. Exhibit 6-2 provides a list of covered motor vehicle exposures, as well as examples.

> The *low power recreational "motor vehicles" endorsement* (HO 24 13) and *snowmobile endorsement* (HO 24 64) can be attached to a homeowners policy to provide liability coverage for some motorized vehicles when used off the insured premises.

EXHIBIT 6-2

Motor Vehicle Exposures Covered by Section II of the HO-3 Policy

Covered Motor Vehicle Liability Exposures	Examples
Motor vehicle in dead storage on an insured location	An unlicensed antique auto is stored in the insured's garage.
Motor vehicle used solely to service an insured's residence	A riding lawn mower is used to maintain the insured's yard.
Motor vehicle designed for assisting people who are handicapped	A motorized wheelchair, or a three- or four-wheeled power scooter, is used by a handicapped person.
Motorized vehicle · designed for recreational use off public roads, and · *not owned* by an insured	An insured borrows an unlicensed dune buggy for a ride through the sand dunes.
Motorized vehicle · designed for recreational use off public roads, and · *owned* by an insured and *on an insured location*	An insured owns an unlicensed dirt bike used by the insured's grandchild on the insured's property.
Motorized golf cart, not capable of exceeding 25 mph, owned by an insured: · used to play golf on a golf course, or · legally used within a private residential association	The insured lives in a gated retirement community and owns a golf cart used for visiting and running errands within the community and also for playing golf on the community's golf course.
Trailer not towed by, hitched to, or carried on a motor vehicle	An insured has parked the family's travel trailer at a campsite for use on a two-week vacation. Once the trailer is unhitched, the liability exposure is covered under the homeowners policy because it is no longer a "motor vehicle," as defined, and therefore is not subject to the motor vehicle exclusion.

Watercraft

In general, small, low-powered watercraft, or watercraft the insured uses but does not own, are included for Section II coverage. Watercraft not covered by the homeowners policy can be insured by a watercraft policy (discussed in Chapter 9).

The watercraft exclusions are similar to the motor vehicle exclusions previously addressed. Coverage does not apply to watercraft that:

- Are involved in an organized race. This exclusion does not apply to sailboats or predicted log cruises. A predicted log contest is like a road rally that takes place on the water. Boaters predict the time their boats will take to get from point to point on a designated course. It is an organized event that tests accuracy, not speed.
- Are rented to others.
- Are used to carry persons or cargo for a charge.
- Are used for any business purpose.

Unless the craft is excluded under one of the preceding categories, it might be covered under one of the exceptions to the watercraft exclusion. Exhibit 6-3 provides a list of covered watercraft exposures as well as examples.

> The *watercraft endorsement* (HO 24 75) provides Coverages E and F for scheduled watercraft.

Aircraft

The homeowners policy flatly excludes all aircraft liability. Because model airplanes or hobby aircraft that do not carry people or cargo are excluded from the "aircraft" definition, they are covered. If an insured flies her radio-controlled model airplane through a neighbor's picture window, the resulting liability claim would be covered.

Hovercraft

As with aircraft, hovercraft liability is flatly excluded. Hovercraft are self-propelled motorized ground effect vehicles. A hovercraft travels over land or water on a cushion of air trapped in a chamber beneath the craft by a flexible curtain, or skirt. The air chamber is continuously supplied with air under pressure to replace the air escaping from the bottom edge of the chamber. Air, usually from a propeller, is also used to propel the vehicle forward.

Other Exclusions That Apply to Both Coverage E—Personal Liability and Coverage F—Medical Payments to Others

Coverages E and F provide very broad coverage to protect the insured from the financial consequences of causing injury to others or damage to their property. However, some injuries and damage are beyond the scope of the homeowners policy or are more effectively covered elsewhere; these types of exposures are excluded from coverage. The following section describes bodily injury and property damage exposures that are excluded for both Coverages E and F.

EXHIBIT 6-3

Watercraft Exposures Covered by Section II of the HO-3 Policy

Covered Watercraft Liability Exposures	Examples
1. Watercraft that are stored	A 30-foot sailboat stored out of the water at a marina for the winter
2. Sailboats (with or without auxiliary power) shorter than 26 feet	A 17-foot catamaran owned by the insured
3. Sailboats (with or without auxiliary power) longer than 26 feet *not owned by or rented to an insured*	A 32-foot sailboat the insured borrowed from her brother for a vacation
4. Inboard or inboard-outdrive watercraft with engines of 50 horsepower or less that are *not owned* by an insured	A 50-horsepower jet ski rented by an insured
5. Inboard or inboard-outdrive watercraft of more than 50 horsepower *not owned by or rented to* an insured	A 150-horsepower inboard motor boat borrowed from a neighbor
6. Watercraft with one or more outboard engines or motors with 25 total horsepower or less	A fishing boat with a 15-horsepower motor, owned by the insured
7. Watercraft with one or more outboard engines or motors with more than 25 total horsepower that are *not owned* by an insured	A boat with a 75-horsepower outboard motor, borrowed from a friend
8. Watercraft with outboard engines or motors of more than 25 total horsepower owned by an insured if acquired during the policy period. If the insured acquires such watercraft before the policy period, they are covered only if the insured: • declares them at the policy inception, or • reports the intention to insure them within 45 days of acquiring them	A new boat with a 100-horsepower outboard motor purchased by the insured after the effective date of the policy

Expected or Intended Injury or Damage

Section II provides liability protection to the insured for a covered *occurrence* and medical payments to others coverage for injuries resulting from an *accident*. "Accident" is not defined, but the definitions section of the policy defines **occurrence** as follows:

Occurrence

Accident that results in bodily injury or property damage, including continuous or repeated exposure to the same general harmful conditions.

> "Occurrence" means an accident, including continuous or repeated exposure to substantially the same general harmful conditions, which results, during the policy period, in: a. "bodily injury"; or b. "property damage".

An occurrence must be accidental; intended harm committed by one or more insureds is not covered. In other words, if an insured intentionally injures another person, coverage is not provided.

Questions arise when an action is intended, but the resulting injury or damage is not expected. For example, an insured might intentionally punch a person but not intend to permanently disfigure the person. The exclusion in the homeowners policy makes it clear that intentional acts are not covered, even if the results of the act are more serious than was intended. However, coverage is not precluded in cases of self-defense, involving reasonable force to protect either people or property:

> **Coverage E—Personal Liability** and **Coverage F—Medical Payments to Others** do not apply to "bodily injury" or "property damage":
>
> a. Which is expected or intended by an "insured" even if the resulting "bodily injury" or "property damage":
>
> (1) Is of a different kind, quality or degree than initially expected or intended; or
>
> (2) Is sustained by a different person, entity, real or personal property than initially expected or intended.
>
> However, this exclusion…does not apply to "bodily injury" resulting from the use of reasonable force by an "insured" to protect persons or property.

Business

The business exclusion is designed to preclude coverage for bodily injury or property damage arising out of the business activities of any insured, but to provide coverage for occasional or part-time activities such as delivering newspapers, maintaining lawns, washing cars, or babysitting.

The business exclusion explicitly states that the policy provides no coverage for bodily injury or property damage relating to a business operated from the residence premises or another insured location.

"Business" is broadly defined in the definitions section of the policy to include a full-time, part-time, or occasional trade, profession, or occupation, or any other activity engaged in for money or other compensation, except:

- Activities for which the insured received $2,000 or less during the year preceding the policy period
- Volunteer activities
- Home daycare services not involving compensation, but possibly involving an exchange of services
- Home daycare services rendered to a relative

As an example, an insured who operates a beauty salon in her home would not have liability coverage under the homeowners policy for activities involving the operation of the salon.

The policy contains some exceptions to this broad business exclusion. Unless otherwise excluded, coverage is available for an "insured" under the age of twenty-one involved in a part-time or occasional, self-employed business with no employees. Thus, coverage is provided for a teenager's newspaper delivery, children's street-side lemonade stands, and the like.

Renting property to others qualifies as a business, as defined. However, three exceptions to this exclusion allow for some common rental situations. These exceptions, along with examples of situations in which coverage would apply, follow:

1. Rental of an insured location on an occasional basis is a covered exposure if the location is used only as a residence. For example, a homeowner lives in a town that hosts a popular annual arts festival. During the festival, the homeowner leaves on vacation and rents her home to festival attendees. Section II coverage would be provided to the insured during the time the home is rented.

2. Rental of part of an insured location as a residence is a covered exposure, as long as the occupying family takes no more than two roomers or boarders in a single family unit. For example, a homeowner renting out an apartment in the residence (perhaps an apartment over an attached garage) would have Section II coverage arising out of the normal rental of that apartment.

3. Rental of part of an insured location is a covered exposure if it is used only as an office or a school, studio, or private garage. For example, an insured could rent out a room or an apartment in the residence for use as an office, and Section II coverage would apply.

Several endorsements are available to provide limited liability coverage for certain business activities of the insured:

*   The *permitted incidental occupancies—residence premises endorsement* (HO 04 42) extends Section I and Section II coverages for a business on the residence premises.

*   The *home business insurance coverage endorsement* (HO 07 01) provides a broader range of property and liability coverages than the above endorsement for a business usually conducted from the insured's home.

*   The *business pursuits endorsement* (HO 24 71) provides Section II coverages for a business engaged in, but not owned or controlled by, the insured (such as sales, clerical, or teaching occupations).

*   The *home day care coverage endorsement* (HO 04 97) extends Section II coverages to a day care business in the home.

*   The *additional residence rented to others endorsement* (HO 24 70) extends Section II coverages to an additional residence of the insured that is rented to one to four families.

For each of the preceding situations, Section II coverage applies to the insured but not to the tenant of the insured. Using the example in 1, above, suppose a guest of the festival attendees was injured in the insured's home. If the guest sued both the insured and the festival attendees renting the insured's home, the insured would have liability coverage under her homeowners policy, but the festival attendees would not be covered under her policy.

Professional Services

Coverages E and F exclude coverage for the insured's rendering or failure to render professional services. For example, an architect might be liable for a loss resulting from improper drawings provided to a client. This exposure should be addressed by a professional liability policy.

Locations That Are Not Insured Locations

Exhibit 6-1 provided descriptions and examples of locations included in the policy definitions as insured locations. A loss that arises out of premises that are not an insured location is not covered.

War

Section II of the homeowners policy excludes any loss that results from war.

Communicable Disease

Any loss that results from the transmission of a communicable disease by an insured is excluded under Section II of the homeowners policy. Consequently, a claim that the insured negligently transmitted herpes, AIDS, or even a common cold, to another person would not be covered.

Sexual Molestation and Physical or Mental Abuse

Any loss that arises out of sexual molestation, corporal punishment, or physical or mental abuse by an insured is excluded under Section II. Corporal punishment is not defined, but generally refers to spanking, slapping, hitting, and similar disciplinary actions.

Controlled Substances

Section II excludes any loss that results from the use, sale, manufacture, delivery, transfer, or possession of controlled substances as defined by the Federal Food and Drug Law (such as cocaine, marijuana, and other narcotic drugs, or steroids). An excluded loss could result if, say, an insured injures a person or causes damage because of a drug-induced hallucination or supplies controlled substances that harm another person. However, this exclusion does not apply to (and thus coverage is provided for) the legitimate use of prescription drugs by a person following the orders of a licensed physician.

Exclusions That Apply Only to Coverage E— Personal Liability

The exclusions previously discussed apply to both Coverages E and F. Following are a group of exclusions that apply only to Coverage E—Personal Liability; they do not apply to the Medical Payments to Others Coverage.

Loss Assessment

Homeowners who belong to a homeowners' association or a community of property owners might face liability exposures. Each individual homeowner could be assessed a portion of the liability claims against the association for any loss that the group has not insured or for which the group has purchased inadequate limits of insurance. For example, a swimming pool is owned and maintained by the local homeowners' association. A child is injured while diving into the pool. The homeowners' association is sued for the child's injuries, and $2 million in damages is awarded to the child and the child's family. The association has a liability policy with a limit of $1 million; the remaining $1 million is assessed against the 100 members of the homeowners' association, each of whom must pay a $10,000 assessment.

Coverage E of the homeowners policy excludes coverage for liability assessments charged to the policyholder. Thus, the full Coverage E limits are not available to pay a liability loss assessment. However, a Section II—Additional Coverage, discussed later in this chapter, provides $1,000 in coverage for this exposure. An endorsement is available to increase the $1,000 limit.

Liability Assumed Under Contract

Coverage does not apply to liability an insured assumes under any contract or agreement. However, exceptions apply, and liability coverage is therefore provided, for two types of written contracts as long as the exposures do not involve coverage excluded elsewhere in the policy:

a. *Contracts relating to the ownership, maintenance, or use of an insured location.* For example, an insured rents a mountain cabin from a friend for a class reunion. (The cabin is an insured location because the insured has temporarily rented it for nonbusiness use.) It is understood by the insured and the friend that the insured will be responsible for any injury occurring on the premises. This informal agreement can be formalized even after an injury occurs to a classmate who was chopping wood, and Coverage E will provide coverage to meet the insured's obligations.

b. *Liability of others assumed by the named insured before an accident occurs.* For example, an insured signs a contract with a roofer to replace the roof on the insured's home. The contract states that if the roofer is sued for negligence in the course of performing his work at the insured's home, the insured will provide a defense and pay any damages on behalf of the roofer. As the roofer is bringing the new shingles up to the insured's roof, a bundle slides from the roof and injures a neighbor. Coverage E will apply to the insured's obligation under the contract with the roofer.

Damage to the Insured's Property

Liability coverage excludes damage to property owned by an insured. This exclusion precludes insured-versus-insured claims arising out of damage of one insured's property by another insured. In addition, an insured cannot collect payment under Section II liability coverage for damage to his or her own property, even if the property repairs might serve to prevent a liability claim. For example, an insured cannot expect his homeowners policy to pay the cost of replacing a rotting wooden fence around his swimming pool, on the basis that the repairs prevent a potential liability claim from a child who might wander into the pool.

Coverage E is intended to be a third-party coverage that protects the insured against liability for damage that might be done to others' property. Insureds can collect payment under Section I of the homeowners policy for damage to their own property that is covered under Section I. Maintenance expenses, such as replacing the rotting fence, are properly borne by the homeowner, not an insurance company.

Property in the Insured's Care

This exclusion, which applies to property of *others*, is similar to the previous exclusion, which excludes coverage for damage to an insured's *owned* property. Coverage E does not apply to damage to property that is rented to, occupied by, or in the care of an insured. To illustrate, an insured who borrows a relative's thirty-foot sailboat might have personal liability coverage for damage done to another boat that the insured strikes with the borrowed sailboat, but Coverage E protection would not apply to the $10,000 damage done to the relative's sailboat, because the sailboat was in the insured's care.

An exception to this exclusion applies to property damage *caused by fire, smoke, or explosion*. If the insured rents a beach cottage for a summer vacation, Coverage E would apply if the insured accidentally starts a fire in the kitchen that results in smoke and fire damage to the cottage. However, Coverage E would not apply if the insured runs into the cottage with a vehicle, because vehicle damage to the cottage is not a result of fire, smoke, or explosion.

Bodily Injury to Persons Eligible for Workers Compensation Benefits

Coverage is excluded under Coverage E for bodily injury to any person who is eligible to receive or who is provided benefits by an insured under a state workers compensation law, nonoccupational disability law, or occupational disease law. Assume that an insured has a housekeeper who is injured by falling from a stepladder while cleaning the insured's windows:

• If the insured lives in a state where the insured is *not required* to provide workers compensation for a domestic worker, the insured *will* have coverage for his or her liability for the housekeeper's bodily injury under Coverage E (unless the insured has voluntarily purchased a workers compensation policy).

- If the insured lives in a state where workers compensation *is required* for a domestic worker, the insured *will not* have coverage for his or her liability for the housekeeper's bodily injury under Coverage E, regardless of whether the insured had actually purchased separate workers compensation insurance.

Nuclear Liability

Bodily injury or property damage liability that would be covered under a nuclear energy liability policy is excluded from homeowners Coverage E. Only unusual circumstances would cause a homeowners insured to become responsible for damages related to a nuclear energy loss, but this standard exclusion is inserted into many types of insurance policies, both personal and commercial. Nuclear liability exclusions limit the insurance industry's overall liability for nuclear occurrences to the coverage provided by specialty nuclear energy liability policies.

Bodily Injury to an Insured

The named insured, resident relatives, and other residents under the age of twenty-one in the insured's care cannot collect damages under Coverage E for their own bodily injury, even if the injury is caused by another insured.

Exclusions That Apply Only to Coverage F—Medical Payments to Others

Four exclusions apply only to Coverage F—Medical Payments to Others.

Residence Employee Off Premises

Coverage F excludes bodily injury to a residence employee if an injury occurs off the insured's location *and* the injury does not arise out of the employee's work. Therefore, Coverage F *would* apply in the following types of situations:

- *The residence employee is away from the insured location, but is working.* For example, the insured's housekeeper is struck by a hit-and-run vehicle while walking to the post office to mail a package for the insured.
- *The residence employee is on the insured location (whether working or not).* For example, the insured's gardener chips a tooth while eating lunch at a table in the insured's kitchen.

Bodily Injury Eligible for Workers Compensation Benefits

Any person eligible to receive payment under *any* workers compensation law, nonoccupational disability law, or occupational disease law will not receive compensation for bodily injury under Coverage F. This exclusion applies whether or not the benefits are to be provided by an insured.

Nuclear Reaction

Coverage F excludes bodily injury from any nuclear reaction, nuclear radiation, or radioactive contamination, regardless of the cause.

Injury to Residents

Bodily injury to any person who regularly resides at the insured location (other than a residence employee) is excluded under Coverage F—Medical Payments to Others.

SECTION II—ADDITIONAL COVERAGES

Like Section I of the homeowners policy, Section II also provides additional coverages. The four additional coverages in Section II include miscellaneous additional items and limited coverage for otherwise-excluded personal liability exposures. All Section II—Additional Coverages are in addition to the limits for Coverage E and Coverage F.

Claim Expenses

As noted earlier, defense expenses are paid by the insurer in addition to the limit of liability for Coverage E. The additional coverage for claim expenses specifies which expenses the insurer will pay in handling a claim.

Expenses We Incur

The insurer will assume the expenses and costs taxed against an insured in any suit the insurer defends. Costs that might be assumed by the insurer include the expenses of defense counsel, filing fees, additional experts, witnesses, or other individuals necessary for testimony.

Premiums on Bonds

The insurer will pay the premiums on bonds required in the defense of a suit, but no more than the premium for a bond in the amount of the Coverage E limit. If a higher bond amount is needed, the insured must pay the premium for any amount above the policy limit.

Even if the insurer also issues surety bonds, the insurer is not required to apply for or furnish any bond required in a suit defended under a homeowners insurance policy. The insurer is only required to pay the premium for the bond obtained by the insured up to the limit mentioned above.

Reasonable Expenses

The insurer will pay for reasonable expenses incurred by an insured, including actual loss of earnings up to $250 per day, when the insurer requests an insured's assistance in the investigation or defense of a claim or suit. Reasonable expenses include parking costs, meals, and mileage.

Postjudgment Interest

After a judgment has been made against an insured, interest can accrue on the amount to be paid to a plaintiff until the insurer pays (up to the limit of Coverage E) the judgment. Postjudgment interest can be substantial if the insurer appeals the judgment to a higher court. If the insurer loses the appeal, the insurer is responsible for paying the interest on the entire judgment, not just the interest on that portion of the judgment that does not exceed the Coverage E limit. For example, if the judgment is $120,000 and the insured has a $100,000 Coverage E limit, the insurer would be responsible for interest on the entire $120,000, in addition to the $100,000 in covered damages.

Interest that might accrue on damages before a judgment is rendered is called *pre*judgment interest. Any *pre*judgment interest awarded against the insured is included within the Coverage E limit rather than being provided as an additional coverage. Prejudgment and postjudgment interest were explained in greater detail in Chapter 3.

First-Aid Expenses

The insurer will reimburse expenses incurred by an insured for first aid to others for any bodily injury covered under the policy. For example, if a guest is injured in the insured's home and the insured uses supplies from her first-aid kit to bandage the wound, the insured could collect reimbursement from her insurer for the supplies used. The insurer will *not* reimburse expenses for first aid to an injured insured.

Damage to Property of Others

The insurer will pay up to $1,000 per occurrence for damage to the property of others caused by an insured. Coverage is provided on a replacement cost basis. Just as the medical payments to others coverage covers minor injuries to others without the need to prove fault, so also the damage to the property of others coverage pays for minor property damage *without the need to prove the insured's negligence.*

Suppose, for example, an insured borrows a friend's lawn mower that sustains water damage when it is driven into a pond because the insured, who was mowing his lawn, lost control of the mower and was unable to stop it. The insured will have coverage up to $1,000 to replace the lawn mower without having to prove that the insured was actually responsible for the loss. This coverage allows the insured to maintain goodwill by paying for relatively minor losses to another person's property, and it allows the insurer to avoid litigation expenses on small property damage claims to determine whether the insured was at fault.

The insurer will *not* pay under this additional coverage for property damage to the extent of any amount recoverable under Section I of the policy. For example, if the mower had been damaged by fire—a peril covered under Section I, the insurer would pay only the deductible amount under the Damage to the Property of Others Coverage; the remaining amount would be payable under Section I. The insurer will not pay for any property damage:

- Caused intentionally by an insured who is thirteen years old or older.
- To property owned by an insured.
- To property owned by or rented to a tenant of an insured or a resident of the named insured's household.
- If the damage arises out of a business engaged in by an insured.
- If the damage is a result of an act or omission in connection with premises (other than an insured location) that the insured owns, rents, or controls.
- If the damage arises out of the ownership, maintenance, or use of any motor vehicle, watercraft, aircraft, or hovercraft (other than a recreational vehicle designed for use off public roads that is not subject to motor vehicle registration and not owned by an insured).

Intentional damage by children under the age of thirteen is covered. For example, when nine-year-old Donnie and seven-year-old Jonnie used a neighbor's freshly-poured cement driveway to create finger art, their parents' homeowners policy would cover the property damage, even though their act was quite intentional.

Loss Assessment

Under this additional coverage, loss assessment coverage is provided up to $1,000 for an insured's share of loss assessment charged against a policyholder during the policy period, as owner of the residence premises, by a corporation or an association of property owners for the following types of losses:

- Bodily injury or property damage that is not excluded under Section II of the homeowners policy
- Liability that results from an act of an elected and unpaid director, officer, or trustee.

Earlier in this chapter, while discussing the loss assessment exclusion to Coverage E, an illustration involved a diving accident at the subdivision's swimming pool for which no Coverage E—Personal Liability coverage applied. A homeowners insured would have $1,000 available for his or her share of that assessment under this additional coverage.

> The *loss assessment coverage endorsement* (HO 04 35) can be attached to the policy to increase the limit for the loss assessment additional coverage in both Section I and Section II.

SECTION II—CONDITIONS

Section II—Conditions establish the duties and responsibilities of the insurer and the policyholder. Part of these duties and responsibilities involves how Section II claims will be handled.

Limit of Liability

The limit of Coverage E—Personal Liability appearing on the declarations page is the total limit of coverage for any one occurrence. This limit will not increase regardless of the number of insureds, claims made, or people injured. For example, an insured and his wife are operating a covered watercraft and accidentally collide with another boat, injuring four passengers in the other boat. If the insured has a $100,000 Coverage E limit, that is the total amount of coverage available for this occurrence even if both the insured and his spouse are listed in a suit and all four passengers of the other boat file suit. However, defense costs for this suit will be paid in excess of the $100,000 Coverage E liability limit.

This Section II condition also states that all bodily injury and property damage that result from continuous or repeated exposure to the same harmful conditions are considered to be one occurrence; therefore, the Coverage E limit is the maximum amount that will be paid for any loss of that type. For example, the insured's gardener becomes ill over a period of weeks after using an insecticide the insured purchased for use in the yard. The gardener is hospitalized as a result. The insured is covered for the gardener's resulting claim (as long as the gardener does not fall under the workers compensation exclusion) even though the occurrence that caused the injury was not a single event but took place over several months. The injury is considered the result of a single occurrence.

This condition further states that the total liability under Coverage F—Medical Payments to Others for all medical expenses for bodily injury to one person as the result of an accident will not be more than the Coverage F limit shown on the declarations page. For example, a policyholder with a $1,000 limit for Coverage F would have $1,000 coverage available for each guest injured in an accident in the policyholder's home. It is not common for a medical payments claim to involve more than one person, but it can happen. For example, a number of people attending a party at the policyholder's home might be injured if they are crowded onto a second-story deck that collapses. In such an incident, up to $1,000 in medical payments to others coverage would be available for each injured guest. (If the policyholder is legally liable for guests' injuries, coverage is also available under Coverage E—Personal Liability.)

Severability of insurance condition

Policy condition that applies insurance separately to each insured; does not increase the insurer's limit of liability for any one occurrence.

Severability of Insurance

Some occurrences might result in a claim involving the alleged negligence of several insureds. Under the **severability of insurance condition,** each insured seeking protection is treated as if he or she has separate coverage under the policy. However, the insurer's limit of liability stated in the policy is not increased for any one occurrence, if more than one insured is involved.

For example, Sharon and Alice are sisters, and both are insureds under their parents' HO-3. They fight with Dora, their neighbor. During the fight, Dora falls and strikes her head on the sidewalk. After lapsing into a coma for four days, Dora awakes with major speech problems and a loss of her short-term memory. Dora's family sues Sharon and Alice for damages. The HO-3 under which Sharon and Alice are insured provides a limit of liability of $500,000. If the court decides against both Sharon and Alice, the most the insurer will pay, in total, is $500,000, even if Sharon is held liable for $550,000 and Alice is liable for $100,000. If the court decides Sharon acted intentionally and Alice acted negligently, the insurer might be able to exclude coverage for Sharon but would still provide coverage for Alice.

Duties After Loss

The insured is required to do certain things after a Section II occurrence. If prejudicial to the insurer, failure to fulfill post-loss duties provides sufficient grounds for the insurer to deny coverage.

- *Give written notice.* The insured must give written notice to the insurer (or its agent) as soon as practical. The notice should identify the policy and the named insured shown in the declarations; provide information about the time, place, and circumstances of the occurrence; and state the names and addresses of the claimants and witnesses.

- *Cooperate with the insurer.* The insured must cooperate with the insurer's investigation, settlement, and defense activities.

- *Forward legal documents.* The insured is required to forward promptly to the insurer every notice, demand, summons, or other process relating to an occurrence. Legal demands or notices of suit usually have a time limit during which a response must be entered with the court.

- *Provide claims assistance.* The insured is required to assist the insurer in making a settlement, enforcing any right of contribution against another party who might be liable, attending hearings and trials, securing and giving evidence, and obtaining the attendance of witnesses.

- *Submit evidence for damage to property of others.* If a claim is made under the additional coverage for damage to property of others, the insured must submit to the insurer, within sixty days after the loss, a sworn statement of loss and show the damaged property to the insurer (if possible).

- *Not make voluntary payments.* If the insured makes any voluntary payment, assumes any obligations, or incurs expenses (other than for first aid to others), it will be at the insured's own expense. The insured is not permitted to make commitments on behalf of the insurer.

Duties of an Injured Person—Coverage F

If a person makes a claim for a loss under Coverage F—Medical Payments to Others, the injured person (or someone acting on his or her behalf) must:

- Give the insurer written proof of the claim as soon as possible; the proof must be given under oath if required.
- Authorize the insurer to obtain copies of medical reports and records.

In addition, the injured person must submit to a physical exam by a doctor chosen by the insurer as often as the insurer requires such examinations.

Payment of Claim—Coverage F

If a claim is paid under Coverage F—Medical Payments to Others, a policy condition makes clear that the payment is not an admission of liability by the insured or the insurer. Sometimes a person with a small medical payments to others claim, apparently involving a minor injury and modest expense, develops complications that require much more expensive treatment that would be covered under Coverage E if the insured is liable for the claimant's injuries. Even if a Coverage F claim has been paid, the insurer still has a right to defend the insured against a Coverage E claim and to pay no damages if an insured is not responsible for the injury.

Suit Against Insurer

This condition makes the following three points regarding compliance with the policy provisions and the insurer's rights under the policy:

- No legal action can be brought against the insurer unless the insured has met all its obligations under Section II of the policy.
- No one has the right to join the insurer as a party to any action against an insured.
- No action with respect to Coverage E can be brought against the insurer until the obligation of the insured has been determined by a final judgment or agreement signed by the insurer.

Bankruptcy of an Insured

If the insured becomes bankrupt or insolvent, the insurer is still obligated to handle the loss as it normally would. The insurer is not relieved of any obligations under the policy by the insured's financial status.

Other Insurance—Coverage E

The other insurance condition for Section II of the homeowners policy is different from Section I's other insurance condition. Coverage E limits are paid as excess over any other collectible insurance unless the other insurance is written specifically to provide excess coverage (such as a personal umbrella liability policy).

For example, an insured might purchase a yacht policy with a $200,000 limit of liability for his twenty-five-foot sailboat. The insured's homeowners policy provides Section II coverage with a limit of $100,000 for Coverage E for injury or damage caused by any sailboats that are less than twenty-six feet long; therefore, both the homeowners policy and the yacht policy would provide liability coverage. If a $250,000 liability loss occurs, the yacht policy will pay $200,000 first. The homeowners policy would pay the remaining $50,000. If the loss in this case had been less than the $200,000 limit provided by the yacht policy, no payment would be made under the homeowners policy for the loss.

Policy Period

Coverage applies only to bodily injury and property damage that occurs during the policy period, which is indicated in the declarations. The claim may be filed at any time, even after the policy has expired. Often there is a delay between the time of an injury and the time a claim is made against an insured.

Concealment or Fraud

Like Section I, Section II of the homeowners policy includes a concealment or fraud provision. There is a subtle, but important, difference between the two provisions. The condition that applies to Section II—Liability Coverages reads as follows:

> We do not provide coverage to an "insured" who, whether before or after a loss, has:
>
> (1) Intentionally concealed or misrepresented any material fact or circumstance;
>
> (2) Engaged in fraudulent conduct; or
>
> (3) Made false statements;
>
> relating to this insurance.

Only the insured or insureds who conceal or misrepresent, commit fraud, or make false statements are barred from liability coverages under Section II. Other innocent insureds would not be precluded from liability coverage. Under Section I, concealment or fraud by any insured bars property coverage for all insureds.

Suppose Andrea becomes angry at her husband, Don, and burns down their house, and the fire also damages a neighbor's house. Although Andrea first denies having set the fire, an investigation uncovers evidence conclusively proving that she did. Because of her misrepresentation, Andrea has no coverage under either Section I or Section II of their homeowners policy.

Don, who is completely innocent in this example, would have no property coverage under Section I of their homeowners policy. If the neighbors make a property damage liability claim against Andrea and Don, the insurer would defend only Don and, should he somehow be found liable, pay the claim on his behalf.

SECTIONS I AND II—CONDITIONS

This final segment of the homeowners policy states conditions that apply to the entire policy, both Sections I and II. Conditions here relate to the policy period, cancellation, nonrenewal, and other matters affecting the policy as a whole.

Liberalization Clause

According to the liberalization clause, if the insurer, during the policy period or within sixty days before the policy period, adopts a revision that broadens the coverage without an additional premium charge, the increased coverage will automatically apply to all existing policies on the date it is implemented within the state. The liberalization clause does not apply to changes introduced when the insurer makes a general homeowners program revision that both broadens and restricts coverage, whether that change is introduced in a later edition of the policy or implemented through an amendatory endorsement. Policyholders insured under the Homeowners 2000 series edition of the homeowners policy would not automatically benefit from any changes that might be introduced in, say, a new policy edition introduced in year 2006.

To illustrate how the liberalization clause might apply, suppose IIA Insurance Company, wanting to attract new customers, provides replacement cost coverage on contents to all insureds at no charge by attaching a personal property replacement cost endorsement (HO 04 90) to all new and renewal homeowners policies. On the date that additional coverage becomes effective, all existing homeowners policies issued by the insurer are automatically entitled to the additional coverage, even if the insureds are unaware of the change.

Waiver or Change of Policy Provisions

This policy condition states that a waiver or change of a policy provision is valid only if the insurer makes it in writing. Nevertheless, courts have permitted oral waivers by claims representatives made during the adjustment of a loss and after the written policy was issued. Claims representatives are considered representatives of the insurer with the apparent authority to modify policy conditions.

As agents of the insurance company, insurance agents with binding authority are authorized to make policy changes through an oral binder that is effective until a written policy change endorsement is produced.

Cancellation

The *policyholder* may cancel the homeowners policy at any time by returning the policy to the insurer or by contacting the insurer in writing and advising the insurer of the date that cancellation is to take effect.

> The *additional interests—residence premises endorsement* (HO 04 10) is used if other persons or organizations with an interest in the property are to be notified if the insurer cancels or nonrenews the policy.

The *insurer* may cancel the policy only for the following reasons, with written notice to the policyholder at the mailing address shown in the declarations:

- The insurer may cancel at any time for *nonpayment of premium* if the policyholder is given at least ten days' notice before the effective date of cancellation.

- *When a new policy has been in effect for less than sixty days*, the insurer may cancel the policy *for any reason* if the policyholder is given at least ten days' notice before the effective date of cancellation.

- *When the policy has been in effect for more than sixty days (or is a renewal)*, the insurer may cancel the policy by giving at least thirty days' notice to the policyholder before the effective date of cancellation if:

  a. There has been a material misrepresentation of fact.

  b. The risk has changed substantially since the policy was issued (such as the establishment of a child daycare business in the home).

When a policy is canceled by either party, a **pro rata refund** of the premium is sent to the policyholder with the cancellation notice (or within a reasonable time afterward).

> *Note:* State law often dictates how and when insurers can cancel and nonrenew policies. Whenever policy language and state laws conflict, state law takes precedence and overrides policy language. State laws involving cancellation requirements and other matters are often reflected in a state-specific amendatory endorsement to the policy.

Nonrenewal

The insurer has the right to decide not to renew the policy when it expires at the end of the policy period. Nonrenewal is accomplished by mailing a notice to the policyholder (at the address shown in the declarations) at least thirty days before the policy expiration date.

Pro rata refund
Unused premium, returned to the policyholder when the policy is canceled, calculated in direct proportion to the portion of the policy term that has not been used. For example, if a one-year (365-day) premium is $365 and the policy is canceled 100 days before it would expire (with 100 of the 365 days of coverage unused), the insured will receive a refund of $100. Rather than calculating unearned premium refunds on a pro rata basis, some insurance policies apply a "short-rate penalty" when the *insured* cancels the policy.

Assignment

The policy cannot be assigned (transferred) to another party without the insurer's written consent. An insurance policy is a personal contract between the insurer and the policyholder, and the insurer needs to be able to choose whom it will insure.

This wording is necessary in the homeowners contract to make it clear that the policy is not transferable, at least not without the insurer's permission. In practice, insurance policies are hardly ever transferred when a house is sold. Usually, the seller just cancels his or her policy, and the buyer purchases his or her own policy.

Subrogation

Subrogation refers to the insurer's right to recover its claim payment to an insured from the party responsible for the loss. Once the insurer pays a claim to or on behalf of an insured, if the insured had any rights to collect from another party responsible for the loss, the insurer may require that these rights be transferred to the insurer. If a fire results from a contractor's negligent installation of a wood stove in an insured home, the insurer will pay for the property loss, because a fire is a covered peril under the homeowners policy. The insurer will then subrogate against the contractor to recover the amount it has paid.

This method of claim settlement allows an insured to pursue a first-party claim against his or her own insurance company. If another party is ultimately responsible for the loss, the insurance company is best equipped to pursue any legal remedy required to recoup the loss from the negligent party.

An insured can waive his or her rights of recovery against another person *before* a loss occurs, but the waiver must be in writing. For example, the homeowner buying a wood stove might sign a contract with the contractor, agreeing to hold the installer harmless if damage results from using the wood stove. If a fire occurs under these circumstances, the homeowners insurer would still pay the property insurance claim, but the insurer could not subrogate against the contractor. The insured had previously signed away its rights of recovery, so there are no rights to transfer to the insurer.

An insured may not waive his or her rights of recovery *after* a loss has occurred. Assuming no hold harmless agreement existed, the insured could not tell the wood stove installer, after the loss, "Don't worry about the damage; my fire insurance will pay for everything." The insured does not have the authority after a loss to waive any rights of recovery related to that loss.

Death

If the insured named in the declarations or the insured's spouse dies, the insurer will insure the legal representative (usually the executor or administrator of the estate) of the deceased person but only with respect to the premises and property of the deceased person covered under the homeowners policy at the time of death. The policy will not extend to the deceased person's entire estate, which might include other property not covered by the policy.

This condition includes a modified definition of "insured" that identifies the parties covered under the policy when a named insured has died.

SUMMARY

This chapter examined Section II—Liability Coverages of the ISO homeowners policy. Section II, which is the same for all forms of the ISO homeowners policy, consists of two principal coverages:

- Coverage E—Personal Liability
- Coverage F—Medical Payments to Others

Section II also includes additional coverages that provide miscellaneous liability and related coverages.

Coverage E—Personal Liability provides coverage if a claim is brought against an insured because of bodily injury or property damage caused by an insured in a covered occurrence. "Insured" has a specific meaning that includes the insured named on the declarations page and a number of other persons; the definitions section of the homeowners policy gives the specific meaning of insured as the word is used in the policy. In addition to the limit of liability for Coverage E, the insurer pays defense costs if an insured is involved in a lawsuit for a loss that is covered under the policy.

Coverage F—Medical Payments to Others provides a limited amount of coverage for necessary medical expenses incurred by others (not an insured) within three years of an injury. These medical expenses include reasonable charges for medical, surgical, X-ray, dental, hospital, funeral, and related services. Coverage applies to accidents that occur on the insured premises or as a result of covered activities of the insured at any location.

Because the Section II coverages are defined in broad coverage terms, the policy lists a number of exclusions that eliminate coverage for specified types of occurrences. Section II exclusions, which are important for the student to learn, are divided into the following categories:

- Exclusions that apply to both Coverages E and F
- Exclusions that apply only to Coverage E
- Exclusions that apply only to Coverage F

Just as additional coverages are provided in Section I of the homeowners policy, Section II also provides additional coverages. The four Section II—Additional Coverages, which are in addition to the limits for Coverages E and F, consist of claim expenses, first-aid expenses, damage to property of others, and loss assessment.

The Section II—Conditions establish the duties and responsibilities of the insurer and the insured. They also describe how Section II claims will be settled. The final segment of the homeowners policy states conditions that apply to both Sections I and II, including cancellation, nonrenewal, and other provisions.

Chapter 7

Direct Your Learning

Homeowners Variations, Endorsements, and Rating

After learning the subject matter of this chapter, you should be able to:

■ Compare each of the following ISO policy forms to the ISO HO-3 Special Form:

- HO-2 Broad Form

- HO-5 Comprehensive Form

- HO-4 Contents Broad Form

- HO-6 Unit-Owners Form

- HO-8 Modified Coverage Form

■ Explain how each of the endorsements described in this assignment changes the ISO homeowners policy coverage.

■ Given a case involving a homeowners loss,

- Explain whether the loss is covered.

- Determine what homeowners endorsement would cover the loss.

■ Identify the factors considered in determining a homeowners policy's premium.

Develop Your Perspective

What are the main topics covered in the chapter?

The ISO HO-3 homeowners policy described in Chapters 5 and 6 does not meet the needs of all homeowners. Indeed, all homeowners are not eligible for that policy form. This chapter compares the HO-3 to other ISO and American Association of Insurance Services (AAIS) homeowners forms regarding their intended use and coverages provided. Endorsements that can be used to modify homeowners policies are also described.

Compare the various homeowners forms described with the HO-3.

- For what type of homeowner are the forms intended?

- How do the coverages provided by these forms benefit the intended policyholders?

Why is it important to know these topics?

Homeowners policies, other than the HO-3, are appropriate to address the wide variations in coverage needs for an array of homeowners. Endorsements can be used to further tailor coverage to the loss exposures of an individual or a family. To apply these forms and endorsements appropriately, you must first understand the coverages they provide.

Contrast the various homeowners forms.

- In broad terms, how are the forms different from the HO-3?

- How can endorsements be used to further modify all policy forms?

How can you use this information?

Develop a chart comparing the HO-3 homeowners forms with the alternative coverage forms described in this chapter. Identify the following for the various forms:

- What property is covered? For what limits? Under what circumstances? What property is excluded from coverage?

- What additional coverages are provided?

- For what perils is coverage provided? Under what circumstances? Who has the burden of proof?

Chapter 7

Homeowners Variations, Endorsements, and Rating

Chapters 5 and 6 examined the popular ISO HO-3 homeowners policy form in detail. Other homeowners policies also exist, because the HO-3 does not fit everyone's needs. For example:

- Apartment dwellers and condominium unit owners do not need full insurance on the building.

- Some customers are willing to accept more-restricted coverage in exchange for a lower premium.

- Some customers want the broadest possible coverage and are willing to pay more for it.

- Some older homes have substantially depreciated and are not well suited for replacement cost coverage.

- Some property or liability exposures are not addressed by the standard, unendorsed HO-3 because they are not faced by the typical family or they require special underwriting attention.

Homeowners forms are not all alike. This chapter describes ISO homeowners forms other than the HO-3 that address the first four situations above, and it compares them with the HO-3 previously studied. This chapter also includes a brief overview of AAIS homeowners forms. Like ISO, the American Association of Insurance Services (AAIS) is an organization that drafts homeowners forms and other policies that many insurance companies use. As mentioned later in the chapter, some insurance companies also draft their own homeowners forms, and state-by-state variations on all forms are common.

The HO-3 and other homeowners forms often must be tailored to address a given homeowner's particular situation. A variety of endorsements can tailor the policy to meet special needs. Many of the endorsements discussed here were referenced in shaded boxes in Chapters 5 and 6, near the sections of the contract that they modify. Others are mentioned here for the first time. Additional endorsements, not mentioned in this chapter, are also available.

Finally, this chapter briefly addresses homeowners policy rating.

VARIATIONS IN ISO HOMEOWNERS FORMS

This section of Chapter 7 compares other ISO homeowners forms with the HO-3 form that was examined in detail in Chapters 5 and 6. It does not review each form in detail but rather summarizes the differences that distinguish the forms from one another. The form numbers HO-2, HO-3, and so forth reflect the order in which various homeowners forms were introduced into the marketplace, not their relative importance. The homeowners forms are discussed here in logical order rather than numerical order. This portion of the chapter discusses, in this sequence, HO-2, HO-5, HO-4, HO-6, and HO-8.

Section II—Liability Coverages is the same in all standard, unendorsed ISO homeowners forms. The Agreement and Sections I and II—Conditions are also the same. The primary differences between the forms occur in Section I—Property Coverages.

HO-2 Broad Form

Like the Homeowners 3—Special Form (HO-3) policy, ISO's Homeowners 2—Broad Form (HO 00 02), commonly known as the "HO-2," is designed for the owner-occupant of a house.

An HO-2 has a slightly lower premium than an HO-3 with similar limits, because it covers the dwelling building and other structures against fewer causes of loss. In the HO-2, covered causes of loss are limited to the named perils listed in the policy, not only for personal property but also for the building and other structures.

Exhibit 7-1 repeats the structure of the ISO homeowners policy (as introduced in Chapter 5) and indicates the difference between the HO-3 and the HO-2, as well as the HO-5 discussed later. Only the Section I—Perils Insured Against segment is different. The HO-3 provides *special-form coverage* (coverage for any direct loss unless excluded, also known as open-perils coverage) for Coverages A and B and *named perils coverage* (perils listed and described in the policy) for Coverage C; the HO-2 provides named perils coverage for Coverages A, B, and C. In both forms, Coverage D is triggered by a loss covered under the other Coverages that makes the building unusable.

The list of named perils in the HO-2 closely resembles the list of named perils in the HO-3 for Coverage C. The long list of named perils covered by the HO-2 encompasses most of the insurable perils that can easily be imagined, but the HO-3 also covers some losses that cannot readily be foreseen. A good example involves ice dams, one of the more common examples of a loss covered by an HO-3 but not an HO-2. An ice dam forms near the edge of a roof, under certain weather conditions, and traps melting ice and snow so it cannot flow off the roof. Instead, the trapped water seeps through the roof and damages interior walls and ceilings.

Another important difference between named-perils coverage and special-form coverage involves the burden of proof, discussed on page 7.6.

EXHIBIT 7-1

Comparison of HO-3, HO-2, and HO-5 Policies

Policy Segments	Differences Between HO-3, HO-2, and HO-5

Section I—Property

Agreement

Definitions

Section I—Property Coverages

Section I—Perils Insured Against ◄

Section I—Exclusions

Section I—Conditions

Note: Section II is the same on all ISO homeowners forms

Section II—Liability

Section II—Liability Coverages

Section II—Exclusions

Section II—Additional Coverages

Section II—Conditions

Sections I and II—Conditions

The difference between the HO-3, HO-2, and HO-5 is the covered perils provided for Coverages A, B, and C.

The HO-3 provides "special-form coverage" for the dwelling and other structures, and "named perils" coverage for the personal property.

The HO-2 provides "named perils" coverage for the dwelling, other structures, and personal property.

The HO-5 provides "special-form coverage" for the dwelling, other structures, and personal property.

Burden of Proof

An important difference between named perils and special-form ("all-risks") coverage involves the burden of proof.

- With a named perils policy, for coverage to apply, the insured must prove that the loss was caused by a *covered* cause of loss.

- With a special-form coverage policy, if a loss to covered property occurs, it is initially assumed that coverage applies. However, coverage may be denied if the *insurer* can prove that the loss was caused by an *excluded* cause of loss.

In the first case, the burden of proof is on the insured; in the second, it is on the insurer.

By shifting the burden of proof, special-form coverage can provide an important advantage to the insured who suffers a property loss by an unknown cause. For example, suppose that after a flood strikes the community, the insured's wrought-iron patio furniture is missing. Assume also that the patio furniture is clearly covered property. It is possible that the furniture was swept away in the flood, but it is also possible that the furniture was stolen following the flood. If a named perils policy covered theft but not flood, the *insured* would have to prove that the property had been stolen. Under a special-form coverage policy, the insurer would have to pay the claim (even if the policy excluded flood losses) unless the *insurer* could prove that the property was swept away in the flood.

The HO-2 might be used by an underwriter who is unwilling to provide the broad coverage of the HO-3 in a particular situation. However, the HO-2 is used mainly to minimize premiums. For example, a retired couple on a fixed income wants to purchase a homeowners policy but does not want to pay the premium charged for the HO-3. The couple believe that the named perils coverage provided by the HO-2 is sufficient to cover their exposures, so they choose the HO-2 to save a little money.

HO-5 Comprehensive Form

The Homeowners 5—Comprehensive Form (HO 00 05), also known as the "HO-5," provides the broadest property coverage of any of the standard, unendorsed homeowners forms. The HO-5 is essentially an HO-3 that has been modified to provide special-form coverage, not only for the dwelling and other structures, but also for Coverage C—Personal Property. In the HO-5, personal property is covered for loss by any peril, subject to the exclusions that also apply to Coverages A and B, as well as some additional exclusions applicable only to personal property:

- The policy provides no coverage for breakage of certain valuable or fragile articles, unless the breakage is caused by a named peril similar to those covered under the HO-3. Breakage coverage does not apply to eyeglasses, glassware, statuary, marble, fragile articles, or cameras if the breakage occurs as a result of carelessness rather than one of the named perils.

- Damage caused by dampness or temperature extremes is not covered unless the direct cause of loss is rain, snow, sleet, or hail.

- Loss caused by refinishing, renovating, or repairing property other than watches, jewelry, and furs is not covered.

- Loss to personal property caused by collision other than collision with a land vehicle, or the sinking, swamping, or stranding of watercraft, is not covered.

- Destruction, confiscation, or seizure of personal property by government authorities is excluded, whether or not the property itself is legally held by an insured.

As compared with the HO-3, coverage on personal property is broadened by the HO-5 in some areas simply because an exposure is not excluded. For example:

- Coverage for water damage, including flood damage, *is* provided for personal property away from a premises or location owned, rented, occupied, or controlled by an insured.

- Coverage *does* apply to personal property damaged by rain through an open window, door, or roof opening even if the building itself is not damaged.

The special limits of $1,500 for jewelry and furs, $2,500 for firearms, and $2,500 for silverware also apply not only to theft, but also to the perils of *misplacing* or *losing* the items. Misplacing and losing are not covered perils under the HO-3. Because misplacing or losing other types of personal property is not subject to a dollar limit, the HO-5 would cover other property that is misplaced or lost, subject to the deductible. Of course, the intentional loss exclusion still applies.

HO-4 Contents Broad Form

Even though it is not designed for people who own homes, the policy discussed here is called a homeowners form because it is part of the homeowners policy series. ISO's Homeowners 4—Contents Broad Form (HO 00 04), known as the "HO-4," often referred to as a "tenant homeowners policy" or a "renters policy," is a homeowners policy form designed specifically for the needs of persons or families who live in a rented house or apartment.

The HO-4 is essentially the same as an HO-3 without Coverages A and B. A few other adjustments, noted here, adapt the HO-4 to meet the needs of tenants.

Tenants obviously do not need coverage for buildings or other structures, because tenants usually do not own the building they live in. An insured who owns and lives in a building that does not qualify for coverage under another homeowners form might also purchase an HO-4. For example, a retired couple might own and reside in a house containing eight apartments. Building coverage would probably be written under a commercial insurance policy.

However, the couple can obtain an HO-4 policy to cover the contents in the apartment they occupy, other personal property they own or use, and also their personal liability exposures.

The HO-4 and the HO-3 provide the same named perils for Coverage C—Personal Property. Exhibit 7-2 illustrates the structural differences between the HO-3 and the HO-4.

The HO-4 differs from the HO-3 in the following ways:

*   Coverages A and B are absent from Section I—Property Coverages; an insured who rents his or her residence does not typically need coverage on a dwelling or other structure.

*   Coverage C is written at a limit the insured selects as adequate to cover the insured's personal property. (In the HO-3, HO-2, and HO-5, the Coverage C limit is typically 50 percent of the Coverage A limit.)

*   Coverage D in the HO-4 is automatically provided at 30 percent of the Coverage C limit (rather than 30 percent of the Coverage A limit, as in the HO-2 and HO-3).

*   An additional coverage, "building additions and alterations," is provided in the HO-4 for a limit up to 10 percent of Coverage C. Although a tenant does not have an insurable interest in the building where he or she resides, the tenant might add fixtures (called "additions and alterations" or "improvements and betterments") to the house. For example, a tenant who uses a wheelchair might install railings in the bathroom and ramps at the doors. If the house were destroyed as a result of a covered peril, the insured would lose the value of these installations.

*   The additional coverage for "landlord's furnishings" is not included in the HO-4 because the occupant-insured of the apartment does not have such property.

*   The additional coverage "ordinance or law" is provided in the HO-3 for a limit up to 10 percent of Coverage A. The HO-4 also provides this ordinance or law additional coverage, but for a limit up to 10 percent of the building additions and alterations limit.

HO-6 Unit-Owners Form

Closely related to the HO-4 is ISO's Homeowners 6 Unit-Owners Form (HO 00 06), known as the "HO-6." The HO-6 is a homeowners policy tailored to cover the exposures faced by people who own a **condominium** unit or a **cooperative** unit. Owners of condominium or cooperative units jointly own a building with other co-owners and individually own or are responsible for a specific unit within the building.

Unit Owners' Coverage Needs

The ownership deed for a condominium (called the "condominium declaration" or the "master deed") establishes the ownership and rights of the unit owners. This ownership deed usually contains a section relating to insurance

Condominium
A building or complex for which the unit owner has a separate title and exclusive ownership of a specific unit as well as the joint ownership of the common areas and facilities.

Cooperative
Housing unit in a complex owned by a corporation, the stockholders of which are the building's residents; corporation owns the real estate title; each unit owner owns corporation stock and has the right to occupy a specific unit.

EXHIBIT 7-2

Comparison of HO-3 and HO-4 Policies

Policy Segments	Differences Between HO-3 and HO-4

Agreement

Definitions

Section I—Property Coverages

Section I—Perils Insured Against

Section I—Exclusions

Section I—Conditions

Note: Section II is the same on all ISO homeowners forms

Section II—Liability Coverages

Section II—Exclusions

Section II—Additional Coverages

Section II—Conditions

Sections I and II—Conditions

Section I—Property

Section II—Liability

Coverages A and B are eliminated from the HO-4 policy because they are not needed by a tenant.

An additional coverage for "Building Additions and Alterations" is included in the HO-4.

The additional coverage "Landlord's Furnishings" is *not* provided in the HO-4.

"Ordinance or Law" is an additional coverage under the HO-3 (up to 10 percent of Coverage A). The additional coverage is provided in the HO-4 for an amount up to 10 percent of the "Building Additions and Alterations" limit.

Perils for Coverages A and B are not listed in an HO-4 because the coverages are not included.

requirements. This section of the deed describes the insurance provided for the property that the unit owners jointly own. Property not insured by this insurance (often called "condominium association insurance" or a "condominium master policy") is usually the responsibility of the individual unit owners. Cooperative associations also have legal documents that dictate the rights and responsibilities of unit owners.

The condominium association insurance might cover a unit owner's entire unit, including the fixtures, plumbing, wiring, or partitions; or the condominium association insurance might provide only "bare walls" coverage. Bare walls coverage means that the condominium association's policy provides coverage for only the building structure and walls that support the structure. The unit owner would be responsible for insuring other walls and fixtures inside the unit.

Coverages Provided by the HO-6

The HO-6 is tailored to provide coverage for unit owners' property exposures. The HO-6 differs from the HO-3 in the following ways:

- The definition of residence premises in the HO-6 is "the unit where you reside shown as the 'residence premises'... "; the HO-3 definition includes a one- to four-family dwelling where the insured resides.
- Reflecting the nature of condominium unit ownership, the HO-6 description of Coverage A under Section I—Property Coverages includes:
  1. The alterations, appliances, fixtures, and improvements that are part of the building contained within the insured unit (such as kitchen cabinets, partitions, and wallpaper)
  2. Items of real property that pertain exclusively to the insured unit (such as awnings or shutters)
  3. Property that is the unit owner's insurance responsibility under a property owners agreement of a condominium or cooperative association
  4. Structures owned solely by the insured at the residence location (such as a storage shed or garage owned by the insured)
- Coverage A—Dwelling in the HO-6 policy provides a basic limit of $5,000. This limit might not be adequate if an insured has extensive property exposures that are not covered by the condominium association insurance, and producers often recommend increasing the basic limit.
- Coverage B—Other Structures is eliminated from the HO-6. In the condominium form, other structures owned solely by the insured are included under Coverage A.
- Coverage C—Personal Property is written for a limit selected by the insured (rather than a percentage of Coverage A).
- Coverage D—Loss of Use is automatically provided at a limit that is 50 percent of the Coverage C limit (rather than 30 percent of the Coverage A limit).

- Section I—Perils Insured Against in the HO-6 provides named perils coverage for Coverages A and C similar to that provided in the HO-2.
- Section I—Conditions in the HO-6 specifies that Coverage A losses are settled on a replacement cost basis as long as the insured makes the repairs "within a reasonable time." There is no requirement that the Coverage A limit be written in an amount that equals a percentage of the replacement cost as is required in the HO-3.

The HO-6 *additional coverages* also reflect the unique aspects of condominium unit ownership:

- Trees, shrubs, and other plants coverage is provided in the HO-6 for a limit up to 10 percent of Coverage C (in contrast to the HO-3, which provides a limit up to 5 percent of Coverage A). In the HO-6, this coverage applies to plants solely owned by the named insured on grounds at the insured unit (such as those in the yard of a townhouse-style condominium).
- Glass or safety glazing material coverage is limited in the HO-6 to only that glass that is part of the insured's unit.
- Landlord's furnishings coverage is not provided in the HO-6.

Exhibit 7-3 shows how the HO-6 differs from the HO-3.

HO-8 Modified Coverage Form

ISO's Homeowners 8—Modified Coverage Form (HO 00 08), known as the "HO-8," is designed for use where the replacement cost of an owner-occupied dwelling significantly exceeds its **market value**. Such a home might be a large, older house with obsolete construction or features, such as hand-carved wooden moldings, that would be expensive to replace.

Market value
Price at which a particular property item could be sold.

For example, such a house could have a market value of $100,000, but the cost to replace the house might be $200,000. Many homeowners are unwilling to pay the high premium necessary to buy $200,000 of insurance on a house they bought for $100,000. Any homeowner who does insure the home to its $200,000 replacement cost value under an HO-3 policy could get more money by collecting the insurance than by selling the house. This situation creates an obvious **moral hazard**, and that is why many insurers are unwilling to write an HO-3 when there is a big difference between a home's market value and its replacement cost value.

Moral hazard
Condition that might lead a person to intentionally cause or exaggerate a loss.

The feature of the HO-8 that addresses this problem appears in the policy under Section I—Conditions. Under the HO-8, if the insured makes repairs after a loss, the insurer will not pay more than the cost of "common construction materials and methods" that are "functionally equivalent to and less costly than obsolete, antique, or custom construction." If the insured does not make repairs, the insurer will not pay more than "market value at the time of loss." For example, if an old home has plaster-over-lathe walls that are damaged by a covered peril, the insurer with an HO-8 might make the repairs using the type of wallboard usually used in new construction.

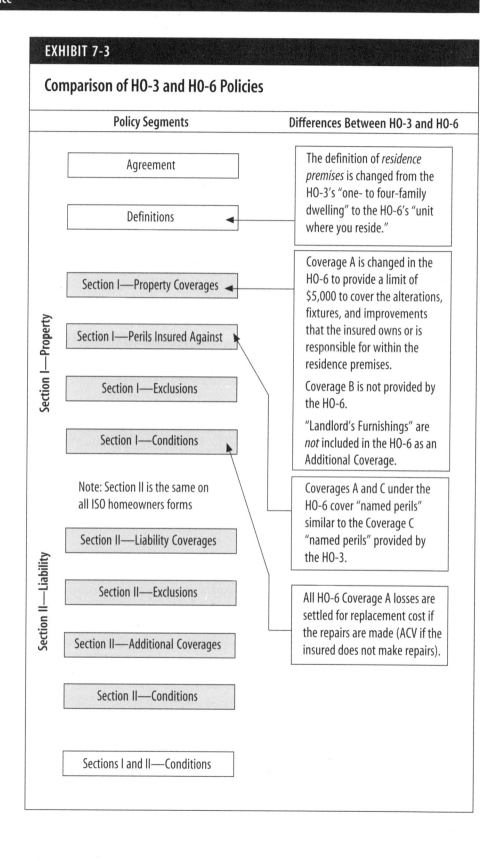

EXHIBIT 7-3

Comparison of HO-3 and HO-6 Policies

Policy Segments	Differences Between HO-3 and HO-6
Agreement	The definition of *residence premises* is changed from the HO-3's "one- to four-family dwelling" to the HO-6's "unit where you reside."
Definitions	
Section I—Property Coverages	Coverage A is changed in the HO-6 to provide a limit of $5,000 to cover the alterations, fixtures, and improvements that the insured owns or is responsible for within the residence premises. Coverage B is not provided by the HO-6. "Landlord's Furnishings" are *not* included in the HO-6 as an Additional Coverage.
Section I—Perils Insured Against	
Section I—Exclusions	
Section I—Conditions	Coverages A and C under the HO-6 cover "named perils" similar to the Coverage C "named perils" provided by the HO-3.
Note: Section II is the same on all ISO homeowners forms	
Section II—Liability Coverages	
Section II—Exclusions	All HO-6 Coverage A losses are settled for replacement cost if the repairs are made (ACV if the insured does not make repairs).
Section II—Additional Coverages	
Section II—Conditions	
Sections I and II—Conditions	

Section I—Property

Section II—Liability

The HO-8 contains a few more coverage limitations, as compared with the HO-3:

- The HO-8 provides *limited named perils* coverage for all Section I losses. The named perils mentioned in Exhibit 7-4 as covered by the HO-8 are fewer and less broad than those in other homeowners policies.

- Theft coverage provided under the HO-8 applies only if the theft occurs at the residence premises, and the total limit for any one theft loss is $1,000. The usual homeowners special limits for loss by theft of jewelry, firearms, and silverware would serve no purpose in this form, and they do not appear in the HO-8.

- The HO-8 limits off-premises coverage for personal property to 10 percent of Coverage C, or $1,000 (whichever is greater). The HO-3 provides coverage for personal property worldwide up to the Coverage C limit.

- The HO-8 does not include the additional coverages of collapse, landlord's furnishings, ordinance or law, and grave markers.

- The HO-8 provides debris removal coverage; however, it is included within the limit that applies to the damaged property rather than as an additional amount of insurance.

Exhibit 7-4 displays the significant areas of difference between the HO-3 and the HO-8.

AAIS HOMEOWNERS FORMS

Like Insurance Services Office (ISO), the American Association of Insurance Services (AAIS) is an advisory organization that develops policies and provides actuarial, statistical, filing, and software support. AAIS will work with its affiliated companies to provide customized policy programs to meet their specific needs.

AAIS offers two separate, complete homeowners programs, the Primary (standard) and the Alternate (a "back-to-basics" program). The AAIS forms described in this text (the Primary or standard forms) are comparable to the ISO HO forms. The Alternate Program (which also includes versions of all the coverage forms—Basic, Broad, Special, etc.) is not discussed here.

Highlights of the AAIS Homeowners Program include:

- Five forms to insure one- to four-family dwellings against a variety of perils, as well as the insured's liability exposures,

- A Contents form to insure the property and liability exposures of a tenant of an apartment or a dwelling,

- A Unit-Owners form to insure the interests of a condominium or cooperative unit owner,

- An assortment of loss settlement terms that allow the company to choose the valuation most appropriate for each risk, and

- A variety of coverage options to tailor the policy to the insured's needs.

EXHIBIT 7-4

Comparison of HO-3 and HO-8 Policies

Policy Segments	Differences Between HO-3 and HO-8

Section I—Property

Agreement

Definitions

Section I—Property Coverages ◄

Section I—Perils Insured Against ◄

Section I—Exclusions

Section I—Conditions ◄

Note: Section II is the same on all ISO homeowners forms

Section II—Liability

Section II—Liability Coverages

Section II—Exclusions

Section II—Additional Coverages

Section II—Conditions

Sections I and II—Conditions

Differences Between HO-3 and HO-8

Coverage C under the HO-8 differs from Coverage C under the HO-3 as follows:

- Only 10 percent of the Coverage C limit (or $1,000, whichever is greater) is provided worldwide (the HO-3 allows 100 percent).

- There are no special limits for the theft of jewelry, firearms, or silver in the HO-8, but any one theft loss is limited to $1,000. Theft is covered only at the residence premises.

HO-8 Additional Coverages differ from those in the HO-3 as follows:

- Debris removal is included within the limit of liability applying to the damaged property (the HO-3 allows an additional 5 percent of the applicable limit).

- Collapse is not provided in the HO-8.

- Ordinance or law, grave markers, and landlord's furnishings additional coverages are not provided in the HO-8.

Coverages A, B, and C are covered under the HO-8 for an abbreviated list of named perils: fire, lightning, windstorm or hail, explosion, riot or civil commotion, aircraft, vehicles, smoke, vandalism and malicious mischief, volcanic eruption, and theft (theft is *only* covered from the residence premises and up to a limit of $1,000).

The Loss Settlement condition for Coverages A and B under the HO-8 differs significantly from that under the HO-3. Under the HO-8, if the insured makes repairs after a loss, the insurer will not pay more than the cost of "common construction materials and methods" that are functionally equivalent to and less costly than obsolete, antique, or custom construction. If the insured does not make repairs, the insurer will not pay more than "market value at the time of loss."

AAIS Coverage Forms

The AAIS program includes seven coverage forms as shown in Exhibit 7-5. Each form provides both property and liability coverages. The liability coverage is identical in each form; however, the property coverage and perils differ.

EXHIBIT 7-5

AAIS Homeowners Forms

Form No.	Title	Property Covered
Form 1	Basic	Residence; Related Private Structures; Personal Property; Additional Living Costs and Loss of Rent
Form 2	Broad	
Form 3*	Special	
Form 5	Special Building and Contents	
Form 8	Limited	
Form 4	Contents Broad Form	Personal Property; Additional Living Costs and Loss of Rent
Form 6*	Unit-Owner's Form	Fixtures, Alterations, Additions, Structures Owned by Insured; Personal Property; Additional Living Costs, and Loss of Rent

*Form 3, the special form, provides special-form coverage (on an "open perils" or "risks not excluded" basis) for the residence and related private structures. Broad named perils apply to loss to personal property. In Form 6, the broad named perils apply to all covered property.

Exhibit 7-6 provides a comparison of the ISO and AAIS programs with respect to the special limits on certain property under Coverage C.

A distinctive feature of the AAIS homeowners *liability* coverage is that it provides incidental liability coverages through an affirmative statement of coverage rather than as an exception to an exclusion. For example, the AAIS forms provide coverage explicitly for liability arising out of the use of certain motorized vehicles and watercraft as specific *Incidental Liability Coverages*. In many other standard homeowners forms such as those provided by ISO, these incidental liability coverages are provided by way of exceptions to exclusions.

Another unique feature of the AAIS Homeowners Program is its simplified fire protection definitions. As mentioned later in this chapter, ISO uses ten protection classes; with AAIS, each home is placed in one of three protection groups: protected, partially protected, or unprotected. This categorization not only simplifies the selection of the appropriate protection class for a given insured but also facilitates the rating process.

EXHIBIT 7-6

Coverage C—Property Subject to Limitations, AAIS and ISO Forms Compared

Covered Property: Money, bank notes, bullion, gold other than goldware and gold-plated ware, silver other than silverware and silver-plated ware, platinum, and numismatic property.	AAIS: $250 ISO: $200
Covered Property: Securities, stamps, letters of credit, notes other than bank notes, tickets, accounts, deeds, evidence of debt, passports, personal records, and manuscripts. **Comments:** AAIS Form 5 limit: $2,500 per occurrence	AAIS: $1,500 ISO: $1,500
Covered Property: Electronic devices, accessories, and antennas that can be operated from the electrical system of a motorized vehicle or watercraft and by other sources of power. This includes films, tapes, wires, discs, records, and other media for use with such devices. **Comments:** (1) In the AAIS program, the limit applies to devices while in or on a **motorized vehicle or watercraft** and to devices used for business and away from the insured premises. (2) The ISO form contains two $1,500 limitations: one applies while in or on a **motor vehicle**, and the other applies to devices used for business and away from the insured premises. The limitation does not apply to property in or on watercraft. (3) AAIS Form 5 limit: $2,500 per occurrence.	AAIS: $1,500 ISO: $1,500
Covered Property: Watercraft, including trailers, furnishings, equipment, and engines or motors. **Comments:** AAIS Form 5 limit: $2,500 per occurrence.	AAIS: $1,500 ISO: $1,500
Covered Property: Trailers not otherwise provided for. **Comments:** AAIS Form 5 limit: $2,500 per occurrence.	AAIS: $1,500 ISO: $1,500
Covered Property: Theft loss to jewelry, watches, precious and semiprecious stones, gems, and furs. **Comments:** (1) AAIS Form 8 does not cover loss caused by theft. (2) In AAIS Form 5 and ISO HO 00 05, the limitation on theft also includes loss from losing or misplacing. (3) ISO HO 08 limit: $1,000.	AAIS: $2,500 ISO: $1,500
Covered Property: Theft loss to silverware, goldware, pewterware, and gold- and silver-plated items. **Comments:** (1) ISO HO 00 08 limit: $1,000. (2) AAIS Form 8 does not include loss from theft. (3) In AAIS Form 5 and ISO HO 00 05, theft also includes loss from losing or misplacing.	AAIS: $2,500 ISO: $2,500
Covered Property: Theft loss to guns **Comments:** (1) ISO HO 00 08 limit: $1,000. (2) AAIS Form 8 does not include loss from theft. (3) In AAIS Form 5 and ISO HO 00 05, theft includes loss from losing or misplacing. The ISO form limitation also applies to related equipment such as ammunition, scopes, etc.	AAIS: $2,500 ISO: $2,500
Covered Property: Business property	AAIS: $2,500 on premises/ $250 away from premises ISO: $2,500 on premises/ $500 away from premises

The ISO and AAIS programs contain comparable exclusions that apply to liability coverages. However, the AAIS program includes three additional exclusions that have been filed as endorsements: punitive damages, lead liability, and pollution. These endorsements are mandatory in most states. Although the ISO program contains a provision for a lead liability limitation, it does not otherwise address these exposures.

COMPANY-SPECIFIC FORMS

Some insurance companies, especially those writing a high volume of home-owners business, create their own policy forms or endorsements to address the needs of various types of customers or to distinguish their products in the marketplace. For example, one insurer might choose to provide property coverage on watercraft for more than the $1,500 special limit of standard ISO homeowners contracts. An insurance company that uses ISO forms but wants to provide this coverage enhancement might draft an endorsement, develop rates, and request approval for use of the endorsement and rates from the regulatory authorities in the insurer's states of operation.

Any given company-specific policy form or endorsement must be evaluated on its own to determine how it differs from standard ISO or AAIS policy forms.

STATE-SPECIFIC ENDORSEMENTS

Every state regulates insurance operations within that state. Policy forms and endorsements that are developed for countrywide use are approved by the various states. States often require that a policy form be modified before they will approve it. A policy can be modified by creating a special version of the form for use within that state. More often, an endorsement is developed that modifies the standard policy form. Some state endorsements provide optional coverages that can be used within the state.

State-specific endorsements vary widely. Insurance professionals should become familiar with the endorsements that are required or available within their states of operation.

ENDORSEMENTS THAT MODIFY ISO FORMS

Many endorsements are available to modify ISO homeowners policies. Endorsements can increase or decrease limits, add or remove coverages, change definitions, clarify policy intent, or recognize specific characteristics that require a premium increase or decrease. This section discusses some of the ISO endorsements that are used frequently and that are approved by most states. Many other endorsements, not mentioned in this text, are also available.

Endorsements That Modify Section I—Property Coverages

This section presents a more complete description of the property-related homeowners endorsements that were briefly mentioned in Chapter 5, as well as some additional endorsements. Most of the endorsements affecting only the property section of the homeowners policy increase dollar limits for some exposures, change the valuation approach, or expand the list of covered perils. The first two endorsements mentioned below serve all three purposes.

Endorsements That Increase Limits, Modify Valuation, and Expand Perils

A few property insurance endorsements modify a standard, unendorsed homeowners policy to provide increased limits of coverage, modify the valuation approach, and provide coverage against more perils.

Scheduled Personal Property Endorsement

Perhaps the most popular homeowners policy endorsement is the *scheduled personal property endorsement* (HO 04 61). The same coverage is also available in a separate inland marine floater policy, the *personal articles floater*, mentioned in Chapter 9. Either a scheduled personal property endorsement or a personal articles floater is used to provide appropriate coverage for insureds who own jewelry, furs, or other eligible property for which an unendorsed homeowners policy does not provide adequate protection. Remember, an unendorsed homeowners policy (except for the HO-5) covers personal property against only named perils, and that might not be satisfactory for a policyholder who owns expensive cameras or musical instruments. Also, all homeowners policies impose special across-the-board sublimits on certain types of property such as stamps and coins, and they include special sublimits on theft of jewelry and other types of property.

Schedule
List of insured property items that are covered, with each item specifically described and having its own coverage limit.

The scheduled personal property endorsement provides coverage for a **schedule** of specific items. The following categories of property can be covered under the scheduled personal property endorsement:

1. Jewelry
2. Furs
3. Cameras
4. Musical instruments
5. Silverware
6. Golfer's equipment
7. Fine arts
8. Postage stamps
9. Rare and current coins

Special-form (open perils) coverage applies to the items scheduled on the endorsement; in other words, such items are covered for "risks of direct loss to property" with only a few exclusions:

- Wear and tear, gradual deterioration, or inherent vice

- Insects or vermin

- War, including civil war, insurrection, rebellion, or discharge of a nuclear weapon

- Nuclear hazards

Breakage of glass and breakage of other fragile items, as well as damage that occurs during restoration, are also excluded for scheduled fine arts. For stamps and coins, the perils of fading, tearing, and loss during shipping (other than by registered mail) are excluded.

The HO-5 is the only homeowners form that includes special-form coverage on personal property, but even the HO-5 has special limits and deductibles. As compared with the HO-3 and other homeowners forms, the scheduled personal property endorsement covers more causes of loss. As compared with all homeowners forms, the insured receives the following benefits for property scheduled on this endorsement:

- The Coverage C special limits do not apply to scheduled items.

- The Section I deductible does not apply to scheduled items.

- Newly acquired property is covered for thirty days (ninety days for fine arts) for 25 percent of the amount of insurance for that category of property (or $10,000, if less, for property other than fine arts).

Unless the homeowners policy has been endorsed to provide replacement cost coverage (this endorsement is discussed later), loss to a scheduled item (other than a fine arts object) is settled at the least of (1) actual cash value, (2) the cost to repair the item, (3) the amount for which the item could be replaced with one substantially identical to the lost or damaged item, or (4) the amount of insurance.

Fine arts losses are settled on a different basis. Because fine arts are often unique, their value is difficult to determine after a loss or disappearance. Therefore, fine arts are written on an **agreed value** basis. If a piece of fine art is lost or damaged, the insurer will settle the loss based on the value listed for the scheduled fine art item. The insured agrees to surrender the fine-arts property (unless it has been lost or stolen) to the insurer. The insured may then repurchase the surrendered property from the insurer at a price they both agree to.

Agreed value approach
Approach to valuation in which the insurer and the insured agree on the value of the insured object and state it in a policy schedule; in case of total loss, the insurer pays the amount specified in the policy.

Scheduling articles in a scheduled personal property endorsement can create a significant difference in the coverage as compared with the amount that would be paid under an unendorsed homeowners policy. Exhibit 7-7 provides examples of the difference in loss settlements for unscheduled and scheduled property.

EXHIBIT 7-7

Examples of Homeowners Loss Settlement Differences for Unscheduled and Scheduled Items

Item insured and type of loss	Loss settlement under the ISO HO-2, 3, 4, or 6 (item not scheduled)	Loss settlement under the ISO HO-5 (item not scheduled)	Loss settlement when the item is scheduled on ISO scheduled personal property form (HO-04-61)
A $5,000 diamond ring is stolen.	$1,500: This is the sublimit that applies for loss by theft of jewelry under Coverage C special limits.	$1,500: This is the sublimit that applies for loss by theft, losing, or misplacing of jewelry under Coverage C special limits.	Coverage applies for the lesser of the item's actual cash value or the amount for which it could be replaced. If the ring is insured for $5,000, the insurer would probably pay $5,000 or the cost to replace the ring with a similar one, if less.
A watch with an ACV of $2,500 is accidentally dropped down the garbage disposal and is destroyed.	$0: This is not a covered peril for personal property items.	$2,500 (or a lesser amount required to replace the watch), minus deductible: This is not an excluded peril under the HO-5.	$2,500 (or a lesser amount required to replace the watch). No deductible is subtracted.
An antique table appraised at $10,000 is ruined beyond repair after a chandelier comes loose from the ceiling and falls onto it.	$0: This is not a covered peril for personal property items.	The actual cash value of the table, minus a deductible: This is not an excluded peril under the HO-5.	If the table is insured for a $10,000 agreed value as fine arts, the insurer would pay the agreed value of $10,000. No deductible is subtracted.

Scheduled Personal Property Endorsement (With Agreed Value Loss Settlement)

The scheduled personal property endorsement described above includes a stated value for each covered item but provides agreed value coverage only on fine arts. For other articles, many insureds did not understand that the amount they would recover after a loss under the aforementioned form might be less than the amount of insurance. For example, a stolen ring scheduled for $1,000 might have a replacement cost value of $900 and an actual cash value of $800, in which case the insurer would pay $800.

To provide coverage more in line with consumers' expectations, the Homeowners 2000 program introduced a *scheduled personal property endorsement (with agreed value loss settlement)* (HO 04 60) that, as the name suggests, provides agreed value coverage on all scheduled property items. For loss to an item that is part of a pair or set, the insurer agrees to pay the full value of the pair or set shown in the schedule.

When the insurer pays the agreed value of an article, pair, or set, the insured agrees to surrender the damaged article(s) or the remaining parts of the pair or set to the insurer. The insured may buy them back from the insurance company at a negotiated price.

Endorsements That Increase Limits

With an HO-3 policy, the insured typically selects a limit of coverage under the dwelling Coverage A and then accepts Coverage B, C, and D limits that are set at a percentage of the Coverage A limit. For example, an HO-3 covering a dwelling for $100,000 would typically cover other detached structures for $10,000; personal property for $50,000; and loss of use for $30,000. Coverage C and D limits can be changed without an endorsement simply by changing the dollar amount shown in the declarations and modifying the premium accordingly.

Apartment dwellers and condominium unit owners select an appropriate limit for Coverage C—Personal Property, and the limits of other coverages are based on a percentage of that figure. Limits on Coverage C—Personal Property and Coverage D—Loss of Use can be increased by indicating the higher limit on the policy declarations and paying a higher premium. Limits for Coverage C can also be reduced as low as 40 percent of the Coverage A limit in exchange for a premium credit.

The standard percentages for other coverages are designed to meet the needs of a typical policyholder. For example, most people do not own personal property whose actual cash value is greater than 50 percent of the replacement cost value of the house the property is in. But some families' needs are not typical, because they own high values of personal property or have valuable outbuildings, swimming pools, tennis courts, or other structures on their property. A variety of endorsements, discussed here, can be used to increase these limits where needed—for an additional premium, of course.

Some endorsements automatically increase Coverage A limits and other limits to reflect changing values. These are also discussed in this section of the chapter.

Other Structures—Increased Limits

Coverage B—Other Structures is provided in the unendorsed HO-2, HO-3, HO-5, and HO-8 policies for 10 percent of the Coverage A—Dwelling limit. This amount applies in addition to the Coverage A limit. For example, an insured with a limit of $150,000 on the house would have $15,000 automatically provided by the homeowners policy for Coverage B—Other Structures. If the insured has a detached garage with a replacement value of $20,000, the *other structures—increased limits endorsement* (HO 04 48) can be used to provide additional coverage for this structure.

Individual structures can be scheduled on the endorsement with a designated amount of additional insurance applying to each. For the example provided, a producer would write this endorsement to indicate an additional limit of $5,000 for the garage. If the insured has additional detached structures, such as storage sheds, swimming pools, or stables, they could also be listed in the endorsement, with a separate limit shown for each.

Increased Limit on Personal Property in Other Residences

In an unendorsed homeowners policy, coverage on personal property items that are usually located at a secondary residence is limited to $1,000 or 10 percent of Coverage C, whichever is more. The *increased limit on personal property in other residences endorsement* (HO 04 50) can be used to increase this limit. The location and limit of additional coverage must be listed on the endorsement. This endorsement might be used, for example, to provide adequate personal property coverage for a student living in a college dormitory (secondary residence), whose computer alone might be worth more than $1,000.

Coverage C Increased Special Limits of Liability

Coverage C—Personal Property includes special limits for certain categories of property (such as $200 for money and $1,500 for theft of jewelry) as explained in Chapter 5. A *Coverage C increased special limits of liability endorsement* (HO 04 65, or HO 04 66 for policies providing special-form coverage), can increase these limits for property in one or more of the categories.

A person with more than $1,500 worth of jewelry might consider either this endorsement, which merely increases the special sublimits, or one of the somewhat broader scheduled personal property endorsements discussed earlier. The "increased special limits" endorsement does not change the perils for which the property is covered. Also, items insured in this endorsement are not listed in a schedule, and agreed amount coverage does not apply. Because it has a $1,000 sublimit for any one article of jewelry, this endorsement would not be well-suited for a person who needs theft coverage on any individual items worth more than $1,000.

Increased Limit on Business Property

In the HO-3, special limits under Coverage C—Personal Property apply to business property on the premises ($2,500) and off the premises ($500). By attaching the *increased limit on business property endorsement* (HO 04 12), these limits can be increased; however, the increased limits do not apply to business property in storage, held as a sample for sale or delivery after a sale, or to property pertaining to a business conducted on the premises.

This endorsement might be useful for an insured who works for an employer but has an office at home. The office furniture, computer equipment, and business supplies with values in excess of the Coverage C special limits could be covered by showing the increase in the limit of coverage on this endorsement. Other endorsements, discussed later, can provide broader coverage on business-in-the-home exposures, addressing both property and liability exposures.

Credit Card, Fund Transfer Card or Access Device, Forgery, and Counterfeit Money Coverage

The credit card, fund transfer card or access device, forgery, and counterfeit money additional coverage under Section I of the homeowners policies provides coverage up to a limit of $500 for losses resulting from the unauthorized use of an insured's credit card, bank transfer card, check forgery, or acceptance of counterfeit money. The *credit card, electronic fund transfer card or access device, forgery and counterfeit money coverage endorsement* (HO 04 53) can be used to increase the limit of insurance for this additional coverage.

Ordinance or Law—Increased Amount of Coverage

The ordinance or law additional coverage under Section I of the homeowners policies provides an additional limit of 10 percent of Coverage A (10 percent of the building additions and alterations limit on an HO-4) to pay for the increased costs of construction incurred because of enforcement of a building code or other ordinance or law. The *ordinance or law—increased amount of coverage endorsement* (HO 04 77) is frequently used to increase the limit of coverage for this type of loss. This endorsement cannot be attached to the HO-8, which does not include the ordinance or law additional coverage.

Inflation Guard

During inflationary periods, the value of real estate can increase rapidly, with the result that an adequate amount of insurance at the beginning of a policy term becomes inadequate before the policy expires. The inflation guard endorsement is a tool designed to help prevent underinsurance caused by economic inflation and rising replacement costs. Rather than increasing coverage by a fixed amount, the popular *inflation guard endorsement* (HO 04 46) gradually increases limits throughout the policy period for Coverages A, B, C, and D.

A percentage increase is selected and noted on the endorsement. The coverage is increased daily, on a pro rata (proportional) basis, during the policy period. For example, James has a homeowners policy with the following Section I limits:

Coverage A—Dwelling $200,000

Coverage B—Other Structures   20,000

Coverage C—Personal Property   100,000

Coverage D—Loss of Use   60,000

James purchases an inflation guard endorsement with a stated annual percentage increase of 6 percent.

James has a covered fire loss that destroys his home and its contents six months after the policy inception date. Because of the inflation guard endorsement, James has an additional 3 percent for Section I coverages when the loss occurs.

$$\left(\frac{6 \text{ months}}{12 \text{ months}}\right) = \frac{1}{2} \times 6\% = 3\%$$

Therefore, James would have the following limits at the time of the loss:

Coverage A: $206,000

Coverage B: 20,600

Coverage C: 103,000

Coverage D: 61,800

Endorsements Changing the Valuation Approach

Homeowners policies, except for the HO-8, usually value building property at its replacement cost and personal property at its actual cash value. Two alternatives, discussed here, do not increase policy limits but (1) agree to pay whatever it costs to repair or replace real property, even if that amount exceeds policy limits, or (2) value personal property on a replacement cost basis.

Additional Limits of Liability for Coverages A, B, C, and D

Except for the inflation guard, previously discussed endorsements increase policy limits on the inception date of the policy (or the inception date of the endorsement if it is added midterm). In contrast, the increases inherent in the *additional limits of liability for Coverages A, B, C, and D endorsement* occur only when there is a total loss to the dwelling and the Coverage A limit shown in the declarations is not enough to pay for its replacement. Once the dwelling's actual replacement cost is known, the Coverage A limit is increased to that amount—retroactively to the date of the loss. The limits for Coverages B, C, and D are automatically increased by the same percentage of increase that applied to Coverage A, also retroactively to the date of the loss.

In exchange for this coverage, the insured agrees to maintain Coverage A limits equal to 100 percent of the full replacement cost of the dwelling *as determined by the insurer* and to report any alterations that increase the dwelling's value by 5 percent or more. Thus, the endorsement, in effect, guarantees that the insurer has required an adequate amount of coverage.

Even a house that is properly appraised and insured to value when the policy period begins does not necessarily have enough insurance to rebuild it after a loss. The cost of repairing or replacing houses sometimes increases dramatically when contractors and building materials are in short supply following damage to many homes in an area from a hurricane, a forest fire, or an earthquake. By ensuring that enough insurance is available to replace the dwelling, this endorsement provides peace of mind for insureds.

Personal Property Replacement Cost Loss Settlement

The endorsement discussed here has become fairly popular, and it provides a valuable expansion in coverage. While the dwelling building and other structures are usually covered for their replacement cost value, losses to Coverage C—Personal Property items are settled on an actual cash value basis under the terms of all unendorsed homeowners forms. The *personal property replacement cost loss settlement endorsement* (HO 04 90) can provide replacement cost coverage on personal property. Replacement cost coverage is also extended to awnings, carpeting, household appliances, and outdoor equipment, which are not covered for their replacement cost by the unendorsed homeowners forms. According to this endorsement, the following property is ineligible for replacement cost coverage:

- Antiques, fine arts, paintings and similar articles of rarity or antiquity that cannot be replaced.
- Memorabilia, souvenirs, collectors items and similar articles whose age or history contribute to their value.
- Articles not maintained in good or workable condition.
- Articles that are outdated or obsolete and are stored or not being used.

If a loss occurs to an item that is covered for replacement cost by this endorsement, the insurer will pay no more than the least of the following amounts:

- Replacement cost at the time of loss without deduction for depreciation;
- The full cost of repair at the time of loss;
- The limit of liability that applies to Coverage C, if applicable;
- Any applicable special limits of liability stated in this policy; or
- For loss to any item separately described and specifically insured in this policy, the limit that applies to the item.

For losses with a replacement value of more than $500, the insured must repair or replace the lost or damaged items before the insurer will pay the replacement cost (ACV is paid until repair or replacement is made). The insured can make an ACV claim at the time of loss and later make a claim for the additional replacement cost, provided the insured notifies the insurer within 180 days after the loss that it intends to make an additional claim to recoup the replacement cost.

The value of personal property on a replacement cost basis is usually higher than property valued on an actual cash value basis. Accordingly, many insurers require a Coverage C—Personal Property limit higher than 50 percent of Coverage A (the usual limit with actual cash value coverage) when this endorsement is used. The endorsement itself does not increase the Coverage C limit, but an increased limit usually accompanies the endorsement.

Endorsements Adding Coverage for More Perils

Some endorsements can be used to provide special-form (open perils) coverage on property otherwise covered for named perils. Other endorsements can add coverage for perils that are otherwise excluded, even under policies providing special-form coverage.

Special Computer Coverage

The *special computer coverage endorsement* (HO 04 14) appeals to many homeowners who own personal computers. Homeowners sometimes want coverage on their computer equipment that is broader than the coverage of an unendorsed homeowners policy such as the HO-3, which provides named perils coverage on personal property.

The special computer coverage endorsement can be attached to a homeowners policy to provide special-form coverage for computers and computer equipment (coverage against risks of direct physical loss subject to specified exclusions). The excluded perils are similar to those for other special-form coverages, such as Coverages A and B of the HO-3. Covered computers and equipment are not scheduled. Computer equipment is defined as:

1. Computer hardware, software, operating systems or networks; and
2. Other electronic parts, equipment or systems solely designed for use with or connected to equipment in 1. above.

Although this endorsement covers this equipment against more perils than an unendorsed HO-3, it does not provide additional amounts of insurance, eliminate the deductible, or change the valuation approach for computer equipment. Coverage C's special limits on electronic apparatus and business property still apply. Other endorsements, discussed later, can be more appropriate for business-related computer exposures.

Special-Form Contents Coverage

All unendorsed homeowners forms, except for the HO-5, provide personal property coverage on a named-perils basis. The homeowners forms for apartment tenants or condominium unit owners can be modified to provide contents coverage similar to that of the HO-5 by using the *special personal property coverage—Form HO 00 04 only endorsement* (HO 05 24) and the *unit-owners Coverage C special coverage endorsement* (HO 17 31), respectively.

Earth Movement, Including Earthquake

Building, contents, and loss of use coverage against any kind of earth movement—including earthquake and landslide—is excluded from all unendorsed homeowners forms.

Optional *earthquake endorsement* (HO 04 54) provides a means to buy coverage only for damage caused by earthquake and land shock waves caused by volcanic eruption. A mandatory deductible applies for each earthquake loss. The standard earthquake deductible is 5 percent of the limit that applies to either Coverage A—Dwelling or Coverage C—Personal Property, whichever is greater. The deductible percentage can be increased for a premium credit. The minimum deductible for any earthquake loss is $250.

Water Back-Up and Sump Discharge or Overflow

Unendorsed homeowners policies exclude property coverage for water or waterborne materials that back up through sewers or drains or that overflow or are discharged from a sump, sump pump, or related equipment. The *water back up and sump discharge or overflow endorsement* (HO 04 95) covers direct losses from such sources up to $5,000 for property covered under Section I. A special deductible of $250 applies to this endorsement and replaces any other deductible that might apply to the policy.

Endorsements That Modify Section II—Liability Coverages

In Chapter 6 of this text, commonly used endorsements that change the liability section of the homeowners policy (Section II) were briefly noted in shaded boxes. A more complete description of those endorsements follows, along with other popular liability endorsements.

Personal Injury

The *personal injury endorsement* (HO 24 82) adds an additional liability insuring agreement expanding the homeowners policy to cover not only bodily injury but also personal injury. **Personal injury** is defined in this endorsement as injuries arising out of one or more of the covered offenses committed during the policy period:

- False arrest, detention or imprisonment
- Malicious prosecution
- Publishing oral or written material involving libel, slander, or invasion of privacy
- Wrongful eviction, wrongful entry, or invasion of privacy involving improper occupancy of a room, dwelling, or premises

Personal injury
Injury arising out of specified offenses, typically including libel, slander, and invasion of privacy.

Coverage provided by this endorsement does not apply to:

- Acts intended to cause personal injury
- Publishing material known to be false
- Material published before the policy period began
- Contractual liability that does not relate to the insured's premises
- A criminal act committed by or at the direction of an insured
- Contractual liability, except related to lease agreements
- Business activities (except as landlord)
- Civic activities
- Personal injury to an insured
- Pollution claims

Business Pursuits

Section II exclusions in the unendorsed homeowners policy forms eliminate coverage for liability "arising out of or in connection with a 'business' conducted from an insured location or engaged in by an 'insured', whether or not the 'business' is owned or operated by an 'insured' or employs an 'insured'." The *business pursuits endorsement* (HO 24 71) can be added to any homeowners form to extend Section II liability coverages to a person and business listed on the endorsement. However, the scope of business exposures covered by the endorsement is limited. This endorsement does *not* apply to:

- A business owned or financially controlled by the insured (or the insured as a member in a partnership)
- Professional liability
- Injury to a fellow employee

When the insured is a teacher, coverage is excluded for losses arising from saddle animals, aircraft, motor vehicles, watercraft, or corporal punishment of a student. The corporal punishment exclusion can be deleted for an additional premium.

Even though this endorsement provides no coverage on business property (a business property endorsement was discussed earlier), and the liability coverage this endorsement provides is limited, it can be useful for persons involved in sales, clerical, and instructional occupations.

Additional Residence Rented to Others

This endorsement is designed for policyholders who also own rental property. The *additional residence rented to others endorsement* (HO 24 70) can be attached to any of the homeowners forms to extend Coverages E—Personal Liability and F—Medical Payments to Others to one- to four-family residences that are owned by the insured and rented to others. The location of the additional residences must be listed on the endorsement along with an indication of the number of families that occupy each.

Incidental Low-Power Recreational Motor Vehicles

The *incidental low power recreational motor vehicles endorsement* (HO 24 13) can be attached to any of the homeowners forms to extend Coverages E and F to cover recreational motorized vehicles that have maximum attainable speeds of less than fifteen miles per hour and that are not subject to motor vehicle registration. Mopeds, motorized bicycles, and motorized golf carts are specifically excluded. This endorsement is generally used to extend liability coverage to miniature automobiles or to other motorized land vehicles designed for use off public roads while the vehicles are away from an insured location.

Just as this edition of the text was being finished, inventor Dean Kamen unveiled the Segway Human Transporter. Perhaps the Segway will also be eligible for coverage under this endorsement.

Owned Snowmobile

The *owned snowmobile endorsement* (HO 24 64) can be attached to any of the homeowners forms to extend Coverages E and F to scheduled snowmobiles while they are off an insured location (liability involving unregistered snowmobiles on the insured location can be covered under an unendorsed homeowners policy). Coverage under the endorsement does not apply to a snowmobile that is (1) subject to motor vehicle registration, (2) used to carry passengers or cargo for a charge, (3) used for any business purpose, (4) rented to others, or (5) operated in or used to practice for any prearranged or organized competition.

Snowmobiles subject to motor vehicle registration can be insured under a Personal Auto Policy, as explained in Chapter 4.

Watercraft

The homeowners forms limit the watercraft covered under Section II— Liability Coverages according to the type and length of the watercraft and the horsepower of the motors. Liability coverage for an otherwise excluded watercraft can be covered under Section II by attaching a *watercraft endorsement* (HO 24 75) scheduling the watercraft.

The endorsement does not extend coverage to the following:

- Watercraft, other than sailboats, used for racing or competitions
- Injuries to employees whose principal duties are the maintenance or use of the watercraft
- Watercraft used to carry persons or cargo for a fee or watercraft rented to others or used for business purposes

The various options for insuring watercraft property and liability exposures are examined more closely in Chapter 9.

Endorsements That Modify Sections I and II

Some commonly used endorsements modify both Section I—Property Coverages and Section II—Liability Coverages of the homeowners policy. The endorsements apply to homeowners who face a situation, not faced by the typical homeowner, involving both property and liability insurance needs.

Endorsements Dealing With Who Is Insured

Some endorsements expand the coverage of an unendorsed homeowners policy to include parties for whom property and liability coverage is not otherwise provided.

Additional Insured

The *additional insured—residence premises endorsement* (HO 04 41) can be used to include the persons or organizations named on the endorsement as insureds with respect to the following coverages:

- Coverages A—Dwelling and B—Other Structures
- Coverages E—Personal Liability and F—Medical Payments to Others, but only with respect to the "residence premises." Bodily injury to an employee of the additional insured is not covered.

For example, a woman purchases her first house with a mortgage that she and her father have obtained jointly. The father, who does not live in this house, requests that he be added to the homeowners policy as an additional insured to protect his interests in the property. If the house is destroyed in a total fire, the father will be covered through this endorsement for his interest in the dwelling, but the father would not have coverage for the contents in the house. Also, in the event of a liability claim involving the property, the father would have coverage as an insured provided by the homeowners policy under Coverage E.

Residence Held in Trust

An increasing number of homeowners have established a separate legal entity, known as a trust, that holds the title to the dwelling building. Trust arrangements are established for various legal reasons beyond the scope of this text. A homeowners policy to which the *residence held in trust endorsement* (HO 05 43) has been added can be used to insure a home owned by a trust. The endorsement modifies various provisions in Sections I and II of the policy that deal with the parties whose interests are insured under the policy.

Assisted Living Care Coverage

An increasing number of people, both with and without disabilities, live in assisted living care facilities. The *assisted living care coverage endorsement* (HO 04 59) was developed to provide limited coverage for personal property, additional living expenses, and liability for relatives of an insured who live in these facilities but are not members of the insured's household.

The insured relative is named and Coverage C (personal property) and Coverage E (liability) limits are shown. Special dollar sublimits apply to coverage on hearing aids, eyeglasses, contact lenses, false teeth, medi-alert devices, walkers or canes, and wheelchairs. Additional living expense coverage is also provided for up to $500 per month.

Endorsements Providing Business-Related Coverage

The business exclusions under Section I and Section II of the standard, unendorsed homeowners policies were described in detail in Chapters 5 and 6. To summarize, coverage on other structures (such as a detached garage) where business is conducted is excluded. Coverage on personal property on the residence premises and used primarily for any business purpose is limited to $2,500, and business property away from the home is covered for a maximum of $500. No coverage applies to business data. Subject to some exceptions described in Chapter 6, bodily injury or property damage arising out of any insured's business activities is also excluded. In exchange for an additional premium, the endorsements described here permit a policyholder with business-related exposures to "buy back" some of the excluded coverage.

Permitted Incidental Occupancies—Residence Premises

The *permitted incidental occupancies—residence premises endorsement* (HO 04 42) deletes or modifies the business exclusions affecting both property and liability coverages. The business described on the endorsement must be "conducted by an 'insured' on the 'residence premises'" in either the dwelling or an "other structure" described in the schedule. This endorsement, which can be used with any of the policy forms, changes the policy in the following ways:

- Coverage B—If an insured conducts business from a separate structure on the residence premises, the insured can purchase property coverage on the scheduled structure for a limit specified in the endorsement. For example, if Judy makes and sells ceramic products in her detached garage, she can use this endorsement to cover the garage building with a specific property limit.

- This endorsement deletes the special limit of $2,500 that applies under Coverage C—Personal Property to property on the residence premises used primarily for business purposes and applies the full limit of Coverage C for business property, as well as other personal property, on the residence premises.

- Section II liability coverage is excluded on an unendorsed homeowners policy for business activities. The permitted incidental occupancies endorsement eliminates this exclusion and provides coverage for the necessary or incidental use of the residence premises to conduct *the business described on the endorsement*. Other business activities are still excluded. Liability and medical payments coverage is specifically excluded for bodily injury to an employee of the insured in connection with the described business.

The permitted incidental occupancies endorsement provides limited coverage for an insured's business activities that are usually conducted from the home. However, it might be appropriate for a business with limited property and liability exposures. A business with more extensive exposures might consider the endorsement discussed next.

Home Business Insurance Coverage Endorsement

The *home business insurance coverage endorsement* (HO 07 01) is also designed for a business that is usually conducted from an insured's home; however, it provides a wider range of coverages. It provides coverages normally found only in a commercial insurance policy and might be appropriate for a home business that has a broad range of property and liability exposures. The endorsement specifically excludes professional liability coverage and lists many examples of professional activities that are excluded, ranging from legal, insurance, or accounting services to body piercing services.

The endorsement changes the homeowners policy to provide coverage as shown in Exhibit 7-8.

Home Daycare Coverage

Home daycare centers, involving both children and geriatric clients, represent a special kind of home business. Increased litigation involving home daycare centers has made this exposure difficult to insure. The *home day care coverage endorsement* (HO 04 97) can be used to extend coverage to a home daycare business—provided an insurer is willing to offer this coverage.

The number of persons receiving daycare services is listed on the endorsement. As with the permitted incidental occupancies endorsement, information is required about the location of the daycare center—that is, whether it is in the dwelling or in another structure on the residence premises.

If another structure is involved, a limit for that structure is indicated and an additional premium is charged.

In addition to providing coverage for the structure (other than the dwelling) in which the daycare business is conducted, the endorsement extends the Coverage C limit to include personal property used in the daycare business. Therefore, the $2,500 limit for personal property on the residence premises used for a business purpose does not apply to the property used in the daycare business.

Section II liability coverages are extended under the endorsement to include bodily injury and property damage arising out of home daycare services; however, damages resulting from saddle animals, aircraft, motor vehicles, or watercraft are not covered.

The limit of liability for Coverage E is changed from an occurrence limit to an annual aggregate limit of coverage (applying to all claims within the policy term). This obviously protects the insurer against the possibility of multiple claims that could develop because of the nature of the exposure.

Structures Rented to Others

This endorsement can meet the needs of a homeowner who has an unattached garage or other structure that has been converted into a rented apartment.

Unendorsed homeowners forms HO-2, HO-3, HO-5, and HO-8 preclude Coverage B—Other Structures coverage for structures rented to anyone who is not a resident of the dwelling (unless it is rented as a garage). Property and liability coverage can be purchased for these structures on the

EXHIBIT 7-8

Coverages Provided by the Home Business Insurance Coverage Endorsement

Coverage C	**Coverage C—Personal Property** is extended to cover business property (of the business named on the home business insurance coverage endorsement), property of others in the insured's care, and property leased by the insured (if there is a contractual requirement to insure such property).
Coverage C Special Limits of Liability	**Money, bank notes, gold, silver, etc.:** The limit is increased to $1,000 (from $200). Business property *on* the residence premises: The coverage for property of the business named on the endorsement is provided up to the limit of Coverage C. The limit continues to be $2,500 for any business that is *not* listed on the home business insurance coverage endorsement. Business property *off* the residence premises: The limit is increased to $5,000 (from $500) for the business named on the endorsement.
Section I Additional Coverages	The following *homeowners* coverages are extended to the business named on the home business insurance coverage endorsement: **Trees, shrubs, and other plants** coverage is extended to trees, shrubs, and plants grown for business purposes. **Credit card, fund transfer card, forgery and counterfeit money coverage** is extended to business losses, and the limit is increased to $1,000 (from $500). The following are *additional* coverages that apply to the business named on the home business insurance coverage endorsement: **Accounts Receivable Coverage** pays up to $5,000 for a loss caused by a covered peril to records of accounts receivable on the premises (up to $2,500 off the premises). **Valuable Papers and Records Coverage** pays up to $2,500 for a loss caused by a covered peril to manuscripts, records, and other documents for which there are no duplicates. **Business Income Coverage** pays for loss of business income when a loss from a covered peril results in a suspension of the business. **Extra Expense Coverage** pays the additional expenses a business incurs after a loss by a covered peril damages the residence where the business is located. **Civil Authority Coverage** pays for the actual loss of business income for three weeks after a civil authority prohibits access to the insured premises because of a nearby direct damage by a covered peril.
Section II	**Coverage E—Personal Liability** applies to personal and advertising injury, and products and completed operations exposures associated with the home business. Liability limits are set as follows: • For products and completed operations, the limit of liability is equal to the Coverage E limit. • For all other business liability and medical expenses, the limit of liability is set at an amount equal to twice the sum of the Coverage E and F limits. • Coverages E and F limits of liability are on an aggregate basis for the annual policy period.
Section II Additional Coverages	**Damage to Property of Others** is extended to the business named on the home business insurance coverage endorsement and the limit is increased from $1,000 to $2,500.
Section II Conditions	**Severability of Insurance** is modified for business liability so that coverage applies separately to each person insured under the policy, but it is subject to the annual aggregate.

residence premises that are rented to others by attaching the *structures rented to others—residence premises endorsement* (HO 04 40) to the home-owners policy. The structure must be described and a property limit shown on the endorsement.

Section II of the unendorsed homeowners policy eliminates liability coverage for property rented to others. This endorsement adds the structure listed on the endorsement as an "insured location," thereby buying back Section II liability coverages for that structure.

Loss Assessment Coverage

As explained in Chapters 5 and 6, standard, unendorsed homeowners policies provide loss assessment coverage as additional coverages, for limits of $1,000, under both Section I and Section II of the policy. *The loss assessment coverage endorsement* (HO 04 35) can be attached to a homeowners policy to provide a higher limit of coverage under both Sections I and II. The limit in the endorsement applies to loss resulting from a single event, whether it involves property, liability, or both. Suppose, for example, a condominium associa-tion's insurance coverage has lapsed when an explosion in the clubhouse injures several guests attending a party. The association will assess its mem-bers for both the property loss to its clubhouse and the bodily injury liability claim. The limit of coverage in this endorsement is the total amount a condominium unit owner's insurance would pay for both the property assess-ment and the liability assessment combined.

The additional limit of coverage available through this endorsement can be especially important to a condominium or cooperative unit owner insured under an HO-6, as well as other homeowners in a gated community or other enclave with a homeowners association. Many homeowners associa-tions have property and liability exposures in the common areas of the property that can easily exceed the $1,000 coverage per member automati-cally provided by an unendorsed homeowners policy. Although the associa-tion should have its own property and liability insurance coverage, the volunteer officers of these associations often pay inadequate attention to the association's insurance needs.

Endorsements for Use With Condominiums

Condominiums have become increasingly popular, especially in some parts of the United States, and several endorsements have been developed to meet the unique needs of condominium and cooperative unit owners. The endorse-ments discussed here customize the HO-6 policy and can be attached only to the HO-6 form.

Unit-Owners Coverage A

As mentioned earlier in this chapter, the HO-6 policy form automatically provides $5,000 of coverage protecting condominium unit owners against loss to building property in which they have an interest. The unendorsed policy insures against named perils for Coverage A. The *unit-owners Coverage A—special coverage endorsement* (HO 17 32) can amend an HO-6 policy to change the Section I—Perils Insured Against to provide special-form coverage that resembles the dwelling coverage provided under the HO-3 and HO-5 forms.

Unit-Owners Coverage C

The HO-6 policy form provides *named perils* coverage for personal property. As mentioned earlier, the *unit-owners Coverage C endorsement* (HO 17 31) can be attached to an HO-6 policy to change the Section I—Perils Insured Against to provide special-form coverage for Coverage C—Personal Property. By adding both this endorsement and the Coverage A endorsement to an HO-6, a condominium unit owner can have the condominium equivalent of HO-5 coverage.

Unit-Owners Rental to Others

Many unit owners rent their condominiums to others. When a unit is rented, the *unit-owners rental to others endorsement* (HO 17 33) can be used to amend the HO-6 policy coverages in two ways:

- Coverage C is extended to include coverage for the insured's personal property (*not* the tenant's property) contained in a rented unit; however, loss caused by theft of money, silverware, precious metals, securities, jewelry, and furs is not covered.

- Section II coverages are extended to cover the insured's (*not* the tenant's) liability exposures for the unit while it is rented.

Endorsements That Provide Rate Credits

Some endorsements recognize a characteristic of the insured property that earns a rate credit. These endorsements also state that the insured is responsible for maintaining any system for which a premium credit is allowed. For example, the *premises alarm or fire protection system endorsement* (HO 04 16) is attached to a homeowners policy to accompany a premium credit for a fire or burglar alarm or a sprinkler system. In exchange, the insured agrees to maintain the system and to notify the insurer if the system is changed or removed.

DEVELOPING A HOMEOWNERS PREMIUM

Rating a homeowners policy according to ISO rules is a relatively simple process. A base premium is first developed. The base premium is determined by the location of the dwelling, the fire protection provided in that area, the type of construction, the amount of coverage, and the policy form. This base premium is then modified if there are unusual construction factors, an increased deductible, or endorsements that increase or decrease the coverage provided.

Developing a Base Premium

The following are the main factors used in developing a base premium for a homeowners policy:

- *Territory.* The territory is a geographical division within a state. Sometimes the territory is defined by the borders of a city or a county; other territories are defined by geographic locations such as major highways or waterways.

- *Public protection class.* The public protection class is a ranking of the fire protection (including available water and water pressure) provided in the area. Each protection class is assigned a number according to its protection ranking. The numbers range from 1 through 10, with 1 being the best protection class. Protection class 10 usually has neither a responding fire department within five miles nor an adequate water supply.

- *Construction.* The two broad classifications of construction used to determine the homeowners base premium are frame and masonry. The frame classification includes structures with exterior walls of wood or other combustible construction (including stucco on wood or plaster on combustible supports). The masonry classification includes structures with exterior walls of combustible construction veneered with brick or stone, or masonry materials (adobe, brick, concrete, gypsum block, hollow concrete block, stone, or tile).

- *Coverage amount.* The amount of coverage required for Coverage A— Dwelling (or Coverage C—Personal Property for the HO-4 or HO-6) must be determined.

- *Policy form.* The policy form also affects the homeowners base premium. For example, a rater calculating the premium for an HO-2 would apply a policy form factor of .85 times the HO-3 base premium. Because the HO-2 policy provides coverage that is less broad than the HO-3 coverage, the HO-2 premium would be lower than the HO-3 premium. Likewise, the HO-5 premium would be higher.

Adjusting the Base Premium

Not all homeowners have the same loss exposures, and the policy forms are frequently altered by changing the deductible or the coverage or by adding endorsements. Alterations made to the standard policy forms usually result in an adjustment made to the base premium. These adjustments are logical: If the coverage or the loss exposure is increased, the base premium is increased; if the coverage or the loss exposure is reduced, the base premium is reduced. The methods for adjusting the base premium vary.

Variation in Construction Type

Dwellings with "superior construction," such as buildings with exterior walls, floors, and roof constructed of metal, gypsum, masonry, or other noncombustible materials, are rated by developing a base premium for masonry construction and applying a factor that lowers the base premium.

For example, the base premium might be multiplied by a factor of .85 for a house with primarily noncombustible construction. The insured would thus receive a 15 percent credit for the reduced fire loss exposure.

Change in Deductible

The standard deductible for all ISO policy forms for Section I—Property Coverages is $250. This deductible can be increased up to $2,500 or decreased to $100. Separate deductibles that apply to the perils of theft and windstorm or hail can also be increased or decreased.

SUMMARY

The HO-3 is the most widely used of the homeowners policy forms. However, the HO-3 does not meet the needs of all homeowners. The following additional policy forms are available to better meet an insured's and an insurer's needs:

- The HO-2 is offered at a lower premium than the HO-3 to meet the basic needs of the insured seeking affordable coverage. It offers a limited number of perils for the dwelling and other structures.

- The HO-5 is offered at a higher premium than the HO-3 and provides special-form coverage on not only the dwelling and other structures but also personal property.

- The HO-4 is designed for a tenant who rents property. It does not have Coverages A and B because renters do not own their dwellings and have no other structures to insure.

- The HO-6 is designed for condominium or cooperative unit owners. It defines a residence as a unit. Coverage A includes the additions and alterations in a unit, and additional coverages are modified to better meet a unit owner's needs.

- The HO-8 provides more limited coverage and perils than an HO-3 and includes loss settlement options to meet the needs of owners of older houses and their insurers.

ISO is not the only source of policy forms. AAIS also provides homeowners forms, which differ from ISO forms in various ways and which can be customized to meet the needs of insurers and their customers. Some companies design their own forms and file them for approval by the state insurance departments.

ISO homeowners policies can be tailored by attaching endorsements that modify the policy forms by adding, changing, or deleting coverage.

Homeowners policies are rated by determining the territory, protection class, construction, coverage amount, and policy form. The base premium is then altered for a variation in the construction, a change in the deductible, or the addition of endorsements.

Chapter 8

Direct Your Learning

Other Residential Insurance

After learning the subject matter of this chapter, you should be able to:

■ Compare the ISO dwelling special form (DP-3) to the ISO HO-3 policy regarding the following:

- Types of property covered

- Other coverages

- Perils insured against

- Exclusions and conditions

- Coverage for liability and theft losses

■ Given a case involving a loss under a DP-3 policy, explain whether coverage applies.

■ Describe how ISO HO-3 policy coverages are modified by the Mobilehome Endorsement (MH 04 01) and other ISO mobilehome endorsements.

■ Describe the coverages in the AAIS farmowners program.

■ Describe the farmowners coverages in the ISO homeowners policy endorsements.

■ Explain how the National Flood Insurance Program operates, and describe the program's coverage.

■ Explain how each of the following programs provides coverage for hard-to-insure residences:

- FAIR plans

- Beachfront and windstorm plans

Develop Your Perspective

What are the main topics covered in the chapter?

Some residential exposures cannot be addressed by homeowners policies. These exposures and the insurance policies that can be used to provide coverage for them are described in this chapter.

Contrast the policies described in this chapter with homeowners policies.

- Are the coverages substantially different?
- What additional coverages do these policies provide?

Why is it important to know these topics?

By understanding unique loss exposures of the owners of other residences, you can appreciate how dwelling policies, mobilehome coverage, farm and ranch coverage, flood insurance, FAIR plans, and beach and windstorm plans fill important needs for these property owners.

Examine the exclusions in the homeowners policies.

- How do other policies fill gaps created by exclusions in homeowners policies?

How can you use this information?

Compare your own residential loss exposures to the homeowners policies and the residential insurance coverages described:

- Which policy best meets your insurance needs?
- What needs are still not met because of the exclusions or limitations of the policy you have selected?
- Would any of the other residential insurance policies described help you address your loss exposures?

Chapter 8

Other Residential Insurance

What types of residential loss exposures exist for individuals and families that cannot be covered by homeowners policies or that can be covered only by special endorsements that were not discussed in previous chapters? Many individuals own houses they do not occupy but rent to others. Other individuals own and occupy multi-family homes that might not qualify for homeowners coverage. In addition, many people live in mobilehomes or manufactured homes, which do not qualify for most homeowners policies because of their value, construction, and potential mobility. Individuals who live on farms and ranches have unique exposures that include both personal and commercial types of losses. All of these property owners have both property and liability loss exposures related to the ownership and use of their property.

Many individuals and families find it difficult to obtain insurance for certain exposures. Coverage for loss caused by flooding is excluded in most property insurance policies. Some residential property does not meet insurer underwriting guidelines for standard coverage because of structural condition, defects in electrical or plumbing systems, or other hazards. Property insurance is often unavailable or unaffordable in coastal areas because of the heavy windstorm exposure.

This chapter describes a variety of policies and endorsements that are available to cover residential loss exposures not covered by standard homeowners policies.

DWELLING POLICIES

Some residences are not eligible for homeowners coverage for various reasons, including the following:

- The residence is not owner-occupied. For example, the house is rented to tenants.
- The value of the dwelling is below the minimum limit for a homeowners policy. For example, an insurer might set a minimum dwelling limit of $30,000 for any new homeowners policy. An insured who owns a home valued at $25,000 would not qualify for a homeowners policy with this insurer.

- The building contains more separate living units than allowed under the homeowners program. For example, a large home that has been divided into five small apartments, each occupied by a different family, would not qualify for most homeowners policies.

- The residence does not otherwise meet an insurer's underwriting guidelines. For example, an insurer might have an underwriting guideline that specifies that no new homeowners policies be written on homes more than fifty years old.

An insured might not want a homeowners policy for one or more of the following reasons:

- The insured might not want or need the full range of homeowners coverages.

- A homeowners policy might be more expensive than the insured is willing to pay.

A dwelling policy can be a valid alternative to a homeowners policy for any of the preceding reasons. Because dwelling policies are widely used, particularly to insure rental dwellings, an understanding of the coverages provided by the dwelling policy and how they differ from homeowners coverages is important.

Structures Eligible for Dwelling Policies

Dwelling policies are designed principally for insuring one- to four-family dwellings, whether owner-occupied or tenant-occupied. However, dwelling policies may also be used for the following:

- Mobilehomes at a permanent location
- Houseboats, in some states
- Certain incidental business occupancies, if they are operated by the owner-insured or by a tenant of the insured location

Dwelling Policy Programs

The discussion of the dwelling policy in this chapter is based on the dwelling forms developed by Insurance Services Office (ISO) and currently used by many of its member companies.[1] Other versions of dwelling policies exist and are used frequently. For instance, the American Association of Insurance Services (AAIS) has developed its own dwelling properties program to provide property insurance on residential property that does not meet the eligibility requirements of a homeowners program or on which the insured does not want to purchase a homeowners policy. In addition, many insurers have developed their own dwelling policy forms. Unlike the ISO dwelling forms, many of the non-ISO dwelling policies automatically include theft and/or liability coverages. Some states require special state endorsements that modify dwelling policies to conform to state regulations. It is important for the insurance professional to become familiar with the particular forms being used. The following discussion of the ISO forms is intended to give a general overview of coverages typically provided in dwelling policies and how they differ from homeowners policies.

The ISO Dwelling Policy

The dwelling policy provides property coverage for dwellings and their contents. The ISO dwelling program includes three forms:

- DP 00 01 (commonly known as DP-1): Dwelling Property 1—Basic Form
- DP 00 02 (or DP-2): Dwelling Property 2—Broad Form
- DP 00 03 (or DP-3): Dwelling Property 3—Special Form

These dwelling forms offer property coverages on a dwelling and its contents similar to the coverages under Section I of the homeowners forms. The following discussion compares the property coverages in the dwelling forms with the property coverages in the homeowners forms.

Although many differences exist between the dwelling and homeowners policies, among the most important differences is the fact that the unendorsed ISO dwelling forms do not provide any theft coverage for personal property or any liability coverages. However, both of these coverages can be added to the dwelling policy by an endorsement or supplement, discussed later in this chapter.

> *Broad theft coverage* (DP 04 72) and *limited theft coverage* (DP 04 73) are endorsements that can be added to a dwelling policy to provide particular coverages for the peril of theft.

> The *personal liability form* (DL 24 01) is used to provide coverage on a dwelling for personal liability and medical payments to others.

Insuring Agreement and Definitions

The format of the dwelling forms is similar to that found in Section I of the homeowners forms. The insuring agreements are identical. The first major difference occurs in the definitions section. Because the dwelling forms do not have liability or medical payments coverage, most definitions are unnecessary in the dwelling forms.

Coverages

The dwelling forms can include the following coverages:

- Coverage A—Dwelling
- Coverage B—Other Structures
- Coverage C—Personal Property
- Coverage D—Fair Rental Value
- Coverage E—Additional Living Expense (not included in the unendorsed form DP-1)

Unlike HO-3 or HO-2 policies, dwelling policies do not automatically include all the property coverages. A limit for each desired coverage (dwelling, other structures, and personal property) must be shown on the declarations page (with appropriate premium charges). Loss of use coverages (fair rental value and additional living expense) are automatically included in forms DP-2 and DP-3; form DP-1 automatically includes fair rental value but not additional living expense.

Although a dwelling policy can be used for insuring only personal property with no dwelling or structures coverage, this is rarely done. The dwelling policy is more commonly used to cover only the dwelling and other structures (for example, to insure a house rented unfurnished to tenants) or to cover the dwelling, other structures, and personal property.

Coverage A—Dwelling

When referring to the dwelling on the described location, the dwelling forms specify that it be used principally for dwelling purposes. The dwelling forms also specifically state that if not covered elsewhere in the policy, building equipment and outdoor equipment used for the service of the premises and located on the described location are covered. For example, if the insured owns a lawn mower kept in the garage of the insured dwelling and uses it to cut the grass at the insured location, the lawn mower would be included under Coverage A (if the insured did not purchase Coverage C—Personal Property). The remainder of the Coverage A language is similar in the dwelling and homeowners forms.

Coverage B—Other Structures

Although there are some minor differences in wording between the dwelling and homeowners forms, the coverage for other structures in both is essentially the same. As in the homeowners policy, Coverage B includes detached structures, such as garages and storage sheds, on the insured premises.

Coverage C—Personal Property

If Coverage C is selected, coverage under the dwelling forms applies to personal property, usual to the occupancy of a dwelling, that is owned or used by the insured or resident family members while the property is on the described location.

Unlike the homeowners forms, no special limits in the dwelling forms apply to any specific type of personal property. For example, the homeowners forms have special limits on theft losses to jewelry, furs, firearms, silverware, and similar types of property; the dwelling forms have no such limits. Because the unendorsed dwelling forms have no theft coverage, such theft limitations are not necessary. The homeowners policy has a special sublimit on money and related items, but the dwelling forms exclude money altogether. The homeowners policy provides a special sublimit on watercraft (including their furnishings, equipment, and outboard motors), but the dwelling forms exclude boats other than rowboats and canoes.

A personal property (Coverage C) limit in the dwelling forms is chosen by the insured if coverage is desired. If an insured is a landlord and has no personal property in the insured dwelling (or chooses not to insure personal property), he or she can choose to purchase only Coverage A under the dwelling program. The homeowners policy has no such option. Furthermore, a tenant may choose to purchase only Coverage C under a dwelling form, thereby obtaining property coverage similar to that provided by an HO-4 policy (except that the dwelling form contains no theft coverage, which is an important difference).

Coverage D—Fair Rental Value and Coverage E—Additional Living Expense

Coverages D and E in the DP-2 and DP-3 forms correspond roughly to Coverage D—Loss of Use in the homeowners policy, which includes both fair rental value and additional living expense. Dwelling form DP-1, the basic form, includes only Coverage D—Fair Rental Value, which covers loss of use of the covered dwelling, or part of the dwelling, that is rented to others. Coverage for additional living expense, which covers loss of use for insureds who live in the covered dwelling, can be added to the DP-1 by endorsement for an additional premium.

Other Coverages

Many of the other coverages provided in the dwelling policy correspond to the additional coverages in the homeowners policy, but there are some differences. Loss assessment coverage, which is included automatically (up to $1,000) in the homeowners policy, can be added to the dwelling policy by endorsement for an additional premium. The additional coverages in the homeowners policy for landlord's furnishings and for credit cards, transfer cards, forgery, and counterfeit money are not available in the dwelling program. The following paragraphs discuss the other coverages in the dwelling policy and compare them with similar coverages provided in the homeowners policy.

Other Structures   The dwelling forms provide up to 10 percent of the Coverage A limit for loss to other structures. Under the broad dwelling form (DP-2) and the special dwelling form (DP-3), this coverage is additional insurance and does not reduce the Coverage A limit for the same loss. In the basic dwelling form (DP-1), however, use of this coverage does reduce the Coverage A limit for the same loss.

Debris Removal   The debris removal coverage of all the dwelling forms is included in the limit applying to the damaged property. In contrast, the homeowners policy provides an additional 5 percent of the applicable coverage limit for debris removal if the amount to be paid for the damage to the property plus the debris removal expense exceeds the coverage limit for the damaged property.

Improvements, Alterations, and Additions   The dwelling forms, like the homeowners contents broad form (HO-4), provide 10 percent of the Coverage C limit to cover a tenant's improvements, alterations, and additions. No comparable coverage is in the other homeowners forms. Under the DP-2 and DP-3 forms, this coverage is additional insurance.

Worldwide Coverage   The dwelling forms provide up to 10 percent of the Coverage C limit for loss to the property covered under Coverage C, except rowboats and canoes, while that property is anywhere in the world. The homeowners policy provides worldwide coverage for personal property owned or used by an insured with no limitation, except that a 10 percent limitation applies to property usually located at a secondary residence of the insured.

Rental Value and Additional Living Expense   The broad (DP-2) and special (DP-3) dwelling forms provide up to 10 percent of the Coverage A limit as an additional amount of insurance for both loss of fair rental value and additional living expense. Under homeowners forms HO-2 and HO-3, the corresponding additional limit for loss of use is 30 percent of the Coverage A limit.

The basic dwelling form (DP-1) automatically provides up to 10 percent of the Coverage A limit for loss of fair rental value only. Payment under this coverage reduces the Coverage A limit by the amount paid for the same loss.

Reasonable Repairs   The dwelling forms, like the homeowners forms, provide coverage for the cost of reasonable repairs made after the occurrence of a covered loss solely to protect covered property from further damage. This coverage does not increase the limit of liability that applies to the covered property.

Property Removed   Under both the dwelling and homeowners forms, covered property is protected if it is removed from the premises because it is endangered by an insured peril. In both cases, this coverage applies to direct loss from any cause (as long as an insured peril necessitated the removal) for thirty days (a limit of five days applies in the DP-1 form). In the dwelling forms, as in the homeowners forms, the limit for this coverage is the same as the limit for the property being moved.

Trees, Shrubs, and Other Plants   In the homeowners forms and the broad (DP-2) and special (DP-3) dwelling forms, the maximum limit that can be applied (as an additional amount of insurance) to trees, shrubs, plants, or lawns is 5 percent of the dwelling (Coverage A) limit. The limit for any one tree, plant, or shrub is $500, and only certain specified perils are covered. This coverage can be added by endorsement to the basic dwelling form (DP-1). Forms DP-2 and DP-3 can be expanded by endorsement to include the perils of wind and hail.

Fire Department Service Charge   The dwelling forms, like the homeowners forms, will pay up to $500 for fire department service charges. Coverage is not provided if the property is located within the limits of the city, municipality, or protection district furnishing the fire department response. This coverage is additional insurance, and no deductible applies.

Collapse   The broad and special dwelling forms offer coverage for building collapse due to specified perils. This coverage is not available in the basic dwelling form (DP-1).

Glass or Safety Glazing Material   Dwelling forms DP-2 and DP-3 provide coverage for breakage of glass or safety glazing material that is part of a building, storm door, or storm window; and for damage to covered property caused by such glass or safety glazing material. The coverage does not apply if the dwelling has been vacant for more than thirty days. Similar coverage is included in the homeowners policy but is not provided in the basic dwelling form(DP-1).

Ordinance or Law   Dwelling forms DP-2 and DP-3 provide coverage for increased costs the insured incurs due to the enforcement of any ordinance or law. If the insured has purchased Coverage A, ordinance or law coverage is provided up to 10 percent of the Coverage A limit. If there is no Coverage A limit, up to 10 percent of Coverage B is provided for ordinance or law coverage.

If the insured is a tenant at the insured location, the limit applying to ordinance or law coverage is up to 10 percent of the limit that applies to improvements, alterations, and additions.

The *ordinance or law—increased amount of coverage endorsement* (DP 04 71) can be used to increase the percentage applied for ordinance or law coverage from 10 percent up to 100 percent.

Perils Insured Against

The dwelling broad form (DP-2) provides coverage against the same perils as those covered by the HO-2 form. The dwelling basic form (DP-1) provides very limited coverage on a named perils basis and is not used as extensively as forms DP-2 and DP-3. As mentioned, there is no theft coverage for personal property under any of the unendorsed dwelling forms, although theft coverage can be added by endorsement.

The following examination of the perils insured against in the dwelling program is based on the dwelling special form (DP-3).

Coverage A—Dwelling and Coverage B—Other Structures

The DP-3, like the HO-3, uses the special-form approach and insures against "risk of direct loss to property" (as opposed to named perils coverage) under Coverage A—Dwelling and Coverage B—Other Structures. In both the DP-3 and the HO-3 forms, the coverage for direct physical loss to real property is determined by the causes of loss that are excluded. Those causes of loss that are not excluded are covered. For example, the DP-3 form excludes coverage for theft of any property that is not part of a covered building or structure. It also excludes loss caused by wind, hail, ice, snow, or sleet to outdoor radio and television antennas and aerials, and to trees, shrubs, plants, or lawns. Other exclusions in the DP-3 are essentially the same as those in the HO-3.

Coverage C—Personal Property

Although the Coverage C perils under the DP-3 form are similar to the perils covered by the HO-3, there are some differences. Theft of personal property is not covered under the DP-3, but coverage is provided for damage to covered property caused by burglars unless the dwelling has been vacant for more than thirty days. For example, if burglars break down a door, damage a table, and steal a television, the damage done to the door and the table would be covered, but the loss of the stolen TV would not be covered. The DP-3 specifically excludes pilferage, theft, burglary, and larceny under the peril of vandalism or malicious mischief.

The windstorm or hail coverage in the DP-3 also differs slightly from the HO-3. The DP-3 specifically excludes wind or hail damage to canoes and rowboats; the HO-3 covers such damage to watercraft and their trailers, furnishings, equipment, and outboard motors, but only while inside a fully enclosed building.

Dwelling Policy General Exclusions

The general exclusions in the DP-3 track closely with the Section I exclusions in the HO-3. These exclusions include loss caused directly or indirectly by any of the following:

* Ordinance or law (except as provided in the other coverages section previously discussed)

- Earth movement, such as an earthquake
- Water damage, such as flood and back-up of sewers and drains
- Power failure that occurs off the described location
- Neglect on the part of the insured
- War
- Nuclear hazard
- Intentional loss
- Weather conditions that contribute to any of the preceding excluded causes of loss
- Acts or decisions of other persons, groups, organizations, or governmental bodies
- Faulty construction, planning, materials, or maintenance

Dwelling Policy Conditions

The DP-3 form contains a single section of conditions. Similar conditions are found in the HO-3 policy, but some HO-3 conditions apply only to Section I, while others apply to both Sections I and II. Because the DP-3 form has no Section II (liability) coverage, there is no need for distinguishing the section to which the conditions apply.

Coverage for Liability and Theft Losses

Although the ISO dwelling forms do not provide coverage for liability or theft losses, such coverages are available by adding a personal liability supplement and a theft endorsement.

Personal Liability Supplement

Liability coverage may be written as an addendum to the dwelling policy or independently as a separate policy through the *personal liability supplement* (DL 24 01). As mentioned in Chapter 7, an insured who has both a homeowners policy on his or her residence and a dwelling policy on a rental dwelling also has the option of obtaining liability coverage for the rental dwelling by purchasing the homeowners additional residence rented to others endorsement (HO 24 70) for an additional premium.

The personal liability supplement provides coverages for personal liability (Coverage L) and medical payments to others (Coverage M). These coverages are similar in format and language to Coverages E—Personal Liability and F—Medical Payments to Others in Section II of the homeowners policy.

The exclusions and additional coverages in the personal liability supplement are virtually the same as those applicable to Section II of the homeowners policy. The main difference is that the additional liability coverage for loss assessment provided (up to a limit of $1,000) in the homeowners policy is not provided in the personal liability supplement. Loss assessment liability coverage for up to three locations can be added to the personal liability supplement for an additional premium.

Residential Theft Coverage

An insured may choose between two endorsements to the dwelling forms (one for owner-occupied dwellings and one for nonowner-occupied dwellings) to provide theft coverage similar to that provided in the homeowners policy:

- *Broad theft coverage* (DP 04 72)—for use with policies covering owner-occupied dwellings. This endorsement provides coverage against the perils of theft, including attempted theft, and vandalism or malicious mischief as a result of theft or attempted theft. Off-premises coverage is available only if the insured purchases on-premises coverage. The endorsement includes special limits similar to the sublimits included in the homeowners policy, such as those for money, jewelry, and firearms.

- *Limited theft coverage* (DP 04 73)—for dwellings that are not owner-occupied. This endorsement is similar to the broad theft coverage endorsement, but the limited theft endorsement excludes certain items of personal property that are subject to special limits under the broad theft endorsement, such as money and jewelry. The limited theft endorsement also excludes coverage for loss caused by a tenant of the described location or by employees or members of the household.

Comparison of HO-3 and DP-3

Exhibit 8-1 shows a brief comparison of the HO-3 and the DP-3 forms.

EXHIBIT 8-1

Comparison of the HO-3 and the DP-3 Forms

Coverage	HO-3	DP-3
A—Dwelling	Limit selected by insured	Same
	Replacement cost coverage if limit is at least 80% of replacement cost	Same
	Automatically included	Included only if limit selected and shown on declarations page
B—Other Structures	10% of Coverage A Automatically included	10% of Coverage A Provided in the Other Coverages section
	Replacement cost coverage if limit is at least 80% of replacement cost	Same

Coverage	HO-3	DP-3
C—Personal Property	50% of Coverage A Automatically included	Included only if limit selected and shown on declarations page
	Worldwide coverage up to Coverage C limit	Worldwide coverage only up to 10% of Coverage C
	ACV coverage	Same
D—Loss of Use	30% of Coverage A Automatically included	10% of Coverage A Provided in the Other Coverages section
Additional/Other Coverages		
• Loss assessment	$1,000	None (can be added by endorsement)
• Credit card, etc.	$500	None
• Landlord's furnishings	$2,500 at residence	None included in the Other Coverages section, but if the dwelling is rented, the owner/landlord's furnishings are covered up to the Coverage C limit
• Debris removal	Additional 5% available	Included in limit of coverage
• Improvements, alterations, and additions	None	Tenant may use up to 10% of Coverage C (additional insurance)
• Reasonable repairs	Included in limit	Same
• Property removed	Covered up to 30 days	Same
• Trees, shrubs, plants	5% of Coverage A, up to $500 per item for limited perils (not including wind or hail)	Same
	Additional insurance	Does not increase coverage
• Fire dept. service charge	$500	Same
• Collapse	Covered for limited perils	Same
• Glass or safety glazing material	Covered	Covered
• Ordinance or law	10% of Coverage A	10% of Coverage A If no Coverage A, 10% of B If insured is tenant, 10% of improvements and alterations limit
Personal Property— Special Limits/Exclusions	$200 money	Money excluded
	$1,500 securities and other documents	Securities and documents excluded
	$1,500 watercraft	Watercraft excluded (except rowboats and canoes)

Continued on next page.

Coverage	HO-3	DP-3
Perils Insured Against		
• Coverages A & B	Special-form coverage (risk of direct loss subject to exclusions)	Same
• Coverage C	Named perils (broad form) Theft coverage included	Named perils (broad form) No theft coverage (theft can be added by endorsement)
Section II—Liability		
• E—Personal Liability	Automatically included	None
• F—Medical Payments to Others	Automatically included	None
		Liability and medical payments can be added by purchase of personal liability supplement

The comparison above is based on ISO forms. It can be used as a quick reference and as an easy method to compare the HO-3 and DP-3 policies. However, only the actual policy forms contain complete coverage information, and those forms should be used to determine coverage wording.

MOBILEHOME COVERAGE

Mobilehomes are generally less expensive than homes built on permanent foundations. In some areas, mobilehomes are popular as seasonal or vacation homes.

Exposures

The owners of mobilehomes face the same exposures to loss that owners of conventional homes face. Therefore, a mobilehome owner might experience loss from any of the following exposures:

- Damage to or destruction of the mobilehome
- Damage to or destruction of other structures on the residence premises
- Damage to or destruction of personal property in the mobilehome or in other structures
- Loss of use of the mobilehome
- Liability loss because of bodily injury to others or damage to the property of others

The Mobilehome

A mobilehome is, by definition, not permanently affixed to the land on which it is located. Consequently, most states consider mobilehomes to be

Vacation Mobilehomes

Many mobilehomes are used in recreational areas as vacation homes. While some are set up in mobilehome parks, many are not. For instance, a mobilehome may be located in the mountains or at the side of a lake or river.

The exposures that owners of vacation mobilehomes face are somewhat different from the exposures that owners of year-round residential mobilehomes face. Often, vacation areas do not have full-time fire departments. Also, the mobilehome owner might have no telephone. Some have no neighbors nearby to report a fire in the owner's absence. All of these factors contribute to the likelihood of increased loss severity if a fire occurs. Vacation mobilehomes located in wooded areas are subject to an unusually high fire hazard. A knowledgeable mobilehome owner can reduce this hazard by removing brush and timber to clear a space around the mobilehome. Nevertheless, a mobilehome in a forest area faces potential loss frequency and severity.

moveable property and not real estate. As moveable property, mobilehomes often have lower property tax rates than do buildings that are permanently affixed to land. However, because mobilehomes are not affixed to masonry foundations, their exposure to some types of losses is greater than the exposure of homes built on permanent foundations. Furthermore, mobilehomes are assembled in a factory and transported to their location in a complete or semi-complete condition, which exposes them to perils of transportation. Mobilehomes are constructed of lighter materials than homes built on permanent foundations, and different construction techniques are used.

A mobilehome is often set up with skirting that conceals the wheels and gives the appearance of a permanent structure. The skirting also reduces the build-up of debris underneath the mobilehome and helps prevent damage that might subsequently result (such as fire caused by burning brush or leaves blown by wind under the mobilehome). Mobilehomes are particularly suscep-tible to damage from windstorm, tornado, and earthquake.

Mobilehomes generally do not remain on their tires but are set up on blocks, piers, or masonry footings. When the mobilehome is set up, it should be tied down to anchors buried in the ground to prevent the unit from moving. The tie-down feature is important, because a windstorm might either move a mobilehome sideways or lift it off the ground. Many insurers will provide coverage for mobilehomes only if they are properly tied down. Some state codes require that they be tied down.

Other Property and Liability Exposures

Mobilehome owners often erect sheds and similar outbuildings on the pre-mises where the mobilehome is located. The contents of mobilehomes and their outbuildings are usually similar to those in conventional dwellings and are subject to the same exposures. However, mobilehomes are more likely than conventional homes to have built-in cabinets, appliances, and furniture; such built-in items are considered part of the mobilehome rather than personal property. If a mobilehome is destroyed or badly damaged by fire or by another cause of loss, the owner will suffer loss of use of the home just like any other homeowner. A mobilehome owner is also subject to the same liability exposures as an owner of a conventional home. Consequently, mobilehome owners have coverage needs for each of these exposures that are similar to the coverage needs of other homeowners.

Mobilehome Coverages

Owners of mobilehomes have several options for insuring their property. Many specialty insurers have developed policies especially for mobilehomes. Such mobilehome policies can also be used to insure prefabricated, manufactured, or modular houses, which are generally manufactured in one location and then transported either in one piece or in several large pieces to be installed at their permanent location. However, prefabricated, manufactured, or modular houses that are installed permanently on masonry foundations are frequently eligible for conventional homeowners coverage. Both Insurance Services Office and the American Association of Insurance Services have developed special forms for insuring mobilehomes.

ISO Mobilehome Endorsements

The following discussion is based on the ISO endorsements designed specifically for mobilehomes and used with an HO-3 policy. According to ISO rules, mobilehome endorsements can also be used with an HO-2 policy. Tenants of mobilehomes may use the HO-4 policy without adding the mobilehome endorsement. A mobilehome is eligible for coverage if it is designed for portability and year-round living. A typical requirement is that it be at least ten feet wide and four hundred square feet in area. Smaller trailers can often be insured under a personal auto policy with an appropriate endorsement, as explained in Chapter 4.

Mobilehome Endorsement

A mobilehome policy is created by attaching the *mobilehome endorsement* (MH 04 01) to a homeowners form and a declarations page. As with all homeowners polices, other endorsements may be attached to modify the coverage. The mobilehome endorsement states that the insurance is subject to all applicable provisions of the homeowners form except as revised by the endorsement. The major ways that the mobilehome policy differs from the HO-3 policy are as follows:

- *Definitions.* The definition of "residence premises" is changed in the mobilehome endorsement to mean the mobilehome and other structures located on land owned or leased by the insured where the insured resides.

This location must be shown as the residence premises on the declarations page.

- *Coverage A—Dwelling.* This coverage applies to a mobilehome used primarily as a private residence as well as to structures and utility tanks attached to the mobilehome. It also applies to floor coverings, appliances, dressers, cabinets, and similar items that are permanently installed.

- *Coverage B—Other Structures.* The limit for other structures in the mobilehome policy is 10 percent of the limit that applies to Coverage A, with a minimum limit of $2,000.

- *Additional Coverages.* The additional coverage for property removed provides up to $500 (with no deductible) for reasonable expenses incurred by the insured for removal and return of the entire mobilehome if it is endangered by an insured peril. An important additional coverage in the HO-3 that does not apply to mobilehomes is the ordinance or law coverage, but this coverage can be added by endorsement.

- *Section I—Conditions.* According to the loss settlement condition in the mobilehome policy, carpeting and appliances are not included as property to be valued on the basis of actual cash value; therefore, these items are included in Coverage A and are covered for replacement cost if the policy has the required amount of insurance.

The mobilehome endorsement amends the homeowners policy in regard to Section I Property Coverages. The endorsement does not amend Section II—Liability Coverages. Therefore, the liability coverage under a mobilehome policy is the same as the liability coverage under a homeowners policy. Because the endorsement changes the definition of residence premises, any reference to the insured location in Section II would include the mobilehome and other structures at the location shown on the declarations page.

Other ISO Mobilehome Endorsements

A mobilehome policy can be endorsed with many of the homeowners endorsements previously discussed. The following five endorsements are available only with the mobilehome policy:

- *Actual cash value–mobilehome endorsement* (MH 04 02). This endorsement changes the loss settlement terms on the mobilehome and other structures from a replacement cost basis to an actual cash value (ACV) basis. Losses to carpeting and appliances would also be settled on an ACV basis. This endorsement would normally be used at the request of an insurer who, for some underwriting reason (such as age of the mobilehome), prefers not to provide replacement cost coverage on the mobilehome.

- *Transportation/permission to move endorsement* (MH 04 03). This endorsement provides coverage for perils of transportation (collision, upset, stranding, or sinking) and coverage at the new location anywhere in the United States or Canada for a period of thirty days from the effective date of the endorsement.

- *Mobilehome lienholder's single interest endorsement* (MH 04 04). This endorsement, required by some lienholders (lending institutions that hold title to the mobilehome until the loan is paid off), provides coverage only to the lienholder for the transportation perils of collision and upset. It also provides coverage to the lienholder for loss due to the owner's conversion, embezzlement, or secretion of the mobilehome.

- *Property removed increased limit endorsement* (MH 04 06). This endorsement allows the insured to increase the basic limit of $500 to cover removal expenses for a mobilehome endangered by an insured peril. Removal costs for a mobilehome could easily run more than $500. The endorsement provides a means for the insured to purchase a sufficiently high removal limit to cover the expenses to take down, transport, and set up the mobilehome.

- *Ordinance or law coverage endorsement* (MH 04 08). This endorsement enables the insured under a mobilehome policy to add ordinance or law coverage for an amount equal to a specified percent of the Coverage A limit. The provisions of this endorsement are virtually identical to those in the ordinance or law additional coverage in the homeowners policy.

AAIS Mobile-Homeowners Program

The American Association of Insurance Services has developed a separate program for insuring mobilehomes, quite similar to its homeowners program, that is used by a number of insurers. Covered property includes the mobilehome, other structures, and personal property. Coverage is provided for personal liability and medical payments, as well as for additional living costs and loss of rent that occur when covered property is damaged by a peril insured against. Several perils options for owner-occupied mobilehomes are available, ranging from limited named perils to special coverage perils (risks of direct physical loss, unless specifically excluded). A separate renters form covers the personal property and additional living costs of a mobilehome tenant.

The AAIS mobile-homeowners program covers the mobilehome on an actual cash value basis, but replacement cost coverage may be added by endorsement. Most other coverages available by endorsement under the AAIS homeowners program are also available, but options that apply only to mobilehomes include consent to move the mobilehome, coverage for collision or upset, and additional coverage for the lienholder of the mobilehome.

PERSONAL INSURANCE FOR FARMS AND RANCHES

Because farmers and ranchers usually live on the land they work, they face loss exposures that need a combination of personal and commercial insurance. The personal exposures are similar to those covered in a homeowners policy, including the farmer's home, household property, loss of use of the home, and personal liability. Because this text does not cover the subject of commercial insurance, this section examines only the types of personal insurance coverages designed for farmers and ranchers. Large commercial farming operations might need more sophisticated commercial lines coverages to treat all of their exposures.

Farm insurance is usually provided by insurers who use their own independently developed policy forms and endorsements. Insurers that specialize in insuring farms and ranches offer various ways to treat farming exposures and use different methods in different states. For example, some insurers offer special farmowners and ranchowners insurance packages for farm families that live on and operate small farms. Insurers also offer homeowners policies, dwelling policies, and mobilehome policies with special endorsements available to cover livestock, animal collision (with motor vehicles), and other farm exposures. Insurers also have special programs for roadside stands and "pick-your-own" operations, where the public is permitted to pick fruits and vegetables on the insured premises. Liability can be provided either by personal liability and farming operation liability policies or by commercial liability policies. Large commercial farms are usually insured under commercial package policies.

Although this text does not examine all the different types of farm coverages available, it presents some of the options commonly used. Insurance professionals who work with farm insurance should review specific farm policies and compare them to others typically in use.

The American Association of Insurance Services and Insurance Services Office also provide farm coverage forms that many of their member insurance companies use.

The AAIS Farmowners Program[2]

The farmowners program of the American Association of Insurance Services is used by many insurance companies to insure personal farm exposures. Many farm operations have a mixture of personal, commercial, and specialty farm exposures, and the AAIS program can be adapted to cover this diversity. AAIS also helps insurance companies develop their own programs to meet specialized farm insurance needs. Because of its flexibility, the AAIS farmowners program is widely used to insure personal farm exposures.

Aside from purely farming enterprises, many agriculture-related operations today are characterized by the blending of agricultural and commercial activity—a combination referred to as "agribusiness." Agribusiness is a broad term that includes the production, processing, and distribution of agricultural products. Common examples of agribusinesses are feed manufacturers, grain elevator operations, and hog processing facilities, to name a few. In response to the growth of this business segment, AAIS developed the Agricultural Output Program (AgOP) to insure the property exposures of agribusiness operations.

Although similarities exist between agribusiness and farmowners risks, there are definite distinctions as well. Farmowner risks tend to consist of owner-operated farms. Dwelling coverage is a key component of farmowners coverage and personal lines-style manual rates predominate. Agribusiness contemplates larger agricultural operations, or combinations of agricultural and commercial operations. Dwelling property is not ineligible for coverage under the AgOP Program, but it is a relatively minor consideration. Inland marine coverages are rolled into the AgOP policy, higher limits are made available, and rating is more judgment-oriented and flexible.

Although insurance for agribusiness is not the subject of this text, students should be aware of the growth of this segment as well as the distinctions between farming and agribusiness insurance.

Policy Overview

The property and liability components of the AAIS farmowners program can be combined or used alone to insure both property and liability or property only. Property coverage forms are available to cover the principal farm dwelling, barns, buildings, structures, and personal property. Mobilehomes used as the primary farm dwelling are also eligible for the farmowners program. Coverage for liability exposures can be provided by using a farm personal liability form or by using commercial liability coverage forms specifically tailored for farm premises and operations. Coverage for personal liability exposures can be added by endorsement when a farm commercial liability coverage form applies.

Property Coverages

Three AAIS forms provide dwelling property coverage similar to the property coverages in the various homeowners and dwelling forms:

- Dwelling Coverage—Basic Form (FO-1)
- Dwelling Coverage—Broad Form (FO-2)
- Dwelling Coverage—Special Form (FO-3)

Principal coverages include the following:

- The farm dwelling
- Related private structures (other than barns and other structures used in the farming operation)
- Household personal property
- Additional living expenses and loss of rent

AAIS also offers a Dwelling Coverage Special Building and Contents Form (FO 0005) that is similar to its homeowners Form 5. This FO 0005 form provides the broadest level of dwelling coverage under the Farmowners Program. The FO 0005 insures property covered under Coverages A, B, *and* C on a special-form (open perils) basis and covers both the dwelling and personal property on a replacement cost basis. In addition, form FO 0005 provides higher limits than do the other dwelling forms for many Coverage C classes of property and incidental coverages.

Dwelling Coverage—Renters Form (FO-4) can be used to cover household personal property and additional living expenses for renters (similar to the property coverages in a tenant homowners policy).

AAIS also offers an endorsement for loss of income coverage for farming operations and farm rentals that is comparable to that typically available under commercial property and businessowners programs.

Farm coverage form (FO-6) is used to insure farm buildings and structures, scheduled farm personal property, and unscheduled farm personal property. Most incidental coverages are similar to those found in a homeowners policy; however, coverage for outdoor antennas, well pumps, private power and light poles, and refrigerated food spoilage are specific to the farm forms. Optional coverages include the following:

- Ordinance or law coverage for farm structures
- Replacement cost and special form coverage for farm structures
- Additional perils for livestock
- Special coverage for certain animals
- Animal boarding

Farm Personal Liability Coverages

The AAIS Personal Liability Coverage (Farm) form (GL-2) offers the same liability coverages found in a homeowners policy: personal liability and medical payments to others. Coverage for most business activities, other than farming, is excluded. Liability coverage for custom farming is provided when receipts for custom farm work do not exceed $5,000 annually and when the custom farm work does not involve the application of pesticides and herbicides. Custom farm work refers to farming activities that the insured performs for others for a fee. For example, a farmer might harvest another farmer's crop for pay.

The flexibility of the AAIS farmowners program is most evident in the liability coverages, which are a separate part of the policy. Coverage for the following liability exposures can be added by endorsement:

- Personal injury
- Expanded custom farming
- Additional business activities
- Fruit or vegetable picking by the public
- Farm chemicals limited liability

ISO Homeowners Endorsements for Farms

Farmowners may be eligible to insure the liability exposures from their farming operations under ISO homeowners policies with the appropriate endorsements. These endorsements cover incidental farming operations on the residence premises or at another location, or larger farms operated away from the residence premises. An insured can purchase either of two ISO farm liability endorsements: the incidental farming personal liability endorsement or the farmers personal liability endorsement. Coverage under both endorsements applies only to Section II—Liability; the endorsements do not provide any additional property coverages. In addition, when one of these endorsements is selected, an insured can purchase optional livestock collision coverage.

The ISO farm liability endorsements can be used only if farming is not the insured's primary occupation. For example, if Bill is an incidental farmer who owns a small farm but also has a full-time job elsewhere, he would probably be eligible for a homeowners policy with a farm liability endorsement.

Incidental Farming Personal Liability

The *incidental farming personal liability endorsement* (HO 24 72) extends the personal liability and medical payments coverage in Section II of the homeowners policy to include an insured's incidental farming operations conducted either at the insured's residence or at a separate location. If the farming is on the insured's residence premises, it must be incidental to the use of the premises as a dwelling. If the incidental farming activities are at a separate location, that location must be specified in the endorsement. Permissible farming activities include the boarding or grazing of animals or the use of land as garden space. The income derived must not be the insured's primary source of income, and no coverage applies if the location is used to race animals.

Farmers Personal Liability

The *farmers personal liability endorsement* (HO 24 73) is designed to cover liability exposures arising out of a commercial farming operation conducted away from the insured's residence premises. Injury to farm employees may be covered under Coverage E—Personal Liability and Coverage F—Medical Payments to Others if a premium is shown in the endorsement for coverage of farm employees.

Each farm premises the insured owns, rents, or operates must be listed in the endorsement and a premium charged for each. Frequently, a farmer will own or use farm land at several locations. Each location must be shown on the endorsement so that coverage will apply to each and the insurer can charge an appropriate premium for the various exposures.

Coverage under the endorsement assumes that no business other than farming is conducted at the insured location. If any other businesses are conducted there, they must be approved by the insurer and listed in the endorsement.

Livestock Collision Coverage

The *livestock collision coverage endorsement* (HO 04 52) provides coverage for a specified amount for death of animals owned by the insured if the death is caused by either of the following:

- The collision or overturn of a vehicle transporting the livestock
- The striking of livestock by a vehicle when the animal is crossing, moving along, or located on a public road

Coverage does not apply if a vehicle that is involved in the collision or that strikes the livestock is owned or operated by the insured or by an employee of the insured.

The livestock collision coverage endorsement can be used when either the incidental farming personal liability or the farmers personal liability endorsement is attached to the homeowners policy.

FLOOD INSURANCE[3]

According to the Federal Emergency Management Agency (FEMA), floods are the most common of all natural disasters. Because buildings, roads, and parking lots are increasingly being built where forests and meadows used to be, floods are becoming more severe. Because of the catastrophic loss potential of floods, the cost to insure against flooding would significantly raise property insurance rates. Therefore, both homeowners and dwelling policies exclude losses caused by flooding. To make flood insurance available to property owners, the federal government provides flood insurance at subsidized rates for both dwellings and commercial buildings, as well as for the contents of both. The **National Flood Insurance Program (NFIP)** was established by the National Flood Insurance Act of 1968 and is administered by FEMA. Under this program, federal flood insurance is available in all states, the District of Columbia, Puerto Rico, Guam, and the U. S. Virgin Islands.

National Flood Insurance Program (NFIP)
Federal program that makes flood insurance available on buildings, both commercial and residential, and their contents in communities that have been approved by the Federal Emergency Management Agency (FEMA).

Community Eligibility

Flood insurance may be written only in communities that FEMA has designated as participating communities in the National Flood Insurance Program. To be eligible for subsidized flood insurance rates under the NFIP, the community must agree to establish and enforce flood-control and land-use restrictions designed to minimize the community's exposure to flood losses. When a community first joins the program, property owners in flood areas are allowed to purchase limited amounts of insurance at subsidized rates under the **emergency program**.

Emergency program
Initial phase of a community's participation in the National Flood Insurance Program in which property owners in flood areas can purchase limited amounts of insurance at subsidized rates.

The government then prepares a flood insurance rate map that divides the community into specific zones to determine the probability of flooding in each zone. When the map is prepared and the community agrees to the required flood-control and land-use restrictions, the community enters the **regular program**. Property owners can then purchase higher amounts of flood insurance.

Regular program
Second phase of the National Flood Insurance Program in which the community agrees to adopt flood-control and land-use restrictions and in which property owners purchase higher amounts of flood insurance than under the emergency program.

Amount of Insurance

The maximum amount of insurance that a property owner can purchase under the emergency program at subsidized rates is $35,000 on a one- to four-family dwelling and $10,000 on the contents. For other residential structures, the maximum dwelling limit is $100,000. (Higher dwelling limits are available under the emergency program in Alaska, Guam, Hawaii, and the U. S. Virgin Islands.)

The maximum amount of insurance available under the regular program is $250,000 for a one- to four-family dwelling or other residential structure and $100,000 on the contents. Exhibit 8-2 shows the maximum amounts available under both the regular and the emergency programs.

Waiting Period

Adverse selection
The tendency for people with the greatest probability of loss to be the ones most likely to purchase insurance.

To avoid **adverse selection**, the National Flood Insurance Program generally requires a thirty-day waiting period for new flood insurance policies and for endorsements increasing coverage on existing policies. In other words, coverage does not become effective until thirty days after the date of the application (or thirty days after receipt by the NFIP or its representative in certain cases). If there were no waiting period, property owners in areas predicted to incur severe flooding within a few days might delay purchase of flood insurance until impending flood endangers their property. An exception to the waiting period is made for flood insurance that is initially purchased in connection with the purchase of property, or the making or increasing of a mortgage on property. In such cases involving property purchase or mortgage transactions, the policy becomes effective at the time the property transfer is settled or the mortgage becomes effective, provided that the policy is applied for and the premium paid at or before the transfer of ownership or date of mortgage. For example, Amy has purchased a home on riverfront property. The settlement (closing) is scheduled for July 25 at noon; the mortgage becomes effective at the same time. Amy submitted an application and paid the appropriate premium to NFIP on July 24 for flood insurance on her new home. Amy's flood policy will become effective at noon on July 25 when the property is transferred to her. Because a new mortgage is involved, Amy's flood policy is not subject to the thirty-day waiting period.

EXHIBIT 8-2

National Flood Insurance Program

Maximum Amounts of Insurance Available for Residential Buildings and Contents

	Emergency Program	Regular Program
Building Coverage		
One- to Four-Family Dwelling	$ 35,000*	$250,000
Other Residential	$100,000**	$250,000
Contents Coverage		
Residential	$ 10,000	$100,000

*In Alaska, Guam, Hawaii, and U.S. Virgin Islands, the amount available is $50,000.
**In Alaska, Guam, Hawaii, and U.S. Virgin Islands, the amount available is $150,000.

Source: *Flood Insurance Manual*, published by Federal Emergency Management Agency, 1994 ed., revised April 1996.

Write-Your-Own Program

The **"Write-Your-Own" (WYO) flood insurance program** is a cooperative undertaking of the insurance industry and the Federal Insurance Administration. WYO allows private insurers participating in the program to sell and service flood insurance under their own names. The insurers receive an expense allowance for policies written and claims processed, while the federal government retains responsibility for losses. Producers have the option of selling flood insurance either through a WYO company or directly through the NFIP. The goals of the WYO program are to increase the number of flood policies written, to improve services, and to involve private insurance companies in the sale of flood insurance. More than 90 percent of all NFIP policies are written through private insurers under the WYO program.

"Write-Your-Own" (WYO) flood insurance program
Cooperative undertaking of the insurance industry and the Federal Insurance Administration that allows participating private insurers to sell and service flood insurance under their own names.

Myths and Facts About Flood Insurance

Although the need for flood insurance is great in many parts of the country, many property owners do not purchase it for various reasons. Of the more than 4 million flood insurance policies in force in 1999, nearly two-thirds were written in the coastal states of California, Florida, Louisiana, and Texas, which have obvious flood exposures. In many other states with heavy flooding exposure, flood policies are not as prevalent. Many people think they do not need flood insurance, particularly if their properties lie in areas that are not considered flood zones. However, between 20 and 25 percent of all claims paid by the NFIP are for policies outside areas with the greatest risk of flooding, designated by FEMA as Special Flood Hazard Areas (SFHAs). Many people think flood insurance is not available to them, while others believe it is prohibitively expensive, and some simply think they do not need it. To offset some of these misconceptions, the NFIP has published twelve interesting myths and important facts about flood insurance, which are reproduced below.

Myths and Facts About the National Flood Insurance Program

Who needs flood insurance? *Everyone*. And everyone in a participating community of the National Flood Insurance Program (NFIP) can buy flood insurance. Nationwide, more than 19,000 communities have joined the program. In some instances, people have been told that they cannot buy flood insurance because of where they live. To clear up this and other misconceptions about federal flood insurance, the NFIP has compiled the following list of common myths about the program and the real facts behind them to give you the full story about this valuable protection.

Myth: *You can't buy flood insurance if you are located in a high-risk flood area.*

Fact: You can buy federal flood insurance no matter where you live if your community belongs to the NFIP, except in Coastal Barrier Resources System (CBRS) areas. The program was created in 1968 to provide affordable flood insurance to people who live in areas with the greatest risk of flooding, called Special Flood Hazard Areas (SFHAs). In fact, under the National Flood Insurance Act, lenders must require borrowers whose property is located within an SFHA to purchase flood insurance as a condition of receiving a federally backed mortgage loan. There is an exemption for conventional loans on properties within CBRS areas.

Lenders should notify borrowers that their property is located in an SFHA and that federal flood insurance is available.

Myth: *You can't buy flood insurance immediately before or during a flood.*

Fact: You can purchase flood coverage at any time. There is a thirty-day waiting period after you've applied and paid the premium before the policy is effective, with the following exceptions: (1) If the initial purchase of flood insurance is in connection with the making, increasing, extending, or renewing of a loan, there is no waiting period. The coverage becomes effective at the time of the loan, provided application and payment of the premium is made at or before loan closing. (2) If the initial purchase of flood insurance is made during the thirteen-month period following the effective date of a revised flood map for a community, there is a one-day waiting period.

The policy does not cover a "loss in progress," defined by the NFIP as a loss occurring as of 12:01 A.M. on the first day of the policy term. In addition, you cannot increase the amount of insurance coverage you have during a loss in progress.

Myth: *Homeowners insurance policies cover flooding.*

Fact: Unfortunately, many homeowners do not find out until it is too late that their homeowners policies do not cover flooding. Federal flood insurance protects your most valuable assets—your home and belongings.

Myth: *Flood insurance is available only for homeowners.*

Fact: Flood insurance is available to protect homes, condominiums, apartments, and nonresidential buildings, including commercial structures. A maximum of $250,000 of building coverage is available for single-family residential buildings and $250,000 per unit for multi-family residences. The limit for contents coverage on all residential buildings is $100,000, which is also available to renters.

Commercial structures can be insured to a limit of $500,000 for the building and $500,000 for the contents.

Myth: *You can't buy flood insurance if your property has been flooded.*

Fact: You are still eligible to purchase flood insurance, provided that your community is participating in the NFIP.

Myth: *Only residents of high flood-risk zones need to insure their property.*

Fact: Even if you live in an area that is not flood-prone, it is advisable to have flood insurance. Between 20 and 25 percent of the NFIP's claims come from outside high flood-risk areas. The NFIP's low-cost policy, available for just over $100 per year, is designed for residential properties located in low-to-moderate flood-risk zones.

Myth: *The NFIP does not offer any type of basement coverage.*

Fact: Yes, it does. The NFIP defines a basement as any area of a building with a floor that is subgrade or below ground level on all sides. Under NFIP building coverage, basements are insured for cleanup and items used to service the building, such as furnaces, hot-water heaters, air conditioners, utility connections, circuit breaker boxes, and pumps and tanks used in solar energy systems, as well as the repair of structural damage to basement walls. Items in basements insured under NFIP contents coverage include clothes washers and dryers and food freezers and the food in them. Improvements to a basement, such as finished walls, floors, or ceilings, as well as personal belongings located in a basement, are not covered in either NFIP building or contents coverage.

Myth: *Federal disaster assistance will pay for flood damage.*

Fact: Before a community is eligible for disaster assistance, it must be declared a federal disaster area. Federal disaster assistance declarations are awarded in fewer than 50 percent of flooding incidents. The premium for an NFIP policy, averaging a little more than $350 per year, is less expensive than interest on federal disaster loans, even though they are always granted on favorable terms.

Furthermore, if you are uninsured and receive federal disaster assistance after a flood, you must purchase flood insurance to receive disaster relief in the future.

Continued on next page.

Myth: *The NFIP encourages coastal development.*

Fact: One of the NFIP's primary objectives is to guide development away from high flood-risk areas. NFIP regulations minimize the impact of structures that are built in SFHAs by requiring them not to cause obstructions to the natural flow of floodwaters. Also, as a condition of community participation in the NFIP, those structures built within SFHAs must adhere to strict flood-plain management regulations.

In addition, the Coastal Barrier Resources Act (CBRA) of 1982 relies on the NFIP to discourage building in the fragile coastal areas covered by CBRA by prohibiting the sale of flood insurance in designated CBRA areas. These laws do not prohibit property owners from building along coastal areas; however, they do transfer the financial risk of such building from federal taxpayers to those who choose to live or invest in these areas.

Myth: *Federal flood insurance can be purchased only through the NFIP directly.*

Fact: NFIP flood insurance is sold through private insurance companies and agents and is backed by the federal government.

Myth: *The NFIP does not cover flooding resulting from hurricanes or the overflow of rivers or tidal waters.*

Fact: The NFIP defines covered flooding as a general and temporary condition during which the surface of normally dry land is partially or completely inundated. Two adjacent properties or two or more acres must be affected. Flooding can be caused by any one of the following:

- The overflow of inland or tidal waters

- The unusual and rapid accumulation or runoff of surface waters from any source, such as heavy rainfall

- The incidence of mudslides or mudflows, caused by flooding, which are comparable to a river of liquid and flowing mud

- The collapse or destabilization of land along the shore of a lake or other body of water, resulting from erosion or the effect of waves, or water currents exceeding normal, cyclical levels

Myth: *Wind-driven rain is considered flooding.*

Fact: No, it isn't. Rain entering through wind-damaged windows, doors, or a hole in the wall or the roof, resulting in standing water or puddles, is considered windstorm rather than flood damage. Federal flood insurance only covers damage caused by the general condition of flooding (defined above), typically caused by storm surge, wave wash, tidal waves, or the overflow of any body of water above normal, cyclical levels. Buildings that sustain this type of damage usually have a watermark, showing how high the water has risen before it subsides. Although the Standard Flood Insurance Policy (SFIP) specifically excludes wind and hail coverage, most homeowners policies provide coverage.

Adapted from FEMA and NFIP bulletin at www.fema.gov/nfip/myth.htm.

INSURANCE FOR HARD-TO-INSURE RESIDENCES

Although most residences are insured under either a homeowners or a dwelling policy, insurers are reluctant to insure some residential dwellings for various reasons. These include homes with a greater-than-average exposure to losses. For example, homes in coastal areas have a greater-than-average exposure to windstorm losses. Several plans are now available to insure such homes that previously were uninsurable or insurable only through the non-standard market at very high premiums.

FAIR Plans

FAIR (Fair Access to Insurance Requirements) plans were set up in response to the urban riots of the 1960s. At that time, property insurance was difficult to obtain in the congested urban areas of many major cities. A majority of states now have FAIR plans that make property insurance available for property located in areas where coverage in the voluntary insurance market is difficult to obtain. Each state with a FAIR plan has enacted its own legislation in response to local market needs, so the coverage provided and the methods of operation among the states that have FAIR plans vary considerably.

FAIR (Fair Access to Insurance Requirements) plans
State-run programs that provide basic property insurance coverage on buildings, dwellings, and their contents for property owners who are unable to obtain coverage in the standard insurance market.

Although procedures differ, FAIR plans provide property insurance to those who have difficulty obtaining insurance, much as automobile insurance ("assigned risk") plans (discussed in Chapter 2) provide coverage for those who have difficulty obtaining auto liability insurance. A property owner unable to obtain property insurance in the voluntary insurance market may apply to the state's FAIR plan through a licensed agent or broker. To be eligible for FAIR plan coverage, the insured must have the property in-spected. Only property that meets the FAIR plan's inspection criteria will be insured in the program. The insured must comply with any recommendations made in the inspection process to be eligible for FAIR plan coverage.

Under most FAIR plans, the following types of exposures are considered uninsurable:

- Vacant property
- Property poorly maintained
- Property subject to unacceptable physical hazards, such as storage of flammable materials
- Property in violation of law or public policy, such as a "condemned building" (one that is considered unfit for human habitation)
- In some states, property not built in accordance with building and safety codes

FAIR plans are not only for properties in poor neighborhoods. The hazard of potential brush fires in wealthy, wooded suburban areas might also cause properties to be uninsurable in the standard market. The current California

FAIR plan, for example, provides coverage for both inner-city properties and suburban homes located in hazardous brush areas.

When FAIR plans were first developed, some people were concerned that well-kept properties in inner cities would be prevented from obtaining coverage solely because of their location. The FAIR plan programs generally require that the inspection of the property must concentrate on that property alone and must ignore any hazardous conditions beyond the control of the property owner that might give rise to loss. An example of such a condition would be neighboring property with highly hazardous conditions that might affect the property to be insured.

Most FAIR plans provide only a small number of coverages common to most homeowners policies; however, limited homeowners coverage is available in about a dozen state FAIR plans. Coverage is typically provided only for fire and a limited number of perils. Limits of insurance available and mandatory deductibles vary widely among plans. To provide coverage greater than that offered by the FAIR plan (such as when an expensive suburban home is written in the FAIR plan), a difference in conditions policy (DIC) can be written by a specialty insurer. A DIC policy can provide coverage for risks of direct loss, while excluding fire and the other perils covered under the FAIR plan policy. Because the peril of fire is the primary loss exposure in these cases, private insurers are willing to provide coverage for other perils.

Beachfront and Windstorm Plans

Beachfront and windstorm plans
State-regulated insurance pools that provide property insurance, both personal and commercial, in coastal areas exposed to the risk of heavy windstorm losses.

Beachfront property in many parts of the country is exposed to heavy windstorm losses during hurricanes and other storms. Much of this property is also vulnerable to damage from unusually high tides and coastal erosion. **Beachfront and windstorm plans** are part of an "assigned risk" property insurance program that is similar to the FAIR plan programs. The origins of the plans differ in that these plans were set up in response to heavy windstorm losses rather than to urban riots, and they exist primarily in the Southeast and Gulf Coast states that are particularly vulnerable to hurricanes. Although beachfront and windstorm plans provide coverage for windstorm losses, losses from tidal water are generally excluded. Such losses should be covered under a flood insurance policy.

Following a number of severe storms, many insurers during the 1960s withdrew from writing property insurance in coastal areas, causing an availability crisis for homeowners, not only for windstorm coverage, but for all property insurance. North Carolina responded to this crisis by creating the North Carolina Insurance Underwriting Association in 1969—the first beachfront plan. Other states soon followed with their own plans.

Each of the beachfront and windstorm plans offers coverage only in designated coastal areas. Owners of most real and personal property in coastal areas can obtain coverage through these plans. However, like the FAIR plans, beachfront and windstorm plans will not insure certain types of property, such as property with poor maintenance or unacceptable physical hazards. The perils insured against in beachfront and windstorm plans vary by state, but many provide only windstorm and hail coverage. In those states, insureds must obtain other property coverages through the standard insurance market or other nonstandard markets. In other states, such as North Carolina, broader property coverages are available through the plan. The maximum limits of insurance available also vary among states, as do deductibles. State plans generally contain a provision that no application for new coverage or increase in limits will be accepted when a hurricane has formed within a certain distance of the beach area where the property lies.

SUMMARY

Although homeowners policies cover many typical loss exposures, other types of residential loss exposures cannot be covered by a homeowners policy or can be covered only with special endorsements. For example, many individuals own houses they do not occupy but rent to others; other people live in mobilehomes or manufactured homes that do not qualify for most homeowners policies. In addition, many individuals find it difficult to obtain insurance for certain exposures, such as flooding or heavy windstorm exposure. This chapter explores policies and endorsements that cover residential loss exposures not covered by standard homeowners policies.

Dwelling policies are designed primarily to insure one- to four-family dwellings, whether owner-occupied or tenant-occupied. The dwelling program developed by Insurance Services Office (ISO) includes three forms: DP-1, the basic form; DP-2, the broad form; and DP-3, the special form. These dwelling policy forms offer property coverages on a dwelling and/or its contents similar to the coverages provided in Section I of the homeowners forms. However, major differences exist between the dwelling and homeowners policies. For example, the unendorsed ISO dwelling forms do not provide any theft coverage for personal property or any liability coverages. These coverages can be added to the dwelling policy by the purchase of a theft coverage endorsement and a personal liability supplement.

Owners of mobilehomes have exposures similar to those faced by owners of other types of homes, but mobilehomes also present unique exposures (such as transportation perils and high susceptibility to windstorm damage) that generally make them ineligible for homeowners policies. However, mobilehome owners have several options for insuring their property and liability exposures. Many specialty insurers have developed policies especially for mobilehomes. Both ISO and the American Association of Insurance Services (AAIS) have developed special forms for insuring mobilehomes. Insurers that use forms developed by ISO can provide coverage for mobilehomes by attaching the ISO mobilehome endorsement to a homeowners policy. In addition, ISO has developed several endorsements that provide unique coverages for use with mobilehomes, such as the transportation/permission to move and the mobilehome lienholder's single interest endorsements. AAIS has developed a separate program for insuring mobilehomes that is similar to its homeowners program and that a number of insurers use.

Other residential exposures that are not adequately covered by standard homeowners policies are the exposures that arise from farming and ranching. Because farmers and ranchers often live on the land they work, they need a combination of personal insurance and commercial insurance. Farm and ranch insurance is usually provided by insurers who use their own independently developed policy forms and endorsements. AAIS has a flexible farmowners program that can be adapted to cover diverse farm exposures and that is used by many insurance companies to insure farms. ISO has developed two farm liability endorsements used with homeowners policies to insure liability exposures from incidental farming operations. The incidental farming personal liability endorsement extends the homeowners Section II coverages to include an insured's incidental farming operations either at the insured's residence or at a separate location. The farmers personal liability endorsement is designed to cover liability exposures arising out of a commercial farming operation conducted away from the insured's residence premises. In addition, a livestock collision coverage endorsement can be added when either of the liability endorsements apply; it provides a specified amount of coverage for the death of an animal owned by the insured if caused by vehicle collision.

Floods are among the most common of all natural disasters, but, because of their catastrophic loss potential, both homeowners and dwelling policies exclude losses caused by flooding. To make flood insurance available to property owners, the federal government provides flood insurance at subsidized rates for both dwellings and commercial buildings, as well as for the contents of both. Under the National Flood Insurance Program (NFIP), flood insurance is now available in all states. The emergency program is the initial phase of the NFIP; during this phase, property owners in flood-prone areas can purchase limited amounts of insurance at subsidized rates. After a community qualifies for the regular program, property owners can purchase higher amounts of flood insurance than under the emergency program.

Insurers are reluctant to insure some residential dwellings that have a greater-than-average exposure to losses, but several plans are available to insure such homes. FAIR plans are state-run programs that provide basic property insurance coverage on buildings, dwellings, and their contents for property owners who are unable to obtain coverage in the standard insurance market. Beach-front and windstorm plans are state-regulated insurance pools whose primary purpose is to provide property insurance, both personal and commercial, in coastal areas exposed to heavy windstorm losses.

CHAPTER NOTES

1. Discussion is based on the 1988 dwelling forms, but points mentioned here are consistent with the Dwelling 2002 program forms released by ISO in December 2001.

2. This section is based on information provided by AAIS.

3. Most of the information in this section is taken from the *Flood Insurance Manual*, published by the Federal Emergency Management Agency, 1994 ed., revised April 1996, and from the FEMA Web site, http://www.fema.gov.

Chapter 9

Direct Your Learning

Other Personal Property and Liability Insurance

After learning the subject matter of this chapter, you should be able to:

■ Describe the general characteristics of inland marine floaters.

■ Describe the coverage provided by and explain why an insured might need the following:

- Personal articles floater

- Personal property floater

- Personal effects floater

■ Describe and, in a given case, analyze the coverages typically provided for watercraft by each of the following:

- The homeowners policy

- The personal auto policy

- Small boat policies

- Boatowners and yacht policies

■ Describe the coverage provided by the typical personal umbrella policy.

■ Given a case involving a liability loss and a personal umbrella policy:

- Explain whether the loss is covered

- Determine the amount the umbrella insurer would pay for covered losses.

- Determine the amount, if any, the underlying insurer would pay.

- Determine the amount, if any, the insured would pay.

Develop Your Perspective

What are the main topics covered in the chapter?

Some property and liability exposures are excluded from residential and personal auto policies. Specialty policies have been created to address some of these exposures. Such policies include inland marine floaters and personal watercraft policies. The personal umbrella provides high coverage limits for residential and auto liability exposures as well as coverage for losses that might be excluded by other policies.

Analyze the coverages these policies provide.

- What gaps do they fill in the coverages provided by the residential and personal auto policies?

Why is it important to know these topics?

Homeowners and personal auto policies are packages of coverages intended to meet the needs of most individuals and families. To include coverages for art with high values or large watercraft would be unfair to policyholders who do not have those exposures, because they would be paying premium for coverages they cannot use. Instead, specific policies are available for those who have the exposures.

Consider the benefits to policyholders who purchase the coverages described in this chapter.

- How can they tailor the coverages to meet their specific exposures?

How can you use this information?

Address your own loss exposures:

- What exposures that are not covered by homeowners and auto policies would be covered by inland marine, watercraft, or umbrella liability policies?

Chapter 9

Other Personal Property and Liability Insurance

This chapter continues the discussion of personal insurance with an examination of other types of property and liability insurance that provide protection to meet the needs of individuals and families: inland marine, personal watercraft, and personal umbrella insurance.

Inland marine insurance is designed to cover property that has special value or that is frequently moved from one location to another, such as jewelry, furs, fine arts, silverware, cameras, stamp and coin collections, clothes and luggage, sports equipment, and musical instruments. Although these types of property are covered under a homeowners policy, they are usually subject to certain limitations. To obtain higher limits and broader coverage on such items, an insured can purchase either an appropriate homeowners endorsement (such as the scheduled personal property endorsement, discussed in Chapter 7) or an appropriate inland marine policy, such as a personal articles floater.

Personal watercraft insurance is designed to cover recreational boats and their motors, equipment, and accessories. The major contracts for insuring pleasure boats are small boat policies, boatowners policies, and personal yacht insurance policies.

Personal umbrella insurance is designed to cover catastrophic claims or judgments arising from personal liability exposures associated with homes, automobiles, boats, recreational vehicles, sports, and other personal activities. A catastrophic claim is one that is so large that if uninsured, or underinsured, it can impair the insured's standard of living. This personal catastrophic liability exposure is insured under a personal umbrella policy, which provides high liability limits in addition to those provided by basic policies such as a homeowners policy and a personal auto policy. Umbrella policies also provide liability coverage that is typically broader than the coverage provided by homeowners and personal auto policies.

INLAND MARINE FLOATERS[1]

Inland marine insurance developed out of the marine insurance industry in the 1920s. Traditionally, marine insurers wrote coverage for the majority of loss exposures associated with transportation because most cargo was transported by

Inland marine insurance
Insurance that covers miscellaneous types of property, such as movable property, goods in domestic transit, and property used in transportation and communication.

sea. With the development of the railroad and trucking industries, a need arose for insurance to cover cargo from the time the goods left the premises of the shipper until they arrived at the final destination. Marine insurers broadened their coverage to include land exposures. Eventually, property and liability insurers began writing inland marine insurance.

The policies that covered movable personal property on land were called personal inland marine **floaters**. The first of these types of policies was the jewelry floater, which was written to include broad *"all-risks"* coverage, followed by the fur floater, fine arts floater, camera floater, and musical instrument floater.

Floater

Inland marine policy that provides coverage for property that "floats" or moves (such as jewelry, furs, or cameras) rather than providing coverage at a fixed location.

> "All-risks" is a term many insurance professionals use to indicate policies that cover all causes of loss that are not specifically excluded. However, this term is misleading because the policies do not cover all risks of loss; some exclusions always apply. Therefore, insurance professionals should avoid the term "all-risks" when talking with customers and others who might misunderstand its meaning. A better term to describe "all-risks" policies would be "special-form coverage" (defined in Chapter 5) or "open perils" (meaning that perils are left "open" rather than being "named" in the policy). Another way to describe the coverage provided by most "all-risks" policies is "risks of direct physical loss" subject to exclusions.

Characteristics of Inland Marine Floaters[2]

Inland marine floater policies share the following general characteristics:

*   The coverage is tailored to the specific type of property to be insured, such as a jewelry floater, camera floater, or musical instruments floater.

*   The insured can select the appropriate policy limits. As discussed in Chapter 5, the homeowners policy automatically covers personal property but with limited amounts on certain types of property. For example, coverage on jewelry has a $1,500 limit for a loss by theft. With the inland marine floater, an insured can obtain higher limits for theft losses.

*   Floaters provide extensive coverage with respect to the perils covered. Floaters are typically written for "all-risks" of direct physical loss or damage subject to policy exclusions and conditions. Named perils coverage is occasionally written.

*   Most floaters provide coverage anywhere in the world.

*   Inland marine floaters are usually written without a deductible.

Inland Marine Floater Policy Provisions

The following provisions commonly appear in inland marine floater policies. Each floater also contains other conditions and exclusions that apply specifically to the particular coverage provided.

Insuring Agreement

Most floater policies insure covered property worldwide on a special-form (open perils) basis subject to exclusions.

Perils Excluded

The following perils are generally excluded:

- Wear and tear, gradual deterioration, or inherent vice
- Insects or vermin
- Mechanical or electrical breakdown or failure
- War and warlike actions
- Nuclear hazard

In addition, some inland marine floaters contain other specific exclusions. For example, floaters covering fine arts usually exclude breakage of fragile articles unless caused by fire, lightning, windstorm, earthquake, flood, or some other specifically mentioned peril.

Persons Insured

Covered persons are generally the named insured and members of the insured's family living in the same household.

General Conditions

With certain exceptions, such as fine arts, the amount paid for a covered loss is the *least* of the four following amounts:

1. The actual cash value of the insured property at the time of loss or damage
2. The amount for which the insured could reasonably be expected to have the property repaired to its condition immediately before loss
3. The amount for which the insured could reasonably be expected to replace the property with property substantially identical to the article lost or damaged
4. The amount of insurance stated in the policy

Other conditions in inland marine policies are similar to those explained in previous chapters.

Types of Personal Inland Marine Floaters

Although many personal inland marine exposures are covered under homeowners policies (often by attaching endorsements), several separate personal inland marine floaters are available to meet specific needs. The following are the most commonly used personal floaters:

- Personal articles floater (PAF)
- Personal property floater (PPF)
- Personal effects floater (PEF)

Personal Articles Floater

The personal articles floater (PAF) developed by ISO is similar to the homeowners scheduled personal property endorsements (HO 04 60 and HO 04 61) discussed in Chapter 7. The PAF provides special-form coverage for nine optional classes of personal property, including jewelry, furs, cameras and photographic equipment, musical instruments, silverware, golfer's equipment, fine arts and antiques, and stamp and coin collections. A specific amount of insurance is shown in the policy for each class of property or for each specific article.

Generally, individuals who own these types of property insure them by adding an endorsement to the homeowners policy, such as the scheduled personal property endorsement. However, some people prefer to obtain coverage under a separate personal articles floater:

- A retired person might own valuable jewelry or golfer's equipment but might be living in a retirement home and have no homeowners policy.

- Two individuals, not residing together, might jointly own valuable photographic equipment. Because they do not reside together, they would be ineligible for a homeowners policy in both names.

- A couple might want to keep their homeowners premium separate from the premium on jewelry or collectibles because the homeowners premium is paid together with the mortgage.

Personal Property Floater

Unscheduled personal property
Personal property not specifically listed (scheduled) on a policy but generally covered with a single limit for all items (or each class) of personal property that are not excluded.

The personal property floater (PPF) provides special-form coverage on **unscheduled personal property** owned or used by the insured and normally kept at the insured's residence. *Scheduled* property may be included with the appropriate floater endorsement. The PPF also provides worldwide coverage on the same property when it is temporarily away from the residence premises. The PPF can be used to insure thirteen classes of unscheduled personal property; a separate amount of insurance applies to each of the following classes:

1. Silverware, goldware, and pewterware
2. Clothing
3. Rugs and draperies
4. Musical instruments and electronic equipment
5. Paintings and other art objects
6. China and glassware
7. Cameras and photographic equipment
8. Guns and other sports equipment
9. Major appliances
10. Bedding and linens
11. Furniture

12. All other personal property, and professional books and equipment while in the residence

13. Building additions and alterations

The total amount of insurance in each category is the maximum limit of recovery for any single loss to property in that category. The total amount for the thirteen categories is the total policy limit. A deductible applies to each loss. As always in special-form policies, specific exclusions apply.

Personal property floaters are rarely used these days, because special-form coverage on personal property is available on an HO-5 policy or under an HO-4 or HO-6 with the appropriate endorsement. The homeowners policies also provide liability coverage.

When Should Personal Property Be Scheduled?

An unendorsed homeowners policy covers unscheduled personal property on a named-perils basis. However, some people own valuable personal property that should be scheduled and specifically insured under a floater policy or an endorsement. In addition to *high-value* property such as valuable jewelry and fur coats, the following types of personal property may be appropriate for scheduled coverage:

1. *Unique objects.* This includes works of art, rare antiques, paintings, and collections of unusual property, such as a valuable stamp or rare coin collection. The value of the property should be established in advance to avoid the problem of proving its value after a loss occurs.

2. *Portable property.* Certain types of portable property such as cameras and camera equipment, musical instruments, or sports equipment can be scheduled and specifically insured under a floater policy.

3. *Fragile objects.* Certain fragile articles with high value can be scheduled and specifically insured, such as glassware or statuary.

Personal Effects Floater

The personal effects floater (PEF) provides special-form coverage on personal property such as luggage, clothes, cameras, and sports equipment normally worn or carried by tourists and travelers. The PEF covers property worldwide, but only while the property is *away from the residence premises*. Coverage applies to property belonging to and used or worn by the named insured, spouse, and unmarried children who permanently reside with the named insured.

Because the homeowners policy covers personal property worldwide, most homeowners do not see any need to purchase a PEF. Coverage is occasionally sold to those who are ineligible for homeowners policies or to travelers who want the broadest possible protection on their luggage and other personal effects.

PERSONAL WATERCRAFT INSURANCE[3]

Boats of many designs and sizes are found on America's waterways. Personal watercraft includes small rowboats, canoes, outboard and inboard motorboats, sailboats, houseboats, and power yachts. This section briefly examines the loss exposures and hazards arising from the ownership and operation of personal watercraft and the major insurance contracts designed for insuring those exposures and hazards.

Property Loss Exposures

Watercraft, boat trailers, and related equipment are exposed to many physical damage and theft losses such as the following:

- Damage to the boat's hull as a result of a collision with another boat
- Theft of the boat's motor or equipment
- Damage to the boat's propeller from hitting an underwater object
- Lightning damage to electrical and navigational equipment aboard the boat
- Wind damage to the sail
- Fire damage to the boat trailer

Liability, Medical Payments, and Uninsured Boaters Exposures

Owners and operators of watercraft face many exposures resulting in claims for bodily injury and property damage liability, medical payments, and uninsured boaters losses. The following are examples:

- *Bodily injury liability loss*: A boat owner fails to take necessary safety precautions while fueling the boat. The engine explodes and passengers are severely burned.
- *Property damage liability loss*: A boat collides with a dock, causing substantial damage to the dock.
- *Medical payments loss*: A guest is injured when she loses her footing while getting off the boat.
- *Uninsured boater loss*: An uninsured boater runs his boat into the insured's boat and causes bodily injury to the insured.

Limited Watercraft Coverage Under Homeowners and Personal Auto Policies

As discussed in earlier chapters, property coverage for watercraft and equipment is limited under the homeowners and personal auto policies.

Homeowners Section I—Property Coverages

The major limitations on property coverage for watercraft in Section I of the homeowners policy are as follows:

- A maximum limit of $1,500 applies to watercraft, including motors, trailers, and equipment. Some insurers offer endorsements to allow insureds to increase this limit.

- Theft of watercraft, trailers, equipment, and outboard motors away from the residence premises is specifically excluded.

- Direct loss to watercraft, trailers, equipment, and outboard motors caused by windstorm or hail is covered (up to the $1,500 limit) only if the property is inside a fully enclosed building.

- Under the HO-3 and other forms providing named-perils coverage on personal property, watercraft and other boating property are covered only for a limited number of perils.

Like all losses to personal property covered under a homeowners policy, a watercraft loss is adjusted on an actual cash value basis unless the personal property replacement cost endorsement is added.

Homeowners Section II—Liability Coverages

As discussed in Chapter 6, the liability section of the homeowners policy covers only certain watercraft loss exposures. Section II of the homeowners policy excludes liability arising out of any of the following:

- The ownership, maintenance, use, loading or unloading of any *excluded watercraft*. (Certain watercraft exposures that are *not* excluded and are therefore covered were shown in Exhibit 6-3 in Chapter 6.)

- The entrustment by an insured of an excluded watercraft to any person.

- Negligent supervision of or failure to supervise any person involved with a watercraft.

- An insured's vicarious liability for the actions of a child or minor using an excluded watercraft.

Coverage Under the Personal Auto Policy

Coverage does not exist for boats, motors, or boat equipment under the Personal Auto Policy. However, physical damage loss to a boat trailer is covered if the trailer is described on the declarations page. For example, if the insured has other than collision coverage on a boat trailer and the trailer is stolen, the PAP will provide coverage. Also, a boat trailer the insured owns is covered for liability (whether it is described on the declarations page or not) if it is designed to be pulled by a private passenger auto, pickup, or van.

Personal Watercraft Policies

Because of the exclusions and limitations under the homeowners and personal auto policies, boat owners usually want to insure their boats with insurance contracts that provide more comprehensive protection. Three types of watercraft policies are discussed below.

Small Boat Policies

Small boat policies are designed to cover boats up to a certain size (such as twenty-six feet in length). Many insurers have developed such policies, which are called by various names (often with a nautical theme) and which contain coverage variations. Although small boat policies are not standard, they have certain common features as described below.

Covered Property

A small boat policy may include the boat, motor, equipment, and trailer. Most small boat policies are written on an actual cash value basis and contain a deductible, such as $100 or more.

Covered Perils

A small boat policy can be written to provide named perils or special-form ("all-risks") coverage. Most of these policies cover all direct physical losses to covered watercraft except those losses that are specifically excluded.

Generally, the policy includes liability insurance for bodily injury, loss of life, illness, and property damage to third parties arising out of the ownership, maintenance, or use of the boat. Typically, medical payments coverage is included for any insured person who sustains bodily injury while in, upon, boarding, or leaving the boat.

Exclusions

The following major exclusions are commonly found in small boat policies:

- *General risks of direct loss.* There is no coverage for loss caused by wear and tear, gradual deterioration, vermin and marine life, rust and corrosion, inherent vice, latent defect, mechanical breakdown, or extremes of temperature.
- *Repair or service.* Loss or damage from refinishing, renovating, or repair is not covered.
- *Business pursuits.* Coverage does not exist if the boat is used to carry passengers for compensation, if the boat or insured property is rented to others, or if the covered property is being operated in any official race or speed contest.

Boatowners and Yacht Policies

Many insurers have developed a special boatowners package policy for boats up to a certain length, such as twenty-six feet. Larger boats are usually written under yacht policies. Both types of policies combine physical damage, liability, medical payments, and sometimes uninsured boaters coverage in one policy. Although boatowners and yacht policies have no standard rules or forms, they contain certain common features.

Warranties

Personal watercraft insurance generally contains several **warranties** or promises that the insured must keep. The boat owner guarantees compliance with the insurer's conditions. If a warranty is violated, higher premiums may be required, or the coverages may not apply, depending on the warranty. The major warranties are as follows:

- *Pleasure use.* The insured warrants that the boat will be used only for private pleasure purposes and will not be hired or *chartered* unless the insurance company approves.
- *Seaworthiness.* The insured warrants that the boat is in a seaworthy condition.
- *Lay-up period.* The insured warrants that the boat will not be in operation during certain periods, such as the winter months. The lay-up period is usually shown on the declarations page.
- *Navigational limits.* The navigation area is stated on the declarations page of the policy. If a loss occurs to the boat in an area not listed in the navigation clause, coverage does not apply. With prior notice and an additional premium, the insurer may allow the boat to be used outside the navigational limits.

Persons Insured

The insured includes those named on the declarations page, resident relatives of the household, and persons under the age of twenty-one in the insured's care. Other persons or organizations using the boat without a charge are covered provided the named insured gives permission.

Physical Damage Coverage (Hull Insurance)

Boatowners and yacht policies contain **hull insurance** on either a named perils or a special-form basis covering the boat (referred to as the **hull**), equipment, accessories, motor, and trailer. Because a special-form policy is broader than a named perils policy, boatowners and yacht policies of various insurers vary greatly in terms of the hull coverage each provides.

The following property exclusions are commonly found in boatowners and yacht policies:

- Wear and tear, gradual deterioration, rust, corrosion, mold, wet or dry rot, marring, denting, scratching, inherent vice, latent or physical defect, insects, animal or marine life, weathering, and dampness of atmosphere.
- Mechanical breakdown or faulty manufacturing, unless the loss was caused by fire or explosion.

Warranties
Promises made by an insured that guarantee compliance with the insurer's conditions.

Hull insurance
Physical damage insurance on a boat, including its sails, machinery, furniture, and other equipment.

Hull
The boat. A vessel's structure, including machinery, spars, sails, tackles, fittings, and other equipment and furnishings that are normally required for the vessel's operation and seaworthy maintenance.

- Freezing and thawing of ice, unless the insured has taken reasonable care to protect the property. For example, an insured could install a circulating water system to keep the water from freezing around the boat in icy conditions.

- Loss that occurs while the boat is used in any official race or speed contest. However, most watercraft policies do not exclude sailboat racing.

- Intentional loss caused by an insured.

- War, nuclear hazard, and radioactive contamination.

Boatowners and yacht policies can be written on either a replacement cost basis or an actual cash value basis. Because replacement cost coverage offers better protection for the insured than coverage on an ACV basis, this difference in valuation is important in any comparison of boat policies. Small boats are usually written with a $100 to $250 deductible. Medium to large boats often carry a deductible equal to 1 percent or higher of the insured value.

Liability Coverage (Protection and Indemnity Insurance)

Protection and indemnity (P&I) insurance
Insurance that covers the insured for bodily injury or property damage liability arising from the ownership, maintenance, or use of the insured boat.

Boatowners and yacht policies also include liability insurance, known as **protection and indemnity (P&I) insurance**, that covers the insured for bodily injury and property damage liability arising from the ownership, maintenance, or use of the boat. Defense costs are also covered. The following exclusions appear in most boatowners and yacht policies:

- Intentional injury or illegal activities.

- Renting the watercraft to others or carrying persons or property for a fee without the insurer's permission.

- Liability arising out of water-skiing, parasailing (a sport using a type of parachute to sail through the air while being towed by a powerboat), or other airborne or experimental devices.

- Using watercraft (except sailboats in some policies) in any official race or speed test.

- Losses covered by a workers compensation or similar law.

- Bodily injury or property damage arising out of transportation of the boat on land. (Coverage can be included with the payment of an additional premium.)

- Liability assumed under a contract.

- Injury to an employee if the employee's work involves operation or maintenance of the watercraft.

- Business use.

- Discharge or escape of pollutants unless sudden or accidental.

- War, insurrection, rebellion, and nuclear perils.

Medical Payments Coverage

Medical payments coverage includes expenses incurred within one to three years from the date of the injury for medical, surgical, X-ray, dental, ambulance, hospital, professional nursing, and funeral services; and for first aid rendered at the time of the accident.

Covered persons include the insured, family members, or any other person (except employees of the insured, trespassers, and racing participants) while in, upon, boarding, or leaving the covered watercraft. Thus, medical payments coverage in boat policies is similar to that provided in personal auto policies because it covers the insured and family members. In contrast, medical payments coverage in homeowners policies does *not* cover the insured or resident family members (and is appropriately named medical payments to others).

Uninsured Boaters Coverage

The **uninsured boaters coverage** is similar to the uninsured motorists coverage found in the personal automobile policy. Coverage is provided for accidental bodily injury incurred by an insured in a boating accident caused by an uninsured owner or operator of another boat who is legally responsible for the injury. See Exhibit 9-1 for a more complete description of this coverage.

Uninsured boaters coverage
Coverage for the insured's bodily injury incurred in a boating accident caused by another boat's owner or operator who is uninsured and who is legally responsible for the injury; similar to the PAP's uninsured motorists coverage.

Other Coverages

Additional coverages may be found in boatowners and yacht policies. These other coverages might include coverage for the following:

- The insured's liability for injury to maritime workers (except crew members) injured in the course of employment who are covered under the **United States Longshore and Harbor Workers' Compensation Act** and for which the insured might be held responsible
- The legal obligation of the insured to remove a wrecked or sunken vessel following a loss
- Bodily injury or property damage arising out of transportation of the boat on land (this coverage can usually be included for an additional premium)
- Damage to or loss of the insured's personal effects, for a limited amount
- The cost of commercial towing and assistance, for a limited amount

United States Longshore and Harbor Workers' Compensation Act
Act that specifies the required benefits to maritime employees (except crew members) who are injured or disabled or who die while working on U.S. navigable waters.

PERSONAL UMBRELLA LIABILITY INSURANCE[4]

Lawsuits arising from personal liability exposures can reach catastrophic levels. A liability judgment might exceed the liability limits of a homeowners, personal auto, or watercraft policy. Once the liability limits under these policies are exhausted, the insured might be forced to pay a substantial amount from personal assets. The personal umbrella policy provides liability protection to insureds for amounts over and above the liability limits on homeowners, personal auto, and watercraft policies. Most personal umbrella policies provide not only higher limits but also broader coverage than the basic policies. Faced with the increasing frequency and severity of liability lawsuits, most individuals and families need this protection.

EXHIBIT 9-1

Uninsured Boaters Coverage

Many boatowners and yacht policies include an optional uninsured boaters coverage, which is similar to the uninsured motorists coverage in an automobile policy. The insurer agrees to pay the damages that a covered person is legally entitled to recover from an uninsured boatowner or operator because of bodily injury the covered person sustained in a boating accident. However, the uninsured boatowner's or operator's liability for the damage must arise out of the ownership, maintenance, or use of a watercraft. For example, if an uninsured boat operator negligently strikes another boat and causes bodily injury to a covered person, the injured person could collect from his or her own insurer.

The uninsured boaters coverage has several exclusions. Bodily injuries arising from the following situations are excluded:

- While occupying or when struck by any watercraft owned by the insured or by any family member insured under the policy

- If the bodily injury claim is settled without the insurer's consent

- While occupying a covered watercraft when it is being used to carry persons or property for a fee or when it is rented to others

- Using or occupying a watercraft without a reasonable belief that the person is entitled to do so

If there is disagreement about whether a covered person is legally entitled to recover damages from the uninsured boatowner or operator, or about the amount of damages, the coverage has an arbitration provision. Each party selects an arbitrator. The two arbitrators then select a third arbitrator or, if they cannot agree within thirty days, a judge appoints the arbitrator. A decision by any two of the three parties is binding on all.

The following are examples of claims covered by personal umbrella insurance:

- The mast on a boat broke and seriously injured a guest on the boat. The amount of the judgment that exceeded the limit of the insured's watercraft policy was paid by the insured's personal umbrella insurer.

- The insured caused an accident involving a school bus and injured several children. The resulting judgments resulted in damages that far exceeded the insured's PAP liability limit. The insured's personal umbrella policy covered the amount in excess of the PAP limit up to the umbrella liability limit.

- The insured slandered two police officers. Although the insured's homeowners policy did not cover this loss, the insured's personal umbrella policy provided protection.

- The insured rented a car in France and was involved in a serious accident. Personal umbrella coverage responded to the loss, although the PAP coverage did not apply because the accident occurred overseas.

- The insured's son rented a motorcycle and was involved in a serious accident. The underlying automobile and homeowners contracts did not cover the resulting third-party claim, but the personal umbrella policy covered the loss.

Although in the first two examples, the claims were covered under the boat and automobile policies, the umbrella policy covered amounts over and above the limits on these policies (subject to its limit). In the last three examples, the personal umbrella policy provided broader coverage than that of the homeowners or auto policies and thus provided the only liability coverage available to the insured.

The Nature of Personal Umbrella Coverage

The personal umbrella policy is designed to provide bodily injury, personal injury, and property damage liability coverage in case of a catastrophic claim, lawsuit, or judgment. The amount of insurance purchased typically ranges from $1 million to $10 million or more. The policy covers the named insured, spouse, and resident relatives; coverage usually applies worldwide.

Because each insurance company has its own forms and rules, there is no standard umbrella policy. The following discussion focuses on the provisions commonly found in personal umbrella policies.

Personal umbrella insurance serves two major purposes: to provide excess liability coverage and to provide broad coverage.

Provides Excess Liability Coverage

The personal umbrella policy provides additional liability limits over any **underlying insurance**, such as homeowners Section II coverage, personal auto liability, and personal watercraft liability policies. A condition of umbrella coverage is that the insured must maintain certain underlying coverages with specified limits. The umbrella insurer pays only after the limits of the underlying policies are exhausted. Each insurance company has specific underlying requirements, but the following requirements are typical:

Personal Auto Policy:

> Bodily injury liability .... $250,000 each person
> $500,000 per occurrence
>
> Property damage liability .... $50,000 per occurrence
> (or $300,000 or $500,000 single limit per occurrence for both BI and PD)

Homeowners Section II .... $100,000 (or $300,000)

Watercraft Liability .... $500,000 (if insured owns a boat)

The relationship between umbrella coverage and underlying policies is shown in Exhibit 9-2. Under the **maintenance of underlying insurance condition** in

Underlying insurance
The basic policies, such as homeowners, personal auto, and watercraft (if the insured owns a boat), that provide primary liability coverages and that the insured is required by a personal umbrella policy to have and maintain.

Maintenance of underlying insurance condition
Condition in personal umbrella policies that requires the insured to keep all required underlying coverages in force during the policy period; also requires the insured to notify the insurer promptly if any underlying policy is changed or replaced by another policy.

personal umbrella policies, if the insured fails to maintain the required limits of underlying liability insurance, the umbrella insurer pays only the amount it would have been required to pay if the underlying policies had been in effect.

Provides Broad Coverage

The personal umbrella policy typically provides broader coverage than that provided by the underlying policies. This broad coverage is called **drop down coverage**. When the underlying insurance does not apply to a particular loss and the loss is not excluded by the umbrella, the umbrella coverage "drops down" to cover the entire loss minus a **self-insured retention (SIR)**. Usually the retention, which is similar to a deductible, is $250 but it can be as high as $10,000. The SIR applies only when the loss is not covered by an existing underlying policy.

For example, losses such as libel, slander, defamation of character, false arrest, and false imprisonment are usually not covered under the homeowners policy; however, these losses would be included under the broad coverage of the personal umbrella after the self-insured retention is met. The following example illustrates how payment for such a loss is made under the personal umbrella policy:

> Mike loses a lawsuit brought by Kevin for defamation of character and must pay damages of $25,000. Underlying coverage does not exist because Kevin did not suffer bodily injury and the homeowners policy does not provide personal injury liability coverage. Mike pays the self-insured retention of $250. Mike's umbrella insurer pays $24,750.

Persons Insured

The personal umbrella covers the named insured and resident relatives and usually persons using (with the insured's permission) cars, motorcycles, recreational vehicles, or watercraft owned by or rented to the named insured. Also, persons under age twenty-one in the care of the named insured or of a resident relative are generally covered.

Personal Umbrella Coverages

The personal umbrella policy includes coverage for personal injury liability (as defined below) and property damage liability, as well as defense costs for covered losses. In some states, uninsured and underinsured motorists protection can be included in the personal umbrella policy.

Personal Injury Liability

The personal umbrella policy covers the insured's liability for personal injury. In addition to bodily injury, the definition of personal injury in the umbrella policy includes false arrest, false imprisonment, wrongful entry or eviction, malicious prosecution or humiliation, libel, slander, defamation of character,

Drop down coverage
Coverage provided by an umbrella policy for a loss that is not excluded by the umbrella policy and that is not covered by underlying policies. The loss is paid by the umbrella insurer in excess of a self-insured retention that the insured must pay.

Self-insured retention
Amount of loss the insured must pay if the loss covered by an umbrella policy is not covered by any underlying insurance.

invasion of privacy, and assault and battery not intentionally committed or directed by a covered person; the definition also includes care, loss of services, and death resulting from any of the above.

EXHIBIT 9-2

Relationship of Personal Umbrella Policy to Typical Underlying Coverages

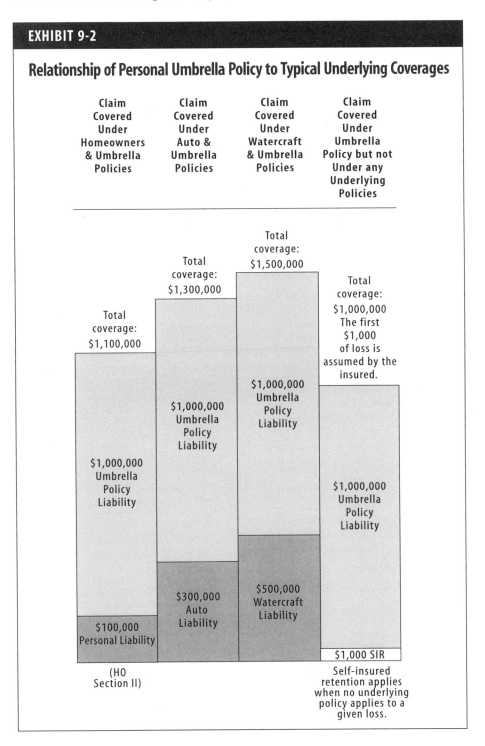

Property Damage Liability

The personal umbrella policy covers the insured's liability for property damage. Similar to the definition in other policies, property damage is defined as physical injury to or destruction of tangible property and includes loss of use of the property.

Defense Costs

The personal umbrella policy includes coverage for the legal defense costs that are not payable by the underlying contracts. Defense costs include payment of attorney fees, premiums on appeal bonds, release of attachment bonds, court costs, interest on unpaid judgments, other legal costs, and loss of earnings up to a certain amount (such as $100) per day to attend court hearings.

For example, Natalie has a personal umbrella policy with a $1,000,000 limit and a $1,000 self-insured retention (SIR).

A personal injury claim is made against Natalie, and a liability judgment is awarded against Natalie in the amount of $1,100,000. The claim is not covered by Natalie's underlying insurance. The umbrella insurer incurs legal costs of $25,000 in defending Natalie. Natalie's insurer would pay the policy limit of $1,000,000 plus $25,000 legal costs. Natalie would pay $100,000 out of her own pocket.

Defense costs are usually paid *in addition* to the liability limit; however, a few personal umbrella policies include the cost of defending the insured as part of the total loss, subject to the policy limit. In the preceding example, if Natalie had an umbrella policy that included defense costs within the policy limit, she would have to pay an additional $25,000 out of her own pocket because the insurer's total obligation would be limited to the umbrella policy limit of $1,000,000.

Uninsured and Underinsured Motorists Coverage

Coverage providing protection to insureds for their own injuries is first-party coverage and would not normally come within the scope of personal umbrella insurance. However, some states require that the insurer offer the insured the option to extend the personal umbrella to cover uninsured and underinsured motorists protection. If the insured does not want this coverage, state laws usually require that he or she must reject the coverage in writing.

Exclusions

Because personal umbrella policies provide broad coverage, certain important exclusions are usually included. The following exclusions are typical:

1. *Workers compensation.* Any obligation for which the insured is legally liable under a workers compensation, disability benefits, or similar law is not covered.

2. *Damage to the insured's property*. All personal umbrella contracts exclude damage to property an insured owns. Most contracts also exclude damage to *nonowned* aircraft or watercraft in the insured's care, custody, or control, such as a plane or a boat that the insured has rented or borrowed.

3. *Nuclear energy*. All personal umbrella policies contain a nuclear energy exclusion.

4. *Intentional injury*. An act committed or directed by a covered person with intent to cause personal injury or property damage is not covered.

5. *Aircraft*. Most personal umbrella policies exclude all liability arising out of the ownership, maintenance, use, loading, or unloading of aircraft.

6. *Watercraft*. The personal umbrella policy covers the insured's liability for smaller boats that are normally covered by the insured's underlying homeowners policy. However, the policy generally excludes coverage for large watercraft such as inboard or inboard-outboard watercraft exceeding fifty horsepower, outboard motorboats with more than twenty-five horsepower engines, and sailing vessels more than twenty-six feet long unless underlying watercraft coverage exists. Generally, if there is underlying watercraft coverage on watercraft excluded from the homeowners policy, the liability coverage for these watercraft may be added to the umbrella for an additional premium.

7. *Business property and pursuits*. Most personal umbrella policies exclude liability arising out of a business activity or business property, other than claims involving an insured's use of a private passenger automobile.

8. *Professional liability*. Personal umbrella policies typically exclude liability for professional services. Some companies may include coverage for professionals such as teachers, barbers, or beauticians; other companies offer such coverage as an option for an additional premium.

9. *Directors and officers*. Most personal umbrella policies exclude liability coverage for acts of directors or officers of a corporation. However, liability coverage for officers and directors of a nonprofit organization is usually included in personal umbrella policies.

10. *Transmission of any communicable diseases*. Some personal umbrella policies exclude liability that results from the insured's transmission of a communicable disease.

11. *Advertising and broadcasting*. Personal umbrella policies may exclude liability arising out of advertising, broadcasting, or telecasting by or for the insured.

12. *Recreational vehicles*. Some personal umbrella policies exclude liability arising out of the ownership, maintenance, or use of recreational vehicles, such as golf carts and snowmobiles, unless there is underlying insurance.

Conditions

The following are among the most important conditions in the personal umbrella policy:

• The insured must maintain the underlying insurance coverages and limits shown in the declarations. Failure to do so will leave the insured without full coverage for a loss.

• The insured must give written notice of loss as soon as practicable.

• The umbrella policy is excess over any other insurance, whether collectible or not.

SUMMARY

Inland marine insurance developed as an extension of marine insurance to provide coverage for property that was transported by land. Today, personal inland marine floater policies cover movable personal property and are sometimes used to insure property with high or special value, such as jewelry, furs, and fine arts. Although personal inland marine floaters are not standardized, they share certain characteristics:

• They can be tailored to the specific type of property being written.

• The insured can select the appropriate policy limits.

• They provide extensive coverage with respect to the perils covered.

• They generally cover the described property anywhere in the world.

• They are usually written without a deductible.

The most commonly used personal inland marine floaters are the personal articles floater (PAF), which is similar to the homeowners scheduled personal property endorsements; the personal property floater (PPF), which can be used to provide special-form ("all-risks") coverage on unscheduled personal property normally kept at the insured's residence and worldwide coverage on the same property when it is temporarily away from the premises; and the personal effects floater (PEF), which travelers use to cover personal property worldwide while it is away from the residence premises.

Although many individuals and families own or operate boats, homeowners policies provide limited coverage for the property and liability exposures arising from the ownership or use of watercraft and related equipment. Various types of personal watercraft policies provide more adequate protection for a variety of personal boats. Small boat policies are designed to cover property and liability exposures for boats up to a certain size. For larger boats, boatowners package policies and yacht policies are available to provide both hull (property) and protection and indemnity (liability) coverages. Boatowners and yacht policies contain several warranties (promises on the part of the insured): that the boat will be used only for private pleasure purposes, that the boat is seaworthy, and that the boat will not be used outside the layup period or the navigational limit. Physical damage coverage under boatowners and yacht policies can be written on either a named perils or an "all-risks" basis. Protection and indemnity insurance covers bodily injury and property damage liability, as well as defense costs, arising from the ownership, maintenance, or use of the boat.

A personal umbrella policy provides a high limit (usually $1,000,000 to $10,000,000) of liability protection over and above the liability limits on the insured's underlying homeowners, personal auto, and watercraft policies. Personal umbrella insurance serves two purposes: (1) to provide excess liability coverage over the underlying policies and (2) to provide broad liability coverage that "drops down" to cover a liability loss, minus a self-insured retention (SIR), when the loss is not covered by an underlying policy. The insured must maintain the underlying coverages and limits; if not, the insurer will pay only the amount it would have been required to pay for a loss if the underlying policies had been in effect. The personal umbrella policy covers the insured for liability for property damage and for personal injury, which is broadly defined to include bodily injury as well as intentional torts such as libel, slander, defamation of character, and invasion of privacy. It also covers defense costs, which are usually paid in addition to the limit of liability. Because the personal umbrella policy provides such broad liability coverage, certain exclusions are important.

CHAPTER NOTES

1. The discussion of the historical development of inland marine insurance is based on David L. Bickelhaupt, *General Insurance*, 11th ed. (Homewood, Ill.: Richard D. Irwin, Inc., 1983).

2. The section on inland marine floaters is based in part on *FC&S Bulletins*, Personal Lines Volume, Miscellaneous Personal section on personal articles form (Cincinnati, Ohio: The National Underwriter Company, March, 1996), pp. A.1-1–A.1-15.

3. The discussion of personal watercraft is based on *FC&S Bulletins*, Miscellaneous section on Boatowners Package Policy; policies from Windsor-Mount Joy Mutual Insurance, Metropolitan Property and Liability Insurance, and CIGNA.

4. The discussion on personal umbrella is based on *FC&S Bulletins*, Personal Lines Volume, Jan. 1996, pp. P.2-1–P.2-11.

Chapter 10

Direct

Direct Your Learning

Personal Loss Exposures and Financial Planning

After learning the subject matter of this chapter, you should be able to:

■ Identify and describe:
- Personal (human) loss exposures
- Steps to develop a financial plan
- Financial goals important for individuals and families
- Basic investment objectives
- Types of investment risks
- Types of investments

■ Explain the importance of retirement planning, including investment planning.

■ Describe private pension plans and individual retirement accounts.

■ Briefly describe other types of tax-deferred retirement plans and types of individual annuities.

■ Describe the Social Security Program's basic characteristics, eligibility requirements, and types of benefits.
- Given a case, explain whether Social Security benefits would be available.

Develop Your Perspective

What are the main topics covered in the chapter?

This chapter describes personal loss exposures that can result from death, illness, or injury. In addition, financial planning and investments that can address these loss exposures, as well as other financial goals and objectives of individuals and families, are illustrated.

Consider the financial consequences for a family whose wage earner has become ill or disabled or has died prematurely. Consider also the financial outcome for a family who has failed to plan adequately for retirement.

- How can financial planning address these potential outcomes?

- What investments might be included in a financial plan?

Why is it important to know these topics?

Personal loss exposures can have a tremendous financial effect on individuals and families. Yet a vast portion of individuals fail to plan adequately for eventualities such as retirement. Effective planning can minimize financial uncertainty.

Explore the investment options that can be part of a financial plan.

- What objectives do various types of investments meet?

- What types of investments are effective for individual investors?

How can you use this information?

Create a table displaying the types of investment objectives:

- What investments are effective for each of the investment objectives? Why?

- What are your own financial goals and investment objectives?

- Identify your current investments. Are they compatible with your investment objectives? If not, what changes might you consider?

Chapter 10

Personal Loss Exposures and Financial Planning

Chapter 1 explained that a loss exposure is any condition or situation that presents the possibility of a financial loss. In addition to property and liability loss exposures, a **personal loss exposure** is a type of exposure that has a tremendous financial effect on individuals and families. In this chapter, the term "personal loss exposure" will be limited solely to loss situations involving the possibility of a direct financial loss to a human being, such as death, illness, or injury.

This chapter deals with personal loss exposures and the related topics of financial and retirement planning. The first part of the chapter discusses important personal loss exposures that can result in financial insecurity for individuals and families. In addition to protection against personal loss exposures, most families have other financial goals and objectives. The second part of the chapter examines some common financial goals and the role of financial planning and investing to attain these goals. The final part of the chapter considers retirement planning, including a discussion of investments, tax-deferred retirement plans, and the Social Security program.

Personal loss exposure (human loss exposure)
Any condition or situation that presents the possibility of financial loss to a person, such as death, sickness, or injury.

PERSONAL LOSS EXPOSURES

Certain personal loss exposures can result in great financial difficulty for individuals and their family members. They include premature death, poor health and disability, unemployment, and retirement. In addition, certain personal loss exposures within the control of the individual, such as failing to engage in financial planning, can result in financial insecurity.[1]

Premature Death

When **premature death** occurs, the family's share of the deceased person's future earnings is lost forever. If replacement income from other sources is insufficient to meet the family's needs, or if present savings and financial assets are limited, the surviving family members might experience considerable financial hardship.

Premature death
Early death of a person with outstanding or unfulfilled financial obligations, such as children to support or mortgage payments.

Poor Health and Disability

Poor health is another important personal loss exposure that can create serious financial problems for individuals and families. First, catastrophic medical bills might be incurred, such as expenses in excess of $100,000, $200,000, or even higher amounts. Unless the sick or injured person has individual or group health insurance or sufficient savings to pay these expenses, he or she will be exposed to financial insecurity. The inability to pay catastrophic medical bills is a major cause of personal bankruptcy.

Second, if a person in the labor force becomes disabled, earnings are also lost. If income from other sources during the period of disability is insufficient or if personal savings are limited, the disabled person will be exposed to considerable lack of financial security.

Finally, a serious illness or injury can result in loss of employee benefits, reduction or exhaustion of personal savings, and additional expenses, such as hiring someone to care for the sick person.

Unemployment

Involuntary unemployment is another personal loss exposure that can result in financial difficulty. Workers can lose their jobs for a number of reasons, which include layoffs during business recessions, downsizing by corporations, changes in the economy, and seasonal factors.

When workers become unemployed, they lose their earnings. Unless they have adequate replacement income or accumulated savings on which to draw, they might experience financial hardship. In addition, because of adverse economic conditions, hours of work might be reduced, and the reduced income might be insufficient for maintaining the worker's previous standard of living. Finally, if the duration of unemployment is prolonged, savings might be substantially reduced or exhausted.

Unemployment Compensation

Unemployment compensation programs
Government programs that pay weekly cash benefits to eligible workers who are involuntarily unemployed.

In the United States, unemployment compensation is a major technique to alleviate financial insecurity from involuntary unemployment. All states have **unemployment compensation programs** that pay weekly cash benefits to covered workers who are involuntarily unemployed. The benefits help workers maintain their previous standard of living during periods of unemployment.

To receive unemployment compensation, workers must meet the following eligibility requirements:

- Become involuntarily unemployed
- Earn qualifying wages during a specified base period
- Actively seek work

- Be free from disqualifying acts (such as refusing suitable work)
- Meet a specified waiting period (one week in most states)

Weekly benefits are based on the worker's covered earnings during his or her base period (a specified period of time before the period of unemployment). Benefits can be paid up to a maximum of twenty-six weeks in virtually all states. With the exception of a few states that require employee contributions, state unemployment compensation programs are financed by employer tax contributions based on the firm's unemployment record.

Extended Benefits

In addition to regular state unemployment compensation programs, a federal-state program of extended benefits exists. This program is important to unemployed workers in states with high rates of unemployment. The extended benefits program pays up to thirteen weeks of additional benefits to claimants who have exhausted their regular benefits during periods of high unemployment. The costs of the extended benefits program are shared equally by the state and the federal government.

Retirement

The possibility of insufficient income during retirement is another important loss exposure. With certain exceptions, workers cannot be forced to retire at a mandatory retirement age. However, as a practical matter, most workers retire voluntarily by age sixty-five. The major financial problem for many retired workers is insufficient income. When workers retire, they lose their regular earnings. If replacement income from Social Security, private retirement plans, and personal savings is inadequate, the retired worker's previous standard of living may be reduced. In addition, the problem of insufficient income is aggravated if the retired worker lives unusually long, incurs catastrophic medical expenses, or needs long-term care in a nursing facility. Planning for retirement is the major challenge of financial planning and is discussed in greater detail later in this chapter.

PLANNING FOR THE FUTURE

The financial insecurity associated with most personal loss exposures can be reduced and possibly eliminated by adequate life and health insurance, disability income insurance, and private or public retirement plans. However, individuals and families often have additional financial goals, such as saving for a down payment on a home or for their children's college education. Attaining these goals requires a financial plan, which includes an effective savings and investment program.

Developing a Financial Plan

Financial planning
Process that helps individuals and families to identify their financial goals and to develop a realistic plan for attaining those goals.

The process of **financial planning** requires five steps:

1. *Gather important financial information.* The first step in financial planning is to gather relevant and important financial information. Important information includes the following:

   - Current income—the amount of monthly and annual earnings, net take-home pay, and other sources of income

   - Assets—present financial assets, including stocks, bonds, mutual funds, and savings accounts; value of individual retirement accounts (IRAs) and employer-sponsored pension or retirement plans; value of life insurance policies and real estate

   - Outstanding liabilities and debts—the amount of present installment debts, remaining mortgage balances, and educational and other loans

   - Current spending—preparation of a monthly or yearly cash-flow statement to determine the amounts spent on food, housing, installment debts, medical bills, insurance premiums, taxes, and other necessary living expenses

   - Number and ages of dependents

Net worth
Excess of assets over liabilities; assets − liabilities = net worth

2. *Analyze the present financial situation.* This step includes a review of spending habits to determine whether the individual is spending more than his or her annual income. It also includes a review of outstanding debts, amounts presently saved and invested, and **net worth**. Periodic calculation of net worth indicates whether the individual or family is making satisfactory financial progress over time. Many families have a negative net worth, which often indicates a serious overspending problem. Recent college graduates often have a negative net worth because of student loans.

3. *Determine specific financial goals and objectives.* Important financial goals and objectives are discussed later in the chapter.

4. *Design a financial plan for attaining these goals.* The financial plan should be realistic and have a time limit. The plan should include drawing up a cash-flow budget so that spending does not continuously exceed income over an extended period with a subsequent increase in consumer debt.

5. *Periodically review and revise the plan.* The financial plan should be reviewed periodically and changed if marriage, birth, divorce, job change, disability, unemployment, or any other change affects finances.

Advantages of Financial Planning

Developing a financial plan offers numerous advantages to individuals and families. Personal wealth can be increased; an improved standard of living is more easily attained; financial goals can be achieved; the family can be protected against major property, liability, and personal loss exposures; credit problems can be avoided or reduced; and taxes can be minimized.

Obstacles to Financial Planning

Despite the preceding advantages, many Americans do not have an effective financial plan because of certain obstacles. These obstacles include the unwillingness of many consumers to save and invest; the excessive use of high-interest credit cards and continued overspending; the natural tendency to procrastinate and delay saving for specific goals, such as retirement and children's college education; and inadequate knowledge about financial planning.[2]

Common Financial Goals

An effective financial plan requires identifying specific financial goals and objectives. Many Americans do not have well-defined financial goals. One national survey revealed that only 21 percent of the respondents had well-defined financial goals; another 45 percent indicated they had general financial goals but had not determined the amounts needed for attaining these goals; the remaining 34 percent indicated they did not have any clearly defined long-term goals.[3] Another national survey revealed that many Americans have little financial expertise and require increased knowledge about personal financial planning, especially with respect to life and health insurance and mutual fund investments.[4]

Because all individuals and families are not the same, financial goals and objectives differ. However, certain financial goals are important to most individuals and families:

- *Increase in personal wealth.* Most Americans would like to increase the amount of their present savings and personal wealth. Investing to attain financial goals is discussed later in the chapter.
- *Higher standard of living.* A higher standard of living means that real income increases over time. Real income (money income adjusted for inflation) refers to the goods and services that can be purchased with money income. An effective saving and investing program can increase future real income and standard of living.
- *Protection of the family and property.* An extremely important financial goal is protection of the family and its property against loss exposures that create financial insecurity. As stated earlier, these exposures include property, liability, and personal loss exposures.
- *Saving for retirement.* Saving for retirement is another important financial goal for most Americans. Social Security retirement benefits provide only a minimum base income. Additional retirement income can be attained by establishing an individual retirement account (discussed later) or by participating in an employer-sponsored retirement plan.

- *Purchase of a home.* Purchase of a home is a high-priority financial goal for many people. However, the down payment and closing costs may require thousands of dollars. The amount needed can be obtained by an effective saving and investing program.

- *College education for children.* For many families, saving for the college education of their children is an important financial goal, requiring financial planning, regular saving, and effective investing.

- *Emergency fund.* Financial planners typically recommend a savings fund, equal to three to six months of take-home pay, for unexpected emergencies. An emergency fund is especially important with respect to the unemployment loss exposure. Many workers will become unemployed several times during their working careers. An emergency fund can reduce the painful financial shock that may result from an extended period of involuntary unemployment.

- *Getting out of debt.* Getting out of debt is an important financial goal for many Americans who are deeply in debt because of overspending, abusing credit cards, and taking out high-interest consumer loans. Consumer loans typically include car loans, appliance and furniture loans, personal loans, education loans, consolidation loans, and similar types of consumer installment loans.

- *Minimizing taxes.* An important financial goal is to minimize the taxes that consumers pay. Average income earners can easily pay 40 percent or more of their total annual income in taxes of all types. These taxes include federal and state income tax, sales tax, property tax, gasoline tax, telephone tax, and numerous other taxes. Taxation does not end at death. In many cases, particularly if the estate is large, state and federal estate taxes apply to the deceased person's estate.

- *Investment goals.* In addition to considering the preceding financial goals, individuals and families should consider their investment goals. The important topic of investing to attain specific financial goals is discussed in the following section.

INVESTING TO ATTAIN FINANCIAL GOALS

Individuals and families must have an effective program of saving and investing to attain their financial goals. They must consider investment objectives, investment risks, and types of investments. Most life insurance products, treated in Chapter 11, have investment characteristics. Thus, to understand life insurance, one must also understand investments.

Saving
The practice of not consuming all income.

Investing
The purchase of assets, either financial or real, that the investor hopes will help achieve financial goals.

Investment Objectives

Investors have different investment objectives. Some investment objectives are primary, while others are secondary. Although the terms are often used interchangeably, **saving** and **investing** are not the same. Saving, which precedes investing, involves not consuming all income. Once a person is saving, he or she should invest the savings. The basic types of investment objectives are summarized as follows:

- *Capital appreciation.* **Capital appreciation** is the primary goal of many investors. This objective is appropriate for investors who have long-term financial goals, such as accumulating a fund for retirement or for their children's college education. A major tax advantage of capital appreciation is that investment gains are not taxable until the investment is sold.

    Capital appreciation
    An increase in the value of investments.

- *Preservation of capital.* Most investments carry some risk of their value decreasing. Many investors are conservative, and **preservation of capital** is of primary importance to them. Preservation of capital is also appropriate for investors who have short-term financial goals, such as saving for a down payment on a home. However, money should not simply be stored in a safety deposit box for safe keeping. To preserve the real purchasing power of the funds, the rate of return on the funds must at least equal the rate of inflation.

    Preservation of capital
    Practice of ensuring that the value of assets does not decrease.

- *Current income.* In addition to seeing the value of their investments increase, many investors are looking for income from their investments. A steady stream of current income is the primary investment objective for many investors, especially for older retired persons and individuals close to retirement. Investment income is a desirable supplement to Social Security and private pension benefits.

- *Growth and income.* Some investors seek both growth in and income from their investments. Investors seek a high total return by investing primarily in stocks that pay high current dividends and that also have the potential for capital appreciation.

- *Liquidity.* Some investors use the term **liquidity** to refer not only to the speed but also to the certainty with which an asset can be turned into cash (liquidated). A passbook savings account, for example, has a high degree of liquidity. Most real estate, however, has a low degree of liquidity because it cannot be easily or quickly converted to cash.

    Liquidity
    Ability to quickly convert an investment into cash with a minimal loss of principal.

- *Minimizing taxes.* High-income investors typically have the objective of minimizing taxes. Such investors might purchase municipal bonds in which the interest is exempt from federal income tax. Municipal bonds may also be exempt from state income tax for residents of the state where the bond is issued.

Investment Risks

Investing involves certain risks. There is a relationship between risk and rate of return. As investment risk increases, the potential total return (or loss) also increases. Total return is the sum of the dividends paid plus capital appreciation.

Investment risk can be defined as the variability of investment outcomes. Certain investments provide a guaranteed rate of return where the investment

Investment risk
Variability of investment outcomes.

outcome is known in advance, such as ninety-day U.S. Treasury bills; thus, they have little investment risk, and the rate of return is relatively low. Other investments are speculative, such as the purchase of stock of a company that sells new computer software; the rate of return and future outcome are unknown, but the potential for profit (or loss) is great.

Investors should be aware of different types of investment risks before they invest:

- *Inflation risk*—the risk associated with the loss of purchasing power because of an overall increase in the price level in the economy.
- *Market risk*—the risk associated with fluctuations in prices of financial securities, such as stocks and bonds.
- *Interest-rate risk*—the risk associated with the future value of a security because of changes in interest rates.
- *Financial risk*—the risk associated with the ownership of securities in a company with a relatively large amount of debt on its balance sheet. If the company defaults on its debt obligations, it may be forced into bankruptcy by its creditors.
- *Business risk*—the risk associated with the fluctuation in a company's earnings and its ability to pay dividends and interest.
- *Liquidity risk*—the risk of being unable to liquidate an investment easily and at a reasonable price.

An investor's willingness to accept risk (called risk tolerance) will have an important influence on the types of investments purchased. Some investors are aggressive risk takers and are comfortable investing in speculative stocks with which the potential profit or loss is high. Other investors are "risk averse" and attempt to avoid or minimize risk in their investments; they tend to invest in conservative investments with lower yields, such as savings accounts, money market funds, certificates of deposit, and government bonds. Still others are middle-of-the-road investors who are willing to accept some risk in their investments but are not speculators; they prefer high-quality stocks and conservative mutual funds and bonds. Many financial planners attempt to determine an individual's tolerance for risk in order to recommend suitable investments.

Types of Investments

Numerous types of investments are available today. The most important include the following:

- Savings accounts and savings instruments
- Stocks
- Bonds
- Mutual funds

- Real estate
- Miscellaneous investments, such as gold and artwork

Savings Accounts and Savings Instruments

Commercial banks, savings and loan institutions, credit unions, and other financial institutions offer a variety of savings accounts and savings instruments. Savings accounts are free of market risk and interest-rate risk and are essentially free of financial risk when insured by the federal government, such as through the Federal Deposit Insurance Corporation (FDIC). Savings accounts involve some inflation risk because the return they pay usually just keeps up with inflation and has failed to do so in the past. The great virtue of savings accounts is their high liquidity. Savings accounts can be used to save money for an emergency fund and for short-term financial goals.

Important types of savings accounts and savings instruments include the following:

- *Regular savings accounts.* Regular savings accounts of financial institutions are highly liquid investments. The funds generally can be withdrawn at any time with no penalty for early withdrawal. In addition, the funds are safe. Each depositor is insured against loss up to $100,000 by the FDIC. However, the yields on regular savings accounts are relatively low.

- *Certificates of deposit.* Financial institutions also issue certificates of deposit (CDs), which are time deposits that mature after a certain period, such as one year. CDs pay higher returns than regular savings accounts, and the funds are also insured by the FDIC. However, a penalty may apply for the early withdrawal of the funds.

- *Money market mutual funds.* Money market mutual funds pool the funds of individual investors and are typically invested in short-term, high-quality securities of the U.S. Treasury, major corporations, large commercial banks, and other government agencies. The interest rate paid is typically higher than that paid on regular savings accounts; however, the funds are not insured by the FDIC. Investors can gain access to the funds by writing checks on their accounts; a check typically must be written for a minimum amount, such as $250 or $500.

- *Money market deposit accounts.* Commercial banks and other financial institutions also offer money market deposit accounts. These accounts are safe, convenient, and insured by the FDIC. Depositors can gain access to the funds by writing checks on their accounts. The yields tend to be less than the yields paid by money market mutual funds.

Stocks

Investors often purchase common stock and preferred stock in their investment programs. **Common stock** represents an ownership interest in a corporation. For example, if a corporation has 100,000 shares of common stock, and an investor purchases 1,000 shares, he or she would own 1 percent of the corporation.

Common stock
Represents an ownership interest in a corporation and gives stockowners certain rights and privileges, such as the right to vote on important corporate matters.

Stockholders participate in the profits and losses of the corporation. If the corporation is profitable, the price of the shares will usually increase; conversely, if the corporation is unprofitable, share price may fall. Stockholders also have the right to receive any dividends declared by the board of directors. Dividends are paid out of the profits of a business. If profits are strong and growing, dividends are likely to increase. If profits are weak or declining, dividends are likely to be cut or eliminated. The stockholders can vote for the board of directors, but the officers and other executives actually manage the corporation. Common stock remains in force indefinitely and has no maturity date.

Because of the uncertainty of corporate earnings and dividends and because stocks are subject to all types of investment risk, stocks are the riskiest of the major types of investments. On a year-to-year basis, stock values can go up or down dramatically. Yet investors are rewarded for accepting this risk. Over long-run periods of ten to twenty years, stocks have outperformed most other investments.

Preferred stock
An investment having characteristics of both common stocks and bonds.

Investors may also purchase **preferred stock**, which has the characteristics of both common stock and bonds. Like common stock, preferred stock represents an ownership interest in a corporation, but most companies restrict the voting rights of preferred stockholders. Preferred stockholders usually receive an annual dividend that is typically stated as a percentage of the value of the stock, such as 8 percent ($8 on a stock with a value of $100). As such, preferred stock is similar to a bond. Dividends to preferred stockholders must be paid first before any dividends are paid to the common stockholders. If the corporation is liquidated, the claims of creditors must be satisfied first. Then, however, the claims of preferred stockholders have priority over the claims of common stockholders.

Bonds

Bonds
Debt obligations issued by corporations and government entities.

Bonds are important to investors who seek current income. Bonds are riskier than savings accounts but less risky than stocks. Thus, the return on bonds is generally greater than on savings accounts but lower than on stocks. Many corporations borrow money to finance corporate projects by issuing bonds. Bonds have a fixed maturity date and typically pay periodic interest payments to the bondholders. Bonds have a coupon rate that states the rate of interest the bondholder will earn. For example, a newly issued twenty-year $1,000 bond with a coupon rate of 6 percent would pay $60 annual interest plus $1,000 when the bond matures at the end of twenty years. Bonds can be sold before their maturity date. However, depending on market conditions and current interest rates, the current market price may be above or below the original price.

Mutual Funds

Mutual fund
Investment mechanism that pools the funds of individual investors and invests in securities.

Diversification
Technique to reduce one's overall investment risk by spreading funds among investments with different risks.

Mutual funds are popular investments. Mutual funds offer numerous advantages to investors, which include wide **diversification**, professional management, record keeping, marketability, and liquidity.

More than 8,000 mutual funds exist at present,[5] and discussing the different types of mutual funds is beyond the scope of this text. The nature of the underlying investments determines the classification of the mutual fund. Investors should pick mutual funds that share their goals and tolerance for risk.

The financial pages of daily newspapers list mutual funds by group or family. A mutual fund group markets its funds and provides or hires the investment manager. The group also takes care of filings with the government and mailings to investors.

Real Estate

Real estate is another important investment. For most families, the purchase of a home is their most important investment. A home is unique among investments. Although homes have performed well as investments, they are much more than an investment and provide shelter, stability, and security for a family. Real estate investments also include commercial office buildings, apartment complexes, shopping centers, mortgages, farmland, undeveloped land, limited partnerships, and real estate investment trusts (REITs).

Investors in rental property receive investment income from the tenants and capital appreciation if the value of the property increases. However, investing in real property has some drawbacks: there are maintenance, tax, and insurance expenses; real estate is not liquid; tax issues are complex; and dealing with problem tenants can be difficult and expensive.

Miscellaneous Investments

Numerous other investments are also available. Some investors purchase gold, silver, and other precious metals. Others invest in artwork and collectibles, such as paintings, coin and stamp collections, antiques, glassware, and baseball cards. As investments, these pursuits are usually risky and not liquid. They are often pursued primarily as hobbies.

RETIREMENT PLANNING

Planning for a comfortable retirement is an extremely important financial goal. When a worker retires, earnings terminate. If replacement income from other sources is inadequate, the retired worker is exposed to financial insecurity. In addition, retirees often incur substantial medical expenses not covered by the current Medicare program, such as the cost of long-term care in a nursing facility.

Importance of Retirement Planning

Most Americans want to retire comfortably, be financially independent, and maintain a high standard of living during retirement. However, the goal of a comfortable retirement might be more difficult to attain in the future because of certain emerging trends.

Increased Proportion of Retirees

The proportion of older people in the population will increase significantly in the future. In 1999, persons aged sixty-five and older accounted for 12.7 percent of the population; by 2020, this proportion is projected to increase to 16.3 percent.[6] If retirement income from Social Security, employer-sponsored retirement plans, and private savings is inadequate, the retiree's standard of living during retirement might decline.

Longer Period of Retirement

The period of retirement has increased over time. The majority of workers retire early (before age sixty-five), and life expectancy has increased. As a result, most workers are spending a relatively longer period of their adult lifetime in retirement and relatively less time in the labor force. Because of the shorter period of employment, some workers might be unable to save enough during their working years to provide for a decent standard of living during the longer retirement period.

Insufficient Money Income

Older married couples living together (at least one of whom is age sixty-five or older) and nonmarried persons age sixty-five or older typically have annual money incomes that are relatively low and far from adequate. In 2000, the median total money income for older couples and singles age sixty-five or older was only $11,673.[7] These income levels might be insufficient for retirees who are faced with high expenses, such as uninsured medical bills, the cost of long-term care in a nursing facility, and property taxes.

Insufficient Financial Assets

The financial assets owned by many individuals nearing retirement are also relatively small. According to a 2001 census bureau publication, the median value of financial assets of families headed by a person aged fifty-five to sixty-four was only $45,600.[8]

In addition, research studies show that many younger workers are saving an inadequate amount for retirement. One study of the baby boom generation (those born between 1946 and 1964) showed that baby boomers must nearly triple their savings rate to maintain their present standard of living during retirement.[9] Another study predicted that most Americans will have only one-third to one-half of the annual income needed to attain a comfortable retirement.[10]

Poor Health

Some older people are in poor health and require long-term care in a nursing facility. The average cost of long-term care is estimated at $46,000 annually.

In some regions, the cost is twice that amount.[11] The current Medicare program does not cover long-term care in a nursing facility, and most retired persons do not have private long-term care policies because of the high cost. As a result, the financial assets of most older patients who require long-term care are quickly depleted, which often forces them to apply for coverage under the Medicaid program. Medicaid is a welfare program that has strict eligibility requirements and a severe means test; it should not be confused with Medicare. Long-term care insurance is discussed in Chapter 12.

Minimum Floor of Income From Social Security

Social Security retirement benefits (discussed later in this chapter) provide only a minimum floor of income. As a result, many retired workers will be exposed to financial insecurity in the future if they rely largely on Social Security retirement benefits as their major source of income.

Investing for Retirement

Based on the preceding discussion, retirement planning should be a high-priority financial goal, involving an effective program of saving and investing. Discussing all aspects of investing for retirement is beyond the scope of this text. However, certain suggestions by financial planners merit a brief discussion:

- *Begin investing early.* One of the most important suggestions is to begin saving and investing for retirement at the earliest possible age. Time is on the side of younger workers who start to invest at an early age because the accumulated deposits and investment earnings can be compounded over a longer period. A delay in investing can significantly reduce the amount available at retirement. Exhibit 10-1 shows the difference between an investment begun at age twenty-five and one starting at age thirty-five.

- *Make maximum contributions to tax-deferred retirement plans.* Another important suggestion for a comfortable retirement is to contribute the maximum allowed under a **tax-deferred retirement plan**. Employers typically make contributions to qualified retirement plans, which are not taxable as current income to the participants. Unfortunately, many employees who have the opportunity to participate in tax-deferred retirement plans do not do so. Failure to participate in an employer-sponsored retirement plan virtually guarantees an insufficient amount of income during retirement for most workers.

Tax-deferred retirement plans
Plans that receive favorable income-tax treatment, such as employer-sponsored Section 401(k) plans.

- *Change the allocation of assets over the life cycle.* The funds set aside for retirement must be allocated among stocks, bonds, and cash reserves. The initial mix of assets depends on the worker's age and willingness to accept risk. The longer the period for investing, the greater is the risk that the investor should assume. Younger workers can afford to invest a larger proportion of their retirement funds in common stocks or mutual funds because of the longer period to retirement. However, as they approach

EXHIBIT 10-1

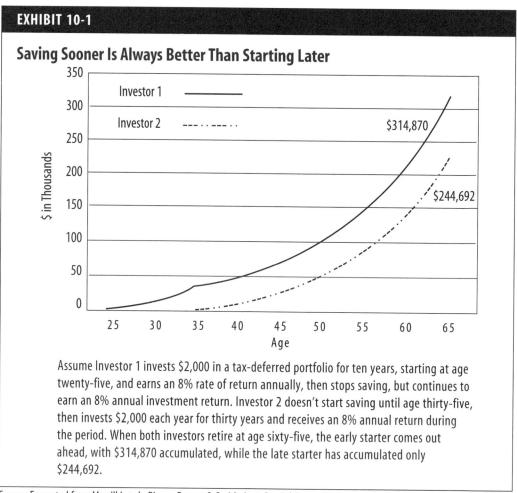

Saving Sooner Is Always Better Than Starting Later

Assume Investor 1 invests $2,000 in a tax-deferred portfolio for ten years, starting at age twenty-five, and earns an 8% rate of return annually, then stops saving, but continues to earn an 8% annual investment return. Investor 2 doesn't start saving until age thirty-five, then invests $2,000 each year for thirty years and receives an 8% annual return during the period. When both investors retire at age sixty-five, the early starter comes out ahead, with $314,870 accumulated, while the late starter has accumulated only $244,692.

Source: Excerpted from Merrill Lynch, Pierce, Fenner & Smith, Inc., *Special Report: Saving and the American Family* (March 1994).

retirement, they might prefer to invest more conservatively by reducing the proportion of assets invested in common stocks. Exhibit 10-2 is one example of recommended asset allocation over a worker's life cycle.

- *Consider dollar-cost averaging.* Dollar-cost averaging is an investment strategy in which a fixed amount is invested at regular intervals, regardless of market price and market conditions. The result is that the average cost per share will be less than average market price. Because they involve periodic (e.g., monthly) investments, most tax-deferred retirement plans use dollar-cost averaging. Although dollar-cost averaging does not guarantee a profit, it has a very impressive record of being profitable for the investor.

- *Do not ignore the effect of inflation after retirement.* Many retired workers will spend twenty or twenty-five years in retirement, especially women (who have a longer life expectancy than men). During that time, inflation can severely erode the purchasing power of a retirement fund invested entirely in fixed-income investments. Depending on the investor's willingness to accept risk, many financial planners recommend that 20 to 40 percent of the financial assets should remain invested in common stocks or stock mutual funds after retirement. Historically, common stock prices have kept pace with or have exceeded the rate of inflation in the long run.

EXHIBIT 10-2

Allocation of Assets Over the Life Cycle

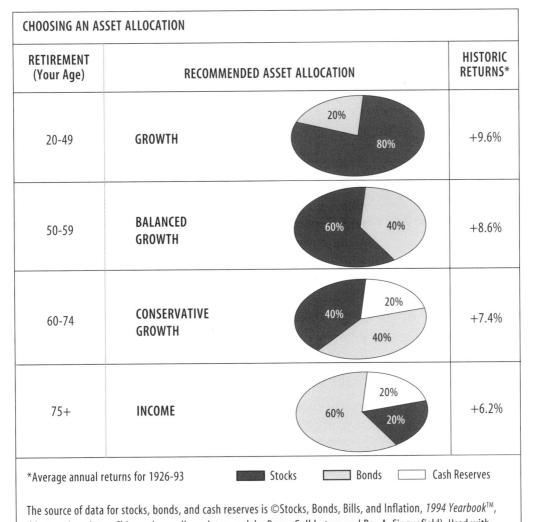

CHOOSING AN ASSET ALLOCATION		
RETIREMENT (Your Age)	RECOMMENDED ASSET ALLOCATION	HISTORIC RETURNS*
20-49	GROWTH — 20% / 80%	+9.6%
50-59	BALANCED GROWTH — 60% / 40%	+8.6%
60-74	CONSERVATIVE GROWTH — 40% / 20% / 40%	+7.4%
75+	INCOME — 20% / 60% / 20%	+6.2%

*Average annual returns for 1926-93   ■ Stocks   ▨ Bonds   ☐ Cash Reserves

The source of data for stocks, bonds, and cash reserves is ©Stocks, Bonds, Bills, and Inflation, *1994 Yearbook*™, Ibbotson Associates, Chicago (annually updates work by Roger G. Ibbotson and Rex A. Sinquefield). Used with permission. All rights reserved.

Adapted from: *Facts on Funds for Your Retirement* (Valley Forge, Pa.: The Vanguard Group of Investment Companies, 1994), p. 5.

TAX-DEFERRED RETIREMENT PLANS

Tax-deferred retirement plans are extremely important in retirement planning. As stated earlier, tax-deferred retirement plans are individual or employer-sponsored retirement plans that receive favorable income tax treatment. Retirement plans are typically sponsored by employers and are designed to provide retirement income in addition to Social Security benefits. The employer's contributions to a qualified retirement plan are income-tax deductible up to certain limits; the employer's contributions are not taxed as current income to the participating employees; investment earnings on plan assets accumulate income-tax free; and the retirement contributions are not taxed until the employee retires or receives a distribution from the plan. At retirement, the taxable income is generally lower, so tax liability is lessened as well. The financial advantages of tax-deferred investments over taxable investments are substantial. Exhibit 10-3 illustrates these long-term advantages.

Private Pension Plans

Many employers have established private pension plans for eligible employees. Plans that meet certain Internal Revenue Service requirements receive favorable income tax treatment and are referred to as qualified plans.

Eligibility Requirements

Most private pension plans have a minimum-age and length-of-service requirement. The law requires coverage of all eligible employees who are at least age twenty-one and have completed one year of service. (In some cases, two years of service are required.)

Basic Types of Pension Plans

There are two basic types of pension plans: defined contribution plans and defined benefit plans.

Defined Contribution Plan

Defined contribution plan (money purchase pension plan)
Pension plan in which the contribution rate or amount is specified, but the retirement benefit is variable.

A **defined contribution plan** is a plan in which the contribution rate is defined, but the retirement benefit is variable. For example, assume that Megan, age twenty-eight, contributes 6 percent of her salary to a defined contribution plan; the employer also contributes 6 percent of her salary amount to the plan. The contribution is defined: 12 percent of Megan's salary. The actual retirement benefit is unknown and will depend on her earnings, investment results, and age of retirement. In recent years, defined contribution plans have become popular. Virtually all new retirement plans are defined contribution plans.

EXHIBIT 10-3

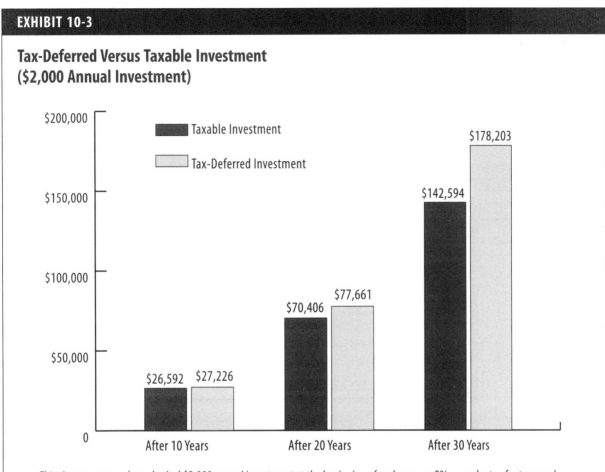

Tax-Deferred Versus Taxable Investment ($2,000 Annual Investment)

This chart assumes a hypothetical $2,000 annual investment at the beginning of each year, an 8% annual rate of return, and a 36% federal tax bracket. The tax-deferred investments are non-deductible, and their earnings grow tax-deferred until withdrawn at the end of the specified period when the earnings are taxed at the rate of 36%. The taxable investments are invested after-tax and their earnings are taxed every year; the tax liability is deducted from the balance.

Source: *Retirement Planning Guide, A Fidelity Common Sense Guide* (Dallas, Tex.: Fidelity Distributors Corporation, 1994), p. 22.

Defined Benefit Plan

A **defined benefit plan** is a plan in which the retirement benefit is specified, but the employer's contributions vary depending on the amount needed to fund the benefit. The retirement benefit can be based on a percentage of the worker's earnings, years of service, or some combination; or it can be a flat amount for all employees. For example, assume that Matthew, age forty, is entitled at age sixty-five to a retirement benefit equal to 40 percent of his average compensation for the three highest consecutive years of earnings. An actuary then determines the amount that must be contributed each year to fund the desired benefit. Defined benefit plans generally require no contributions or investment management by employees. Employers must fund and manage their employees' retirement plans.

Defined benefit plan
Pension plan in which the retirement benefit is specified and the employer's contributions vary depending on the amount needed to fund the benefit; typically requires no employee contributions.

Retirement Age

Pension plans have provisions dealing with the age of retirement. The normal retirement age is the age that an employee can retire and receive full, unreduced benefits; pension plans often specify age sixty-five as the normal retirement age.

Most pension plans also permit early retirement. The early retirement age is the earliest age that an employee can retire and receive retirement benefits; for example, the plan may allow retirement at age fifty-five for employees with ten or more years of service. In a defined contribution plan, the retirement benefit is based on the amount in the employee's account at the time of retirement. However, there are tax penalties for withdrawal before age fifty-nine and one-half. In a defined benefit plan, the benefits are actuarially reduced for early retirement because less interest is earned on the funds and the benefits are paid over a longer retirement period.

A pension plan may also have a provision for late retirement, which is any age beyond the normal retirement age. With certain exceptions, pension benefits continue to accrue for employees who continue working beyond the normal retirement age.

Vesting

Vesting refers to an employee's ownership of pension contributions made by the employer. Employees automatically have ownership rights to any amounts they have contributed themselves. The purposes of vesting are to reward long-term employees, to reduce labor turnover, and to avoid forfeiture by employees who change jobs.

Vesting
Employee's right to part or all of the pension contributions made by the employer if employment terminates before retirement.

Annual Limits on Contributions and Benefits

Qualified retirement plans are subject to certain annual limits on contributions and benefits.

Early and Late Distributions

Qualified private pension plans are designed to encourage employees to save for retirement. If funds are withdrawn before age fifty-nine and one-half, the distribution is subject to a penalty tax of 10 percent. However, the penalty tax does not apply to distributions involving death or permanent total disability of the employee, medical expenses deductible under the IRS code, substantially equal payments paid over the employee's life expectancy, and certain other exceptions.

The law also applies to late distributions. Plan distributions must start no later than April 1 of the calendar year following the year in which the individual attains age seventy and one-half. However, if the participants are still working, the law allows workers age seventy and one-half or older to delay receiving minimum distributions from qualified retirement plans, such as a 401(k) plan (but not from an individual retirement account). The law allows workers to delay receiving distributions either until April 1 of the year following attainment of age seventy and one-half or until April 1 of the year after retirement.

Traditional Individual Retirement Account (IRA)

To set up a **traditional individual retirement account (IRA)**, the worker must have taxable compensation during the year and must not attain age seventy and one-half by the end of the year. Compensation includes wages and salaries, tips, commissions, fees, bonuses, self-employment income, and taxable alimony and separate maintenance payments. Investment income, pension or annuity income, and rental income do not qualify.

Traditional individual retirement account (IRA)
Retirement plan that allows workers with taxable compensation below certain thresholds to make limited annual contributions and receive favorable income-tax treatment. Not employer sponsored.

Tax-Deductible Contributions

For 2002, annual IRA contributions are limited to $3,000 or a maximum of 100 percent of taxable compensation, whichever is less. (Individuals age fifty or older may contribute up to $3,500.) These limits will increase in future years. If the participant has a nonworking spouse, a spousal IRA (two separate IRAs at $3,000 each in 2002) is available with a maximum annual contribution of $6,000. ($7,000 when both spouses are fifty or older.)

Contributions to a traditional IRA can be deducted in full for federal income-tax purposes in two general situations. First, if the worker is not an active participant in an employer-sponsored retirement plan, he or she can make a fully deductible IRA contribution up to the maximum annual limit. Second, even if the worker is a participant in the employer's retirement plan, a full deduction is allowed if the worker's modified adjusted gross income is below certain thresholds. Modified adjusted gross income generally is adjusted gross income without taking into account the IRA deduction and certain other items. For the year 2002, a full deduction is allowed if the taxpayer's modified adjusted gross income is $34,000 or less ($54,000 or less for married couples filing jointly). The income limits for a full deduction will increase gradually in the future.

The full IRA deduction under a traditional IRA is gradually phased out as modified adjusted gross income increases. For the year 2002, the phase-out range is $34,000 to $44,000 for single taxpayers and $54,000 to $64,000 for married taxpayers filing jointly. The phase-out limits will also gradually increase in the future.

Taxpayers with incomes above the phase-out limits can contribute to a traditional IRA but cannot deduct the contributions. In such cases, a Roth IRA (discussed later) should be considered.

Finally, a special phase-out rule applies to married couples in situations in which one spouse is not an active participant in an employer-sponsored retirement plan, but the other spouse is. As a result, most homemakers can make a fully deductible contribution to a traditional IRA even though the other spouse is covered under a retirement plan at work. The maximum annual IRA deduction for a spouse who is not an active participant is currently $3,000 even if the other spouse is covered under a retirement plan at work. Eligibility for a full deduction is limited to married couples with modified adjusted gross incomes below a certain amount.

Withdrawing IRA Funds

An IRA is designed for retirement income. If IRA funds are withdrawn before age fifty-nine and one-half, a 10 percent penalty tax must be paid on the taxable portion of the distribution. Ordinary income tax must also be paid on the taxable amount. The penalty tax does not apply to distributions that result from death, disability, substantially equal payments paid over the worker's life expectancy, and a return of nondeductible contributions that have already been taxed.

In addition, the 10 percent penalty tax does not apply to withdrawals to pay deductible medical expenses in excess of 7.5 percent of adjusted gross income. Also, individuals who have received unemployment compensation benefits for twelve consecutive weeks may withdraw IRA funds without penalty to pay health insurance premiums for themselves and their families. Withdrawals to pay qualified higher-education expenses or for purchasing a first-time home (maximum withdrawal of $10,000) are also exempt.

Funds cannot remain in the plan indefinitely. Owners of a traditional IRA must make annual withdrawals at least equal to certain minimum amounts no later than April 1 following the calendar year in which they reach age seventy and one-half. A tax penalty applies if the minimum amount is not withdrawn. All withdrawals are taxed as ordinary income except for a return of nondeductible IRA contributions, which have already been taxed.

Roth IRA

Roth IRA
Individual retirement plan that allows (1) investment earnings to accumulate free of federal income taxes and (2) tax-free withdrawals at age 59 ½ or later; does not allow federal income-tax deduction of annual contributions.

The Taxpayer Relief Act of 1997 made available a **Roth IRA**, which provides substantial tax advantages over a traditional IRA. Annual contribution limits are the same as for a traditional IRA. The annual contributions to a Roth IRA are not income-tax deductible. However, investment earnings accumulate free of federal income taxes, and qualified distributions are not taxable if the account has been held for at least five years and the distribution is made for any of the following reasons: (1) the account holder is age fifty-nine and one-half or older, (2) the account holder is disabled, (3) the distribution is paid to a beneficiary upon the account holder's death, or (4) the money is used for a first-time home purchase (maximum distribution of $10,000).

The five-year holding period begins with the first tax year for which a contribution was made to a Roth IRA.

In addition, unlike a traditional IRA, a Roth IRA does not require the account holder to make minimum annual withdrawals after attaining age seventy and one-half.

Roth IRAs are subject to income limits. The maximum annual IRA contribution can be made by single filers whose modified adjusted gross incomes are $95,000 or less, and by married couples filing jointly whose modified adjusted gross incomes are $150,000 or less. Maximum annual contributions are phased out for single taxpayers with modified adjusted gross incomes between $95,000 and $110,000, and for married couples filing jointly with modified adjusted gross incomes between $150,000 and $160,000.

A traditional IRA can be converted to a Roth IRA. However, the right to convert is limited to taxpayers with annual adjusted gross incomes of $100,000 or less. The amount converted is subject to ordinary income taxation without an early-withdrawal penalty. Many investment firms have interactive calculators on Internet Web sites that can be used to determine whether a conversion is financially desirable.

Other Tax-Deferred Retirement Plans

In addition to private pension plans and IRAs, a number of other tax-deferred retirement plans are available. A brief description of each is given below.

- *Section 401(k) plan*—an arrangement that allows participants the option of contributing before-tax dollars into the plan or receiving the funds as cash. The amount of salary deferred is invested in the employee's Section 401(k) plan and receives favorable income tax treatment. The law limits the maximum amount of salary that a worker can defer ($11,000 in 2002). A 401(k) plan can be established with both employee and employer contributions, employee contributions only, or employer contributions only. In a typical plan, both the employee and the employer contribute.

- *Profit sharing plan*—a defined contribution plan that pays part of the firm's profits to participating employees. If there are no profits, employers are not required to make contributions. The maximum amount an employer can contribute to a qualified profit sharing plan is 15 percent of the covered compensation of all participants in the plan.

- *Thrift plan (or savings plan)*—a defined contribution plan to which eligible employees contribute voluntarily up to a certain percentage of their salary. The employer also contributes an amount that is typically some fraction of the employee's contribution. For example, if the employee contributes $2, the employer might contribute one-half that amount, or $1.

- *Keogh plan (HR-10 plan)*—a qualified retirement plan that allows self-employed individuals to make tax-deductible contributions to a defined contribution plan or a defined benefit plan. Unincorporated sole proprietors and partnerships can establish a Keogh plan and receive most of the tax advantages that participants in other qualified retirement plans enjoy. Keogh plans have annual limits on contributions and benefits, depending on the type of plan.

- *Simplified employee pension (SEP)*—a retirement plan in which the employer contributes to an IRA established for each eligible employee. However, the annual contribution limits are substantially higher than those allowed for IRAs.

- *SIMPLE plan (Savings Incentive Match Plan for Employees)*—established in 1996, this plan is limited to employers who do not maintain another employer-sponsored retirement plan and who employ 100 or fewer eligible employees. Under a SIMPLE plan, these employers are exempt from complex reporting requirements and administrative rules that apply to qualified pension plans. By simplifying the pension rules, Congress is encouraging smaller employers to establish pension plans for their employees.

- *Section 403(b) plans (also called tax-sheltered annuities)*—tax-deferred retirement plans for qualified tax-exempt employers and public schools as defined in the Internal Revenue Code. Eligible employers include churches, charities, nonprofit hospitals, public and private schools, colleges, and universities. In a typical 403(b) plan, a participating employee can elect to contribute a percentage of his or her salary up to a certain annual limit. The employer also contributes to the plan. As a result, the employee's taxable income is reduced, and plan contributions and investment income accumulate free of income taxes until the employee actually receives the funds.

INDIVIDUAL ANNUITIES

Individual annuities can also be purchased to provide additional retirement income. Although the premiums are paid with after-tax dollars, the investment income is not currently taxable to the policyholder. The funds accumulate on a tax-deferred basis until they are actually received.

Annuity
Provides periodic payments for a fixed period or for the duration of a designated life or lives.

The fundamental purpose of an **annuity** is to provide periodic income that an individual cannot outlive. An annuity provides lifetime income and protection against the exhaustion of one's savings.

Life insurers sell a variety of individual annuities, including the following:[12]

- An *immediate annuity* is purchased with a single sum, and the first payment is one payment interval from the date of purchase. If the income is paid monthly, the first payment starts one month from the date of purchase. For example, if Helen, age sixty-five, purchases a life annuity by making a lump-sum payment of $100,000, the first monthly payment of $750 would be paid to her one month later.

- A *deferred annuity* pays income at some future date. One type of deferred annuity is a retirement annuity. The premiums paid, less expenses, accumulate interest before retirement. At retirement, the cash in the annuity can be paid to the annuitant in a lump sum or as income under one of the annuity options stated in the policy.

- A *flexible-premium annuity* allows the policyholder to vary the premium payments with no requirement that a specified premium be paid each year. The amount of retirement income will be based on the value of the accumulated payments at retirement.

- A *fixed annuity* is one whose periodic payments are fixed in amount. Because the payments are fixed, the annuitant generally has no protection against inflation, which reduces the real purchasing power of the benefits.

- A *variable annuity* is one whose payments vary depending on the investment returns of the fund in which the premiums are invested. The purpose is to provide protection against inflation by maintaining the real purchasing power of the benefits during retirement. The long-run investment returns of most variable annuities have increased more rapidly than inflation as measured by the Consumer Price Index (CPI).

SOCIAL SECURITY

The Old-Age, Survivors, Disability, and Health Insurance program (OASDHI), or Social Security program, is one of the most important retirement programs in the United States. Most retired persons age sixty-two and older receive retirement benefits from the Social Security program that provide an important base of financial security during retirement. In addition, the program provides survivor, disability income, and Medicare benefits to covered beneficiaries.

When only the monthly cash benefits are being discussed, the program is customarily called the OASDI program. However, when Medicare is also included, the total program is called the OASDHI program.

Basic Characteristics of OASDI

The OASDI program is a social insurance program. Social insurance programs have certain characteristics that distinguish them from other government insurance programs. The following section discusses the basic characteristics of the OASDI program.[13]

Compulsory Program

With few exceptions, the OASDI program is compulsory. Most employers and employees are covered and must contribute to the program. A compulsory program has two major advantages: (1) the social objective of providing a base of financial security to the population is achieved more easily, and (2) adverse selection is controlled because all healthy and unhealthy people are essentially covered.

Minimum Floor of Income

The OASDI program provides only a minimum floor of income with respect to covered losses. Individuals are expected to supplement the minimum floor of income with their own personal program of private pensions, savings, investments, and insurance.

Emphasis on Social Adequacy

The OASDI program pays benefits based on social adequacy, which means the benefits should provide a certain standard of living to all beneficiaries. To accomplish this objective, the benefit formula is heavily weighted in favor of certain groups, such as low-income people, the aged, and people with large families. The emphasis on social adequacy helps achieve the social objective of providing a minimum floor of income to all covered groups in the population.

Benefits Loosely Related to Earnings

OASDI benefits are loosely related to the worker's earnings. The higher the covered earnings, the greater the cash benefits received. Although the relationship between benefits and earnings is loose and disproportionate, it does exist.

Benefits Prescribed by Law

OASDI benefits are based on federal law, not on a contract. Benefit amounts, eligibility requirements, method of financing, and other provisions are established by law. Benefits can change if the law is changed.

Financially Self-Supporting

Congress has always intended that the OASDI program should be financially self-supporting. The funds needed to pay benefits and expenses are derived primarily from the payroll tax contributions of covered employees, employers, and the self-employed; interest on the trust fund investments; and taxation of part of the OASDI benefits.

Full Funding Unnecessary

The OASDI program is *not* fully funded. Full funding means that if the program should terminate, the assets already accumulated under the plan are sufficient to discharge all liabilities for the benefits accrued to date.

A fully funded OASDI program is considered unnecessary for several reasons:

- The program is expected to operate indefinitely and not terminate in the future.
- Because the program is compulsory, new entrants into the workforce will always pay taxes to support the program.

- If the program has financial problems, the federal government can use its taxing and borrowing powers to raise additional revenues.

No Means Test

Monthly OASDI cash benefits do not require a means test. A means test requires applicants for benefits to show that their income and financial assets are below a certain level. A means test is used to determine whether applicants are eligible for public assistance or other welfare benefits. However, applicants for OASDI benefits have a statutory right to the benefits if they meet the eligibility requirements discussed later.

Covered Occupations

Most occupations in the private sector are covered on a compulsory basis. Self-employed workers with annual net earnings of $400 or more are also covered on a compulsory basis. Employees of nonprofit charitable, educational, and religious organizations must be covered if they are paid $100 or more during the year. Federal civilian employees hired after 1983 are also covered under the program. In addition, state and local government employees can be covered by a voluntary agreement between the state and the federal government.

Insured Status

To become eligible for benefits, a worker must have credit for a certain amount of work in covered employment. For 2002, a worker received one credit (also called a quarter of coverage) for each $870 of covered annual earnings. A worker can earn a maximum of four credits during the calendar year. The amount of covered earnings needed for one credit will automatically increase as average wages in the economy increase. To become eligible for the various benefits, a worker must attain insured status. There are three types of insured status.

Fully Insured

A worker must be fully insured to receive retirement benefits. Workers who have forty credits or have worked full-time for ten years are fully insured for life even if they never work again.

Currently Insured

A worker is currently insured if he or she has earned at least six credits during the last thirteen calendar quarters ending with the quarter in which death, disability, or entitlement to retirement benefits occurs.

Disability Insured

To be eligible for disability income benefits, the worker must be disability insured. The number of credits depends on the worker's age. Workers age thirty-one or older must be fully insured and have at least twenty credits out of the last forty quarters ending with the quarter in which the worker became disabled. Special rules apply to younger workers and to blind people to make it easier for them to qualify for disability benefits.

Types of Benefits

The OASDHI program has four major benefits:

- Retirement benefits
- Survivor benefits
- Disability benefits
- Medicare benefits

Retirement Benefits

Retirement benefits require a fully insured status. Full benefits are payable at the normal retirement age, which is also called the full retirement age. The full retirement age is currently age sixty-five. However, beginning in 2003, the full retirement age will gradually increase from sixty-five to sixty-seven. The higher retirement age will affect beneficiaries born in 1938 and later. Exhibit 10-4 illustrates these changes.

EXHIBIT 10-4

Age To Receive Full Social Security Benefits (Beginning in 2003)

Year of Birth	Full Retirement Age
1937 or earlier	65
1938	65 and 2 months
1939	65 and 4 months
1940	65 and 6 months
1941	65 and 8 months
1942	65 and 10 months
1943 to 1954	66
1955	66 and 2 months
1956	66 and 4 months
1957	66 and 6 months
1958	66 and 8 months
1959	66 and 10 months
1960 and later	67

Source: Social Security Administration.

All monthly retirement benefits are based on the worker's primary insurance amount (PIA). The PIA is the monthly amount paid to the worker at the full retirement age or to a disabled worker. The PIA is based on the worker's average indexed monthly earnings. The worker's actual earnings are indexed or updated to take into account changes in average wages from the year the earnings were received. The purpose of the indexing method is to ensure that workers who retire today and workers who retire in the future will have about the same proportion of their earnings restored at retirement by OASDI benefits.

After the worker's average indexed monthly earnings are computed, a benefit formula is used to determine the worker's PIA. As stated earlier, benefits are heavily weighted in favor of low-income groups. Exhibit 10-5 provides examples of monthly retirement benefits for selected beneficiaries.

EXHIBIT 10-5

Examples of OASDI Retirement Benefits

Approximate Monthly Benefits If You Retire at Full Retirement Age and Had Steady Lifetime Earnings

Your Age in 2002	Your Family	Your Earnings in 2001						$84,900 or More[1]
		$20,000	$30,000	$40,000	$50,000	$60,000	$70,000	
45	You	$ 876	$1,143	$1,409	$1,574	$1,699	$1,824	$1,977
	You and your spouse[2]	1,314	1,714	2,113	2,361	2,548	2,736	2,965
55	You	876	1,143	1,409	1,574	1,697	1,815	1,925
	You and your spouse[2]	1,314	1,714	2,113	2,361	2,545	2,722	2,887
65	You	820	1,072	1,323	1,453	1,536	1,611	1,660
	You and your spouse[2]	1,230	1,608	1,984	2,179	2,304	2,416	2,490

1. Maximum earnings are greater than or equal to the OASDI wage base and are determined to be $80,400 for 2001 and $84,900 for 2002 and later.

2. Your spouse is assumed to be the same age as you and recieves a benefit equal to one-half that of the worker. Your spouse may qualify for a higher benefit based on his or her earnings.

Note: The accuracy of these estimates depends on your actual earnings, which may vary significantly from those shown here.

Source: Social Security Administration.

Cost-of-Living Adjustment

The monthly cash benefits are automatically adjusted each year for changes in the cost of living, which maintains the real purchasing power of the benefits. Whenever the Consumer Price Index increases from the third quarter of the previous year through the third quarter of the present year, the benefits are automatically increased by the same percentage for the December benefit (payable in early January).

Early Retirement Age

Workers can retire early at age sixty-two with reduced benefits. At the present time, the full benefit payable at age sixty-five is reduced five-ninths of one percent for each month that the person is below age sixty-five. For example, a worker retiring at age sixty-two receives only 80 percent of the full benefit. The reduction in benefits for early retirement at age sixty-two will gradually increase from 20 to 30 percent when the new higher-retirement-age provisions become fully effective.

Delayed Retirement Credit

To encourage working beyond the full retirement age, the OASDI program gives a credit for delayed retirement. The delayed retirement credit applies to the period beyond the full retirement age and up to age seventy. For individuals attaining age sixty-five in 1997, the worker's PIA is increased 5 percent for each year of delayed retirement (prorated monthly) beyond the normal retirement age and up to age seventy. The delayed retirement credit will gradually increase until it reaches 8 percent for workers who were born in 1943 or later.

Monthly Retirement Benefits

Monthly retirement benefits can be paid to the following persons:

- Retired workers age sixty-two or older.
- A retired worker's spouse if he or she is at least age sixty-two. An unmarried divorced spouse is also eligible for benefits if he or she is at least age sixty-two, the marriage had lasted at least ten years, and the divorce has been in effect for at least two years. The two-year waiting period is waived if the worker received benefits before the divorce.
- A retired worker's unmarried children under age eighteen (under nineteen if full-time elementary or high-school students).
- A retired worker's unmarried disabled children age eighteen or older if they were severely disabled before age twenty-two and continue to be disabled.
- A retired worker's spouse at any age if caring for dependent children under age sixteen or for disabled children as defined above.

Survivor Benefits

Survivor benefits can be paid to the dependents of a deceased worker. The worker must be either fully or currently insured at the time of death, but for certain survivor benefits, a fully insured status is required.

Survivor benefits can be paid to various beneficiaries, which include the following:

- Unmarried children under age eighteen (under nineteen if full-time elementary or high-school students)
- Unmarried disabled children as defined above

- Surviving spouse caring for children under age sixteen or for unmarried disabled children as defined above
- Surviving spouse age sixty or older if the deceased is fully insured
- Disabled widow or widower, age fifty through fifty-nine, under certain conditions if the deceased is fully insured
- Dependent parent age sixty-two and older if the deceased is fully insured

In addition, a lump sum benefit of $255 can be paid to an eligible surviving spouse or to a child entitled to benefits. The benefit is not paid if there is no surviving spouse or child entitled to benefits.

The value of OASDI survivor benefits is substantial. The value of the survivor benefits for an average wage earner who dies and has a spouse and two eligible children is equivalent to $403,000 of private life insurance.[14] The benefits, however, are paid monthly and not in a lump sum.

Disability Income Benefits

Disability income benefits are paid to disabled workers and eligible dependents if strict eligibility requirements are met. The disability income program is discussed in Chapter 12.

Medicare Benefits

Medicare benefits are also available under the OASDHI program. The Medicare program covers most people age sixty-five or older and certain other people with disabilities. The Medicare program is also discussed in Chapter 12.

SUMMARY

A personal loss exposure can be defined as any condition or situation that presents the possibility of a direct financial loss to a human being. Important personal loss exposures include premature death, poor health, unemployment, and insufficient income during retirement. Financial insecurity from personal loss exposures can be reduced or even eliminated by life and health insurance, disability income insurance, private and public retirement plans, and an effective saving and investing program.

Financial planning is a process that helps individuals and families to identify their financial goals and to develop a realistic plan for attaining these goals. Common financial goals include an increase in personal wealth, a higher standard of living, protection of the family and property, accumulating a fund for retirement, the purchase of a home, a college education for the children, an emergency fund, getting out of debt, and minimizing federal and state income and estate taxes.

Investing to attain specific financial goals involves certain risks. Major investment risks include inflation risk, market risk, interest-rate risk, financial risk, business risk, and liquidity risk. Major types of investments include savings accounts and savings instruments (including certificates of deposit and money market funds), stocks, bonds, mutual funds, and real estate.

An important personal loss exposure is insufficient income during retirement. Planning for a comfortable retirement is especially important because the proportion of retirees in the population will increase significantly in the future; the period of time spent in retirement has increased; many individuals and families on the threshold of retirement have not accumulated sufficient financial assets; some older retirees require long-term care in a nursing facility and are faced with catastrophic costs; and Social Security retirement benefits provide only a minimum floor of retirement income.

Tax-deferred retirement plans receive favorable income tax treatment and are important in retirement planning. Employer-sponsored tax-deferred plans include defined contribution and defined benefit pension plans. An individual retirement account (IRA) allows workers with taxable compensation to make annual contributions to a retirement plan and receive favorable income tax treatment. Other tax-deferred retirement plans include Section 401(k) plans; profit sharing and thrift plans; Keogh plans for the self-employed; simplified employee pension (SEP) plans; SIMPLE retirement plan for smaller firms; and Section 403(b) plans.

Individual annuities also receive favorable income tax treatment. There are various types of annuities. An immediate annuity pays periodic benefits one payment interval from the date of purchase. In contrast, a deferred annuity pays benefits at some future date. A flexible-premium annuity allows the policyholder to vary the premiums, and no specified premium must be paid each year. A fixed annuity pays periodic payments that are fixed in amount, while a variable annuity pays benefits that vary depending on the investment returns of the fund in which the premiums are invested.

The Social Security program has certain basic characteristics. The program is compulsory; it provides only a minimum floor of income; benefits are based on social adequacy; benefits are loosely related to the worker's earnings; the benefits, eligibility requirements, and other provisions are prescribed by law; Congress intends the program to be financially self-supporting; full funding is unnecessary; and a means test is not required.

An insured status is necessary to receive Social Security benefits. There are three types of insured status: fully insured, currently insured, and disability insured. There are four major Social Security benefits: retirement benefits, survivor benefits, disability benefits, and Medicare benefits.

CHAPTER NOTES

1. This section is based on George E. Rejda, *Social Insurance and Economic Security*, 5th ed. (Englewood Cliffs, N.J.: Prentice-Hall, Inc., 1994), pp. 5-12.
2. Robert M. Crowe and Charles E. Hughes, eds., *Fundamentals of Financial Planning*, 2d ed. (Bryn Mawr, Pa.: The American College, 1993), pp. 18-21.

3. *Confronting the Saving Crisis, Perceptions and Attitudes About Retirement and Financial Planning* (Merrill Lynch & Co., 1995), p. 22.

4. Neal E. Cutler and Steven J. Devlin, "Financial Literacy 2000," *Journal of the American Society of CLU & ChFC*, vol. L, no. 4 (July 1996), pp. 32-37.

5. Investment Company Institute, *2001 Mutual Fund Fact Book*, 41st ed. (Washington, D.C.: Investment Company Institute, 2001), p. 39.

6. U.S. Census Bureau, Statistical Abstract of the United States: 2001 (Washington, D.C.: U.S. Census Bureau, 2001), pp.14-15.

7. Social Security Administration, "Income of the Population 55 or Older, 2000," April 15, 2002. World Wide Web: http://www.ssa.gov/statistics/incpop55/2000/exp_toc.html (15 April 2002).

8. U.S. Census Bureau, *Statistical Abstract of the United States: 2001* (Washington, D.C.: U.S. Census Bureau, 2001), p. 726. This figure is based on 1992 to 1998 data expressed in 1998 dollars.

9. *Confronting the Savings Crisis, Perceptions and Attitudes About Retirement and Financial Planning*, p. 6.

10. John L. Buckman, "Part I, Countdown to Retirement," *Barron's*, August 30, 1993, p. 24.

11. Health Insurance Association of America, "Guide to Long-Term Care Insurance" (Washington, D.C.: Health Insurance Association of America, 1999), p.7.

12. George E. Rejda, *Principles of Risk Management and Insurance*, 5th ed. (New York: HarperCollins College Publishers, 1995), pp. 343-344.

13. Rejda, *Social Insurance and Economic Security*, pp. 22-30.

14. Social Security Administration, *Social Security: Basic Facts*, SSA Publication no. 05-10080, May 2002. World Wide Web: http://www.ssa.gov/pubs/10080.html (11 June 2002).

Chapter 11

Direct Your Learning

Life Insurance

After learning the subject matter of this chapter, you should be able to:

◼ Explain the costs associated with premature death.

◼ Describe the need for life insurance for different family structures.

◼ Describe the needs approach to determining the amount of life insurance to own.

◼ Describe the following types of life insurance:

• Term insurance

• Whole life insurance, including ordinary life and limited-payment life insurance

• Universal life insurance

◼ Explain various life insurance contractual provisions.

◼ Explain the purpose of additional benefits that can be added to a life insurance policy by riders.

◼ Identify and describe factors used in underwriting individual life insurance.

◼ Regarding group life insurance:

• Describe the basic characteristics

• Describe underwriting factors

• Explain typical eligibility requirements

• Describe typical benefits provided

◼ Given a case involving a life insurance claim:

• Explain whether the claim would be paid.

• Determine the amount of payment for covered losses.

• Explain how a given settlement option would affect payment.

Develop Your Perspective

What are the main topics covered in the chapter?

Life insurance addresses a major loss exposure for individuals and families. This chapter describes the fundamentals of life insurance, including the need for life insurance, methods for determining the amount of insurance to purchase, and the major types of life insurance.

Examine the types of life insurance and the way that they meet specific needs.

- How do the various types address specific loss exposures?
- How do the contract provisions differ from those in property and liability insurance contracts?

Why is it important to know these topics?

Life insurance provides a vital safety net for families. The loss of a working family member can create significant financial uncertainty for the surviving family members.

Consider the need for continued income by most families.

- How does life insurance replace the flow of income?
- How can life insurance provide funds for college and retirement?

How can you use this information?

Assess your life insurance needs:

- Who depends on you for the income that you generate now and the income that you will probably generate in the future?
- How can life insurance help you accumulate cash values as an investment or for future income?

Chapter 11

Life Insurance

Premature death of a working person is a devastating personal loss exposure that should receive high priority in a financial plan. If a working member of a family dies prematurely, the surviving family members might be exposed to considerable financial insecurity. For example, assume that Jennifer, age thirty-five, is the major source of financial support for her disabled husband and two small children. She earns $25,000 annually and has saved only $10,000. If she is killed suddenly in an auto accident and has only $25,000 of life insurance, could her family survive on the $35,000 left to them? Although Social Security survivor benefits might be available, other financial needs must be considered, such as financial support for the disabled spouse, paying off the mortgage, and providing a college education for the children. The $35,000 left to the family will not go far. Jennifer's sudden death would create financial difficulty for the surviving family members. Additional life insurance could have been used to restore the family's share of the income lost because of her death.

This chapter discusses the fundamentals of life insurance, a major technique for reducing or even eliminating the adverse financial consequences of premature death. Topics include premature death, the need for life insurance based on the type of family structure, the amount of life insurance to own, and the characteristics of the major types of life insurance sold today. The chapter also discusses important contractual provisions of life insurance policies and additional benefits that can be added. The chapter concludes with a discussion of life insurance underwriting and group life insurance.

PREMATURE DEATH

Chapter 10 notes that premature death can be defined as the early death of a working person with outstanding or unfulfilled financial obligations, such as dependents to support, children to educate, or a mortgage and other installment debts to pay off. If replacement income from other sources is inadequate, or if the assets already accumulated by the family are relatively small, the surviving family members will be exposed to financial hardship.

At least four costs are associated with premature death:

- The income earned by the deceased terminates, and the family's share of that income is lost forever.

- Additional costs are incurred for funeral expenses, uninsured medical bills, probate and estate settlement costs, child-care expenses for young dependent children, and federal and state taxes for large estates.
- Because of insufficient replacement income, some families might experience a reduction in their standard of living.
- Certain emotional and noneconomic costs are incurred, such as the grief of a surviving spouse and the loss of a role model and moral guidance for the children.

NEED FOR LIFE INSURANCE

Life insurance is economically justified if a family member earns an income and if others are dependent on that income for part or all of their financial support. However, the financial impact of premature death is not uniform for all families but varies enormously depending on the type of family structure.[1]

Singles

The number of single people in the United States has increased over time. Many people are delaying marriage, often beyond age thirty or thirty-five; many adults are single because of divorce; and adults often become single once again because their spouses die.

If a single person dies leaving no dependents or outstanding financial obligations, that death is not likely to create a financial problem for others. Thus, such a person needs only a modest amount of life insurance for funeral expenses and uninsured medical bills. However, single persons should realize that their insurance needs could change in the future, and they might be wise to purchase life insurance early in life. Premiums will be lower and insurance might be more easily available than later in life when the need might be greater.

Single-Parent Families

The number of single-parent families with children under age eighteen has increased substantially in recent years because of the large numbers of children born outside of marriage, widespread divorce and separation, and the incarceration or death of a parent. In most cases, single-parent families are headed by women.

Premature death of an income earner in a single-parent family can result in great financial insecurity for the surviving dependent children despite the possibility of receiving Social Security survivor benefits. Thus, the need for life insurance is great. However, many single-parent families have low incomes, and their ability to purchase large amounts of life insurance is limited.

Two-Income Families

In many families, both spouses are employed. The proportion of women in the labor force has increased dramatically over time, especially married women with children. In two-income families with children, premature death of either spouse can cause financial insecurity for the surviving family members because both incomes are normally needed to maintain the family's customary standard of living. The need for life insurance on both spouses, in addition to Social Security benefits, is substantial. Life insurance can replace the lost earnings, so the family can maintain its previous standard of living.

In the case of a married working couple without children, premature death of one spouse might not create severe financial problems for the surviving spouse. The surviving spouse is already in the labor force, child-care costs are not being incurred, and the cost of a college education for children is not an issue. Thus, the need for large amounts of life insurance on both spouses might be reduced. However, other concerns, such as indebtedness and current or future financial support of parents or other relatives, might increase the need for life insurance.

Traditional Families

"Traditional families" are those in which only one parent (historically the father) is in the labor force, and the other parent stays at home and takes care of the dependent children. Statistically, traditional families have declined in relative number over the last few decades. Premature death can cause great financial loss for a traditional family if the parent in the labor force dies. The need for life insurance in this group is significant. Although the surviving family members might be eligible for Social Security survivor benefits, the benefits will probably be inadequate to meet the family's needs. If the amount of life insurance on the deceased parent is insufficient, the family's standard of living is likely to decline.

The need for life insurance on the spouse staying at home can be equally important. The death of this spouse can result in significant expenses, such as those for child-care and housekeeping. While the life insurance amounts needed might not be as high as those of the working spouse, the lack of insurance can have negative effects on the surviving family's standard of living.

Blended Families

A "blended family" is one in which a divorced person with children marries someone who also has children. Premature death of a working spouse in a blended family can cause great financial difficulty for the surviving family members, and the need for life insurance is great. Both spouses might be in the labor force, and two incomes are needed to support the blended family. The premature death of one spouse may result in a reduction in the family's standard of living. In addition, older children may be present from the previous marriage, and additional children may be born in the new marriage. As a result, child-care costs may be incurred over a longer period, and funds for the parents' retirement and children's college education may be limited.

Sandwiched Families

The increase in life expectancy over the last few decades has proportionately increased the number of older people in the total population. Often, an aged parent receives financial assistance or other assistance from a son or daughter. A "sandwiched family" is one in which a son or daughter with children provides financial support or other types of assistance, such as physical care, to one or both parents. Thus, the son or daughter is "sandwiched" between the older and younger generations. Premature death of an income earner in a sandwiched family can cause great financial hardship to the surviving family members. Life insurance can be used to replace the lost income.

DETERMINING THE AMOUNT OF LIFE INSURANCE TO OWN

Once the need for life insurance has been established, the next step is to determine the amount of life insurance to own. Most families are underinsured. In 2000, the average amount of life insurance in force per household in the United States was only $196,200.[2] Some life insurers have proposed certain arbitrary rules for determining the amount of life insurance to own, such as six to ten times annual earnings. These rules, however, are imprecise and might not reflect a particular family's needs.

Needs Approach

Needs approach
Method used to determine an adequate amount of life insurance based on the survivors' needs and the amount of existing life insurance, financial assets, and expected Social Security benefits.

The **needs approach** is widely used to determine the amount of life insurance to own. Under the needs approach, a family's financial needs are estimated after taking into account any Social Security survivor benefits or other benefits that might be available. The amount of existing life insurance and financial assets is then subtracted from the family's financial needs to determine the additional amount of life insurance required, if any, to meet these needs.

The most important family needs include the following:

- An estate clearance fund
- Income during the readjustment period
- Income during the dependency period
- Income to the surviving spouse during the blackout period
- Retirement income
- Special needs, such as paying off a mortgage, an emergency fund, or a college fund for children

Illustration of Needs Approach

The needs approach can be illustrated by analyzing the insurance needs of a family, with children, in which both spouses work. For example, Karen and Christopher Swift are married and have a son, age three. Karen, age thirty-five, earns $48,000 annually as a marketing analyst for a national public relations firm. Christopher, age thirty-six, earns $35,000 as an accountant for a local public utility firm. Both want the family to be financially secure if either spouse should die prematurely.

Exhibit 11-1 is a worksheet for estimating the amount of life insurance needed. In determining the amount of life insurance, Karen recognizes that certain needs, such as the college fund, will increase because of inflation. However, Karen assumes that, in the event of her death, life insurance proceeds could be invested at a rate of interest equal to the rate of inflation. An explanation of certain items in Exhibit 11-1 follows:

- *Estate clearance fund.* Cash would be needed immediately in an estate clearance fund for funeral expenses, uninsured medical bills, car loans and installment debts, and estate administration expenses. Karen estimates that $28,000 will be needed to pay these expenses.

- *Readjustment period.* In addition to Social Security survivor benefits and her husband's take-home pay, Karen would like her family to receive an additional $1,000 monthly during a two-year readjustment period following her death. A total of $24,000 would be needed to meet this need.

- *Dependency period.* Karen would like her family to continue receiving $1,000 monthly for another fifteen years until her son reaches age eighteen. An additional $180,000 would be needed to meet this need during the dependency period.

- *Blackout period.* Under current law, Social Security survivor benefits can be paid to a surviving spouse with eligible children under age sixteen. The benefits paid to the surviving spouse terminate when the youngest child reaches age sixteen and do not resume until the spouse reaches age sixty. The children's benefits, however, continue until the youngest child reaches age eighteen. Because Karen's husband would continue to work after her death, additional income during the blackout period would not be needed.

- *Retirement income.* Retirement income to a surviving spouse is another important need to consider. Christopher will be eligible for Social Security benefits when he retires, and he plans to receive additional retirement income from his employer's Section 401(k) plan. In addition, Christopher has an individual retirement account (IRA). Karen believes that retirement benefits from these sources will be adequate, and additional income from life insurance will probably not be needed.

- *Special needs.* Karen also has three special needs: (1) a fund to pay off the mortgage, (2) an education fund for her son, and (3) an emergency fund for unexpected events. Karen estimates that a total of $235,000 would meet these needs.

EXHIBIT 11-1

Illustration of Needs Approach

Karen Swift's Needs			Your Needs	
Estate Clearance Fund				
Funeral costs	$ 10,000		$_____	
Uninsured medical bills	3,000		_____	
Installment debts	12,000		_____	
Probate costs	3,000		_____	
Federal estate taxes	0		_____	
State inheritance taxes	0		_____	
Total estate clearance fund		$ 28,000		$_____
Income Needs				
Readjustment period	$ 24,000		$_____	
Dependency period	180,000		_____	
Blackout period	0		_____	
Retirement income	0		_____	
Total income needs		$ 204,000		$_____
Special Needs				
Pay off mortgage	$ 110,000		$_____	
College education fund	100,000		_____	
Emergency fund	25,000		_____	
Total special needs		$ 235,000		$_____
Total needs		$ 467,000		$_____

Karen Swift's Assets			Your Assets	
Present Life Insurance and Financial Assets				
Checking and savings accounts	$ 10,000		$_____	
Mutual funds and securities	25,000		_____	
IRAs and Keogh plan	4,000		_____	
Section 401(k) plan and employer savings plan	4,000		_____	
Private pension death benefit	10,000		_____	
Current life insurance	50,000		_____	
Other financial assets	0		_____	
Total assets		$ 103,000		$_____
Additional Life Insurance Needed				
Total needs		$ 467,000		$_____
Less total assets		103,000		_____
Additional life insurance needed		$ 364,000		$_____

Karen has estimated that cash needs, income needs, and special needs total $467,000. Because Karen's current financial assets and life insurance total only $103,000, Karen needs an additional $364,000 of life insurance.

TYPES OF LIFE INSURANCE

After determining the amount of life insurance needed, an individual must determine the type of life insurance to purchase. Life insurers sell a variety of insurance contracts, many of which are designed specifically for certain needs.[3]

Term Insurance

Term insurance is the most basic type of life insurance. If the insured dies within the term or policy period, the face amount of the policy is paid; if the insured survives beyond that period, nothing is paid.

Basic Characteristics of Term Insurance

Term insurance has four basic characteristics:

- Term insurance provides temporary protection for a specified period, such as one, five, or ten years, or until the insured reaches a specified age, such as age sixty-five or seventy.

- Term insurance policies have no **cash value** or savings element. The insurance provides protection but no investment, and cash values do not accumulate.

- Most term insurance policies are **renewable** and **convertible**. Insurers typically do not allow renewal after a certain age, such as sixty-five, seventy, or seventy-five. However, some insurers guarantee renewability to an older age, such as ninety-five or ninety-nine.

- Term insurance premiums increase with the insured's age and are based on mortality rates. Because **mortality rates** increase with age, term insurance premiums must also increase.

Types of Term Insurance

Insurers today sell many term insurance policies, including the following:

- *Yearly renewable term.* With this type of policy, the policyowner has the right to renew for successive one-year periods.

- *Specified period term.* The premium for this type of term policy does not change during the policy term. However, if the policy is renewed at the end of the term, the premium will increase.

- *Decreasing term.* An example of a decreasing term policy is a $50,000 policy issued for thirty years that gradually declines to $25,000 by the end of the twentieth year, and to zero by the end of the thirtieth year.

Term insurance
Insurance that provides temporary protection (for a certain period of time) with no cash value; usually renewable and convertible.

Cash value
Fund that accumulates in a whole life insurance policy and that the policyholder can access in several ways, including borrowing, purchasing paid-up life insurance, and surrendering the policy in exchange for the cash value.

Renewable
Characteristic of a term life insurance policy that permits the policyholder to renew it for additional periods without evidence of insurability.

Convertible
Characteristic of a term insurance policy that allows the policy to be exchanged for some type of permanent life insurance policy with no evidence of insurability.

Mortality rates
Probabilities of death at specific ages. Life insurers have been able to predict mortality rates with a high degree of accuracy for large groups of people.

Decreasing term policies are frequently used as protection to pay off a mortgage at the death of a homeowner.

- *Reentry term.* The premiums for this type of policy are increased substantially if the insured cannot provide satisfactory evidence of insurability.

Uses of Term Insurance

Term insurance is appropriate in three general situations:

- *When income is limited and substantial amounts of life insurance are needed.* Term insurance premiums have declined over time because of intense price competition and increases in life expectancy. Substantial amounts of term insurance can be purchased with relatively modest annual premiums.

- *To meet a temporary need, such as the need for income during the readjustment, dependency, and blackout periods.* Decreasing term can be used to pay off a mortgage or a loan if the insured should die while a balance remains.

- *To guarantee the future insurability of the insured.* The insured might wish to buy permanent insurance but might be unable to pay the higher premiums. He or she can purchase term insurance and convert it later into a permanent policy without **evidence of insurability**.

Although term insurance can play a valuable role in an insurance program, two major limitations exist. First, term insurance premiums gradually increase with age and eventually reach prohibitive levels at older ages. Thus, term insurance is not suitable for lifetime protection. Second, term insurance policies typically do not develop cash values. Thus, term insurance cannot be used to save money, such as saving for retirement or accumulating a fund for the children's college education.

Whole Life Insurance

Whole life insurance provides permanent (lifetime) protection as opposed to the temporary protection of term insurance. Two basic types of whole life insurance are ordinary life insurance and limited payment life insurance.

Ordinary Life Insurance

Premiums under an **ordinary life insurance** policy do not increase with age and are paid periodically until the insured dies or reaches age 100. If the insured is still alive at age 100, the face amount of insurance is paid to the policyowner at that time.

Cash Values

An ordinary life policy develops cash values. The policyholder can borrow the cash value or use it to purchase a **paid-up policy**. If the policyowner no

---

Evidence of insurability
A requirement by a life insurer that the insured demonstrate that he or she still meets the insurer's underwriting standards. The insured is usually required to submit a medical questionnaire or have a physical examination to show that he or she is in good health.

Whole life insurance
Level-premium insurance that provides lifetime protection and builds cash values.

Ordinary life insurance
Whole life insurance that requires periodic premiums until the insured dies or reaches age 100. (Also called straight life insurance.)

Paid-up policy
Life insurance that does not require additional premium payments to remain in force.

longer desires the life insurance protection, the policy can be surrendered for its cash value.

Uses of Ordinary Life Insurance

Ordinary life insurance can be used when the policyowner desires life insurance protection beyond age sixty-five. As noted earlier, term insurance is not suitable for lifetime protection because the premiums continually increase with age. In addition, ordinary life insurance can be used to save money for general or specific purposes. The cash value can be used as an emergency fund, or cash can be accumulated for specific purposes, such as children's college education or additional retirement income to the insured.

The major disadvantage of ordinary life insurance is that the policyowner might be substantially underinsured after purchasing the policy because ordinary life insurance premiums are generally higher than term insurance until the insured reaches a certain age. Attracted by the savings feature, some policyowners might purchase an ordinary life insurance policy and, as a result, have an insufficient amount of insurance protection. For example, Megan, age twenty-eight, is a single parent with a son, age one. Based on her limited income, she cannot spend more than $400 annually for life insurance. Based on the rates of one insurer, she could buy about $64,000 of ordinary life insurance. The same premium would purchase more than $400,000 of term insurance, which would provide substantially greater financial protection for her son if she should die.

Limited-Payment Life Insurance

Limited-payment life insurance policies can be issued with various premium payment periods, such as ten, twenty, or thirty years. Policies paid-up at age sixty-five or seventy are also available. For example, Scott, age thirty-two, purchases a twenty-year limited payment policy in the amount of $100,000. After twenty years, no additional premiums are required, and the policy is completely paid-up.

Limited-payment life insurance might be appropriate for policyowners who want their life insurance to be paid-up after a certain period; for instance, individuals may want their insurance paid-up before they retire. The major disadvantage, however, is that limited-payment life insurance is expensive. Policyowners with limited amounts to spend on life insurance might be substantially underinsured with a limited-payment policy. If a person desires permanent protection, an ordinary life policy will be less expensive.

> **Limited-payment life insurance**
> Whole life insurance in which the premiums are level but are paid only for a certain number of years. After that time, the policy is paid-up.

Universal Life Insurance

Another type of life insurance is **universal life insurance**, which has become popular in recent years. Universal life policies are frequently sold as an investment that combines life insurance protection with savings. The policyowner has a cash value account that is credited with the premiums paid

> **Universal life insurance**
> Flexible-premium life insurance that separates the protection, savings, and expense components.

less a deduction for the cost of the insurance protection and expenses charged. The balance in the account is then credited with interest at a specified rate. If the policy is surrendered, the cash value account may be reduced by a surrender charge to determine the surrender value paid to the policyowner. Surrender charges typically apply over some time period, such as ten to fifteen years.

Basic Characteristics of Universal Life Insurance

There are two forms of universal life insurance. The first type has an initial level death benefit; as the cash value increases, the amount of pure insurance protection declines. The second type has an increasing death benefit; the death benefit is equal to the face amount of insurance plus the cash value. As the cash value increases, the total death benefit also increases. A higher premium is charged for the latter type of policy.

Universal life insurance has several basic characteristics:

- Separation of protection, savings, and expense components
- Stated rate of interest
- Considerable flexibility
- Partial cash withdrawals option

First, there is separation ("unbundling") of the protection, savings, and expense components under the policy. The policyowner receives an annual disclosure statement that shows the premiums paid, death benefit, expense charges, interest credited to the cash value account, and cash surrender value.

Second, the interest rate credited to the cash value account is specifically stated. There are two interest rates. There is a current interest rate (or advertised rate), which is higher than the guaranteed rate and fluctuates with the market. A guaranteed minimum interest rate is also stated in the policy, such as 4 or 4.5 percent. The interest rate credited to the cash value account can never be less than the guaranteed rate.

In addition, universal life insurance provides considerable flexibility. Premiums can be decreased, increased, or skipped as long as the cash value account is sufficient to pay the mortality costs and expenses; the death benefit can be increased (with evidence of insurability); the policyowner can add to the cash value at any time subject to any insurer restrictions; policy loans are permitted; and certain insureds can be added to the policy.

Finally, partial cash withdrawals can be made. A surrender charge or transaction fee may be imposed for each withdrawal. Unlike a policy loan, a partial cash withdrawal does not obligate the policyowner to pay interest on the funds withdrawn or to repay the insurance company. The withdrawal simply reduces the cash value account. Funds withdrawn can be restored through voluntary additional premium payments.

Uses of Universal Life Insurance

Universal life insurance is appropriate for policyowners who want both an investment vehicle and life insurance protection in one policy. It is also appropriate for policyowners who want flexibility in their life insurance program as financial circumstances change over time. For example, premiums can be decreased or even eliminated by policyowners who become unemployed or have children in college. Premiums may be increased by policyowners who are nearing retirement in order to accumulate higher cash values for retirement purposes. Finally, universal life insurance can be used to save money for specific financial goals, such as a down payment on a home, the children's college education, or supplemental retirement income.

One disadvantage of universal life insurance is the flexibility that allows policyowners to reduce or eliminate premiums; policyowners might not be firmly committed to pay regularly. As a result, the policy might lapse because of insufficient cash value to keep the insurance in force.

Exhibit 11-2 compares universal life insurance with other major types of life insurance discussed in the previous sections.

Other Types of Life Insurance

In addition to term insurance, whole life insurance, and universal life insurance, several other types of life insurance are available, including the following:

- *Variable life insurance* is a life insurance policy in which the face amount of insurance and cash value vary according to the investment experience of a separate account maintained by the insurer. The policy provides permanent protection with level premiums that are invested in common stocks, bonds, or other investments. Variable life insurance is appropriate for policyowners who want some protection against inflation in the long run in their life insurance program.

- *Variable universal life insurance* is similar to universal life insurance with two major exceptions. First, the cash values are not guaranteed, and there is no minimum interest rate guarantee. The cash value of the policy is determined by the investment experience of a separate account maintained by the insurer. The second major difference is that the policyowner can select the separate account in which the premiums are invested. Variable universal life insurance is appropriate for policyowners who would like an investment product and want to determine how the premiums are to be invested.

- *Current assumption whole life insurance* (also called interest-sensitive life insurance) is a generic name for a whole life policy in which the cash values and premiums are determined by the insurer's current investment and loss experience.[4]

  Current assumption whole life insurance might be appropriate for policyowners during times when interest rates earned by the insurer are

EXHIBIT 11-2

Life Insurance Policy Comparison Chart

Product	Death Benefit	Premium	Cash Value	Cash Value or Dividends Use Current Interest?	Partial Surrenders Permitted?	Policy Elements Unbundled?
Term (Yearly Renewable)	Fixed, Level	Increasing	None	N.A.	N.A.	No
Ordinary Life (Participating)	Fixed, Level	Fixed, Level	Fixed with minimum interest rate guaranteed.	Yes	Yes, but through paid-up additions only.	No
Universal Life	Adjustable	Flexible	Varies depending on face amount and premium. Minimum guaranteed interest. Excess interest increases cash values.	Yes	Yes	Yes

Source: Adaptation of Table 6-2 in Kenneth Black, Jr., and Harold D. Skipper, Jr., *Life Insurance* (Englewood Cliffs, N.J.: Prentice-Hall, Inc., 1994), p. 146.

increasing. However, because of declining interest rates during the late 1980s and early 1990s, some unhappy policyowners have filed class action lawsuits against insurers selling such policies, alleging misrepresentation in the sales presentations.

- *Endowment insurance* pays the face amount of insurance to the designated beneficiary if the insured dies within a certain period; if the insured survives to the end of the period, the face amount is paid to the policyowner. Endowment insurance is seldom sold today because most new endowment policies cannot meet the tax definition of life insurance. Thus, adverse tax consequences have discouraged the sale of new endowment policies. However, many older endowment policies are still in force, and endowment contracts are sometimes used in retirement plans.

LIFE INSURANCE CONTRACTUAL PROVISIONS

This section discusses some of the important contractual provisions that appear in life insurance policies.

Incontestable Clause

According to the **incontestable clause**, the insurer has a specified period, such as two years, to discover any irregularities affecting the contract, such as a material misrepresentation or concealment on the part of the insured. If the insured dies after that time, the death benefit must be paid. For example, assume that Scott concealed a cancer operation when his life insurance application was filled out, and he dies three years after the policy becomes effective. Because the two-year contestable period has expired, the insurer must pay the death benefit without contesting the validity of the policy.

The purpose of the incontestable clause is to protect the beneficiary if the insurer attempts to deny payment of the death benefit several years after the policy is issued. Because the insured is dead, the insurer's allegations concerning statements in the application cannot be easily refuted. After the contestable period has expired, the insurer must pay the death benefit.

Suicide Clause

A typical **suicide clause** states that the death proceeds will not be paid if the insured commits suicide within two years after the policy is issued. In some policies, suicide is excluded for only one year. The only payment the beneficiary receives is a refund of the premiums paid less any policy loans. The purpose of the suicide clause is to provide the insurer with some protection against an insured who purchases a life insurance policy with the intention of committing suicide.

Grace Period

A typical **grace period** gives the policyowner thirty-one days to pay an overdue premium. Universal life policies usually have a longer grace period, such as sixty-one days. If death occurs during the grace period, the overdue premium is deducted from the death benefits. The purpose of the grace period is to give the policyowner some flexibility in the payment of premiums so that the policy does not immediately lapse if a premium is received late.

Reinstatement Clause

If the premium is not paid during the grace period, the policy may lapse for nonpayment of premium. The **reinstatement clause** allows the policyowner

Incontestable clause
Clause that states that the insurer cannot contest the policy after it has been in force for a specified period, such as two years, during the insured's lifetime.

Suicide clause
Clause that states the insurer will not pay the death benefit if the insured commits suicide within a certain period (usually two years) after policy inception.

Grace period
Provision that continues a life insurance policy in force for a certain number of days (usually thirty or thirty-one) after the premium due date, during which time the policyowner can pay the overdue premium without penalty.

Reinstatement clause
Clause that gives the policyowner the right to reinstate a lapsed life insurance policy if certain requirements are met.

the right to reinstate a lapsed policy if certain requirements such as the following are met:

- The lapsed policy must be reinstated within five years.
- All unpaid premiums plus interest must be paid.
- The policy must not be surrendered for its cash value.
- All policy loans must be repaid or reinstated.
- Evidence of insurability may be required. However, evidence of insurability is often waived if the policy is reinstated within thirty-one days after the grace period ends.

Misstatement of Age or Sex

Misstatement of age or sex provision

Clause stating that if the insured's age or sex is misstated in a life insurance policy application, the amount of death benefit the insurer will pay is the amount that the premium would have purchased at the insured's correct age and sex.

The **misstatement of age or sex provision** states that if the insured's age or sex is misstated in the application, the amount of death benefit payable is the amount that the premiums paid would have purchased at the correct age and sex. For example, Michelle's correct age is thirty-one but is recorded in the application as thirty. Assume that the premium for an ordinary life policy is $15 per $1,000 at age thirty and $16.50 per $1,000 at age thirty-one. Michelle purchased $110,000 of ordinary life insurance with an annual premium of $1,650 ($15 × 110). If Michelle dies, the insurer will pay only $100,000 ($1,650 / $16.50), the amount the premium of $1,650 would have purchased at the correct age of thirty-one.

Beneficiary Designations

Beneficiary

Person(s) designated in a life insurance policy to receive the death benefit.

Types of **beneficiaries** that can be designated in life insurance policies include the following:

- The *primary beneficiary* is the first party entitled to receive the death benefit at the insured's death.
- The *contingent beneficiary* is the beneficiary who is entitled to receive the death benefit if the primary beneficiary is not alive.
- A *revocable beneficiary* designation means that the policyowner has the right to change the beneficiary without the beneficiary's consent.
- An *irrevocable beneficiary* designation means that the policyowner cannot change the beneficiary without the beneficiary's consent.
- A *specific beneficiary* designation means that the beneficiary is named and can be identified, such as "Christian Louis Swift, son of the insured."
- A *class beneficiary* designation means that a specific individual is not identified but is a member of a group to whom the proceeds are paid. One example of a class designation is "children of the insured."

Assignment Clause

A life insurance policy can be assigned by the policyowner to another party. There are two types of assignments:

- An *absolute assignment* transfers all ownership rights in the policy to a new owner.

- A *collateral assignment* assigns the life insurance policy to another party as collateral for a loan. Under this type of assignment, only certain policy rights are transferred to the creditor to protect its interest.

In life insurance, the *insured* and the *policyowner* are not necessarily the same person or party. The death of the insured is the event that triggers payment of the death benefit to the beneficiary. However, it is the policyowner who owns the policy and has the right to assign the policy, make policy loans, or receive dividends. For example, if Judy buys a life insurance policy covering the life of her twelve-year-old son, Mark, Judy would be the policyowner, and Mark would be the insured.

Dividend Options

Some life insurance policies pay dividends to the policyowners. Policies that pay dividends are called **participating policies**.

Policies that do not pay dividends are called **nonparticipating** (or **guaranteed cost**) **policies**. Dividends can be paid if the insurer has favorable loss, investment, and expense experience. However, because the insurer's expenses and investments cannot be guaranteed, the dividends are not guaranteed.

The policyowner of a participating policy has a choice of several dividend options:

- *Cash.* When this option is chosen, the policyowner receives a check from the insurer, usually on the anniversary date of the policy. The dividend is relatively small in the early years but can increase to sizable amounts in later years.

- *Reduction of premium.* Under this option, the current dividend is used to reduce the next year's premium. This option is appropriate if the premiums become financially burdensome to pay.

- *Accumulate at interest.* The dividends can be accumulated at interest with the insurer. Interest is credited at a specified rate stated in the policy, but the insurer can pay a higher rate at its discretion. The policyowner can withdraw the accumulated dividends and interest at any time. If left with the insurer, the accumulated dividends and interest become part of the death proceeds and are paid in addition to the death benefit amount.

- *Paid-up additions.* Under this option, the dividends are used to purchase additional amounts of paid-up whole life insurance. The dividend is applied as a net single premium at the insured's attained age to

Participating policies
Life insurance policies that pay dividends to policyowners.

Nonparticipating (guaranteed cost) policies
Life insurance policies that do not pay dividends to policyowners.

buy an additional increment of paid-up whole life insurance. For example, a dividend of $40 may purchase about $100 of paid-up whole life insurance for a twenty-year-old woman. The paid-up insurance becomes part of the death proceeds when the insured dies. This option is appropriate if the insured becomes uninsurable and needs additional insurance.

- *One-year term insurance.* Some policies allow the dividend to be used to purchase one-year term insurance. If the insured dies while the insurance is in force, the amount of term insurance is added to the basic death benefit.

Nonforfeiture Options

A cash value life insurance policy contains provisions that protect the policyowner from forfeiture of the cash value if the policy is discontinued. All states have nonforfeiture laws that require insurers to pay at least a minimum amount if a cash value policy is surrendered.

Nonforfeiture options
Provisions in a life insurance policy that give the policyowner a choice of ways to use the cash value if the policy is terminated and that protect the policyowner from forfeiting the cash value.

There are three **nonforfeiture options**:

1. *Cash.* The policy can be surrendered for its cash surrender value, and protection under the policy ceases. The cash values are relatively low during the early years but can accumulate to sizable amounts over time.

2. *Reduced paid-up insurance.* The cash value in the policy can be applied as a net single premium to purchase a reduced amount of paid-up insurance. The amount of paid-up insurance depends on the insured's attained age, the amount of cash value, and the interest and mortality assumptions stated in the policy. The paid-up policy is the same as the original policy, but the face amount of insurance is reduced.

3. *Extended term insurance.* Under this option, the cash value is used to extend the face amount of insurance (less any indebtedness) as paid-up term insurance. The death benefit is equal to the full face amount of insurance, but the period of protection is limited to a certain number of years and days.

A cash value policy contains a table of nonforfeiture options that shows the value of each option at various attained ages. Exhibit 11-3 illustrates a nonforfeiture option table.

Policy Loan Provision

Cash value policies also contain a policy loan provision that allows the policyowner to borrow the cash value. However, with the exception of a policy loan to pay a premium, the insurer can delay granting a policy loan for up to six months.

Most insurers charge a fixed interest rate stated in the policy. Some insurers charge a variable rate of interest.

Any unpaid interest is added to the loan. If the insured dies before the loan is repaid, the face amount of insurance is reduced by the amount of the total policy debt.

In addition, the automatic premium loan provision can be added at no cost to a cash value policy. An overdue premium is automatically borrowed from the cash value at the expiration of the grace period. The purpose of this provision is to prevent the policy from lapsing because an overdue premium has not been paid.

EXHIBIT 11-3

Nonforfeiture Options (Dollar Amount for Each $1,000 of Ordinary Life Insurance Issued at Age 21)

End of Policy Year	Cash or Loan Value	Paid-up Insurance	Extended Term Insurance	
			Years	Days
1	$0.00	$0	0	0
2	0.00	0	0	0
3	4.79	15	1	315
4	16.21	48	6	161
5	27.91	81	11	15
6	39.91	113	14	275
7	52.20	145	17	158
8	64.78	176	19	157
9	77.66	206	20	342
10	90.84	236	22	29
11	104.33	265	22	351
12	118.13	294	23	231
13	132.25	322	24	54
14	146.69	350	24	191
15	161.43	377	24	290
16	176.47	403	24	356
17	191.79	429	25	28
18	207.38	454	25	42
19	223.22	478	25	36
20	239.29	502	25	13
Age 60	563.42	806	17	26
Age 65	608.49	833	15	272

Source: George E. Rejda, *Principles of Risk Management and Insurance*, 5th ed. (New York: HarperCollins College Publishers, 1995), Table 17.1, p. 364.

Settlement Options

Life insurance death benefits are typically paid in a lump sum to a designated beneficiary or beneficiaries. However, the death proceeds can also be paid out under various **settlement options** in a life insurance policy. The policyowner can elect a settlement option before the insured's death. If the policyowner has not selected a settlement option, the beneficiary has the right to select the method of payment after the death occurs.

Common settlement options include the following:

- *Interest option.* Under the interest option, the insurer retains the death proceeds, and interest is paid periodically to the beneficiary. The rate of interest paid is stated in the policy. However, the insurer can pay a higher rate at its discretion. The beneficiary may be given the right to withdraw part or all of the proceeds at any time. The interest option is appropriate when the funds will not be needed until a later date.

- *Fixed-period option.* This option pays the policy proceeds to a designated beneficiary or beneficiaries over some fixed period, which typically ranges from one to thirty years. The policyowner or beneficiary selects the number of years over which the proceeds are to be paid. If the primary beneficiary dies before receiving all payments, the remaining payments are paid to a contingent beneficiary or to the primary beneficiary's estate. The fixed-period option is appropriate when income is needed over some fixed period, such as income during the readjustment, dependency, or blackout periods.

- *Fixed-amount option.* This is an option that pays a fixed amount periodically to the beneficiary. The payments are typically paid monthly, but longer payment intervals are possible. The policyowner or beneficiary selects the amount of monthly income, and the payments continue until both principal and interest are exhausted. Assuming that the death proceeds are adequate, the fixed-amount option can be used to provide monthly income during the readjustment and dependency periods.

- *Life income options.* The death proceeds can also be paid out under a life income option. Several life income options are available. A life income with no-refund option pays periodic income to the beneficiary only while the beneficiary is alive; no additional payments are made after the beneficiary dies. The life income with a period-certain option pays a lifetime income to the beneficiary, but payments are guaranteed for a stated time, such as ten or twenty years. If the primary beneficiary dies before receiving all of the guaranteed payments, the remaining payments are paid to a contingent beneficiary or to the beneficiary's estate. Finally, a joint-and-survivor income option pays periodic income to two persons, such as a husband and wife, during their lifetime.

ADDITIONAL LIFE INSURANCE BENEFITS

Several optional benefits can be added to a life insurance policy by an appropriate **rider**. Some common riders include the following:

- Waiver of premium
- Accidental death benefit

- Guaranteed insurability
- Cost-of-living rider
- Accelerated death benefits

Each of these options can typically be purchased for an additional premium.

Waiver of Premium

A **waiver of premium** can be added to most individual life insurance policies. In some policies, it is automatically included as part of the contract.

Certain requirements must be met before premiums are waived. First, the insured must become totally disabled before a certain age, such as age sixty or sixty-five. Second, the insured must be continuously disabled for six months (four months in some policies). Third, the definition of disability in the policy must be satisfied.

> **Waiver of premium**
> Clause stating that the insurer will waive premiums due during the period of disability if the insured becomes totally disabled before a certain age.

Accidental Death Benefit

The **accidental death benefit** (sometimes called "double indemnity") doubles the face amount of insurance if the insured dies as a result of an accident. In some contracts, the face amount of insurance is tripled.

Several requirements must be satisfied to collect accidental death benefits. First, the death must result directly from an accidental bodily injury. Death from disease, suicide, war, inhalation of gas or fumes, commission of a felony, and certain aviation activities other than as a fare-paying passenger are typically excluded. Second, the death must occur within a certain number of days, usually ninety, after the accident. Some riders have a longer period, such as 180 days, one year, or as long as the rider is in effect. Finally, the death must occur before some stated age, such as age sixty-five or seventy.

> **Accidental death benefit**
> Provision in a life insurance policy that doubles (or triples) the face amount of insurance payable if the insured dies as a result of an accident.

Guaranteed Insurability

The purpose of the **guaranteed insurability rider** is to guarantee the insured's future insurability even though he or she might become uninsurable because of poor health.

The typical option permits additional amounts of life insurance to be purchased every three years without evidence of insurability up to some stated age, such as forty. For example, assume that Allison, age twenty-five, purchases a $25,000 ordinary life insurance policy with a guaranteed insurability rider. After the policy is issued, she becomes uninsurable because of a serious illness. At ages twenty-eight, thirty-one, thirty-four, thirty-seven, and forty, she could purchase an additional $25,000 of ordinary life insurance with no evidence of insurability. If all of these options are exercised, she would have a total of $150,000 of coverage. She might

> **Guaranteed insurability rider (guaranteed purchase option)**
> Rider that permits the policyowner to buy additional amounts of life insurance at standard rates without evidence of insurability.

also be able to exercise a purchase option early if certain events occur, such as the birth of a child, adoption, or marriage.

Cost-of-Living Rider

The cost-of-living rider allows the policyowner to purchase, without evidence of insurability, one-year term insurance equal to the face amount of the policy times the percentage change in the Consumer Price Index (CPI). The purpose of the cost-of-living rider is to preserve the real purchasing power of the face amount of insurance by adjusting it for inflation. For example, assume that Kelly, age thirty, purchases a $100,000 ordinary life insurance policy, and that the CPI increases 3 percent during the first year. The total amount of life insurance would be increased to $103,000 with the addition of a cost-of-living rider.

Accelerated Death Benefits

An accelerated death benefits rider allows insureds who have certain catastrophic diseases or who are terminally ill to receive part or all of the available life insurance proceeds before death occurs. There are three basic types of accelerated death benefits riders:

- *Terminal illness rider.* This rider allows insureds with a life expectancy of six months or one year to collect part or all of the available proceeds.
- *Catastrophic illness rider.* Insureds who have certain catastrophic diseases, such as life-threatening cancer, coronary artery disease, or AIDS, can receive part of the face amount of insurance.
- *Long-term care rider.* Insureds who require long-term care can receive part of the face amount to help pay for the cost of care. For example, a benefit equal to 2 percent of the policy face amount may be paid each month up to a maximum of 50 percent.

LIFE INSURANCE UNDERWRITING

The underwriting of individual life insurance is discussed briefly in this section; group life insurance underwriting is discussed later in this chapter. Life insurance underwriting refers to the process of selecting and classifying applicants for life insurance. Acceptable applicants should be placed in the correct underwriting class and pay an appropriate premium that reflects the exposure for that class. This process can be done only by the careful selection and classification of individual applicants for insurance.

Life insurance underwriting is based, in part, on the basic principle of emphasizing the standard acceptable group.[5] The insurer's underwriting standards should be sufficiently broad so that most applicants are accepted at standard rates. A large number of rejections increases the insurer's cost of doing business, reduces the morale of the sales force, and may also lead to a loss of goodwill among potential insureds.

Underwriting Factors

Life insurers use a number of important underwriting factors to determine whether applicants for individual life insurance are acceptable, substandard, or uninsurable. The major factors are summarized as follows:[6]

- *Age.* The mortality rate correlates with age. Generally, the older the applicant, the higher the premium.

- *Sex.* Women have a longer life expectancy than men the same age. As a result, women typically are charged lower premiums than men.

- *Build.* Build refers to the relationship between height, weight, and girth (the comparison of an expanded chest with the abdomen). Mortality rates are substantially higher for overweight people.

- *Physical condition.* Depending on the amount of life insurance desired, certain tests may be required to determine the applicant's physical condition. These tests include a blood pressure test, a urinalysis test to detect kidney disease, a blood test for AIDS, and an electrocardiogram to detect heart disease.

- *Personal health history.* Personal health history is also important. Applicants are asked whether they have had certain diseases, whether they have received treatment for drug or alcohol addiction, and whether they have been refused life insurance in the past or offered insurance at higher than standard rates.

- *Family health history.* Certain health characteristics are hereditary. Applicants are asked questions concerning the health history of family members, such as heart disease, cancer, diabetes, and other serious diseases.

- *Smoking.* Smokers have higher mortality rates than nonsmokers. Applicants are asked whether they smoke or when they discontinued smoking.

- *Hazardous sports and hobbies.* Some sports and hobbies are hazardous and can increase the insurer's mortality risk. These activities include sky diving, hang gliding, scuba diving, and race car driving.

- *Habits and morals.* Applicants are asked questions concerning the use of alcohol and drugs. However, alcoholics who have successfully undergone treatment or have not consumed alcohol for a number of years may be insurable at standard rates. Moral factors are also considered, including serious financial problems such as bankruptcy.

- *Residence.* Mortality rates vary throughout the world because of living standards, climate, disease, sanitation, war, and other factors. The applicant might plan to live in a foreign country or might have recently traveled or resided in a foreign country.

- *Occupation.* Certain occupations have relatively high accident rates, while other occupations expose workers to certain types of occupational disease. Hazardous occupations include underground mining, lumber mills, construction, farming, and jobs in which the workers are exposed to dust and poisons.

Underwriting Decisions

After evaluating the information provided by the applicant and other sources noted above, several underwriting decisions are possible. First, the applicant may be rated as standard and charged the normal premium for the desired coverage. More than 90 percent of life insurance applicants are accepted at standard rates.[7] Second, the applicant may be rated as substandard and charged a higher premium. About 6 to 7 percent of applicants are insured at substandard rates. Finally, the applicant may be rejected. About 3 percent of applicants are denied insurance.

In addition, some applicants apply for life insurance as a preferred risk. Life insurance is provided at reduced rates to individuals who belong to a group whose mortality experience is expected to be lower than average. The insurance is carefully underwritten and sold only to applicants whose physical condition, personal health history, weight, occupation, and personal habits indicate more favorable mortality experience than the average. A minimum amount of life insurance must also be purchased, such as $200,000 or $250,000.

GROUP LIFE INSURANCE

In addition to individual life insurance, group life insurance is also important in providing financial security to families. In 2000, group life insurance accounted for about 40 percent of the total amount of life insurance in force in the United States.[8] It is an important benefit that many employers provide to their employees.

Basic Characteristics

Group life insurance has certain basic characteristics.[9] First, numerous individuals are insured under a master contract, which contains relevant provisions concerning the coverage provided. There are only two parties to the master contract: the insurer and policyowner. In most cases, the group policyowner is the employer. Each individual insured receives a certificate of insurance, which provides evidence of coverage.

Second, if the group is sufficiently large, experience rating is used to determine premiums. Under experience rating, past losses sustained by the group are considered in determining the policy premium. The actual loss experience is a major factor in determining the premiums charged.

Third, individual members are not normally required to provide evidence of insurability. Group insurance underwriters evaluate the overall characteristics of the group of persons to be insured rather than the individual characteristics of each person in the group to determine whether the group is acceptable to the insurer.

Finally, for covered employees, the cost of group life insurance is generally lower than individual coverage because the employer may pay part or all of the cost, which reduces the cost to the employees. In addition, the life insurance provided is usually term insurance, which provides low-cost protection at younger ages.

Group Underwriting Factors

Based on state law and insurer practices, most groups today are eligible for group life insurance. These groups include individual employer groups, multiple-employer groups, trade associations, labor unions, and miscellaneous groups such as professional and alumni associations. However, before a group can be covered, insurers consider certain underwriting factors to determine whether the group is acceptable.

First, the group must not be formed solely for the purpose of purchasing insurance. This requirement protects the insurer against the possibility of a substandard group being formed solely to obtain insurance.

Second, ideally there should be a low turnover of persons in the group. Groups with high turnover will increase the administrative expenses under the plan. However, groups with low turnover will increase the average age of the group, which might result in higher premiums.

Third, the size of the group is an important underwriting factor. If the group is large, prior group loss experience can be used to determine the premium. In addition, experience rating can be used to adjust premiums for an adverse claims record.

Smaller groups are less desirable from an underwriting viewpoint. Traditionally, insurers required a minimum of ten lives, but insurers today often insure groups with as few as three lives. A small group, however, presents two important problems: (1) administrative expenses tend to be relatively higher than for large groups and (2) the employer or major stockholder might be interested in getting the insurance because of his or her own serious health problems. To deal with these problems, the insurer's underwriting practices might be more restrictive for small groups, such as less liberal contractual provisions and individual underwriting in some cases.

Noncontributory plan
Group plan in which the employer pays the entire cost.

In addition, minimum participation requirements are important in group underwriting. A minimum percentage of eligible employees must participate in the plan. The employer pays the entire cost in a **noncontributory plan**, and employees pay part or all of the cost in a **contributory plan**. If the plan is noncontributory, most insurers and many state laws require coverage of 100 percent of the eligible employees. If the plan is contributory, a lower

Contributory plan
Group plan in which employees pay part or all of the cost.

percentage of employees is required, such as 75 percent. A minimum participation requirement helps to protect the insurer against the possibility of insuring a large proportion of unhealthy lives.

Finally, some additional factors are considered in group underwriting. These include efficient administration, such as payroll deduction by employers; prior loss experience of the group; age and sex composition of the group; and occupational hazards in the industry that the group represents.

Eligibility Requirements

Employees must meet certain eligibility requirements before the coverage becomes effective. First, the employer may limit coverage to full-time employees. The employer determines the number of hours for full-time employment, which must be at least thirty hours weekly. However, depending on insurer practices, part-time employees may also be covered.

Second, in some group plans, new employees must satisfy a probationary period, which is a short waiting period of one to six months, before they can participate in the plan. The purpose of the probationary period is to eliminate coverage of transient workers who work for firms with high labor turnover.

In addition, if the plan is contributory, new employees must sign up for the insurance either before or during their eligibility period. The eligibility period is typically a thirty-one-day period during which the employee can sign up for the insurance with no evidence of insurability. If the employee requests coverage after the eligibility period expires, the insurer requires evidence of insurability to protect the insurer against adverse selection.

Finally, before the coverage becomes effective, the employee must be actively at work. If the employee is absent from work because of sickness or injury, coverage begins when the employee returns to work.

Group Life Insurance Benefits

Most group life insurance plans provide yearly renewable term insurance to the members. The amount of insurance is determined by a schedule. The amount can be based on earnings, position, or length of service, or it can be a flat amount for all. Most group term insurance plans provide an amount of insurance equal to some multiple of the employee's annual earnings, such as one or two times annual earnings. If service with the employer is terminated, the employee has the right to convert the term insurance to an individual cash value policy within thirty-one days with no evidence of insurability.

Many group life insurance plans also provide accidental death and dismemberment benefits that pay additional benefits if the employee dies in an accident or incurs certain types of injuries, such as the loss of both hands or the sight in both eyes. The amount paid for an accidental death is some multiple of the basic amount of insurance (called the principal sum), such as two times the principal sum.

Finally, many group plans make available dependent life insurance that provides modest amounts of life insurance on the lives of the employee's dependents. Dependents include the employee's spouse and unmarried dependent children over fourteen days of age but under a certain age, such as nineteen or twenty-one. The insurance on the life of the employee's spouse can be converted to a cash value policy. Some states, however, require that the conversion option apply to all dependents.

SUMMARY

Premature death can be defined as the death of a working person with outstanding or unfulfilled financial obligations, such as family members to support, children to educate, and a mortgage to pay off. The costs of premature death include the loss of income to the family, additional family expenses, possible decline in the family's standard of living, and noneconomic costs, such as grief and the loss of a role model for the children.

The financial impact of premature death on the surviving family members varies by type of family. If a single person with no dependents dies or a spouse in a two-income family with no children dies, that death is not likely to cause a serious financial problem for others. In contrast, premature death can cause great financial insecurity in a single-parent family; in a family with children in which both spouses work; and in a traditional, blended, or sandwiched family. The needs approach can be used to estimate the amount of life insurance these families need.

Term insurance provides only temporary protection and does not build cash values; however, term insurance policies are typically renewable for additional terms and also convertible to cash-value policies. In addition, premiums for term insurance increase with age, which makes term insurance unsuitable for lifetime protection. Typical term insurance policies provide level protection for a specified term, such as one, five, ten, or twenty years, or up to age sixty-five or seventy. Decreasing term insurance provides protection that declines over some time period, such as twenty or thirty years.

Whole life insurance provides level premiums and lifetime protection. Two basic types of whole life insurance are ordinary life and limited-payment life insurance. Ordinary life insurance provides lifetime protection to age 100 with level premiums paid periodically until the insured dies or reaches age 100. Limited-payment life insurance requires level premium payments for only a specified number of years, although the protection is for a lifetime. All whole life policies have cash values.

Universal life insurance is a flexible premium policy that has an investment feature and separates the protection, savings, and expense components. The policy has a guaranteed minimum interest rate and guaranteed cash values.

The policy also provides for the crediting of the cash value account with excess interest based on a higher current market rate of interest.

Life insurance policies contain a number of important contractual provisions, which include the incontestable clause, suicide clause, grace period, reinstatement clause, misstatement of age or sex provision, beneficiary designations, and assignment clause.

A participating policy is one that pays dividends. Several dividend options are typically available: cash, reduction of future premiums, accumulation at interest, paid-up additions, and one-year term insurance.

All states have nonforfeiture laws that require insurers to pay at least a minimum nonforfeiture value if a policyowner surrenders a cash value policy. There are three nonforfeiture options: cash, reduced paid-up life insurance, and extended term insurance. The cash value can also be borrowed under the policy loan provision in the policy.

Settlement options refer to the various ways that the policy proceeds can be paid other than in a lump sum. Typical settlement options include the interest option, fixed-period option, fixed-amount option, and various life income options.

Benefits can be added to a life insurance policy by an appropriate rider. Optional benefits include the waiver of premium provision, accidental death benefit rider, guaranteed insurability rider, cost-of-living rider, and accelerated death benefits rider.

Life insurance underwriting is based, in part, on the general principle of emphasizing the standard acceptable group in which most applicants are acceptable at standard rates. Important underwriting factors for individual life insurance include age, sex, build, physical condition, personal and family health history, smoking habits, involvement in hazardous sports or hobbies, personal habits and morals, country of residence, and occupation.

Group life insurance differs from individual life insurance in several respects. Many individuals can be insured under a master contract between the insurer and policyowner; experience rating is used in larger groups to determine the premiums charged; individual evidence of insurability is usually not required because group underwriters evaluate the overall characteristics of the group; and the coverage is usually low-cost protection to the employee.

Yearly renewable term insurance is the most common type of group life insurance used today. If membership in the group terminates, the employee can convert the term insurance to a cash-value policy within thirty-one days without evidence of insurability.

CHAPTER NOTES

1. George E. Rejda, *Social Insurance and Economic Security*, 5th ed. (Englewood Cliffs, N.J.: Prentice-Hall, Inc., 1994), pp. 52-55.

2. American Council of Life Insurers, *Life Insurers Fact Book 2001*(Washington, D.C.: American Council of Life Insurers, 2001), p. 104.

3. The material on individual life insurance in this chapter is based on George E. Rejda, *Principles of Risk Management and Insurance*, 5th ed. (New York: HarperCollins College Publishers, 1995), Chapters 15-17.

4. The discussion of current assumption whole life is based on Kenneth Black, Jr., and Harold D. Skipper, Jr., *Life Insurance*, 12th ed. (Englewood Cliffs, N.J.: Prentice-Hall, Inc., 1994), pp. 109-113.

5. Edward E. Graves, ed., *McGill's Life Insurance* (Bryn Mawr, Pa.: The American College, 1994), pp. 437-438.

6. Graves, pp. 438-451.

7. Graves, p. 451.

8. *Life Insurers Fact Book 2001*, p. 107.

9. This section is based on Graves, pp. 687-716, and Burton T. Beam, Jr., and John J. McFadden, *Employee Benefits*, 4th ed. (Chicago: Dearborn Financial Publishing, 1996), pp. 112-113.

Chapter 12

Direct

Direct Your Learning

Health and Disability Insurance

After learning the subject matter of this chapter, you should be able to:

■ Describe various healthcare problems in the United States.

■ Identify and describe types of private health insurance providers.

■ Describe the benefits provided by basic medical expense coverage.

■ Describe the basic types of major medical insurance.

■ Describe important provisions that apply to most group health insurance policies.

■ Describe the types of plans and cost control provisions of dental insurance.

■ Describe the typical benefits provided by and eligibility provisions required by long-term care insurance.

■ Describe the characteristics of managed care plans.

■ Describe the distinguishing features the following types of disability income insurance:

  • Individual disability income insurance

  • Group disability income plans

  • Social Security disability income benefits

■ Describe the following government programs for providing healthcare benefits:

  • Medicare

  • Medicare + Choice

  • Medicaid

  • Workers compensation

Develop Your Perspective

What are the main topics covered in the chapter?

Health and disability insurance provides protection against the loss exposures of poor health and injury. The major types of insurance that address these exposures are described in this chapter, along with healthcare problems in the United States.

Examine the healthcare and disability programs.

- What role does each of the programs play in addressing the potential financial loss that individuals and families face?

Why is it important to know these topics?

Access to adequate healthcare is considered a right in the United States. However, the expense of healthcare can be overwhelming without adequate insurance. For this reason, healthcare insurance is considered by many to be a necessity.

Assess the problems in healthcare in the United States.

- How do these problems change the healthcare that segments of the population receive?
- How is insurance involved in each of the healthcare problems?

How can you use this information?

Evaluate your own health and disability insurance needs:

- What would the financial consequences be without these coverages if you faced a serious illness?
- Which of the coverages best meets your needs?
- How might your coverage needs change as you age?

Chapter 12

Health and Disability Insurance

The adverse financial consequences of poor health are an important loss exposure that should receive high priority in a personal insurance program. When a person becomes seriously ill or injured, he or she might incur catastrophic medical bills. If the individual is in the labor force, wages are also lost. The loss of earnings can be substantial if the disability extends over a long period. Without proper protection, the sick or injured person might have to pay thousands of dollars in medical bills out of pocket and absorb the loss of earnings. For example, Tim, age twenty-eight, is a self-employed carpenter who experienced a sharp pain in his head. Diagnosis revealed a large tumor that required immediate surgery. The surgeon's fee, hospital bills, and other medical expenses exceeded $100,000. Tim did not have any health insurance. In addition, he was unable to work for several months after the surgery. He did not have any disability income insurance to restore the lost earnings. As a result, his savings were wiped out, and he was deeply in debt. He was eventually forced to declare bankruptcy. Because he had no health and disability insurance, Tim experienced serious financial difficulty as a result of his sickness.

This chapter discusses the major individual and group health insurance coverages available today. Topics include healthcare problems in the United States, private health insurance providers, basic medical expense coverages, major medical insurance, dental insurance, long-term care insurance, and disability income insurance. In addition, the chapter discusses various managed care plans, which are rapidly increasing in popularity. The chapter concludes with a discussion of government health insurance and healthcare plans.

HEALTHCARE PROBLEMS IN THE UNITED STATES

The United States can provide higher quality medical care than any other nation in the world. The high quality is due largely to new technology, scientific breakthroughs in medicine, and highly skilled medical personnel. However, despite the tremendous gains in medical knowledge and the development of new technology, there is considerable dissatisfaction with the present healthcare delivery system. The present system has four major problems:

- Rising healthcare expenditures
- Inadequate access to medical care

- Uneven quality of medical care
- Considerable waste, inefficiency, and fraud[1]

Rising Healthcare Expenditures

The first problem is that healthcare expenditures have increased substantially over time. Several factors explain the rise in healthcare spending. They include new and expensive medical technology, population growth that increases the demand for medical care, general price inflation, increased spending under Medicare and Medicaid and cost shifting by these programs to private insurers, aging of the population, and state-mandated private health insurance benefits. In addition, the tax subsidy and favorable tax treatment of group health insurance have encouraged the growth of expensive health insurance plans. Finally, the growth of private health insurance is another factor; private health insurance removes a financial barrier to care and increases the demand for medical care.

Inadequate Access to Medical Care

Another problem is inadequate access to care by certain groups. First, millions of Americans are uninsured and have no private or public health insurance. Groups with a high proportion of uninsured persons include small firms that cannot afford health insurance for their employees, single adults under age twenty-five, low-income families not eligible for government health insurance programs, and noncitizens, such as illegal and legal immigrants. Certain states also have a high proportion of uninsured residents, including Arizona, California, New Mexico, and Texas. In addition, people in rural areas often have inadequate access to healthcare because of the shortage of physicians in many small rural communities. Finally, because of inadequate reimbursement rates, some welfare recipients have experienced problems finding physicians who will treat them promptly.

Uneven Quality of Medical Care

A third problem is that the quality of medical care is not uniformly high throughout the United States but varies widely depending on geographic location and physician specialty.

In addition, treatment for the same medical condition varies by geographic location. For example, one study showed that residents of New Haven, Connecticut, were twice as likely to have coronary artery bypass surgery as residents of Boston, Massachusetts.[2]

Finally, many physicians are sued for medical malpractice, which indicates that many patients think physicians do not always provide high-quality medical care or adequate information. The cost of malpractice litigation and the resulting high cost of medical professional liability insurance also contribute substantially to the cost of healthcare.

Considerable Waste, Inefficiency, and Fraud

A final problem is waste and inefficiency in the present system. For example, healthcare providers and insurers are inundated by excessive paperwork; claim forms are not uniform; fraud and abuse by healthcare providers and patients are widespread; there is duplication of expensive technology in many cities; and the practice of defensive medicine by physicians in order to avoid lawsuits results in many unnecessary tests and procedures. Excess hospital capacity is another source of inefficiency, and statistics show that many hospitals could be closed with no resulting capacity problems.

In addition, research studies suggest that many surgical operations are unnecessary. One study showed that 20 percent of the operations for the installation of permanent pacemakers were not justified, and another 36 percent were of questionable value.[3]

PROVIDERS OF PRIVATE HEALTH INSURANCE

Most individuals and families are insured under private or group health insurance plans. Coverage is available from a number of sources. Major private health insurance providers include commercial insurers, Blue Cross and Blue Shield, and self-insured plans by employers.

Private insurers sell both individual and group medical expense coverages. However, most individuals and families are insured under some type of group health insurance plan. Individual coverages are relatively unimportant in terms of the total amount of health insurance. Group insurance premiums under various group arrangements, Blue Cross and Blue Shield plans, and self-insured plans now account for more than 90 percent of the total premiums paid for health insurance.[4]

Commercial Insurers

Private life and health insurers and some property and casualty insurers sell individual and group health insurance coverages. Most medical expense insurance coverages are written by fewer than 100 insurers, and more than half of the business is written by approximately 30 insurers.[5]

In addition, commercial insurers sponsor various managed care plans, including health maintenance organizations (HMOs) and preferred provider organizations (PPOs). Managed care plans are discussed in greater detail later in the chapter.

Blue Cross and Blue Shield Plans

Blue Cross and Blue Shield plans are typically nonprofit plans that cover hospital expenses, physician and surgeon fees, and related medical expenses.

The "Blues" also offer major medical insurance. The various plans provide individual, family, and group coverages.

Blue Cross plans cover hospital expenses and other related medical expenses. Service benefits rather than cash benefits are typically provided, and payment is made directly to the hospital instead of to the insured. Blue Shield plans pay for the services of physicians and surgeons and related medical expenses. Blue Cross and Blue Shield plans also sponsor managed care plans, which typically include HMOs and PPOs. Most plans today include both Blue Cross and Blue Shield coverages.

Self-Insured Plans

Many employers self-insure part or all of the health insurance benefits provided to their employees. Self-insurance, also called self-funding, means that the employer pays part or all of the employee's health claim costs.

Employers that self-insure typically purchase stop-loss insurance to cover excess losses. Stop-loss insurance means that a commercial insurer will pay claims in excess of certain dollar amounts up to some maximum limit specified in the contract.

In addition, employers that self-insure frequently enter into contracts with third-party administrators (TPAs) to manage the plans. A TPA contract is an arrangement by which an insurer or another independent organization receives a fee for handling certain administrative details, such as enrollment of employees, record keeping, and claim payments.

Self-insurance has several advantages to employers. Health insurance costs might be reduced or might increase less rapidly because of the savings in state premium taxes, commissions, and the insurer's profit. In addition, cash flow may be improved. The employer retains part or all of the funds needed to pay claims and earns interest on the money until the claims are paid. Finally, self-insured plans are usually exempt from state laws that require insured plans to offer certain mandated benefits.

Basic medical expense coverages
Coverage for medical expenses, such as hospital and surgical expenses, physicians' visits, and miscellaneous medical services.

BASIC MEDICAL EXPENSE COVERAGES

Some individual and group plans provide only basic protection. These plans generally cover routine medical expenses and might be inadequate if a catastrophic loss were to occur. **Basic medical expense coverages** include hospital expense insurance, surgical expense insurance, physicians' visits insurance, and coverage for additional medical services.

Hospital expense insurance
Insurance that covers medical expenses while the patient is in the hospital, such as daily room-and-board and miscellaneous expenses incurred during the hospital stay.

Hospital Expense Insurance

Hospital expense insurance pays for covered medical expenses while the patient is in the hospital. A typical policy pays daily room-and-board benefits and benefits for miscellaneous services and supplies provided during the hospital stay.

Two methods are commonly used to pay the daily room-and-board charge. An indemnity plan pays the actual daily charge up to some maximum dollar limit for a specified number of days, such as $500 daily for 120 days. A second type of plan provides service benefits, which means it pays up to the full cost of a semiprivate room for up to a specified number of days, typically from 31 to 365 days.

Hospital expense insurance typically includes ancillary charges, which are miscellaneous hospital charges such as drugs, laboratory fees, use of an operating room, and X-rays. Payment of such miscellaneous charges varies among insurers. Some plans pay the full cost up to a maximum dollar limit; the maximum limit may be a multiple of the daily room-and-board benefit, such as twenty times the daily benefit. Other plans pay the full cost up to a certain limit and a specified percentage after that limit is reached. For example, the plan may pay the first $2,000 in full and 75 percent of the next $3,000.

Surgical Expense Insurance

Basic plans commonly provide **surgical expense insurance**. Different methods are used to reimburse surgeons. Some older plans use a schedule approach in which the various surgical operations are listed in a schedule, and a maximum dollar amount is specified for each procedure. For example, the plan may pay a maximum of $600 to repair a broken leg and $3,000 for a heart valve replacement.

The majority of surgical expense plans reimburse physicians on the basis of their **usual, reasonable, and customary (URC) charges**. Physicians are reimbursed on the basis of their usual fee as long as the fee is reasonable and customary. Insurers differ in how they determine reasonable and customary fees. Many insurers consider a fee to be reasonable and customary if it does not exceed the ninetieth percentile for the same medical procedure performed by other physicians in the same geographic area. The patient must pay that portion of the fee in excess of the maximum allowed unless the physician accepts the amount allowed by the insurer.

Physicians' Visits Insurance

Physicians' visits insurance is another basic medical expense coverage. The coverage usually applies when the patient is in the hospital, but some plans also cover office and home visits.

Additional Benefits

Basic plans often provide coverage for additional medical services. They include the following:

- Outpatient surgery when surgery is performed in a hospital or an office but the patient recovers at home

Surgical expense insurance
Insurance that covers part or all of a physician's fee for a surgical operation.

Usual, reasonable, and customary (URC) charges
Charges for which physicians are reimbursed on the basis of their usual fee as long as the fee is reasonable and customary.

Physicians' visits insurance
Insurance that covers nonsurgical care provided by an attending physician other than a surgeon.

- Preadmission testing when diagnostic tests are given as an outpatient before admission to the hospital
- Diagnostic X-ray and laboratory expenses
- Home healthcare services by health professionals
- Extended-care facility services
- Hospice care

MAJOR MEDICAL INSURANCE

The basic coverages just discussed may be inadequate if a catastrophic loss occurs. The purpose of **major medical insurance** is to prevent the insured from being financially ruined by a catastrophic illness or injury. Although major medical insurance is sold on both individual and group bases, most insureds are covered under group plans.

Major medical insurance
Insurance that covers medical expenses resulting from illness or injury that are not covered by a basic medical expense plan.

Types of Major Medical Plans

There are two basic types of major medical plans: supplemental plans and comprehensive plans. The benefits payable under a basic plan may be exhausted, or the basic plan may not cover certain expenses. The supplemental major medical insurance plan covers medical expenses that exceed the limits of the underlying basic medical expense policy. The supplemental plan may also cover certain medical expenses not covered by the basic policy. A corridor deductible (discussed later) is used to integrate the basic medical expense plan with the supplemental major medical plan.

The second type of major medical insurance is the comprehensive major medical policy, which combines basic medical expense coverages and major medical insurance into one policy. This type of policy is widely used by employers who want both basic and major medical benefits in a single group plan.

Basic Characteristics

Both individual and group major medical insurance plans have certain basic characteristics.

Broad Coverage

Major medical insurance provides broad coverage for reasonable and necessary medical expenses from a covered illness or accident. Covered expenses typically include hospital room-and-board charges, miscellaneous hospital services and supplies, X-rays, diagnostic tests, physician and surgeon fees, prescription drugs, home healthcare services, durable medical equipment, and numerous additional expenses. The full cost of a semiprivate room is usually paid in full after the deductible is satisfied. Physicians are often reimbursed on the basis of their usual, reasonable, and customary charges.

High Lifetime Limits

Major medical plans are typically written with high lifetime limits of $250,000; $500,000; $1 million; or even higher. Some plans have no maximum limits. High limits are necessary to prevent the insured's financial ruin from a catastrophic illness or injury.

Deductible

Major medical insurance plans typically have deductible provisions. The purpose is to eliminate small claims and to hold down premiums. The deductible amount can range from $100 to $1,000 or higher amounts. The higher the deductible, the lower the premium.

Major medical plans contain different types of deductibles. A **calendar-year deductible** is widely used in comprehensive major medical plans. Once the deductible is satisfied, no additional deductible applies during the calendar year.

Calendar-year deductible
Medical insurance deductible an insured must meet only once during the calendar year.

The calendar-year deductible applies separately to each family member. However, to reduce the financial burden on the family, most major medical plans have a family deductible provision. A typical provision states that additional deductibles for family members will not be required if two separate deductibles have been satisfied by individual family members during the calendar year.

Many plans with calendar-year deductibles also have a deductible carry-over provision. Covered medical expenses incurred during the last three months of the calendar year that are applied to this year's deductible can be carried over to satisfy next year's deductible. For example, assume that Matthew is covered under a major medical plan with a $300 calendar-year deductible. He incurs covered medical expenses of $50 in May, $100 in October, and $125 in December, for a total of $275. Under the carry-over provision, the medical expenses incurred during October and December, a total of $225, can be applied towards next year's deductible. No carry over, however, is allowed if the deductible is satisfied before the last three months of the current year.

In addition, most major medical plans contain a common accident provision. This provision states that if two or more family members are injured in the same accident, the deductible for only one insured will apply to all covered medical expenses resulting from the common accident.

A **corridor deductible** is commonly used to integrate a basic medical expense plan with a supplemental major medical plan. A corridor deductible applies to medical expenses not paid or covered by the basic plan. The insured must satisfy a deductible before the supplemental major medical plan pays any benefits. As stated earlier, benefits under a basic plan may be exhausted, or certain expenses may not be covered. The supplemental major medical policy will cover these expenses after the deductible is satisfied. For example, assume that Jennifer is covered under both her employer's basic medical

Corridor deductible
Medical insurance deductible amount an insured must pay under a supplemental major medical insurance plan after the insured's medical expenses exceed the limits of the underlying basic medical expense plan.

expense plan and a supplemental major medical plan with an annual deductible of $300. Assume that she incurs covered medical expenses of $20,000, and that the basic plan pays only $18,000. The remaining $2,000 of medical expenses will be covered under the supplemental plan after the $300 deductible is satisfied. The supplemental plan will pay $1,700 less any coinsurance charges. This example is summarized as follows:

Covered medical expenses	$20,000
Paid by basic medical expense plan	– 18,000
Remaining expenses	2,000
Corridor deductible paid by Jennifer	– 300
Paid by supplemental major medical plan	$ 1,700

Coinsurance Provision

Coinsurance

Medical insurance provision that requires the insured to pay part of the covered medical expenses in excess of the deductible.

Major medical plans typically contain a **coinsurance** provision (also called a percentage participation clause). Major medical plans typically require the insurer to pay 80 percent of the covered expenses in excess of the deductible; the insured pays 20 percent. The purposes of coinsurance are to hold down premiums and to reduce overuse of plan benefits by requiring the insured to pay part of the cost.

For example, assume that Michelle has a comprehensive major medical plan with a $1 million lifetime limit, an 80 percent coinsurance percentage, and a $500 calendar-year deductible. She incurs covered medical expenses of $20,500 during the calendar year. The insurer will pay $16,000, and she will pay $4,000 (plus the $500 deductible). This example is summarized as follows:

Covered medical expenses	$20,500
Less calendar-year deductible	– 500
Remaining expenses	20,000
80 percent paid by insurer	– 16,000
20 percent paid by Michelle	$ 4,000

Stop-loss provision

Insurance provision that limits the amount the insured must pay by reimbursing 100 percent of covered expenses in excess of this limit for the rest of the calendar year.

Major medical plans typically have a **stop-loss provision** that limits the amount the insured must pay. All covered expenses in excess of the stop-loss limit are reimbursed at a rate of 100 percent for the rest of the calendar year. Some plans allow the deductible to be included in the stop-loss limit, but others do not. In addition, many group plans have a per-person stop-loss limit, such as $1,000, and a stop-loss limit for the entire family, such as $2,000. In the previous example, Michelle had to pay $4,000 plus the $500 deductible, for a total of $4,500. If Michelle's plan had a per-person stop-loss limit of $1,000 applying to covered expenses in excess of the deductible, Michelle would pay only $1,000 plus the $500 deductible, for a total of $1,500. If Michelle's plan allowed the deductible to be included in the stop-loss limit, Michelle would pay only $1,000.

Exclusions and Internal Limits

Although major medical plans provide broad coverage, they contain several exclusions. Common exclusions include eyeglasses and hearing aids, elective cosmetic surgery, experimental surgery, expenses covered by a workers compensation law, expenses in excess of usual and customary charges, and services furnished by governmental agencies unless the patient has an obligation to pay. To control cost, major medical plans also contain internal limits, which are maximum amounts payable for certain covered medical services. For example, there may be limits on the maximum amounts paid each year for alcohol and drug addiction treatment.

IMPORTANT GROUP HEALTH INSURANCE PROVISIONS

Group health policies do not have standard policy provisions, and coverages vary widely. However, certain important provisions apply to most group health insurance policies, and some are mandated by law.

Preexisting Conditions

Group major medical plans and other group health insurance plans may contain a **preexisting conditions clause** that excludes coverage for a preexisting medical condition for a limited period after an insured enters the plan. A preexisting condition is a medical condition that existed before the effective date of the policy. After the waiting period expires, the condition is no longer considered preexisting and would be covered subject to any other limitations in the plan. The purposes of this clause are to reduce adverse selection against the insurer and to hold down the employer's costs.

Preexisting conditions clause
A health insurance provision that excludes coverage for any preexisting medical condition (one that existed before the policy effective date) for a limited period after an insured enters the plan.

In 1996, Congress enacted the Health Insurance Portability and Accountability Act, which restricts the right of employers and insurers to exclude or limit coverage for preexisting conditions. This law guarantees that most workers who change jobs or lose jobs will have access to health insurance coverage. It prohibits employers and insurers that offer health insurance plans from dropping people from coverage because they are sick, or from imposing waiting periods for preexisting conditions for more than twelve months (eighteen months for late enrollees). It also requires employers and health insurers to give credit for previous coverage so that workers who maintain continuous health insurance coverage (without a gap of sixty-three days) can never be excluded because of a preexisting condition.

The major provisions of the law dealing with preexisting conditions are summarized as follows:

- Employer-sponsored group health insurance plans are prohibited from excluding or limiting coverage for a pre-existing condition for more than twelve months (eighteen months for late enrollees). A preexisting condition is defined in the law as a medical condition that is diagnosed or treated during the six months before the enrollment date in the plan.

In addition, a preexisting condition exclusion cannot be applied to pregnancy, newly born children, or adopted children.

- Once the twelve-month period expires, no new preexisting condition period may ever be imposed on workers who maintain continuous coverage, with no more than a sixty-three day gap, even if they change jobs or health plans.

- Employers and insurers must give credit for previous coverage of fewer than twelve months with respect to any preexisting condition exclusion under a new health insurance plan. For example, a person previously covered for nine months under a group plan when he or she changes jobs or health plans would face a maximum additional exclusion of three months for a preexisting condition, rather than the normal twelve months.

- Discrimination against employees and dependents based on health status is prohibited. Employers offering health insurance coverage to employees and dependents are prohibited from excluding or dropping an individual's coverage based on health status. Charging higher premiums based on an individual's health status is also prohibited. Health status is broadly defined to include medical condition, which includes both physical and mental illness, claims experience, receipt of healthcare, medical history, genetic information, evidence of insurability (including conditions arising out of acts of domestic violence), and disability.

- The legislation guarantees the availability of health insurance coverage for small employers. Insurers, HMOs, and other entities issuing health insurance coverages are prohibited from denying coverage to employers that employ between two and fifty employees.

Because the new law places limits on preexisting conditions and provides credit for prior continuous coverage, workers are no longer locked into their jobs for fear of losing their health insurance protection. As a result, workers can change jobs and still be assured health insurance coverage.

Portability
Characteristic of a health plan that requires a new employer or health plan to give credit for prior, continuous health insurance coverage.

However, **portability** does not mean that workers can take their present health insurance coverage with them when they leave their current jobs. Instead, it means that when workers change jobs, the new employer or health plan must give them credit for prior, continuous health insurance coverage. When an employee leaves a job, the employer or insurer must provide information showing how long the employee was covered while working at that job. He or she will then be required to present this documentation to the new employer or health plan. If a worker has been covered for twelve months or more by the previous employer or health plan and does not have a gap in coverage of more than sixty-three days, the worker is eligible for coverage under the new employer's plan even if he or she has a preexisting condition.

The law establishes only federal minimum standards for preexisting conditions and portability. States are free to adopt shorter preexisting condition periods to provide greater protection to workers and dependents.

Continuation of Group Health Insurance

Workers frequently quit their jobs, are laid off, or are fired. Terminated employees and covered dependents can retain their group health insurance for a limited period by electing to remain in the employer's plan under the Consolidated Omnibus Budget Reconciliation Act of 1985 (COBRA). The COBRA law applies to employers of twenty or more employees. Under COBRA, employees and covered dependents can elect to remain in the employer's plan for a limited period after a qualifying event occurs that results in the loss of coverage. Qualifying events include termination of employment for any reason (except gross misconduct), death of the employee, divorce or legal separation, and attainment of a maximum age by dependent children. If employment terminates, or if the worker no longer satisfies the requirements for hours worked, the terminated employee and insured dependents can elect to remain in the group plan for up to eighteen months. If the employee dies, is divorced or legally separated, or has a child who is no longer eligible for coverage, insured dependents can elect to remain in the group plan for up to thirty-six months. Insureds who elect to remain in the group plan can be required to pay up to 102 percent of the group rate.

After the period of COBRA protection expires, many persons with preexisting conditions often cannot obtain individual health insurance coverage, and employees in firms with fewer than twenty employees do not have access to COBRA at all. The Health Insurance Portability and Accountability Act guarantees the availability of individual health insurance to eligible individuals who meet the following criteria: (1) they have had employment-based health insurance for at least eighteen months, (2) they are ineligible for COBRA or have exhausted their COBRA coverage, and (3) they are ineligible for coverage under any other employment-based health plan. As a result, eligible individuals who meet the preceding requirements are guaranteed individual health insurance coverage.

Coordination-of-Benefits Provision

In many families, a spouse or dependent child may be covered under two group medical expense plans. Duplication can occur when each spouse is covered as an employee under a separate group health insurance plan, and one spouse or child is also covered as a dependent under the other spouse's plan. To prevent overinsurance and duplication of benefits, group medical expense plans typically contain a **coordination-of-benefits provision.**

The coordination-of-benefits provisions in group medical expense plans are usually based on the rules developed by the National Association of Insurance Commissioners (NAIC). These rules are complex and cover numerous family situations. The major rules are as follows:[6]

- The plan covering the employee is primary; the other plan pays second.
- If the claimant is a dependent child whose parents are not divorced or

Coordination-of-benefits provision
Provision that indicates the order of payment when an insured is covered under two or more group health insurance plans; limits the insured's total recovery under all applicable policies to 100 percent of covered expenses.

separated, the plan of the parent whose birthday occurs first during the year is primary; the other plan pays second.

- The claimant may be a dependent child whose parents are divorced or separated. If a court decree states that one parent is responsible for health insurance on the child, that parent's plan is primary. The other plan pays second.

- If no court decree requires a parent to provide health insurance on a dependent child, the plan of the parent who has custody and has not remarried is primary. The other plan pays second.

- If the parent who has custody of a dependent child has remarried, that parent's plan is primary. The stepparent's plan pays second, and the plan of the parent without custody pays third.

- If none of the preceding rules applies, the plan that has covered the claimant for the longest period of time will pay its benefits first.

DENTAL INSURANCE

Dental insurance is a form of health insurance that covers normal dental care and damage to teeth in an accident. The coverage is available under individual plans, but most insureds are covered under group plans. Dental insurance has the major advantage of helping employees and covered dependents pay for the cost of routine dental care. The coverage also encourages insureds to regularly see a dentist, who can detect or prevent serious dental problems.

Types of Group Dental Plans

There are two major types of group dental plans.[7] One type is a scheduled plan in which covered dental services are listed in a schedule and a specific dollar amount is paid for each service. Most scheduled plans do not have deductibles or coinsurance. However, the benefits paid are usually lower than the usual, reasonable, and customary charges of dentists. If a dentist charges a fee in excess of the specified amount, the patient must pay the difference unless the dentist agrees to accept the insurer's scheduled amount.

A nonscheduled dental plan is the most common type of dental plan. In a nonscheduled plan (also called a comprehensive plan), most dental services are covered, and dentists are reimbursed on the basis of their usual, reasonable, and customary charges subject to any limitations on benefits stated in the plan. Covered services typically include oral examinations, cleaning, fillings, X-rays, orthodontia, extractions, and dentures.

Nonscheduled plans usually have an annual deductible and a coinsurance provision, such as a $50 annual deductible and 80 percent coinsurance. However, to encourage regular visits to a dentist, diagnostic and preventive services (such as routine oral exams) may not be subject to the annual deductible or coinsurance requirement. Expensive services, such as crowns, dentures, and orthodontics, may be reimbursed at a lower percentage, such as 50 percent.

Cost Controls

Dental insurance plans have a number of provisions to help control costs. They include the following:

- In addition to deductibles and coinsurance, the plan may have maximum limits on benefits, such as $2,000 annually.

- New employees may have to meet a waiting period before certain dental expenses are covered, such as twelve months for orthodontia.

- To deal with adverse selection, employees desiring coverage after their eligibility period expires might have to meet a waiting period, such as one or two years, or might have reduced benefits.

- Certain dental expenses are excluded, such as cosmetic dental work, lost or duplicate dentures, and expenses covered by workers compensation.

- Most plans contain a predetermination-of-benefits provision. If the estimated cost of treatment exceeds a certain amount, such as $200, the dentist submits to the insurer a plan of treatment, which specifies the services needed. The insurer then determines the amount the plan will pay. If the amount to be paid is lower than the estimated cost of treatment, the patient can seek less costly care.

LONG-TERM CARE INSURANCE

Long-term care insurance is an important coverage that merits some discussion. Studies show that at least 40 percent of all persons who have reached age sixty will enter a nursing home at some time during their lifetime. The majority of people live in a nursing home for less than one year, and the average nursing-home stay is often said to be 2.5 years. It can be misleading to use these "typical" or "average" statistics as a basis for financial planning. People face a significant risk of a lengthy stay. According to one analysis based on 1999 survey data, 4 percent of men and 7 percent of women discharged from nursing homes had stayed in a nursing home longer than five years.[8]

Long-term care insurance
Insurance that pays for extended medical care or custodial care received in a nursing home, hospital, or home.

The cost of long-term care is staggering. The average cost of a year in a nursing home is estimated at $46,000, and it can be twice that amount in some areas.[9] The Medicare program does not cover long-term care in a nursing facility. Medicare covers only skilled nursing care up to a maximum of 100 days; custodial care is excluded altogether. In addition, most aged patients in nursing homes do not initially qualify for long-term care under the Medicaid program, which is a welfare program with stringent eligibility requirements. As a result, many older Americans have purchased long-term care insurance to pay for the huge medical bills that result from an extended stay in a nursing home.[10]

Benefits Provided

Purchasers of long-term care insurance typically have a choice of benefits, such as a daily benefit of up to $80, $120, or $160, that are paid over a maximum period of two, three, or four years, or for the insured's lifetime. Some plans allow purchasers to select maximum lifetime benefits, such as a $300,000 lifetime maximum.

The policies typically cover skilled nursing home care, intermediate nursing care, and custodial care. Skilled nursing care is medical care provided by skilled medical personnel twenty-four hours a day under the supervision of a physician, such as care by registered nurses or physical therapists. Intermediate nursing care is care for a stable condition that requires daily care but not twenty-four hour nursing supervision. Custodial care assists the patient in the activities of daily living, such as dressing, bathing, eating, and using the toilet.

Many policies also cover home healthcare services. Some plans cover only skilled nursing care provided in the home by registered nurses and other skilled personnel. Other plans are broader and also cover home health aides provided by licensed agencies. However, few policies cover the cost of having someone come into the home to cook meals, clean the house, or run errands.

Elimination Period

Elimination period
Initial time period in a health insurance or disability income policy during which benefits are not paid.

Most long-term care plans are sold with an **elimination period** that functions like a "time deductible." In other words, coverage does not begin until after a certain time has elapsed. Elimination periods can range from 0 to 365 days. A longer elimination period can substantially reduce the annual premium. Common elimination periods are 30, 60, 100, or 180 days.

Eligibility for Benefits

All long-term care policies have "gatekeeper" provisions that determine whether the insured is eligible for benefits under the policy. A gatekeeper provision states the requirements that the insured must meet to receive benefits. A common type of gatekeeper provision requires that the insured be unable to perform a certain number of activities of daily living, commonly referred to as ADLs. These activities include eating, bathing, walking, dressing, moving from the bed to a chair, using the toilet, and maintaining continence. Benefits can be paid if the insured cannot perform a certain number of ADLs (such as two out of five) without help from another person.

Protection Against Inflation

Inflation can substantially erode the real value of long-term care insurance benefits, especially if the policy is purchased by a young person. For example, assuming an annual inflation rate of 5 percent, a daily charge of $120 will increase to $318 in twenty years.[11]

Protection against inflation is usually available as an optional benefit. Insurers use two major methods for providing protection against inflation. Some plans allow insureds to purchase additional amounts of insurance in the future with no evidence of insurability. The premium is based on the insured's current age, but evidence of insurability is not required.

Some plans provide for an automatic benefit increase in which the daily benefit is increased by a specified percentage for a number of years, such as 5 percent annually for the next ten or twenty years. Adding an automatic benefit increase to a long-term policy is expensive and may double the annual premium in some cases, especially if an older person purchases the policy.

Guaranteed Renewability

Most individual long-term care policies sold today are guaranteed renewable. Once the policy has been issued, it cannot be canceled. However, premiums can be increased for the underwriting class in which the insured is placed.

Cost

Long-term care insurance is expensive, especially if the policy is purchased by older individuals. For example, one plan that pays a daily benefit of $100 for a maximum of four years with a seven-day elimination period has an annual premium of $740 if a sixty-year-old purchases it. If purchased when that person is seventy-nine, the same policy would cost $5,190 annually.

MANAGED CARE PLANS[12]

To control the escalation in healthcare costs, insurers and employers have developed **managed care** plans that differ substantially from traditional group health insurance plans described earlier. These plans generally limit the choice of physicians and other healthcare providers to those who are affiliated with the plan. The plans monitor the quality of medical care provided and emphasize preventive care and healthy lifestyles for plan members.

Managed care
Medical insurance plans that provide coverage for cost-effective medical services provided to plan members.

Many managed care plans exist today, including the following:

- Health maintenance organizations
- Preferred provider organizations
- Exclusive provider organizations
- Point-of-service plans

Health Maintenance Organization

A **health maintenance organization (HMO)** is a managed care plan that provides a wide range of comprehensive healthcare services to a specific group for a fixed, prepaid fee. In 1998, about 30 percent of employees in an employer-sponsored health plan were enrolled in HMOs.[13]

Health maintenance organization (HMO)
Managed care plan that provides a range of comprehensive healthcare services to its members for a fixed, prepaid fee; members' choice of healthcare providers is usually restricted to those in the HMO network.

HMOs have certain common characteristics. First, an HMO provides comprehensive healthcare services to its members. Covered services typically include hospital care, physicians' and surgeons' services, laboratory and X-ray services, outpatient services, maternity care, and numerous other services. Most services are covered in full with few maximum limits on individual services. In addition, office visits to HMO physicians are covered in full, or a nominal fee is charged for each visit.

Second, plan members' choice of physicians and other healthcare providers is usually restricted to providers who are part of the plan network. However, some plans cover medical care obtained outside the network. Because an HMO operates in a limited geographic area, coverage of medical care received outside that geographic area is usually limited to emergency medical treatment.

Third, plan members pay a fixed, prepaid premium for the services provided. Most covered services are not subject to deductibles or coinsurance. However, many HMOs impose copayment charges for treatment of alcohol and drug addiction and outpatient treatment of mental illness. Also, as stated earlier, nominal fees may be charged for certain services, such as $10 for a prescription drug or a doctor's office visit.

In addition, HMOs emphasize cost controls. Physicians may be paid a salary and an incentive bonus based on plan experience; costs may be reduced because physicians have no financial incentive to provide unnecessary services for additional fees. In addition, the HMO enters into contracts with specialists and other healthcare providers who agree to provide certain services at predetermined, negotiated fees. Also, if patients want to see a specialist, they must first get approval from a "gatekeeper physician." The gatekeeper physician is a primary-care physician who determines whether a patient should be referred to a specialist. HMOs also monitor network physicians to determine whether certain physicians are prescribing excessive or unnecessary diagnostic tests and procedures. Finally, physicians may be required to get approval from the HMO before certain types of treatment can be given.

Preferred Provider Organization

Preferred provider organization (PPO)
Managed care plan that contracts with healthcare providers for medical services provided to plan members at discounted fees; members' choice of healthcare providers is not restricted, but members have a financial incentive to choose contracted providers.

A **preferred provider organization (PPO)** is a plan that contracts with healthcare providers to provide medical services to plan members at discounted fees. To encourage plan members to receive treatment from preferred providers, deductibles and coinsurance charges are reduced or eliminated. Plan members are not required to receive treatment from a preferred provider but have a financial incentive to do so because their out-of-pocket cost will be less.

Exclusive Provider Organization

Exclusive provider organization (EPO)
Managed care plan that pays only for medical care received within the network of preferred providers.

An **exclusive provider organization (EPO)**, unlike a PPO, is a managed care plan that does not pay for medical care received outside the network of preferred providers. As a result, if plan members receive care outside the network, they must pay the cost themselves.

Point-of-Service Plan

A **point-of-service (POS) plan** is a newer type of managed care plan that combines the characteristics of an HMO and a PPO. The point-of-service plan has a network of preferred providers. If plan members receive care from healthcare providers who are part of the network, they pay little or nothing out of pocket. However, if care is received outside the network, the care is covered, but the patient must pay substantially higher coinsurance charges and a deductible. For example, if the patient sees a physician outside the network, he or she might pay an annual deductible of $500 and a coinsurance charge of 30 percent.

A point-of-service plan has the major advantage of preserving freedom of choice for plan members by making it possible to see a physician or specialist of their choice. However, the major disadvantage is the higher out-of-pocket cost that the member must pay.

Advantages of Managed Care Plans

Managed care plans offer a number of advantages to insurers, employers, and employees. One advantage is that healthcare costs can be held down because these plans emphasize cost controls. One study showed that the average cost per enrollee was less under managed care plans than under traditional group indemnity plans.[14]

Another advantage is that plan members often pay little or no out-of-pocket costs for covered medical services. Under HMOs, most covered services are covered in full without deductibles or coinsurance charges (except modest copayment charges for office visits and prescription drugs). Under PPOs, deductibles and coinsurance charges are reduced when preferred providers are used. As a result, out-of-pocket costs for covered services are reduced.

In addition, managed care plans provide many loss-prevention services, such as routine physical examinations, Pap smears, immunizations, well-child care, and eye examinations.

Finally, managed care plans generally have lower hospital and surgical utilization rates, and employees do not have to file claim forms.

Disadvantages of Managed Care Plans

One major criticism of managed care plans is that the emphasis on cost control may reduce the quality of care provided to some patients. For example, critics argue that some HMO gatekeeper physicians are slow in referring sick patients to specialists because of the additional cost to the plan; certain diagnostic tests might not be prescribed; and some patients who should be hospitalized are not.

Point-of-service (POS) plan
Managed care plan that combines the characteristics of an HMO and a PPO; has a network of preferred providers who, if used by the member, charge little or nothing for services; healthcare received out of the network is covered, but members must pay substantially higher coinsurance charges and a deductible.

In addition, managed care plans often provide a financial incentive, such as a bonus to network physicians, to hold down costs. As a result, critics argue that plan physicians have a conflict of interest between providing high-quality medical care to their patients and holding down costs in order to improve the profitability of the plan.

Some HMO network physicians are also critical of managed care plans. HMO physicians are not free to treat patients without restrictions. For example, plan physicians may be required to obtain approval from plan administrators before certain tests and procedures are given; physicians often must justify the medical care provided to patients and may have to argue for additional hospital days or additional care for the patients; and prescription drugs may be limited to drugs on an approved list. As a result, many plan physicians believe that an outside third party is now compromising the traditional doctor-patient relationship.

DISABILITY INCOME INSURANCE

Disability income insurance
Insurance that pays periodic income payments to an insured who is unable to work because of sickness or injury.

If a serious illness or accident occurs, individuals could lose their earnings in addition to incurring catastrophic medical expenses. **Disability income insurance** is important in a personal insurance program because the financial consequences of a long-term disability can be severe, especially if the disability occurs at a young age. For example, the probability that a person age twenty-five will be disabled for at least ninety days before age sixty-five is 54 percent, as shown in Exhibit 12-1. If the disability extends over a long period, the disabled person loses his or her earnings; medical bills are incurred; employee benefits might be lost; savings might be depleted; and someone might have to care for the disabled person. Disability income insurance should receive high

EXHIBIT 12-1

Probability of Becoming Disabled for at Least Ninety Days Before Age Sixty-Five

Age	Probability
25	54%
30	52
35	50
40	48
45	44
50	39
55	32
60	9

Based on 1985 Commissioners Disability Table

Source: Adapted from Edward E. Graves, ed., *McGill's Life Insurance* (Bryn Mawr, Pa.: The American College, 2000), Table 7-2, p. 168.

priority in a personal insurance program. Disability income insurance is available from several sources, including the following:

- Individual disability income insurance
- Group disability income insurance
- Social Security disability income benefits

Individual Disability Income Insurance

An individual disability income insurance policy pays monthly cash benefits to an insured who becomes totally disabled from sickness or injury. Specific limits and provisions apply to individual disability policies.

Limit on Amount of Disability Income

Most insurers limit the amount of disability income to no more than 60 to 80 percent of the worker's earnings for several reasons. Benefits received under group plans paid by the employer are taxable income to the disabled worker, but the worker might not have to pay withholding tax if he or she is disabled under Social Security rules. Because the insured will have no taxes, or fewer taxes to pay on disability income benefits, the benefits can be lower than the insured's normal, taxable income and provide the same amount of spendable income. Also, if disability benefits match or exceed an insured's (after-tax) pre-disability income, the insured might be tempted to malinger (pretend to be incapacitated in order to avoid work). An insured with a relatively high disability income might attempt to extend the period of disability, thus postponing the return to work.

Definition of Total Disability

The meaning of total disability varies among insurers. According to the most liberal definition, *total disability means that the insured is unable to perform the major duties of his or her own occupation.* For example, a dentist who loses a hand in a hunting accident would be considered totally disabled under this definition. The dentist could no longer engage in his or her own occupation.

In a second, less liberal definition, *total disability means that the insured is unable to perform the duties of any gainful occupation for which he or she is reasonably suited by education, training, and experience.* Thus, in the previous example, if the dentist could work as a research scientist for a dental supply firm, he or she would not be considered disabled because this position is consistent with the dentist's training and experience.

Many policies use a dual definition of total disability that combines the two preceding definitions. For some initial time period, such as one to five years, total disability is defined in terms of the insured's own occupation. After the initial period expires, the insured is considered totally disabled only if he or she is unable to perform the duties of any gainful occupation to which he or she is reasonably suited by training, education, and experience.

Finally, a definition of presumptive disability may also appear in the policy. Total disability is presumed to exist if the insured loses the sight of both eyes or the use of both hands, both feet, or one hand and one foot.

Residual Disability

Many plans have a residual disability benefit or make it available as an additional benefit. A residual disability benefit means a pro rata benefit is paid when a disabled person returns to work but has a reduction in earned income. The insured must experience an earnings reduction of at least 20 or 25 percent before a pro rata benefit is paid. If the loss of earnings exceeds 75 or 80 percent, many plans will pay the full monthly disability benefit. For example, Megan, age twenty-eight, earns $2,000 monthly. She is totally disabled because of a broken leg suffered in a skiing accident. When she returns to work, she can work only part-time. Her monthly earnings average only $1,000, or a reduction of 50 percent from her normal earnings. If she has a disability income policy that pays $1,200 monthly, she would receive a monthly residual benefit of $600 (50 percent of the full monthly benefit).

Elimination Period

Disability income policies typically have an elimination period during which disability income benefits are not paid. The policyowner has a choice of elimination periods, such as thirty, sixty, or ninety days; six months; or one or two years. Premiums are reduced as the length of the elimination period increases.

Most insurers have discontinued selling policies with an elimination period of fourteen days or less, and elimination periods of thirty days or more are now the rule. In recent years, insurers have increased the rates on policies sold with elimination periods of thirty or sixty days, which have made them unattractive to many insurance consumers.[15] As a result, many policyowners now choose a ninety-day elimination period, which lowers their premiums.

Benefit Period

The policyowner has a choice of benefit period, the period of time that disability benefits are payable after the elimination period has been satisfied. Typical benefit periods are one, two, five, or ten years, or up to age sixty-five or seventy.

Most disabilities are of short duration; about 98 percent of all disabled individuals recover within the first year of becoming disabled.[16] Although most disabilities are short, a one-year benefit period is generally not adequate for most insureds. For example, if an insured becomes disabled at age twenty-two and remains disabled for one year, the probability of remaining disabled for at least five more years is 32 percent.[17] The longer the disability lasts, the less likely a disabled person will recover promptly. Thus, because of uncertainty concerning the duration of disability, most insureds should elect a benefit period longer than one year. Although more expensive, a policy that pays benefits to age sixty-five or seventy is highly desirable.

Renewability of the Policy

The renewability provisions in an individual disability income policy refer to the length of time the disability income policy can remain in force. The most important renewability provisions are as follows:

- Guaranteed renewable
- Noncancelable
- Conditionally renewable

Most policies sold today are guaranteed renewable. A **guaranteed renewable policy** cannot be canceled after it has been issued, and the insurer guarantees renewal to some stated age, such as age sixty-five or seventy. However, the premiums are not guaranteed. The insurer has the right to increase premiums for the underwriting class in which the insured is placed.

A **noncancelable policy** cannot be canceled, and the insurer guarantees renewal to some stated age, typically to age sixty-five. In addition, the premiums are guaranteed and cannot be increased by the insurer during that period. If the insured is working full-time, the policy may permit renewal beyond age sixty-five. When the insured reaches age sixty-five, the insurer has the right to increase the premiums if the insured decides to renew and is employed full-time. As long as the higher premium is paid and the insured is employed full-time, the policy can be continued to some stated age, typically age seventy-five.[18]

Finally, a disability policy may be conditionally renewable, a provision often used to cover individuals who work in hazardous occupations. A **conditionally renewable policy** is one in which the insurer agrees to renew the policy to some stated age, provided the insured meets certain qualifications. Full-time employment is the most common requirement to continue the policy. In addition, some association or franchise plans require the insured to be a member of the association to continue the policy.[19] Premiums can be increased under a conditionally renewable policy. However, the policy cannot be canceled as long as the insured meets the qualification requirements and the premium is paid on time.

Waiver of Premium

Disability income policies typically contain a waiver-of-premium provision, which states that if the insured is totally disabled for ninety days, premiums due after the initial ninety-day period will be waived as long as the insured remains disabled. There is also a refund of the premiums paid during the initial ninety-day period.

Guaranteed renewable policy
Policy that cannot be canceled after it has been issued; insurer maintains the right to increase premiums for classes of insureds.

Noncancelable policy
Policy that cannot be canceled or non-renewed until some stated age; insurer cannot increase premiums before that time.

Conditionally renewable policy
Policy that guarantees renewal to a specified time, provided the insured meets certain qualifications.

Optional Disability Income Benefits

Several optional benefits are available, depending on the insured's needs and desires. They include the following:

- *Social Security offset rider*. To prevent overinsurance, the amount of disability income insurance an individual can purchase may be reduced by estimated Social Security disability benefits. However, Social Security disability benefits are difficult to obtain because of strict eligibility requirements. The Social Security offset rider pays an additional amount of disability income benefits if the insured is denied Social Security benefits.

- *Cost of living rider*. Under this rider, the disability benefits payable to a disabled person are periodically increased based on the Consumer Price Index. The purpose is to maintain the real purchasing power of the benefits during an extended disability. The rider is costly and can increase premiums by 25 to 50 percent.

- *Guaranteed insurability rider*. The insured's income might increase, and he or she might desire additional disability income benefits. Under this rider, the insured has the right to purchase additional amounts of disability income coverage with no evidence of insurability.

Group Disability Income Insurance

Many employers have disability income insurance plans that pay weekly or monthly cash benefits to disabled workers. These plans fall into two categories: short-term plans and long-term plans.[20]

Short-Term Plans

Short-term plans pay disability income benefits to eligible workers for relatively short periods, typically ranging from thirteen weeks to two years. Most plans pay benefits for thirteen or twenty-six weeks. The benefit amount is usually a specified percentage of weekly earnings up to some maximum limit, such as 50 to 70 percent of earnings but not to exceed a stated amount.

Short-term plans typically have a short elimination period that ranges from one to seven days for sickness. However, accidents are covered from the first day of disability. The elimination period holds down cost and reduces absenteeism and malingering.

Most short-term plans cover only nonoccupational disabilities that occur off the job; workers compensation (covered later in the chapter) pays benefits for job-related disabilities. Disability is usually defined in terms of an individual's own occupation; workers are considered totally disabled if they are unable to perform every duty of their regular occupation. Partial disabilities are not covered.

Long-Term Plans

Many employers also have long-term disability plans that pay disability benefits for longer periods than short-term plans. Maximum benefit periods typically range from two years to age sixty-five; however, for disabilities occurring after age sixty-five, the benefits are paid for a limited duration. A common approach today is to pay benefits to age sixty-five to workers who become disabled before a specified age; for workers disabled after that age, the duration of benefits is reduced. Exhibit 12-2 shows a sample maximum benefit period.

EXHIBIT 12-2

Sample Maximum Benefit Period for a Long-Term Disability Insurance Plan

Age at Disability	Maximum Benefit Period
Younger than age 60	To age 65
60	60 months
61	48 months
62	42 months
63	36 months
64	30 months
65	24 months
66	21 months
67	18 months
68	15 months
69 and older	12 months

Most long-term plans cover both occupational and nonoccupational disability. A dual definition of disability is commonly used. For some initial time period, such as two years, workers are considered disabled if they are unable to perform the major duties of *their regular occupation*. After that time, the workers are considered disabled only if they are unable to work in *any gainful occupation* for which they are reasonably suited by training, education, and experience.

Maximum monthly benefits are usually limited to 50 to 70 percent of the worker's normal earnings up to some monthly maximum. The monthly benefits are substantially higher than those in short-term plans. Some plans pay maximum monthly benefits of $4,000, $5,000, or other amounts.

The disabled worker must satisfy an elimination period of three to six months before benefits are paid. In addition, if the disabled worker is receiving Social

Security disability benefits or workers compensation benefits, the monthly benefit is reduced to prevent overinsurance and malingering.

Certain supplemental benefits may also be available. The plan may have a pension accrual benefit; the insurer makes a contribution to the disabled worker's retirement plan so that retirement benefits continue to accrue. In addition, the plan may also provide a cost-of-living adjustment by which the disability income benefits paid are periodically adjusted for increases in the cost of living. Finally, the plan may pay a monthly survivor income benefit to an eligible spouse or children for a limited period, such as two years following the disabled worker's death.

Social Security Disability Income Benefits

Disability income benefits may also be available under the Social Security program for disabled workers who can meet strict eligibility requirements.

Eligibility Requirements

Three eligibility requirements must be met to qualify for benefits. First, the disabled worker must earn a certain number of credits, also called quarters of coverage, for work in covered employment. (Most occupations today are covered under the Social Security program.) For 2002, a worker earns one credit for each $870 of covered earnings. A maximum of four credits can be earned annually. The amount of earnings needed for one credit is adjusted annually based on increases in national average wages.

The number of credits needed to qualify for benefits depends on the worker's age when he or she becomes disabled. The following rules apply:

- *Age thirty-one or older*. In general, workers age thirty-one or older must have earned the number of credits shown in Exhibit 12-3. Unless the worker is blind, at least twenty of the credits must be earned during the ten years immediately before the worker becomes disabled.

- *Ages twenty-four through thirty*. Workers under age thirty-one can qualify for benefits with fewer credits. For ages twenty-four through thirty, the worker must have worked half the time between age twenty-one and the time he or she becomes disabled. For example, a worker disabled at age twenty-seven needs credit for only three years of work out of the prior six years.

- *Before age twenty-four*. If the worker becomes disabled before age twenty-four, he or she must have earned six credits in the three-year period ending when the disability starts.

A second requirement is that the worker must satisfy a five-month waiting period. The waiting period is five full calendar months, which eliminates a large number of short-term disabilities. For example, a worker disabled on June 3 would not receive any benefits for June or for the next five months, July through November. The first benefit check would be for December and would normally be paid in January.

EXHIBIT 12-3

Number of Work Credits Needed To Qualify for Social Security Disability Benefits

Born After 1929, Become Disabled at Age	Credits You Need
31 through 42	20
44	22
46	24
48	26
50	28
52	30
54	32
56	34
58	36
60	38
62 or older	40

Source: Social Security Administration.

A third requirement is that the disability must meet the stated definition. The definition of disability is rigid: *the worker must have a physical or mental condition that prevents him or her from doing any substantial gainful work, and the condition must be expected to last at least twelve months or result in death.* If the worker is unable to work in his or her own occupation but can engage in any other substantial work, the disability claim will not be allowed. In 2002, monthly earnings of $780 or more are considered substantial, and the worker would not be considered disabled. Special rules, however, apply to blind people and make qualifying for benefits easier for them.

Benefits

A monthly cash benefit is paid to disabled beneficiaries who meet the preceding eligibility requirements. Benefits also can be paid to unmarried children under age eighteen; to unmarried children age eighteen or older who became disabled before age twenty-two and are eligible for benefits based on the disabled worker's earnings; to a spouse at any age who is caring for a child under age sixteen (or for a child who became disabled before age twenty-two); and to a spouse age sixty-two or older even if he or she is not caring for children.

Exhibit 12-4 shows the approximate monthly disability income benefits for workers who become disabled in 2002. However, qualifying for benefits is difficult because of the stringent eligibility requirements and rigid definition of disability. More than half of the initial claimants who apply for disability are denied benefits.[21] Because qualifying for benefits is difficult, workers should not rely on Social Security as their major source of income during a period of disability. A high-quality individual or group disability income policy is also necessary.

EXHIBIT 12-4

Examples of Monthly Social Security Disability Benefits

Approximate Monthly Benefits if You Became Disabled in 2002 and Had Steady Earnings

Your Age	Your Family	Your Earnings in 2001						
		$20,000	$30,000	$40,000	$50,000	$60,000	$70,000	$84,900 or More[1]
25	You	$ 876	$1,143	$1,409	$1,574	$1,699	$1,824	$1,921
	You, your spouse, and child[2]	1,314	1,714	2,114	2,361	2,549	2,737	2,882
35	You	876	1,143	1,409	1,574	1,699	1,824	1,932
	You, your spouse, and child[2]	1,314	1,714	2,114	2,361	2,549	2,737	2,899
45	You	876	1,143	1,409	1,574	1,699	1,824	1,918
	You, your spouse, and child[2]	1,314	1,714	2,114	2,361	2,549	2,737	2,878
55	You	876	1,143	1,409	1,574	1,684	1,783	1,847
	You, your spouse, and child[2]	1,314	1,714	2,114	2,361	2,527	2,674	2,771
64	You	839	1,095	1,351	1,487	1,572	1,648	1,689
	You, your spouse, and child[2]	1,259	1,643	2,027	2,231	2,359	2,473	2,547

[1] Maximum earnings are greater than or equal to the OASDI wage base and are determined to be $80,400 for 2001.
[2] Disability maximum family benefit

Note: The accuracy of these estimates depends on your actual earnings, which may vary significantly from those shown here.

Source: Social Security Administration.

GOVERNMENT HEALTH INSURANCE AND HEALTHCARE PROGRAMS

Most individuals and families are insured under private health insurance plans. However, certain groups receive valuable protection under government insurance and healthcare programs. Three important government programs that merit discussion are Medicare, Medicaid, and workers compensation.

Medicare

Medicare
Social insurance program that covers the medical expenses of most individuals age sixty-five and older.

Medicare is part of the OASDHI program mentioned in Chapter 10. Medicare covers medical expenses of most individuals age sixty-five and older. In addition, Medicare benefits can be paid to disabled individuals under age sixty-five who have been entitled to Social Security disability benefits for twenty-four months (which need not be continuous). The program also covers persons under age sixty-five who need long-term kidney dialysis treatment or a kidney transplant. The original Medicare program consists of two parts—Hospital Insurance (Part A) and Supplementary Medical Insurance (Part B).[22] An alternative Medicare + Choice Program (also called Part C) was introduced in 1997.

Hospital Insurance (Part A)

Part A of the Medicare program, Hospital Insurance, provides five major benefits:

- Inpatient hospital care
- Skilled nursing facility care
- Home healthcare services
- Hospice care
- Blood transfusions

Additional benefits are also provided.

Inpatient Hospital Care

Inpatient hospital care is provided to a patient for up to ninety days for each benefit period. A benefit period starts when the patient first enters the hospital and ends when the patient has been out of the hospital or skilled nursing facility for sixty consecutive days. For the first sixty days, the hospital patient must pay an initial deductible, after which all covered hospital expenses are paid in full. For the sixty-first through ninetieth day of hospitalization, a daily coinsurance charge must also be paid. If the patient is still hospitalized after ninety days, a lifetime reserve of sixty additional days can be used. The lifetime reserve is also subject to a daily coinsurance charge. The inpatient hospital deductible and various coinsurance charges are automatically adjusted each year to reflect changes in hospital costs.

Skilled Nursing Facility Care

Inpatient skilled nursing facility care is also covered. To be eligible for coverage, the patient must be hospitalized for at least three days and must require skilled nursing care. Intermediate care and custodial care are not covered. A maximum of 100 days are covered in a benefit period. The first twenty days of covered services are paid in full. For the next eighty days, a daily coinsurance charge must be paid.

Home Healthcare Services

Healthcare services in the patient's home are covered if the patient requires skilled care for an injury or illness. A prior hospital stay is not required. Part A pays for skilled nurses, home health aides, medical social workers, and various types of therapists. The number of visits is unlimited as long as certain conditions are met. In addition, the home healthcare benefit covers the full cost of some medical supplies and 80 percent of the approved amount for durable medical equipment, such as wheelchairs, hospital beds, and oxygen supplies.

Hospice Care

Hospice care for terminally ill beneficiaries is covered if a physician certifies that the patient is terminally ill and the hospice is certified by Medicare. A hospice program provides inpatient, outpatient, and home healthcare services to terminally ill beneficiaries, such as cancer patients. Curative treatment, however, is not provided.

Blood Transfusions

Except for the first three pints of blood per calendar year, Part A pays for the cost of blood transfusions furnished by a hospital or skilled nursing facility during a covered stay.

Additional Benefits

Medicare also provides additional benefits. These benefits include annual mammograms for female beneficiaries ages forty and older; Pap smears and pelvic and breast examinations; diabetes glucose monitoring and diabetes education; colorectal cancer screening; bone-mass measurements; and annual prostate-cancer screening for men over age fifty.

Supplementary Medical Insurance (Part B)

Supplementary Medical Insurance, or Part B of Medicare, is a voluntary program that covers physicians' fees, most outpatient hospital services, and certain related medical services. Part B covers medical services only when they are medically necessary. Beneficiaries who enroll in Part A of Medicare are also automatically enrolled in Part B unless the coverage is declined. The major benefits under Part B are summarized as follows:

- Physicians' services in a hospital, an office, or elsewhere
- Medical supplies and durable medical equipment
- Clinical laboratory services, such as blood tests and urinalyses
- Home healthcare visits if the beneficiary is not covered by Part A
- Outpatient hospital services for the diagnosis or treatment of illness or injury
- Blood, except for the first three pints
- Ambulatory surgical services

Part B excludes numerous medical services and items, including routine physicals, most dental care, dentures, routine foot care, hearing aids, and most prescription drugs. Eyeglasses are covered only if the patient needs corrective lenses after a cataract operation.

The patient must pay an annual Part B deductible, which is the first $100 of covered charges approved by Medicare. After the $100 calendar-year deductible has been met, Part B pays 80 percent of the Medicare-approved amount for most covered services.

Financing Medicare

Medicare Part A is financed largely by a payroll tax percentage, which is paid by both the employee and employer. The self-employed pay a tax rate that is double the employee rate. The payroll tax rate applies to all earned income, even earnings in excess of the Social Security taxable earnings base ($84,900 in 2002).

Medicare Part B is financed largely by a monthly premium paid by insured persons and by the general revenues of the federal government. The Part B premium is adjusted each year based on plan experience.

Medicare + Choice

The Balanced Budget Act of 1997 created a **Medicare + Choice** program (also called Part C) as an alternative to Parts A and B of Medicare. Medicare beneficiaries now have the following options.

Original Medicare Plan

Beneficiaries can elect coverage under the original fee-for-service Medicare plan and can use any provider that accepts Medicare patients. Some services are not covered, and beneficiaries must pay certain out-of-pocket costs.

Original Medicare Plan With Supplemental Policy

Beneficiaries can choose coverage under the original Medicare plan and can also purchase one of up to ten standard supplemental policies (also called Medigap insurance) from private insurers. Depending on the policy, there is coverage for at least some deductible and coinsurance costs. The supplemental policy may also provide additional benefits not covered by Medicare. A beneficiary pays a premium for the supplemental policy.

Medicare Managed Care Plan

Beneficiaries can choose coverage under a managed care plan, which is a Medicare-approved network of physicians, hospitals, and other healthcare providers that provide care for a fixed monthly fee. Managed care plans include the following:

* *Health Maintenance Organization (HMO)*. Beneficiaries can elect an approved HMO, which usually requires members to use healthcare providers that are part of the network. Beneficiaries usually pay little or no out-of-pocket cost for covered services if they use network providers. Some HMOs provide additional benefits not covered by Medicare.

Medicare + Choice
Medicare alternative that allows beneficiaries to select the original Medicare plan, original Medicare plan with supplementary policy, Medicare managed care plan, private fee-for-service plan, or Medicare medical savings account (MSA).

- *Health Maintenance Organization with Point of Service Option (PSO).* Under this arrangement, beneficiaries have the option of receiving care from providers outside the network. However, beneficiaries must pay substantially higher out-of-pocket costs when care is received outside the network.
- *Preferred Provider Organization (PPO).* Beneficiaries can elect coverage under a PPO. Beneficiaries typically pay a lower deductible and coinsurance costs if they use providers that are part of the network. However, beneficiaries can use providers outside the network by paying an additional out-of-pocket cost.
- *Provider Sponsored Organization (PSO).* Beneficiaries can elect coverage under a PSO, which is a closed network operated by healthcare providers, such as a group of physicians.

Private Fee-for-Service Plan

Beneficiaries can choose coverage under an approved private health insurance plan. Medicare pays a premium to the private plan for covered Medicare services. However, the private plan rather than Medicare determines the amounts paid for covered services. Healthcare providers can bill the patient for an amount in excess of what Medicare pays (up to a limit). The patient must pay the difference between the provider's full fee and the Medicare payment. It is likely that the beneficiary will pay a premium for the private plan.

Medicare Medical Savings Account (MSA)

Beneficiaries can elect to be covered by a medical savings account, which is a health insurance policy with a high annual deductible. Medicare pays the premium for the MSA plan and deposits the money into a separate MSA plan established by the beneficiary. The beneficiary then uses the money in the MSA account to pay for medical expenses. There are no limits on the amounts providers can charge beneficiaries above what is paid by the Medicare MSA plan. Beneficiaries can enroll in an MSA plan only during November and must stay in the plan for a full year.

Medigap Insurance

Because of numerous exclusions, deductibles, cost-sharing provisions, and limitations on approved charges, Medicare does not pay all medical expenses incurred by the aged. As a result, many older persons have purchased a Medigap policy that pays part or all of the covered charges not paid by Medicare.

Medigap policies are sold by private insurers and are strictly regulated by federal law. There are ten standard policies, and each policy offers a different combination of benefits. Each policy has a letter designation ranging from A through J. Insurers are not allowed to change the various combinations of benefits or the letter designations. Insurers and agents are subject to fines and penalties if they engage in deceptive sales practices, such as the sale of a policy that is not an approved standard policy.

Insurers must have an open enrollment period of six months from the date the applicant enrolls in Medicare Part B and is age sixty-five or older. Applicants cannot be turned down or charged higher premiums because of poor health if they buy a policy during this period. After the open enrollment period ends, beneficiaries may be unable to buy the policy of their choice and may have to accept whatever Medigap policy an insurer is willing to provide.

Medicaid

Medicaid is an important government program that provides valuable protection to low-income groups. States vary with respect to persons covered and types of medical services offered. However, certain medical services are provided in all states, including inpatient and outpatient hospital services, physicians' services, prenatal care, laboratory and X-ray services, long-term care in nursing homes, and certain other services.

To qualify for benefits, Medicaid applicants must satisfy a stringent means test, which requires applicants to show that their income and financial assets are below certain limits. If financial assets are above the allowable limits, applicants must "spend down" (reduce) their assets in order to qualify for benefits. In particular, many aged patients in nursing homes have been forced to spend down their financial assets to qualify for long-term care coverage under Medicaid. As a result, a relatively high proportion of the total Medicaid budget is now spent on long-term care of the aged in nursing homes.

Medicaid
Federal-state welfare program that covers the medical expenses of low-income persons, including those who are aged, blind, or disabled; members of families with dependent children; and pregnant women as well as certain children.

Workers Compensation

Workers compensation is an important social insurance program that provides valuable health and disability insurance protection to employed workers. All states have workers compensation laws that require covered employers to pay benefits to workers who have a job-related injury or disease. Workers compensation is based on the liability-without-fault principle, which means that employers are held absolutely liable for job-related injuries or disease incurred by their workers, regardless of fault. Disabled workers are not required to sue their employers or prove negligence to receive benefits but instead are paid based on a schedule of benefits established by law.

Eligibility Requirements

Workers must meet two major eligibility requirements to receive benefits. First, the worker must be working in a covered occupation. Most occupations are covered for workers compensation. However, many states exclude or provide less-than-complete coverage for certain occupations, such as for farm workers and domestic employees, and for firms with fewer than a specified number of employees. Second, the worker must have an injury or a disease that arises out of and in the course of employment; benefits can be paid only for a job-related accident or disease.

Workers Compensation Benefits

Workers compensation benefits vary among the states. However, four basic benefits are typically available to workers who incur a job-related injury or illness. First, medical expenses in all states are paid in full without deductibles or coinsurance.

Second, weekly disability income benefits are paid to disabled workers after a short elimination period, typically ranging from three to seven days. The weekly benefit is a percentage of the worker's average weekly wage, typically two-thirds, and the degree of disability. Most states limit the maximum benefits paid.

Third, death benefits can be paid if the worker dies from a job-related accident or disease. Funeral expenses are paid up to some maximum limit. In addition, weekly cash benefits based on a proportion of the deceased worker's wages can be paid to eligible dependents, such as a surviving spouse or children under a certain age.

Finally, rehabilitation services and vocational retraining are available in all states. The quality and scope of rehabilitation services vary among the states. The purpose, however, is to restore disabled workers to productive employment.

SUMMARY

The healthcare delivery system in the United States has four major problems: rising healthcare expenditures over time, inadequate access to medical care for certain groups, uneven quality of medical care, and considerable waste and inefficiency.

The major providers of private health coverages are commercial insurers, Blue Cross and Blue Shield plans, and employer self-insured plans. Basic medical expense coverages include hospital expense insurance, surgical expense insurance, physicians' visits insurance, and additional benefits. Many hospital expense plans pay the full cost of a semiprivate room up to a specified number of days. Physicians are commonly reimbursed on the basis of their usual, reasonable, and customary charges.

There are two types of major medical insurance plans. A supplemental plan covers medical expenses that exceed the underlying limits of the basic medical expense policy. A supplemental plan may also cover certain expenses not covered by the basic policy. The other type of plan is comprehensive major medical insurance that combines basic medical expense benefits and major medical insurance into one policy.

Individual and group major medical plans have common characteristics. Both plans provide broad coverage with high lifetime limits; a deductible, such as a calendar-year deductible, must be satisfied before any benefits are paid; the plans have a coinsurance provision, which typically requires the insured to pay 20 or 25 percent of covered expenses up to some maximum stop-loss limit; and certain exclusions and internal limits control costs.

Group health insurance plans typically contain important contractual provisions, including a preexisting conditions clause, a coordination-of-benefits provision, and provisions for allowing terminated employees and covered dependents to remain in the group plan for a limited period under the COBRA law.

There are two major types of group dental insurance plans. One type is a scheduled plan in which covered dental services are listed in a schedule, and a specific dollar amount is paid for each service. The other type is a non-scheduled plan (comprehensive plan) in which most dental services are covered, and dentists are reimbursed on the basis of their reasonable and customary charges.

Long-term care insurance is a medical expense plan that pays benefits for medical care or custodial care received in a nursing home, hospital, or private home. Long-term plans have certain common characteristics. Purchasers typically have a choice of daily cash benefits for a specified period of time; the plans are commonly sold with an elimination period ranging from 0 to 365 days; and all plans have gatekeeper provisions that state the requirements the insured must meet to be eligible for benefits.

Managed care plans are medical insurance plans that provide cost-effective coverage for medical services to plan members. Managed care plans include health maintenance organizations (HMOs), preferred provider organizations (PPOs), exclusive provider organizations (EPOs), and point-of-service (POS) plans.

An individual disability income policy pays periodic cash benefits to individuals who are totally disabled from sickness or injury. The insured has a choice of benefit periods, and benefits are paid after an elimination period has been satisfied. A split definition of total disability is commonly used. For some initial time period, total disability means the insured is unable to perform the major duties of his or her own occupation. After the initial period expires, the insured is considered totally disabled only if he or she is unable to perform the duties of any gainful occupation for which he or she is reasonably suited by training, education, and experience.

Group short-term disability income plans are plans that pay benefits ranging from thirteen weeks to two years. Short-term plans typically cover only nonoccupational disabilities. Group long-term disability income plans pay benefits for longer periods, typically to age sixty-five and even beyond if the worker is employed. Long-term plans cover both occupational and nonoccupational disabilities.

Disability income benefits may also be available under the Social Security program if certain eligibility requirements are met. The disabled worker must have a certain number of credits for work in covered employment; the number of credits required depends on the disabled worker's age. In addition, a full five-month waiting period must be satisfied. Finally, the disability must meet a strict stated definition.

Medicare is part of the Social Security program. Medicare covers the medical expenses of most persons age sixty-five and older and certain disabled individuals under age sixty-five. The Medicare program consists of two parts: Hospital Insurance (Part A) and Supplementary Medical Insurance (Part B). A Medicare + Choice program, also called Part C, is available as an alternative to Parts A and B.

Medicaid is a welfare program that covers the medical expenses of low-income persons, including those who are aged, blind, or disabled; members of families with dependent children; and certain children and pregnant women. To qualify for benefits, Medicaid applicants must satisfy a stringent means test.

All states have workers compensation laws that require employers to pay benefits to workers who have a job-related accident or disease. Under the liability-without-fault principle, employers are held absolutely liable for job-related injuries or disease incurred by workers, regardless of fault. To qualify for benefits, the worker must be working in a covered occupation, and the injury or disease must arise out of and in the course of employment.

CHAPTER NOTES

1. George E. Rejda, *Social Insurance and Economic Security*, 5th ed. (Englewood Cliffs, N.J.: Prentice-Hall, Inc., 1994), pp. 191–207.

2. Rejda, p. 204.

3. Rejda, p. 203.

4. Health Insurance Association of America, *Source Book of Health Insurance Data*, 1995 (Washington, D.C.: Health Insurance Association of America, 1996), Table 2.10a, p. 45.

5. Kenneth Black, Jr., and Harold D. Skipper, Jr., *Life Insurance*, 12th ed. (Englewood Cliffs, N.J.: Prentice-Hall, Inc., 1994), p. 757.

6. Burton T. Beam, Jr., and John J. McFadden, *Employee Benefits*, 4th ed. (Chicago, Ill.: Dearborn Financial Publishing, Inc., 1996), p. 206.

7. Beam and McFadden, pp. 302–305.

8. ElderWeb, "Average Length of Nursing Home Stay," 16 May 2002. World Wide Web: http://www.elderweb.com/default.php?PageID=2770 (12 June 2002).

9. Health Insurance Association of America, "Guide to Long-Term Care Insurance" (Washington, D.C.: Health Insurance Association of America, 1999), p.7.

10. The discussion of long-term care insurance is based on National Association of Insurance Commissioners, *A Shopper's Guide to Long-Term Care Insurance* (Kansas City, Mo.: National Association of Insurance Commissioners, 1996).

11. *A Shopper's Guide to Long-Term Care Insurance*, p. 11.

12. The discussion of managed care plans is based on Beam and McFadden, Chapter 11, and George E. Rejda, *Principles of Risk Management and Insurance*, 5th ed. (New York: HarperCollins College Publishers, 1995), pp. 453-457.

13. Health Insurance Association of America, *Source Book of Health Insurance Data, 1999–2000* (Washington, D.C.: Health Insurance Association of America, 1999), pp. 22 & 23.

14. A. Foster Higgins, *News*, February 15, 1994.

15. Jeff Sadler, *Disability Income, The Sale, The Product, The Market*, 2d ed. (Cincinnati, Ohio: The National Underwriter Company, 1995), p. 30.

16. Sadler, p. 157.

17. Edward E. Graves, ed., *McGill's Life Insurance* (Bryn Mawr, Pa.: The American College, 1994), Table 7–4, p. 143.

18. Sadler, p. 128.

19. Sadler, p. 130.

20. This section is based on Beam and McFadden, pp. 161–175, and Rejda, *Principles of Risk Management and Insurance*, pp. 449–451.

21. Rejda, *Social Insurance and Economic Security*, p. 257.

22. The discussion of Medicare is based on U.S. Department of Health and Human Services, Healthcare Financing Administration, *Your Medicare Handbook*, 1996, Publication No. HCFA-10050, Revised April 1996.

Glossary

Absolute liability (strict liability) — Legal liability that arises from inherently dangerous activities or dangerously defective products that harm another, regardless of the degree of care used; does not require proof of negligence.

Accidental death benefit — Provision in a life insurance policy that doubles (or triples) the face amount of insurance payable if the insured dies as a result of an accident.

Actual cash value (ACV) — Replacement cost of property minus an allowance for depreciation and obsolescence.

Add-on plan — Endorsement that provides certain benefits to injured automobile victims regardless of fault; the injured person retains the right to seek compensation from the negligent party who caused the accident.

Adverse selection — The tendency for people with the greatest probability of loss to be the ones most likely to purchase insurance.

Agreed value approach — Approach to valuation in which the insurer and the insured agree on the value of the insured object and state it in a policy schedule; in case of total loss, the insurer pays the amount specified in the policy.

Annuity — Provides periodic payments for a fixed period or for the duration of a designated life or lives.

Appraisal (as used in Part D of the PAP) — A provision that describes how the insured and insurer will settle disputes about the amount of loss. Each party selects a competent appraiser, and the two appraisers select an umpire. A decision by any two of the three is binding. Procedurally, the appraisal process resembles the arbitration process described under uninsured motorists coverage.

Arbitration (as used in the PAP) — Process for settling disputes between the insured and the insurer concerning whether or for what amount uninsured motorists coverage applies.

Assignment — The transfer of a policy from the named insured to another party; insurer's written consent is required.

Automobile insurance plan — Plan for insuring high-risk drivers in which all auto insurers doing business in the state are assigned their proportionate share of such drivers based on the total volume of auto insurance written in the state. For example, if one insurer writes 10 percent of all the auto insurance in the state, it would be assigned 10 percent of the state's high-risk drivers.

Avoidance — Risk management technique by which an individual or a family avoids a loss exposure by choosing not to own a particular item of property or not to engage in a particular activity.

Bailee — Person or business that has in its care, custody, or control, property belonging to another.

Basic medical expense coverages — Coverage for medical expenses, such as hospital and surgical expenses, physicians' visits, and miscellaneous medical services.

Beachfront and windstorm plans — State-regulated insurance pools that provide property insurance, both personal and commercial, in coastal areas exposed to the risk of heavy windstorm losses.

Beneficiary — Person(s) designated in a life insurance policy to receive the death benefit.

Bodily injury (BI) (as used in HO policies) — Bodily harm, sickness, or disease, including required care, loss of services, and death that result.

Bodily injury (BI) (as used in the PAP) — Bodily harm, sickness, or disease, including death that results.

Bonds — Debt obligations issued by corporations and government entities.

Calendar-year deductible — Medical insurance deductible an insured must meet only once during the calendar year.

Cancellation — A decision by the insurer or the insured to terminate coverage during the policy period (before the expiration date of the policy).

Capital appreciation — An increase in the value of investments.

Cash value — Fund that accumulates in a whole life insurance policy and that the policyholder can access in several ways, including borrowing, purchasing paid-up life insurance, and surrendering the policy in exchange for the cash value.

Cause of loss — Means by which property is damaged or destroyed (e.g., fire and theft); also called peril.

Choice no-fault plan — Plan that gives an insured the option, at the time an auto insurance policy is purchased or renewed, of choosing whether to be covered on a no-fault basis.

Civil law — Body of law that deals with the rights and duties of citizens regarding one another.

Coinsurance — Medical insurance provision that requires the insured to pay part of the covered medical expenses in excess of the deductible.

Collision (as used in the PAP) — The upset of a covered auto or a nonowned auto or its impact with another vehicle or object.

Common stock — Represents an ownership interest in a corporation and gives stockowners certain rights and privileges, such as the right to vote on important corporate matters.

Comparative negligence law — Law that requires both parties to a loss to share the financial burden of the injury according to their respective degrees of fault. For example, under one type of comparative negligence law, if Driver A is judged to be 20 percent responsible for an accident and Driver B is judged to be 80 percent responsible, Driver A can collect for his or her injury, but the damages to which Driver A would otherwise be entitled are reduced by 20 percent. In a number of states, if Driver A is 50 percent or more responsible for the accident, he or she can collect nothing from Driver B.

Compensatory damages — Damages, including both special damages and general damages, that are intended to compensate a victim for harm actually suffered.

Compulsory auto insurance law — Law that requires the owners or operators of automobiles to carry automobile liability insurance at least equal to certain minimum limits before the vehicle can be licensed or registered.

Concurrent causation — A loss involving two or more perils, occurring either simultaneously or sequentially.

Conditionally renewable policy — Policy that guarantees renewal to a specified time, provided the insured meets certain qualifications.

Condominium — A building or complex for which the unit owner has a separate title and exclusive ownership of a specific unit as well as the joint ownership of the common areas and facilities.

Contractual liability — Liability assumed under any contract or agreement.

Contributory negligence law — Law that prevents a person from recovering damages if that person contributes in any way to his or her own injury. Thus, if Driver A is judged to be 20 percent responsible for an accident, and Driver B is judged to be 80 percent responsible, Driver A cannot collect any damages.

Contributory plan — Group plan in which employees pay part or all of the cost.

Convertible — Characteristic of a term insurance policy that allows the policy to be exchanged for some type of permanent life insurance policy with no evidence of insurability.

Cooperative — Housing unit in a complex owned by a corporation, the stockholders of which are the building's residents; corporation owns the real estate title; each unit owner owns corporation stock and has the right to occupy a specific unit.

Coordination-of-benefits provision — Provision that indicates the order of payment when an insured is covered under two or more group health insurance plans; limits the insured's total recovery under all applicable policies to 100 percent of covered expenses.

Corridor deductible — Medical insurance deductible amount an insured must pay under a supplemental major medical insurance plan after the insured's medical expenses exceed the limits of the underlying basic medical expense plan.

Damages — Monetary award that one party is required to pay to another who has suffered loss or injury for which the first party is legally responsible.

Declarations page — A required component of an insurance policy; in an auto policy, it provides information about the insured, a description of the insured autos, a schedule of coverages, and other important details.

Defined benefit plan — Pension plan in which the retirement benefit is specified and the employer's contributions vary depending on the amount needed to fund the benefit; typically requires no employee contributions.

Defined contribution plan (money purchase pension plan) — Pension plan in which the contribution rate or amount is specified, but the retirement benefit is variable.

Diminution in value — Actual or perceived loss in market or resale value resulting from a direct and accidental loss.

Disability income insurance — Insurance that pays periodic income payments to an insured who is unable to work because of sickness or injury.

Diversification — Technique to reduce one's overall investment risk by spreading funds among investments with different risks.

Drop down coverage — Coverage provided by an umbrella policy for a loss that is not excluded by the umbrella policy and that is not covered by underlying policies. The loss is paid by the umbrella insurer in excess of a self-insured retention that the insured must pay.

Elimination period — Initial time period in a health insurance or disability income policy during which benefits are not paid.

Emergency program — Initial phase of a community's participation in the National Flood Insurance Program in which property owners in flood areas can purchase limited amounts of insurance at subsidized rates.

Employee (as used in HO policies) — An employee of an insured who is not a residence employee.

Ensuing loss — Loss caused by a peril that occurs after or as a result of an initial peril; e.g., fire damage following an earthquake.

Errors and omissions (E&O) — Negligent acts (errors) committed by a person while conducting insurance business that give rise to legal liability for damages; can also involve a failure to act (omission) that creates legal liability.

Evidence of insurability — A requirement by a life insurer that the insured demonstrate that he or she still meets the insurer's underwriting standards. The insured is usually required to submit a medical questionnaire or have a physical examination to show that he or she is in good health.

Exclusive provider organization (EPO) — Managed care plan that pays only for medical care received within the network of preferred providers.

FAIR (Fair Access to Insurance Requirements) plans — State-run programs that provide basic property insurance coverage on buildings, dwellings, and their contents for property owners who are unable to obtain coverage in the standard insurance market.

Financial planning — Process that helps individuals and families to identify their financial goals and to develop a realistic plan for attaining those goals.

Financial responsibility law — Law that requires motorists, under certain circumstances, to provide proof that they have the ability to pay, up to certain minimum amounts, for damage or injury that they might cause as a result of operating a vehicle.

First party — The insured.

Floater — Inland marine policy that provides coverage for property that "floats" or moves (such as jewelry, furs, or cameras) rather than providing coverage at a fixed location.

General damages — Compensatory damages awarded for losses, such as pain and suffering, that do not have a specific economic loss.

Grace period — Provision that continues a life insurance policy in force for a certain number of days (usually thirty or thirty-one) after the premium due date, during which time the policyowner can pay the overdue premium without penalty.

Guaranteed insurability rider (guaranteed purchase option) — Rider that permits the policyowner to buy additional amounts of life insurance at standard rates without evidence of insurability.

Guaranteed renewable policy — Policy that cannot be canceled after it has been issued; insurer maintains the right to increase premiums for classes of insureds.

Health maintenance organization (HMO) — Managed care plan that provides a range of comprehensive healthcare services to its members for a fixed, prepaid fee; members' choice of healthcare providers is usually restricted to those in the HMO network.

Hospital expense insurance — Insurance that covers medical expenses while the patient is in the hospital, such as daily room-and-board and miscellaneous expenses incurred during the hospital stay.

Hull — The boat. A vessel's structure, including machinery, spars, sails, tackles, fittings, and other equipment and furnishings that are normally required for the vessel's operation and seaworthy maintenance.

Hull insurance — Physical damage insurance on a boat, including its sails, machinery, furniture, and other equipment.

Incontestable clause — Clause that states that the insurer cannot contest the policy after it has been in force for a specified period, such as two years, during the insured's lifetime.

Inherent vice — Type of deterioration that is characteristic of a material; e.g., the tendency of metal to rust.

Inland marine insurance — Insurance that covers miscellaneous types of property, such as movable property, goods in domestic transit, and property used in transportation and communication.

Insurable interest — Interest in property that exists if a person could suffer a financial loss if the property is damaged or destroyed or cannot be used.

Intentional tort — A deliberate act that causes harm to another person.

Investing — The purchase of assets, either financial or real, that the investor hopes will help achieve financial goals.

Investment risk — Variability of investment outcomes.

Joint underwriting association (JUA) — Organization created in a few states that designates servicing insurers to handle high-risk auto insurance business; all auto insurers in the state are assessed a proportionate share of the losses and expenses based on their percentage of the voluntary auto insurance premiums written in the state.

Liability loss — A claim for money damages because of injury to another party or damage to another party's property.

Liability loss exposure — Any condition or situation that presents the possibility of a liability loss.

Limited-payment life insurance — Whole life insurance in which the premiums are level but are paid only for a certain number of years. After that time, the policy is paid-up.

Liquidity — Ability to quickly convert an investment into cash with a minimal loss of principal.

Long-term care insurance — Insurance that pays for extended medical care or custodial care received in a nursing home, hospital, or home.

Loss control — Risk management technique to reduce the frequency or severity of losses.

Loss exposure — Any condition or situation that presents the possibility of a financial loss, whether or not loss occurs.

Maintenance of underlying insurance condition — Condition in personal umbrella policies that requires the insured to keep all required underlying coverages in force during the policy period; also requires the insured to notify the insurer promptly if any underlying policy is changed or replaced by another policy.

Major medical insurance — Insurance that covers medical expenses resulting from illness or injury that are not covered by a basic medical expense plan.

Managed care — Medical insurance plans that provide coverage for cost-effective medical services provided to plan members.

Market value — Price at which a particular property item could be sold.

Material misrepresentation — A false statement by an insured of an important (material) fact on which the insurer relies to make an underwriting decision.

Medicaid — Federal-state welfare program that covers the medical expenses of low-income persons, including those who are aged, blind, or disabled; members of families with dependent children; and pregnant women as well as certain children.

Medical payments to others — A homeowners coverage for necessary medical expenses incurred by others (not an insured) within three years of an injury.

Medicare + Choice — Medicare alternative that allows beneficiaries to select the original Medicare plan, original Medicare plan with supplementary policy, Medicare managed care plan, private fee-for-service plan, or Medicare medical savings account (MSA).

Medicare — Social insurance program that covers the medical expenses of most individuals age sixty-five and older.

Misstatement of age or sex provision — Clause stating that if the insured's age or sex is misstated in a life insurance policy application, the amount of death benefit the insurer will pay is the amount that the premium would have purchased at the insured's correct age and sex.

Modified no-fault laws — Laws that prevent an injured person from seeking compensation for damages from a negligent driver unless damages exceed the monetary or verbal threshold; if the claim is below the threshold, the injured person collects benefits from his or her own insurer.

Monetary threshold — The level of monetary damages in a no-fault system at which one injured party can seek compensation from the at-fault party.

Moral hazard — Condition that might lead a person to intentionally cause or exaggerate a loss.

Mortality rates — Probabilities of death at specific ages. Life insurers have been able to predict mortality rates with a high degree of accuracy for large groups of people.

Mutual fund — Investment mechanism that pools the funds of individual investors and invests in securities.

Named insured (as used in the PAP) — Policyholder whose name (or names) appears on the declarations page.

Named perils — Perils listed and described in the policy as being covered; also called specified perils or specified causes of loss.

National Flood Insurance Program (NFIP) — Federal program that makes flood insurance available on buildings, both commercial and residential, and their contents in communities that have been approved by the Federal Emergency Management Agency (FEMA).

Needs approach — Method used to determine an adequate amount of life insurance based on the survivors' needs and the amount of existing life insurance, financial assets, and expected Social Security benefits.

Negligence — The failure to act in a manner that is reasonably prudent, causing damage to another.

Net worth — Excess of assets over liabilities; assets – liabilities = net worth.

Newly acquired auto (as used in the PAP) — An eligible private passenger auto, pickup, or van of which the named insured becomes the owner or that the named insured leases during the policy period; it can be a replacement auto or an additional auto.

No-fault automobile insurance — Insurance that covers automobile accident victims on a first-party basis, allowing them to collect damages from their own insurers regardless of who was at fault.

Noncancelable policy — Policy that cannot be canceled or non-renewed until some stated age; insurer cannot increase premiums before that time.

Noncontributory plan — Group plan in which the employer pays the entire cost.

Nonforfeiture options — Provisions in a life insurance policy that give the policyowner a choice of ways to use the cash value if the policy is terminated and that protect the policyowner from forfeiting the cash value.

Noninsurance transfer — A risk management technique that transfers loss exposures from one party to another party that is not an insurer.

Nonowned auto (as used in the physical damage coverage section of the PAP) — Any private passenger auto, pickup, van, or trailer that is not owned by or made available for the regular use of the named insured or any family member. Physical damage coverage applies to such a vehicle while it is in the custody of or is being operated by the named insured or any family member. With respect to physical damage coverage, a temporary substitute vehicle is also considered a nonowned auto.

Nonparticipating (guaranteed cost) policies — Life insurance policies that do not pay dividends to policyowners.

Nonrenewal — An insurer's decision to terminate coverage on the expiration date of the policy; in other words, the insurer refuses to renew the policy when it expires.

Occupying (as used in the PAP) — In, upon, getting in, on, out, or off.

Occurrence — Accident that results in bodily injury or property damage, including continuous or repeated exposure to the same general harmful conditions.

Ordinary life insurance — Whole life insurance that requires periodic premiums until the insured dies or reaches age 100. (Also called straight life insurance.)

Other structures — Structures on the residence premises, other than the dwelling building, that are not attached to the dwelling.

Other-than-collision (OTC) coverage — Coverage for auto physical damage losses that are not caused by collision and that are not specifically excluded by the policy.

Out-of-state coverage (as used in Part A of the PAP) — Provision that automatically provides any higher limits and types of coverage required by the state in which an auto accident occurs if such an accident occurs in a state other than the one in which the covered auto is principally garaged.

Package policy — Policy that includes two or more lines of insurance. In personal insurance, such as property and liability, examples of package policies are the homeowners policy and the personal auto policy.

Paid-up policy — Life insurance that does not require additional premium payments to remain in force.

Participating policies — Life insurance policies that pay dividends to policyowners.

Personal injury — Injury arising out of specified offenses, typically including libel, slander, and invasion of privacy.

Personal injury protection (PIP) endorsement — Endorsement to an auto insurance policy describing the no-fault benefits that are provided.

Personal insurance — Insurance that covers the financial consequences of losses to individuals and families caused by death, illness, injury, disability, and unemployment.

Personal loss exposure (human loss exposure) — Any condition or situation that presents the possibility of financial loss to a person, such as death, sickness, or injury.

Personal property — Tangible or intangible property that is not real property.

Personal risk management — The risk management process applied to the loss exposures of individuals or families.

Physical damage coverage — Coverage for damage to your auto.

Physical damage coverage ("coverage for damage to your auto") — Insures against loss resulting from damage to or theft of an auto owned or operated by the insured; a type of property insurance and includes both collision coverage and "other-than-collision" coverage.

Physicians' visits insurance — Insurance that covers nonsurgical care provided by an attending physician other than a surgeon.

Point-of-service (POS) plan — Managed care plan that combines the characteristics of an HMO and a PPO; has a network of preferred providers who, if used by the member, charge little or nothing for services; healthcare received out of the network is covered, but members must pay substantially higher coinsurance charges and a deductible.

Portability — Characteristic of a health plan that requires a new employer or health plan to give credit for prior, continuous health insurance coverage.

Postjudgment interest — Interest in damages that accrues after a judgment has been rendered and before the damages are paid; can be in addition to the liability limits and other legal defense costs.

Preexisting conditions clause — A health insurance provision that excludes coverage for any preexisting medical condition (one that existed before the policy effective date) for a limited period after an insured enters the plan.

Preferred provider organization (PPO) — Managed care plan that contracts with healthcare providers for medical services provided to plan members at discounted fees; members' choice of healthcare providers is not restricted, but members have a financial incentive to choose contracted providers.

Preferred stock — An investment having characteristics of both common stocks and bonds.

Prejudgment interest — Interest on damages that accrues between the time the accident or suit occurs and when a judgment is rendered indicating that the insured is responsible for damages; subject to the policy limit of liability.

Premature death — Early death of a person with outstanding or unfulfilled financial obligations, such as children to support or mortgage payments.

Preservation of capital — Practice of ensuring that the value of assets does not decrease.

Pro rata refund — Unused premium, returned to the policyholder when the policy is canceled, calculated in direct proportion to the portion of the policy term that has not been used. For example, if a one-year (365-day) premium is $365 and the policy is canceled 100 days before it would expire (with 100 of the 365 days of coverage unused), the insured will receive a refund of $100. Rather than calculating unearned premium refunds on a pro rata basis, some insurance policies apply a "short-rate penalty" when the insured cancels the policy.

Proof of loss — Document that describes the details of the loss, property values, and interest(s) in the property.

Property damage (PD) (as used in HO policies) — Physical injury to, destruction of, or loss of use of tangible property.

Property damage (PD) (as used in the PAP) — Physical injury to or destruction of tangible property. It also includes loss of use of tangible property.

Property loss exposure — Any condition or situation that presents the possibility of a property loss.

Protection and indemnity (P&I) insurance — Insurance that covers the insured for bodily injury or property damage liability arising from the ownership, maintenance, or use of the insured boat.

Punitive damages — Damages awarded by a court to punish wrongdoers who, through malicious or outrageous actions, cause injury or damage to others; some states do not permit insurers to award payment for punitive damages because such payment would not punish the insured.

Pure no-fault system — System that would prevent an injured person from seeking compensation for damages from the at-fault party, regardless of the injury's severity; the injured person would collect no-fault benefits directly from his or her own insurer.

Real property — Land, as well as buildings and other structures attached to the land or embedded in it.

Regular program — Second phase of the National Flood Insurance Program in which the community agrees to adopt flood-control and land-use restrictions and in which property owners purchase higher amounts of flood insurance than under the emergency program.

Reinstatement clause — Clause that gives the policyowner the right to reinstate a lapsed life insurance policy if certain requirements are met.

Reinsurance facility — A state-wide reinsurance pool to which insurers can assign premiums and losses for high-risk drivers; original insurers service the policies, but all insurers in the pool share the losses and expenses of the facility in proportion to the total auto insurance they write in that state.

Renewable — Characteristic of a term life insurance policy that permits the policyholder to renew it for additional periods without evidence of insurability.

Residence employees — Domestic workers whose duties include maintaining or using the household premises or performing domestic or household services.

Residence premises (as defined in ISO HO policies) — The one-family dwelling where the named insured resides; the two-, three-, or four-family dwelling where the named insured resides in at least one of the units; that part of any other building where the named insured resides; and other structures and grounds; all at the location shown in the declarations.

Residual market (shared market) — Term referring collectively to insurers and other organizations that make insurance available to those who cannot obtain coverage in the standard market.

Retention — A risk management technique that draws on the financial resources of an individual or a family to pay for part or all of the consequences of a particular loss exposure. If individuals or families do not transfer their loss exposures to an insurance company or to anyone else, they retain their losses (either intentionally or unintentionally) and must pay for such losses themselves.

Rider — Similar to an endorsement; modifies a life insurance policy.

Risk management — The process of making and carrying out decisions that will decrease the adverse effects of potential losses.

Roth IRA — Individual retirement plan that allows (1) investment earnings to accumulate free of federal income taxes and (2) tax-free withdrawals at age 59 ½ or later; does not allow federal income-tax deduction of annual contributions.

Saving — The practice of not consuming all income.

Schedule — List of insured property items that are covered, with each item specifically described and having its own coverage limit.

Self-insured retention — Amount of loss the insured must pay if the loss covered by an umbrella policy is not covered by any underlying insurance.

Settlement options — Various ways of paying life insurance policy proceeds to the beneficiary.

Severability of insurance condition — Policy condition that applies insurance separately to each insured; does not increase the insurer's limit of liability for any one occurrence.

Single limit — Maximum amount an insurer will pay for the insured's liability for both bodily injury and property damage per accident.

Special damages — Compensatory damages allowed for specific out-of-pocket expenses, such as doctor and hospital bills.

Special-form coverage — Coverage for any direct physical loss to property unless the loss is caused by a peril specifically excluded by the policy; also called "all-risks" or open perils coverage.

Split limits (as used in the PAP) — The maximum amounts a PAP insurer will pay for the insured's liability for bodily injury per person, bodily injury per accident, and property damage per accident.

Standard market — Insurers who voluntarily offer insurance coverages at rates designed for customers with average or better-than-average loss exposures.

Statutory liability — Liability imposed by a specific statute or law.

Stop-loss provision — Insurance provision that limits the amount the insured must pay by reimbursing 100 percent of covered expenses in excess of this limit for the rest of the calendar year.

Structured settlement — Periodic and guaranteed pay-ments made for damages over a specified time period; an alternative to lump-sum payment.

Subrogation — Insurer's right to recover payment from a negligent third party. When an insurer pays an insured for a loss, the insurer takes over the insured's right to collect damages from the other party responsible for the loss. The insurer has the right to subrogate against the party directly responsible for the loss.

Suicide clause — Clause that states the insurer will not pay the death benefit if the insured commits suicide within a certain period (usually two years) after policy inception.

Supplementary payments (as used in the PAP) — Amounts paid in addition to the liability limits for items such as premiums on bail bonds and appeal bonds, postjudgment interest, loss of earnings for attendance at trials, and other reasonable expenses incurred at the insurer's request.

Surgical expense insurance — Insurance that covers part or all of a physician's fee for a surgical operation.

Tax-deferred retirement plans — Plans that receive favorable income-tax treatment, such as employer-sponsored Section 401(k) plans.

Temporary substitute vehicle (as used in the PAP) — A nonowned auto or trailer that the insured is using because of the breakdown, repair, servicing, loss, or destruction of a covered vehicle.

Term insurance — Insurance that provides temporary protection (for a certain period of time) with no cash value; usually renewable and convertible.

Third party — Someone not party to the insurance contract who might assert a claim against a first party.

Tort — A wrongful act, other than a crime or breach of contract, committed by one party against another.

Tort reform — Proposed or actual legislation intended to reduce legal costs or settlement awards resulting from negligence lawsuits.

Traditional individual retirement account (IRA) — Retirement plan that allows workers with taxable compensation below certain thresholds to make limited annual contributions and receive favorable income-tax treatment. Not employer sponsored.

Trailer (as used in the PAP) — A vehicle designed to be pulled by a private passenger auto, a pickup, or a van; farm wagon or farm implement when towed by one of these vehicles.

Transportation expenses (as used in the PAP) — Additional coverage reimburses up to $20 per day, to a maximum of $600, for temporary travel expenses for each covered physical damage loss.

Underinsured motorists coverage — Coverage that applies when a negligent driver has liability insurance at the time of the accident but has limits lower than those of the injured person's coverage.

Underlying insurance — The basic policies, such as homeowners, personal auto, and watercraft (if the insured owns a boat), that provide primary liability coverages and that the insured is required by a personal umbrella policy to have and maintain.

Underwriting — The process by which insurers decide which potential customers to insure and the coverage that insureds will be offered. Underwriting activities include selecting insureds, pricing coverage, determining policy terms and conditions, and monitoring underwriting decisions.

Underwriting loss — An insurer's loss incurred when losses and expenses for a given period are greater than its premium income for the same period.

Unemployment compensation programs — Government programs that pay weekly cash benefits to eligible workers who are involuntarily unemployed.

Unfair discrimination — Involves applying different standards or methods of treatment to insureds that have the same basic characteristics and loss potential. Examples of unfair discrimination in auto insurance rating include charging higher-than-normal rates for an applicant based solely on the applicant's race, religion, or ethnic background.

Uninsured boaters coverage — Coverage for the insured's bodily injury incurred in a boating accident caused by another boat's owner or operator who is uninsured and who is legally responsible for the injury; similar to the PAP's uninsured motorists coverage.

Uninsured motor vehicle — Any type of land motor vehicle or trailer that is not insured for bodily injury liability, is insured for less than the financial responsibility limits, is a hit-and-run vehicle, or whose insurer denies coverage or becomes insolvent.

Uninsured motorists (UM) coverage — Coverage that reimburses an insured auto accident victim who sustains bodily injury (and, in some states, property damage) caused by an uninsured motorist, a hit-and-run driver, or a driver whose insurer is insolvent.

United States Longshore and Harbor Workers' Compensation Act — Act that specifies the required benefits to maritime employees (except crew members) who are injured or disabled or who die while working on U.S. navigable waters.

Universal life insurance — Flexible-premium life insurance that separates the protection, savings, and expense components.

Unsatisfied judgment funds — Funds established by some states to compensate auto accident victims who have obtained a court judgment that is uncollectible because the negligent party cannot pay.

Unscheduled personal property — Personal property not specifically listed (scheduled) on a policy but generally covered with a single limit for all items (or each class) of personal property that are not excluded.

Usual, reasonable, and customary (URC) charges — Charges for which physicians are reimbursed on the basis of their usual fee as long as the fee is reasonable and customary.

Verbal threshold — The level of severity of injury in a no-fault system, including death and certain specified injuries, such as disfigurement or dismemberment, at which the injured party can seek compensation from the at-fault party.

Vesting — Employee's right to part or all of the pension contributions made by the employer if employment terminates before retirement.

Waiver of premium — Clause stating that the insurer will waive premiums due during the period of disability if the insured becomes totally disabled before a certain age.

Warranties — Promises made by an insured that guarantee compliance with the insurer's conditions.

Whole life insurance — Level-premium insurance that provides lifetime protection and builds cash values.

"Write-Your-Own" (WYO) flood insurance program — Cooperative undertaking of the insurance industry and the Federal Insurance Administration that allows participating private insurers to sell and service flood insurance under their own names.

Your covered auto (as used in the PAP) — Any vehicle shown in the declarations; a trailer owned by the insured; a temporary substitute auto or trailer; a newly acquired auto (subject to certain restrictions).

Index

Page numbers in boldface refer to definitions of Key Words and Phrases. Page numbers in italics refer to exhibits.